Property-Liability Insurance Accounting and Finance

TERRIE E. TROXEL, Ph.D., CPCU, CLU

Senior Vice President
National Association of Independent Insurers

GEORGE E. BOUCHIE, CPA, CPCU

Director of Insurance Company Services Group
Coopers & Lybrand

Coordinating Author

LOWELL S. YOUNG, M.B.A., CLU

Assistant Director of Curriculum
American Institute for Property and Liability
Underwriters

Third Edition • 1990

AMERICAN INSTITUTE FOR
PROPERTY AND LIABILITY UNDERWRITERS
720 Providence Road, Malvern, Pennsylvania 19355-0770

Property-Liability Insurance Accounting and Finance

Third Edition • June 1990

Library of Congress Catalog Number 89-82258
International Standard Book Number 0-89463-056-3

Printed in the United States of America

Foreword

Over the years, the American Institute for Property and Liability Underwriters and the Insurance Institute of America have responded to the educational needs of the property and liability insurance industry by developing courses and administering national examinations specifically for insurance personnel. These independent, nonprofit educational organizations receive the support of the insurance industry in fulfilling this need.

The American Institute confers the Chartered Property Casualty Underwriter (CPCU®) professional designation on those who meet the experience, ethics, and examination requirements.

The Insurance Institute of America, founded in 1909, offers a wide range of associate designations and certificate programs in technical and managerial disciplines.

Accredited Adviser in Insurance (AAI®)
Associate in Claims (AIC)
Associate in Underwriting (AU)
Associate in Risk Management (ARM)
Associate in Loss Control Management (ALCM®)
Associate in Premium Auditing (APA®)
Associate in Management (AIM)
Associate in Research and Planning (ARP®)
Associate in Insurance Accounting and Finance (AIAF)
Associate in Automation Management (AAM®)
Associate in Marine Insurance Management (AMIM®)
Associate in Reinsurance (ARe)
Certificate in General Insurance
Certificate in Supervisory Management
Certificate in Introduction to Claims
Certificate in Introduction to Property and Liability Insurance

This new edition of the *Property-Liability Insurance Accounting and Finance* text is assigned in four Institute programs. It is used in the IIA Associate in Insurance Accounting and Finance program, the Associate in Premium Auditing program, and the Associate in Reinsurance program, as well as in CPCU 8—Accounting and Finance. This revision was prompted to a large extent by recent changes in the tax laws and their impact on the property-liability insurance business. We were fortunate in being able to draw on the expertise of a number of industry people to prepare this new edition of the text. Lowell S. Young, M.B.A., CLU, assistant director of curriculum at the Institutes, served as coordinating author for this revised edition.

As with all Institute publications, this text has been extensively reviewed by a group of academic and industry experts, and they are recognized in the preface. Throughout the development of this series of texts, it has been—and will continue to be—necessary to draw on the knowledge and skills of Institute personnel. These individuals receive no royalties on texts sold; their writing responsibilities are seen as an integral part of their professional duties. We have proceeded in this way to avoid any possibility of conflict of interests.

We invite and welcome any and all criticisms of our publications. It is only with such comments that we can hope to provide high quality study materials. Comments should be directed to the Curriculum Department of the Institutes.

Norman A. Baglini, Ph.D., CPCU, CLU, AU
President

Preface

This text is designed to serve as part of the CPCU accounting and finance course. The other texts used in this course provide a generalized collegiate-level treatment of basic accounting and finance principles as they apply to commercial enterprises. This text describes the principles and procedures of accounting and finance that specifically relate to property-liability insurance companies.

Individuals who are familiar with general accounting and finance but unacquainted with technical aspects of the insurance business too often regard the accounting and finance practices of property-liability insurers to be abstruse. This book attempts to explain how the administrative and quasi-legislative power of state insurance regulatory authorities, acting principally through the National Association of Insurance Commissioners, has been used to develop and impose insurance accounting and finance practices that safeguard the public interest. This traditionally has meant promulgation of accounting rules that encourage continuity of operations. For example, the asset structure and capital structure of property-liability insurance companies are directly affected by NAIC accounting regulations and other legislative and administrative rules. The focus of insurance accounting and finance therefore differs from the more general principles and practices encountered in other businesses. The variations between generally accepted accounting principles and insurance regulatory accounting are identified in the text. This text also examines the rationale that gives rise to the differences.

More specifically, Chapter 1 describes various financial reports prepared by property-liability insurance companies. Emphasis is placed on an overview of the NAIC Annual Statement. The origin and scope of GAAP are traced, and a comparison is made between GAAP and statutory insurance accounting. Chapter 2 discusses asset valuation and the factors that influence the size and composition of a property-liability insurance company's investment portfolio. In Chapter 3 the principal liability accounts of nonlife insurers are identified, and the methods used to estimate or otherwise determine their values are examined. The balance sheet categories used to classify net worth are also described. Attention turns from balance sheet accounts to income statement variables in Chapter 4. Chapter 5 exposes the reader to a compendium of financial ratios useful in analyzing and comparing property-liability insurance companies. Analysis is based on both regulatory insurance accounting data and on financial information adjusted to a more conventional basis. Methods used to detect financial distress and regulatory tools designed to help assure continued company solvency are also discussed in Chapter 5. The 1989 NAIC Annual Statement for fire and casualty insurance companies referred to throughout the text is reproduced in an appendix, as are the Insurance Expense Exhibit, a summary of the Annual Statement Schedules, and a description of the NAIC cash flow ratios.

This text is not meant to be a comprehensive handbook on property-liability insurance accounting and finance. A number of significant issues relating to this general subject area have been intentionally omitted simply because these topics are beyond the scope of the CPCU course of study. For instance, whether anticipated investment income should be included in the computation of premium deficiencies is not discussed in this volume, nor is the actuarial certification of loss reserves. Nevertheless, the text is sufficiently detailed to give CPCU candidates a working knowledge of the fundamental aspects of this subject area and to allow them to apply this knowledge to actual situations.

No review exercises or discussion questions appear in this text. These are included in a companion study aid—the CPCU 8 Course Guide. The course guide contains educational objectives, outlines of study material, key terms and concepts, review questions, and discussion questions for each chapter.

Preliminary drafts of chapters that made up the first edition of this book benefited from the critical comments and suggestions of reviewers. The authors wish to thank these persons, especially Glenn L. Wood, Ph.D., CPCU, CLU, Professor of Finance and Insurance, California State College at Bakersfield; and Robert A. Zelten, Ph.D., Associate Professor of Insurance, University of Pennsylvania. Ruth E. Salzmann, FCAS, Vice President and Actuary, Sentry Insurance Company, also furnished valuable comments. The first edition of this text was used through 1983. Reviewers of the manuscript for the second edition included Jan R. Bednarz, M-J Insurance, Inc.; Irving Feldmesser, CPCU, CPA; Katherine S. Perry, Senior Vice President and Chief

Financial Officer, Intracorp; and Paul A. Synott, Jr., CPCU, CLU, ARM, Executive Vice President, Society of CPCU.

Cormick L. Breslin was one of the principal authors of the first edition but was not involved in the revisions. He is acknowledged along with two contributing authors, who are listed elsewhere. Their participation in preparing or revising first edition material added significantly to the book.

Special thanks go to Angela K. Cullen, CPA, Assistant Treasurer, The Harleysville Insurance Companies, and Thomas P. Ward, CPA, Director of Financial Reporting, National Association of Independent Insurers, who reviewed the third edition.

A number of people have worked diligently on the editing, proofreading, and production of this text; we wish to thank them for their work. Because insurance and accounting are dynamic disciplines, more changes inevitably will be needed in the text. Constructive comments and suggestions should be communicated to the Institutes so that the study material's usefulness may be maintained.

Terrie E. Troxel
George E. Bouchie

Contributing Authors

The American Institute for Property and Liability Underwriters and the authors acknowledge, with deep appreciation, the work of the following contributing authors:

Dan R. Anderson, Ph.D., CPCU
Associate Professor
Risk Management and Insurance
University of Wisconsin

James E. Bachman, Ph.D.
Controller
The St. Paul Fire & Marine Insurance Co.

Cormick L. Breslin
Vice President—Finance and Treasurer
CIC Financial Corporation

Table of Contents

CHAPTER 1

Introduction to Insurance Accounting and Finance

The purpose of this book is to demonstrate and explain how principles of accounting and finance are practiced in the property-liability insurance business. A basic knowledge of elementary accounting and finance is assumed. From this base, the application of accounting and finance principles to property-liability insurers is developed. Chapter 1 gives an overview of insurance accounting. Chapters 2, 3, and 4 investigate the principal elements of financial accounting—assets, liabilities, revenues, and expenses—for property-liability insurance companies. Chapter 5 discusses how the tools of financial analysis can be used to define, establish, and maintain insurance company solvency.

USES OF ACCOUNTING INFORMATION

The objective of an accounting system is to provide information for decision making. Generally, the four major decision-making areas in which accounting information is used involve (1) resource allocations, (2) administrative control, (3) management stewardship, and (4) social equity. A decision to commit assets to a particular purpose is the most fundamental economic choice that can be made. An affirmative decision to invest in a project gives rise to the second decision-making area, administrative control.

In this second area, accounting information gives administrators a means of evaluating the effectiveness with which objectives and goals are being achieved. Information produced by the accounting system is used in a third decision-making area to gauge management's stewardship of resources. Separate groups with ownership and management

1

control make an accounting information system essential in order for the external owners to judge the manager's performance. Finally, society has a need for information on which to base decisions concerning equity among various groups. Accounting systems are called upon to provide this information.

The nature and scope of the accounting system must consider the uses of its information. Security analysts and stockholders, for instance, are primarily interested in financial accounting information, especially income and cash flow measurements. Internal management is charged with establishing and meeting objectives and goals. Performance of this duty is facilitated by accounting techniques such as budgets and pro forma financial statements. Management evaluation and control require information on cost-volume-profit relationships. Cost accounting systems, therefore, concentrate on classifying, allocating, and assigning costs incurred in the production process to various segments of that process. Similarly, tax accounting provides information from which compliance with tax laws can be judged. Accounting reports to governmental regulatory agencies furnish information that indicates whether or not regulatory objectives are being met. Because there are multiple audiences addressed by the accounting system, there are separate and distinct accounting systems, each with its own purposes. There is legitimate reason for an organization to "keep more than one set of books."

Different users of financial statements have different objectives. While financial statements compiled in accordance with generally accepted accounting principles (GAAP) are most common and usually expected by the business community, bankers, and investors, such statements may not be the most suitable for use by others. GAAP financial statements are compiled using principles that evolved over time and which are acceptable to the Financial Accounting Standards Board and, for publicly held companies, the Securities and Exchange Commission. The format of GAAP financial statements emphasizes the statement of income and the proper matching of income with expense. In some areas of GAAP accounting, alternatives are available, such as the choice between the straight line method of calculating depreciation and an accelerated method or between a LIFO and a FIFO method of valuing inventory, either of which would produce a different financial statement result. Under GAAP, the methods selected must present the information fairly, be appropriate for the circumstances, and be used on a consistent basis.

All insurance companies must report their results to the regulators in states in which they are licensed using the prescribed format of the NAIC Annual Statement. The rules for preparing the NAIC Annual Statement constitute statutory accounting principles which differ from

GAAP. Statutory accounting principles are balance sheet oriented and emphasize the valuation of assets and liabilities on a "liquidation basis" rather than on the "going concern basis" used for GAAP financial statements. Generally, statutory financial statements display a more conservative financial position and results of operations than the results reported under GAAP. Statutory accounting principles give less attention to the matching of income with expense. Many insurers (often mutuals) produce only statutory financial statements, as they have no need for presentations on any other basis. Other insurers (especially stock insurers) produce both statutory and GAAP financial statements because they are required to do so.

For federal income tax purposes, the measurement of taxable income is based on still another format. Internal Revenue Form 1120PC, which property-liability insurance companies use to report their taxable income, follows neither GAAP nor statutory insurance accounting principles entirely. It incorporates elements of both, however, and recognizes the NAIC Annual Statement format as the starting point in the calculation of net income.

A study of insurance accounting requires that the many uses of the information system's audiences be kept in mind. Historically, regulatory uses of accounting have defined the nature and scope of insurance accounting. Regulatory accounting remains important and continues to shape accounting practices within the insurance business. But in recent years, other users of insurance accounting information have become more precise in formulating and more vocal in stating their needs for information. This has expanded the scope of insurance accounting and further complicated a complex subject.

STATUTORY INSURANCE ACCOUNTING PRINCIPLES

Statutory insurance accounting principles are those rules of accounting prescribed or permitted by state law or regulatory authorities for use by insurance companies. An understanding of insurance regulatory objectives helps to clarify statutory insurance accounting principles. Various reasons have been given to explain the need for insurance regulation. In a 1914 case involving the right of the state of Kansas to regulate rates, the United States Supreme Court declared that the business of insurance was "affected with a public interest" and, therefore, subject to governmental regulation.[1] In a subsequent case, the court implied that insurance company operations and regulation should seek to fulfill certain public policy objectives.[2] The objectives most frequently discussed seek to (1) preserve and enhance solvency; (2) promote adequate and fair premium rates; (3) ensure fairness, equity, and reasonableness in insurance markets; and (4) fulfill certain social goals not necessarily pertinent to a successful insurance operation. An external regulatory objective might be assuring access to insurance coverage for marginal loss exposures at a lower cost than dictated by economic considerations.

Uniform statutory accounting principles and reporting practices are not an end in themselves but a means to monitor solvency. Without maintenance of solvency, all other regulatory objectives are meaningless.[3]

Most insurance accounting practices seek to assure solvency, and, therefore, statutory accounting principles have concentrated on conservative valuation rules for balance sheet items. Concern over operating results has always been of secondary importance to analysis of financial position. Generally, a liquidation view of the company applies in the formulation of statutory accounting principles. However, regulators may use a going concern view when perpetuation of company operations is beneficial to the public. What may appear to be unorthodox and inconsistent accounting practices become understandable when placed in the context of the solvency goal.

Insurance accounting practices and rules follow from regulatory objectives. Some rules clearly relate to guaranteeing company solvency and are justified on this basis. Some statutory insurance accounting practices share a theoretical foundation with GAAP accounting (for example, both assume a stable monetary unit, both use a specified time period, and so on), but the theoretical structures are different. Most insurance accounting principles can be traced to the practical selection of accounting concepts and techniques useful in achieving regulatory objectives. The general framework of statutory insurance accounting is based on concepts of valuation, continuity, and realization.

Valuation Concepts

Stating assets and liabilities in terms of a monetary unit is the valuation process. Valuation rules of statutory accounting have been designed to satisfy two criteria:

1. Valuation should result in a *conservative statement of policyholders' surplus.*
2. Valuation should, as much as is reasonably possible, *prevent sharp fluctuations in policyholders' surplus.*

Surplus is a statutory accounting term equivalent to "owners' equity" in usual accounting terms. A conservative measurement of surplus results when the lowest of several possible values is selected for assets and the highest of several possible values is selected for liabilities. Surplus values are stabilized by selecting asset and liability values that experience the least amount of change from period to period. At times, conflicts arise between these two criteria; when this occurs, a compromise must be made taking into consideration the need for the insurance business to continue and to consider values based on what money could be received for the sale of an asset.

Statutory accounting imposes an unusually harsh valuation rule by excluding some assets from the balance sheet altogether. This is accomplished by assigning these so-called *nonadmitted assets* a zero value. Items that cannot be readily converted to cash at or near a known amount are not liquid and generally are not recognized in the statutory balance sheet. Included among the nonadmitted assets are furniture, fixtures, equipment, supplies, automobiles, uncollected premiums over ninety days due, overdue reinsurance, and loans or advances to certain company personnel. As the value of nonadmitted assets is not included in assets, policyholders' surplus is reduced by a similar amount.

The majority of assets admitted to the balance sheet are monetary items (see Illustration 1-1). These *admitted assets* are cash or can be converted to cash reasonably quickly without loss of value. Admitted assets are valued according to rules established by the NAIC. Stocks are shown at their "association values," which usually correspond to year-end market values. Unrealized appreciation or loss from the cost of stock immediately increases or decreases policyholders' surplus. This valuation rule results in a lower statement of surplus than would be obtained by using cost when current market prices fall below original cost. However, the second criterion of the valuation process, stabilization of surplus, is not achieved. Because investing a large portion of portfolio assets in stock exposes surplus to market price fluctuations, the states regulate the relative amount a company can invest in this asset. Constraints vary among the states, but their common intent is to force portfolio diversification and prevent excessive investment in equity securities. On several occasions association values have differed significantly from year-end market prices. In 1937, companies were authorized to use "stabilized values" for stock equal to an average of the previous year's month-end market prices. This practice resulted in an overstatement of surplus according to the usual rule but prevented numerous technical insolvencies due to temporarily depressed market prices. The rationale was that insurance companies are ongoing operations that do not necessarily realize capital losses unless forced to liquidate invested assets. Since the depressed stock prices were regarded as a temporary aberration in the market, forced liquidation and capital impairment under the normal valuation rule were not recognized.

The standard rule for the admitted asset value of bonds is to show them at *amortized cost*. Amortized cost is the price paid for the bond adjusted to the current period in such a way as to equal eventually the precise sum that is payable at the bond's maturity date. A bond that is purchased above (at a premium) or below (at a discount) par value is gradually written down or up to par value between the date of purchase and date of maturity. This amortization accomplishes two things. First, bond values based on amortized cost are more stable than values based on market prices. Policyholders' surplus thus is shielded from fluctuations occurring in the bond market due to interest rate changes. Second, a portion of the bond's premium or discount is allocated to investment income proportionally over the period the bond is held. This allocation has a stabilizing effect on income and, consequently, on surplus. Regulatory authorities permit several methods to be used for amortization; these will be discussed in Chapter 2.

Basing admitted asset values for bonds on amortized cost recognizes that insurance companies are going concerns. They normally do not have to liquidate securities at depressed prices but can rely on normal cash flow from underwriting and scheduled investment maturities to meet disbursement requirements. This reasoning explains why the first valuation criterion (conservative valuation of assets) often is violated by the standard bond valuation rule, especially during periods of rising interest rates.

To illustrate the impact that the use of amortized costs has on company valuation, consider the data in Illustration 1-1. The average stock property-liability insurer at the end of 1988 held 58.9 percent of its assets in bonds. Assume that the bonds were all recently purchased at par, that their coupon or nominal annual interest rate was 8 percent, and that they are fifteen years from maturity. If the values shown in Illustration 1-1 were based on original cost and the market interest rate for bonds of this type had increased to 10 percent by year end, the adjustment necessary to bring these bonds to their market value would reduce policyholders' surplus by 37 percent (see Illustration 1-2).

Only bonds "in good standing" are eligible for amortized cost valuation. A bond is considered "in good standing" if it is not in default, has a maturity date, is amply secured, and is among the classes of bonds approved by the NAIC. Other bonds are shown at market value unless there is a reason to believe a lower value would be realized from their disposal.

Property liability insurers do not invest heavily in mortgages, real estate, or collateral loans. These assets are not considered to possess the degree of liquidity desired for nonlife insurance company opera-

Illustration 1-1

Consolidated Assets of Property-Liability Organizations (as of 12/31/88)

Type of Asset	Industry Total 940 Property-Casualty Organizations (Mill. of $)	%	Stock Company Total 593 Property-Casualty Organizations (Mill. of $)	%	Mutual Company Total 301 Property-Casualty Organizations (Mill. of $)	%	Reciprocal Total 38 Property-Casualty Organizations (Mill. of $)	%	Lloyds Total 8 Property-Casualty Organizations (Mill. of $)	%
Bonds	281,142	58.9	180,674	56.4	84,415	64.9	15,949	61.2	103.3	22.9
Preferred Stocks	9,071	1.9	7,213	2.3	1,356	1.0	500	1.9	1.4	0.3
Common Stocks	41,034	8.6	25,165	7.9	13,179	10.1	2,687	10.3	4.2	0.9
Mortgages, Real Estate, and Collateral Loans	6,465	1.4	6,008	1.9	399	0.3	58	0.2	.2	0.0
Cash, Short Term Investments, and Other	44,193	9.3	32,529	10.2	9,324	7.2	2,025	7.8	314.9	69.7
Investment in Affiliates	22,897	4.8	17,281	5.4	4,759	3.7	852	3.3	5.1	1.1
Real Estate, Offices	4,069	0.9	1,743	0.5	1,670	1.3	655	2.5	.8	0.2
Premium Balances	42,308	8.9	29,483	9.2	10,829	8.3	1,984	7.6	11.6	2.6
Reinsurance	11,857	2.5	10,089	3.1	1,640	1.3	121	0.5	7.1	1.6
Other	13,893	2.9	10,098	3.2	2,574	2.0	1,218	4.7	3.0	0.7
Total Assets	476,929	100.0	320,285	100.0	130,145	100.0	26,048	100.0	451.8	100.0

Based on data from *Best's Aggregates and Averages*, Property-Casualty, 1989.

Illustration 1-2
Effect of Bond Valuation on Surplus

	Bonds at Cost	Bonds at Market	Change Due to Market
Assets			
Bonds	281,142	237,924	43,218
Other	195,787	195,787	—
	476,929	433,711	43,218
Liabilities	358,735	358,735	—
Surplus	118,194	74,976	43,218

tions. Only first lien real estate mortgages are admitted assets at a value equal to the balance of the unpaid principal. Accrued interest is shown separately. Direct real estate investments are valued at cost adjusted for additions, improvements, and depreciation. Encumbrances due to mortgages on company property serve to reduce the balance sheet value of real estate. If the market value exceeds cost, no adjustment is made. However, market values below cost require a reduction of the asset's value to reflect the difference. Thus, real estate values are cost or market, whichever is lower. While this valuation rule appears inconsistent with valuations placed on other assets, especially stocks, the low liquidity characteristics of real estate justify the distinction. Since real estate values do not often fall precipitously, the stability of surplus valuation is not unduly threatened by this method of valuation. State laws limit the amounts insurance companies can invest in real estate. Separate limits apply to property held by the company for its own use and to total real estate investment. Collateral loans are valued at the amount of the unpaid loan or the market value of the pledged collateral, whichever is lowest. Loans made to company officers and directors are nonadmitted assets in some states.

Valuation of liabilities is also subject to standards of conservatism. If more than one possible value exists for a liability, the *highest* value usually is selected. Balance sheet conservatism in the treatment of liabilities may impact on both underwriting income and surplus or on surplus alone, as will be shown.

The increase or decrease in reserves for losses and loss adjustment expenses during an accounting period for the current and/or prior years are included in losses and expenses incurred during the current year in determining statutory underwriting income:

> Premiums Earned
> Less:
>> Losses Incurred
>> Loss Adjustment Expenses Incurred
>> Other Underwriting Expenses Incurred
>
> Equals:
> Statutory Underwriting Income

To the extent that conservative reserve valuations overstate the actual value at which claims are settled, underwriting income is temporarily and artificially reduced. Overstatement of loss reserves also temporarily distorts the company's loss experience record. For insurers that are taxed on underwriting income it may result in deferral of income tax, and it may affect future insurance rates.

Loss reserves for automobile liability, other liability, medical malpractice, workers compensation, and credit lines of business are subject to statutory minimums. Loss reserves can be estimated from individual claims files or by aggregating the average value of claims that have been classified into predetermined loss categories. Regardless of the statistical method used, the resulting estimate is compared to loss reserves determined by statutory formula. If the formula value exceeds reserve values based on claims file estimates, the excess formula value must be added to balance sheet reserves. This procedure results in a direct reduction of surplus and does not affect underwriting income for the period. The purpose of requiring minimum reserves is to make sure insurers do not underestimate losses and provide less than an adequate amount for claims settlements. The minimum reserve requirement applies year-by-year and line-by-line rather than in the aggregate for all those lines.

Continuity Concept

Continuity and the transferability of ownership interest allow a corporation to be treated separately from its owners. General accounting principles assume that the company will continue to operate, and financial statements are prepared accordingly. If there is reason to believe that the business will not continue, general accounting principles are not used and a disclosure of the company's limited life is made.

Illustration 1-3

Hypothetical Insurance Company Balance Sheet—July 1, 19X7

Assets		Liabilities	
Cash	$1,000,000	Reserves	$ 0
		Common stock, paid-up	200,000
Total Assets	_____	Surplus, paid-in	800,000
	$1,000,000	Total Liabilities and Surplus	$1,000,000

Statutory insurance accounting does not employ a consistent continuity concept. Using amortized cost to value bonds assumes that the securities will be held until maturity. This assumption treats the insurer as a going concern. On the other hand, the statutory treatment given premium revenues and the costs associated with writing new business is based on a liquidation concept. This will be illustrated in the discussion of the realization concept. Use of a liquidation view helps assure that if the insurer does not continue in operation long enough to fulfill its existing commitments, it can transfer sufficient funds to another insurer so that the assuming company may carry out the contracts.

Realization Concepts

The term *realization* is used to mean the recognition of revenues, expenses, gains, and losses into income measurement and valuation. Statutory accounting's realization concepts reflect the regulatory emphasis placed on liquidity and solvency.

A simplified example using an unearned premium reserve illustrates statutory realization of premium revenues and the related expenses. Assume that the Hypothetical Insurance Company (HIC) recently was authorized to begin operations. HIC is a stock company that intends to write fire and allied lines. Its initial capitalization consists of 100,000 shares of common stock with a stated value of $2 per share. Promoters who organized the company and who will serve as its management sold all the original shares at $10 each. If organizational costs are ignored and certain other simplifying assumptions made, the beginning balance sheet is as shown in Illustration 1-3.

Assume that on the first day of operations agents bound 1,000 one-year fire insurance policies generating premium revenues of $210,000. Annual premiums were paid in cash and transmitted instantaneously to HIC. Premium *cash* has been received, but because it will be a year

Illustration 1-4

Hypothetical Insurance Company Balance Sheet—July 2, 19X7

Assets		Liabilities	
Cash (includes premium collection)	$1,210,000	Unearned premium reserves	$ 210,000
		Common stock, paid-up	200,000
		Surplus, paid-in	800,000
		Unassigned surplus	0
		Total policyholders' surplus	1,000,000
Total Assets	$1,210,000	Total Liabilities and Surplus	$1,210,000

before the contract provisions are completed, *revenues* are not realized into income at this point. Instead, the insurer must establish a reserve for unearned premiums. This liability represents its unfulfilled obligation to provide coverage under the contracts. At the close of HIC's first day of operations, the balance sheet is as shown in Illustration 1-4. Premium revenues become income on a pro-rata basis over the coverage period. However, expenses associated with writing the coverage—agents' commissions, policy printing and mailing, inspection reports, premium recording, record keeping, and so forth—are charged against income immediately. Assume that the expenses shown in Illustration 1-5 were paid on the day after the coverage was put in force. Payment of these "front-end" expenses results in the balance sheet shown in Illustration 1-6. Incurring expenses immediately while deferring revenue realization produces a decline in surplus as new business is written. Therefore, a stock insurance company that begins operations with the minimum statutory capitalization must have paid-in capital in excess of its stock's stated (or par) value before it can write business. Similarly, mutuals require initial contributed surplus in excess of subsequent minimum capitalization. Even after a company has been operating for a number of years, the realization rules used for premium revenues and acquisition expenses require surplus in order for the company to expand. The level of surplus, therefore, gives a measure of the company's underwriting capacity.

Balance sheets are not prepared daily. The sequential balance sheets shown here are used only to illustrate the impact of realization rules on the insurer's financial position. More realism can be added to the example by computing underwriting results for the years during which the 1,000 original policies are in force. The example assumes that

Illustration 1-5
Assumed Expense Distribution

Agent commissions (20%)	$42,000
Other issue expenses (18%)	37,800
Premium Taxes (2%)	4,200
Total Expenses incurred	
at issue (40%)	$84,000

Illustration 1-6
Hypothetical Insurance Company Balance Sheet—July 3, 19X7

Assets		Liabilities and Surplus	
Cash	$1,126,000	Unearned premium	
		reserves	$ 210,000
		Common stock, paid-up	200,000
		Surplus, paid-in	800,000
		Unassigned surplus	(84,000)
		Total policyholders'	
		surplus	916,000
		Total Liabilities	
Total Assets	$1,126,000	and Surplus	$1,126,000

no new business is written after the initial policies and that none of the policies is canceled.

Between July 1 and December 31, 19X7, HIC incurred claims of $47,250, claims adjustment expenses equal to $5,250, and $7,350 in other maintenance expenses. Statutory accounting's revenue realization rule allows HIC to release half the premiums received on July 1 from the unearned premium reserve to determine underwriting income for 19X7. The statutory income statement appears in Illustration 1-7.

Illustration 1-8 shows the balance sheet at the end of 19X7. Comparing the year-end balance sheet to the company's financial position on July 3 shows changes in three of the four accounts. Cash has been reduced by $59,850. This amount equals the sum of payments for losses, loss adjustment expenses, and other underwriting expenses incurred. Since one-half the coverage has expired, a $105,000 reduction in the unearned premium reserve occurs. Policyholders' surplus has increased by $45,150 between July 3 and December 31. Overall, HIC's first year in business has produced a $38,850 underwriting loss; this is the difference between the beginning and ending balance of the

Illustration 1-7

Hypothetical Insurance Company Abbreviated Income Statement—
December 31, 19X7

Premiums earned ($210,000 x 0.50)		$105,000
Acquisition expenses incurred	$84,000	
Losses incurred	47,250	
Loss adjustment expenses	5,250	
Other underwriting expenses	7,350	143,850
Statutory underwriting loss		($ 38,850)

Illustration 1-8

Hypothetical Insurance Company Balance Sheet—December 31, 19X7

Assets		Liabilities and Surplus	
Cash	$1,066,150	Unearned premium reserves	$ 105,000
		Common stock, paid-up	200,000
		Surplus, paid-in	800,000
		Unassigned surplus	(38,850)
		Total policyholders' surplus	961,150
Total Assets	$1,066,150	Total Liabilities and Surplus	$1,066,150

policyholders' surplus account. Without any more new business, the surplus level is restored as the contracts run their course. This process continues in the next accounting period.

In order to keep the illustration simple, assume that all the policies continue in force until June 30, 19X8. No new policies are issued. Losses, claims settlement costs, and other underwriting expenses are the same as in 19X7. An abbreviated income statement for 19X8 shows a statutory underwriting profit (Illustration 1-9). During this accounting period no new premiums are received and no additional acquisition expenses are incurred. One-half the premiums paid in the previous accounting period are released into income. Costs associated with underwriting are expensed as incurred. At the close of 19X8, the balance sheet shows HIC's financial position to be as shown in Illustration 1-10. A summary of the revenues and expenses associated

Illustration 1-9

Hypothetical Insurance Company Abbreviated Income Statement — December 31, 19X8

Premiums earned ($210,000 x 0.50)		$105,000
Losses incurred	$47,250	
Loss adjustment expenses	5,250	
Other underwriting expenses	7,350	59,850
Statutory underwriting income		$ 45,150

with this block of policies reveals some interesting relationships (Illustration 1-11). The insurance policies written in 19X7 ultimately made a profit for the insurer equal to 3 percent of the premiums earned (and 3 percent of the premiums written, in this case). Accounting for expenses on a cash basis instead of matching them evenly with the related revenues causes an unequal realization of income in the two accounting periods. In 19X7 approximately 71 percent of the total costs associated with this block of business was matched with one-half of the premiums received. A $38,850 underwriting loss was incurred. The remaining revenue was realized in the second period, but only about 29 percent of the total expenses was left to be absorbed. The insurer showed a $45,150 underwriting profit. Statutory realization rules in this area of revenue and expense recognition are conservative in the sense that revenue realization is deferred while expense realization is anticipated. These rules force the insurer to maintain greater liquidity than would be achieved if it were allowed to hold deferred acquisition costs on the balance sheet as assets and amortize them against revenue as they were released into income.

Concepts of valuation, continuity, and realization highlight the rules and conventions that make up regulatory insurance accounting. Additional statutory accounting principles will be discussed throughout the remainder of this book. These principles are designed to meet the informational needs of a particular group—insurance regulators—and make reporting among insurers uniform. They also are intended to force insurers to follow certain practices in their operations. Statutory insurance accounting principles differ significantly from the generally accepted principles of accounting normally applied to other business enterprises. The following section discusses some of the most important areas of difference.

Illustration 1-10

Hypothetical Insurance Company Balance Sheet—December 31, 19X8

Assets		Liabilities and Surplus	
Cash	$1,006,300	Unearned premium reserves	$ 0
		Common stock, paid-up	200,000
		Surplus, paid-in	800,000
		Unassigned surplus	6,300
		Total policyholders' surplus	1,006,300
Total Assets	$1,006,300	Total Liabilities and Surplus	$1,006,300

Illustration 1-11

Revenue and Expense Summary

Premiums earned (100%)		$210,000
Acquisition expenses incurred (40%)	$84,000	
Losses incurred (45%)	94,500	
Loss adjustment expenses (5%)	10,500	
Other underwriting expenses (7%)	14,700	203,700
Underwriting income (3%)		$ 6,300

DIFFERENCES BETWEEN STATUTORY ACCOUNTING AND GENERALLY ACCEPTED ACCOUNTING PRINCIPLES

In the late 1920s and early 1930s, general accounting underwent a fundamental change.[4] Instead of presenting information to management and creditors, accounting was reoriented to provide information for investor decision making. This reorientation made income measurement by means of a uniform income concept more important than valuation. The balance sheet became a repository of account balances between periodic income statements. Full disclosure of relevant financial information and consistent application of accounting practices became major concerns, and footnote information appeared more frequently as a result.

Statutory insurance accounting did not share in this realignment of objectives. It continues to emphasize solvency by use of the balance sheet formula. Income measurement is of secondary importance. If financial statements of insurance companies were used only for regulatory purposes, the differences between statutory accounting and generally accepted accounting principles would not be especially troublesome. However, the broad based and increasing public ownership and trading of equity shares in insurance companies requires accountants and analysts to reconcile statutory financial statements to the needs of nonregulators.

Origin and Scope of Generally Accepted Accounting Principles

Accountants use the term GAAP to encompass the conventions, rules, and procedures developed from experience and believed to be the tools best suited for the purposes intended at a particular time. Generally accepted accounting principles include not only the broad guidelines of general application, but also detailed practices and procedures needed to establish reliable financial and operating information for business enterprises.

Businesses are required to use GAAP in preparation of their financial statements in order to receive an unqualified auditor's opinion. The privilege of having the company's stock traded on the national securities exchanges necessitates receipt of an unqualified opinion. Because of these indirect pressures, most businesses find it expedient to follow GAAP in preparation of their financial statements.

Although uniformity would enhance comparability of financial reports among businesses, more than one procedure may be considered a generally accepted method of dealing with a particular transaction. For example, several inventory valuation methods are allowed (FIFO, LIFO, and so forth). Choice of accounting methods within the range defined as GAAP is left to management discretion. It is the auditor's responsibility to render an opinion on whether the accounting rules used by management are within the scope of GAAP, have been applied on a consistent basis, and result in a fair disclosure of all relevant information.

Applying GAAP to Property-Liability Insurers

Solvency oriented statutory accounting reports are not designed for nonregulatory purposes. Investors making buy, hold, or sell decisions regarding insurance company stocks are more interested in the company's future earnings than in a conservative measurement of its financial position. As early as the 1930s, A. M. Best Company reported "adjusted earnings" for property-liability insurance companies. Adjustments were made to statutory statements for such things as the insurer's equity in the unearned premium reserve that arose from the mismatching of acquisition expenses and premium revenues.

With the increased trading of insurance company stocks after World War II, the investment community's interest in financial reporting practices of insurance companies grew. Security analysts, the SEC, institutional investors, the American Institute of Certified Public Accountants (AICPA), and representatives of the insurance business called for uniformity in the procedures used to adjust statutory accounting statements. In 1957 the AICPA's Committee on Insurance Accounting and Auditing undertook the development of an audit guide for nonlife insurance companies. Nine years later the Committee published a booklet, *Audits of Fire and Casualty Insurance Companies*, intended as a guide for auditors of insurance companies.

The type of audit opinion given corporate financial statements follows generally accepted auditing standards developed by the accounting profession. These standards are spelled out in AICPA publications. The following excerpt from Chapter 10 of the AICPA's *Statement on Auditing Procedure No. 33* is pertinent to opinions given insurance company financial statements:

> The basic postulates and broad principles of accounting comprehended in the term "generally accepted accounting principles" which pertain to business enterprises in general apply also to companies whose accounting practices are prescribed by authorities or commissions. (Such companies include public utilities, common carriers, insurance companies, financial institutions, and the like.) Accordingly, the first reporting standard is equally applicable to opinions on companies presented for purposes other than filings with their respective supervisory agencies, and material variances from generally accepted accounting principles, and their effects, should be dealt with in the independent auditor's report in the same manner followed by companies which are not regulated. Ordinarily, this will require either a qualified or adverse opinion on such statements.[5]

The most recent pronouncement of GAAP as applied to insurance companies is contained in the Financial Accounting Standard Board's (FASB) Statement of Financial Accounting Standards No. 60 issued in June, 1982. SFAS NO. 60, *Accounting and Reporting by Insurance Enterprises*, sets forth standards of financial accounting and reporting for all insurance enterprises other than mutual life insurance enterprises, assessment enterprises, and fraternal benefit societies. The Statement extracts and consolidates the specialized principles and practices from the AICPA insurance-related Guides and Statements of Position. Together with earlier pronouncements of the AICPA, it describes acceptable procedures for presenting insurance company financial statements on a basis that merits an unqualified audit opinion;

that is, it sets forth areas where statutory financial statements must be adjusted to bring them into conformity with GAAP.

There are seven major areas of difference between statutory insurance accounting and GAAP for property-liability insurers stated as adjustments to statutory statements:

1. Nonadmitted assets
2. Unauthorized reinsurance
3. Excess loss reserves
4. Prepaid expenses
5. Deferred federal income taxes
6. Business combinations and consolidated financial statements
7. Premium deficiency

Nonadmitted Assets. For GAAP and federal income tax purposes, nonadmitted assets are not distinguished from other items of value. They must be capitalized (shown as an asset) and, where applicable, depreciated over their estimated useful lives.

Unauthorized Reinsurance. Reinsurance placed with a company not authorized to transact business in a particular state, and hence not subject to that state's regulation, is not recognized under statutory rules unless funds have been deposited with the ceding insurer. This regulatory lever encourages primary insurers to place reinsurance with companies subject to regulation of the jurisdiction in which the annual statement is filed. Financial statements conforming to GAAP seek to reflect economic rather than regulatory circumstances by eliminating the liability for unauthorized reinsurance.

Excess Loss Reserves. Minimum estimated liabilities for loss and loss adjustment expense reserves associated with particular types of coverage are established by statutory formula irrespective of the adequacy of case reserves. GAAP adds current increases in these special reserves back to policyholder surplus.

Prepaid Expenses. Statutory accounting treats the costs of acquiring new business as period expenses when these costs are incurred but realizes the corresponding premium revenue into income over the contractual coverage period. The insurer is said to have "invested" in the unearned premium reserve an amount equal to these prepaid expenses. GAAP capitalizes acquisition expenses by creating an asset account for deferred charges amortized over the same period during which revenues are realized. Expense deferral removes the statutory paradox of decreasing earnings and surplus in periods of expanding sales (such as in the Hypothetical Insurance Company example used earlier). Under statutory accounting rules the relevant

Illustration 1-12
Abbreviated Statutory Revenue and Expense Allocation

	19X7	19X8
Premiums written	$210,000	$ 0
Increase in unearned premiums	105,000	(105,000)
Premiums earned	105,000	105,000
Acquisition costs incurred	84,000	0
Revenue net of acquisition costs	21,000	105,000
Losses and expenses		
subsequently incurred	59,850	59,850
Statutory Underwriting Profit (loss)	($38,850)	$ 45,150

Illustration 1-13
Abbreviated GAAP Revenue and Expense Allocation

	19X7	19X8
Premiums written	$210,000	$ 0
Increase in unearned premiums	105,000	(105,000)
Premiums earned	105,000	105,000
Amortization of deferred		
acquisition costs	42,000	42,000
Adjusted net revenue	63,000	63,000
Losses and expenses		
subsequently incurred	59,850	59,850
Adjusted Underwriting Profit	$ 3,150	$ 3,150

revenue and expense items for 19X7 and 19X8 were as shown in Illustration 1-12.

The GAAP procedure adjusts these figures to provide matching of expenses and revenues in the manner shown in Illustration 1-13. As before, the policies yielded an overall underwriting income of $6,300. Under GAAP, a profit appears in each of the two accounting periods; when statutory rules were employed, a large underwriting loss was followed by a large underwriting profit. Adjusting for the insurer's equity in the unearned premium reserve due to prepayment of expenses conforms the statutory expense recognition rule to GAAP.

Deferred Federal Income Taxes. No adjustment appears in statutory financial statements for federal income tax charges or credits that arise out of differences between pretax statutory income and taxable income as shown on the company's income tax return. When financial statements are adjusted to GAAP, deferred income taxes arising from any timing difference are reflected in the statements. A timing difference results from the fact that income recognition rules under GAAP are not identical to those of the federal tax code. GAAP may recognize income earlier than the tax rules and although a tax is not immediately owed the government on the differential income, a deferred liability must be shown currently in the financial statements. In later periods when the amount of income tax actually paid exceeds the tax on GAAP income for that period, the deferred tax liability is discharged.

Prior to 1987 the calculation of federal income tax liability for property-liability insurance companies followed statutory accounting rules with adjustments to restore nonadmitted assets and other minor adjustments for depreciation and reserves. The Tax Reform Act of 1986 expanded the differences between tax and GAAP statements. These differences involve discounting loss reserves and accruing salvage and subrogation for tax calculation purposes and including portions of the unearned premium reserve in taxable income and tax exempt income. These factors can create a deferred tax asset.

Three points need to be emphasized here. First, deferred federal income taxes are not amounts currently owed to or receivable from the government. This account does not reflect benefits of "creative accounting" or the keeping of a "hidden set of books." Indeed, the existence of the deferred income tax account shows that GAAP income is measured differently from taxable income. Second, deferred income taxes are not unique to insurance companies. Many types of business transactions may result in timing differences between a corporation's tax return and its financial statements, such as use of accelerated depreciation on a tax return and straight-line depreciation on other statements. Third, it is incidental that insurance company income as reported in stockholder financial statements is derived by adjusting statutory income. Timing differences creating deferred income taxes are due to the divergence between GAAP and federal tax code. Two principal areas where GAAP and statutory financial statements differ due to dissimilar treatment of federal income taxes are prepaid expenses and unrealized capital gains and losses.

Tax Treatment of Prepaid Expenses. Expenses incurred on the statutory income statement generally are deductible for income tax purposes. GAAP income capitalizes acquisition costs and amortizes them against income in later periods. This gives rise to higher GAAP income during the current period and hence a deferred federal income tax liability must be recognized. A further extension of the Hypothetical Insurance Company example illustrates the calculation of the deferred tax liability and shows how the account reverses itself in a later period (Illustration 1-14). For the sake of illustration, net investment income is assumed to be $50,000 in both years and an effective tax rate of 34 percent is applied to combined underwriting and investment income.

Net income for the two years totals $70,158 on HIC's tax returns and on its financial statements. Because a 34 percent tax rate is assumed, provision for federal income taxes totals $36,142 for the two years in each set of statements. However, GAAP makes a uniform provision for taxes in each year. In 19X7, HIC pays $3,791 income tax, and establishes a $14,280 deferred tax liability. The total provision for federal income taxes is $18,071. A $32,351 income tax payment is made in 19X8, but of this only $18,071 is current expense and a $14,280 reduction occurs in the deferred tax account. Thus, the timing difference reverses itself in the second year and the balance in the deferred income tax account goes to zero. In an actual case, as some timing differences reverse, others arise so that a balance in the deferred income tax account should be expected.

Tax Treatment of Unrealized Capital Gains and Losses. Realized capital gains and losses are included in the statutory income statement and are subject to taxation during the current year. This treatment parallels GAAP requirements. However, unrealized appreciation or depreciation in the value of stocks on the statutory balance sheet is credited or charged directly to surplus without any adjustment for the tax effect which would occur if such gains or losses were realized. SFAS No. 60 requires that unrealized gains and losses on invested assets be shown as a separate component of surplus, *net of income taxes for GAAP*.

Business Combinations and Consolidated Financial Statements. Combination of two or more corporations through intercorporate investments is common business practice. Within the insurance business, corporate combinations take many forms, including mergers, consolidations, and parent-subsidiary relationships. When the parent holding company and the subsidiary corporations operate in similar or related activities, the combined entities are called a "congeneric." For example, a property and liability insurance company may be part of a congeneric that includes corporations involved in leasing operations, computer services, real estate development, insurance marketing, consulting and research activities, investment banking, and other

Illustration 1-14
Income Effect of Timing Differences

Taxable Income		
	19X7	19X8
Premiums written	$210,000	$ 0
Change in unearned premiums	105,000	(105,000)
Premiums earned	105,000	105,000
Acquisition expenses incurred	84,000	0
Subtotal	21,000	105,000
Losses and expenses		
subsequently incurred	59,850	59,850
Net underwriting profit (loss)	(38,850)	45,150
Net investment income	50,000	50,000
Income before federal income taxes	11,150	95,150
Provision for federal income taxes	3,791	32,351
Net Income	$ 7,359*	$ 62,799*

*(The effects of discounting loss reserves and the unearned premium
  reserve and the alternative minimum tax have been ignored.)

GAAP Income				
Premiums written		$210,000		$ 0
Change in unearned premiums		105,000		(105,000)
Premiums earned		105,000		105,000
Amortized acquisition costs		42,000		42,000
Adjusted net revenue		63,000		63,000
Losses and expenses				
subsequently incurred		59,850		59,850
Adjusted underwriting profit		3,150		3,150
Net investment income		50,000		50,000
Income before federal income taxes		53,150		53,150
Provision for federal income taxes:				
Taxes currently payable	$ 3,791		$32,351	
Taxes deferred	14,280	18,071	(14,280)	18,071
Net Income		$ 35,079		$ 35,079

related financial services. Affiliated corporations engaged in unrelated
operations that provide products and services to distinguishable
markets are called collectively a "conglomerate." Such an organization
might include, for instance, an insurance company, a steel manufacturer, and a fast-food restaurant chain. Property-liability insurance

companies can be found in both congeneric and conglomerate organizational structures.

Statutory Consolidation. For property-liability insurers, regulators require two types of consolidation of financial statements when one insurance company controls another through stock ownership. The first type of consolidation is for the statutory statements filed with individual state insurance departments. The second type of consolidation is for the NAIC offices. For the state statutory statements, the surplus of a subsidiary appears on the parent company's balance sheet as the amount of the parent's investment in the subsidiary. For the NAIC's consolidation, all assets and equities of a subsidiary are brought into the parent's financial statements. For example, The Queen City Indemnity (QCI) is a wholly owned subsidiary of the Cincinnati Insurance Company (CIC). CIC is, in turn, owned by the Cincinnati Financial Corporation (a congeneric). Since QCI is 100 percent owned by CIC, QCI's financial statements are fully consolidated into CIC. All of the assets, liabilities, and surplus of QCI are brought into CIC's NAIC consolidated statutory statements. The net effect is to increase CIC's surplus by the amount of QCI's surplus. In consolidating the financial statements, intercompany transactions are eliminated.

The question of consolidation revolves around "control" as defined by the regulators. In Virginia, any property-liability insurance company owning 10 percent or more of the stock of another insurance company is deemed to be "in control" unless company management can prove otherwise. Assume Crowley Fire and Marine owns 15 percent of Synnott Fire Insurance Company. Under the Virginia provisions, 15 percent of Synnott Fire's assets, liabilities, and surplus would be consolidated into Crowley Fire and Marine's statutory statements. If Crowley Fire and Marine can prove that it does not control Synnott Fire, that it is only an "investment" like any other stock purchase, no consolidation would be required. In the noncontrol case, the value of Synnott Fire's stock would be treated as any other stock in determining its value for Crowley Fire and Marine statutory balance sheet. The only income for Synnott Fire that would appear on Crowley Fire and Marine's income statement would be any dividends Synnott Fire paid (again, just like any other investment).

GAAP Consolidation. Methods of accounting for business combinations in conformity with GAAP are set forth in *Accounting Research Bulletin No. 51, Opinion No. 16* and *Opinion No. 17* of the Accounting Principles Board (APB), and subsequent pronouncements of the FASB. The two APB *Opinions* contain criteria to determine whether a business combination should be treated according to the "pooling of interest method" or the "purchase method."

The details of GAAP consolidation are beyond the scope of this course. However, property and liability insurers use appropriate GAAP methods to account for business combinations and to prepare consolidated financial statements. Companies such as The Home Insurance Company, The Hartford Insurance Group, Allstate Insurance Company, the Crum and Forster Group, and similar property and liability insurers are parts of larger organizations. The format of financial statements issued to stockholders by the parent corporations of such companies differs from that of nonaffiliated insurers. Some years ago, a survey of the annual reports of 100 stock and 48 mutual property-liability insurance companies indicated that 91 percent of the stock companies were affiliated with other corporate entities.[6] The most typical relationship witnessed in these business combinations is that of a noninsurance holding company parent, which has subsidiary insurance companies. Less typically, a property-liability insurance company may act as parent for other insurance and noninsurance subsidiaries. Financial statements of 78 percent of the stock insurers with intercorporate affiliations were presented on a fully consolidated basis, 10 percent were one-line consolidations, 8 percent were partially consolidated, and 4 percent were not consolidated. Only 27 percent of the stock insurers affiliated with other corporations presented separate financial statements for significant property-liability subsidiaries to supplement their consolidated statements.

Premium Deficiency. During periods of intense price competition, some lines of insurance may generate predictable net underwriting losses. A probable loss on insurance contracts exists if the related unearned premiums will not cover the sum of (1) expected claim costs, (2) loss adjustment expenses, (3) expected dividends to policyholders, (4) policy maintenance costs, and (5) unamortized deferred acquisition costs. Each group of insurance contracts is considered separately to determine whether a premium deficiency exists. Contracts are grouped in a manner consistent with the insurer's method of acquiring, servicing, and measuring the profitability of its insurance contracts. At a minimum, a premium deficiency is recognized under GAAP if a loss is expected on an entire line of business.

For the most part, contracts issued by property-liability insurers are for a relatively short, fixed period and include provisions which allow cancellation or revision at the end of the contract period. A GAAP premium deficiency on such short-duration contracts is recognized first by charging any unamortized acquisition costs to current expenses to an extent necessary to eliminate the deficiency. Then a liability must be established for any deficiency in excess of unamortized acquisition costs. No premium deficiency is calculated for statutory accounting.

Notes to Financial Statements. Financial statements based on GAAP are accompanied by a set of notes that disclose information which cannot be presented adequately otherwise. Notes are an integral part of financial statements. While the use of notes in general purpose financial statements is not a difference between statutory insurance accounting principles and GAAP, their use changes the form of presentation. The statutory annual statement uses both notes and interrogatories to facilitate disclosure of nonquantitative information. Notes in general purpose statements have a similar purpose but their content is different.

The initial notes usually explain the significant accounting policies on which the statements are based and disclose any changes in these policies that have occurred since the previous accounting period. These notes state the basis of presentation (GAAP), consolidation policies, and methods of asset and liability valuation. Notes accompanying property-liability insurance company statements discuss the composition of reserves, the nature of the unearned premium reserve, treatment of deferred acquisition costs, restrictions on the distribution of policy-holders' surplus, and other important information. The number of notes appearing in financial statements varies among companies and between accounting periods but it rarely is less than six and often exceeds ten.

ACCOUNTING REPORTS OF PROPERTY-LIABILITY INSURANCE COMPANIES

Property-liability insurers prepare accounting reports for distribution to a number of distinct audiences. The dominant influence that regulatory accounting practices have on insurance company financial operations explains the importance of regulatory reporting requirements. Reports to users other than state insurance regulators also are important. These reports may differ materially from the statutory statements because they are intended to satisfy informational needs of stockholders, the Securities and Exchange Commission (SEC), the stock exchanges, and the Internal Revenue Service (IRS). Eight accounting reports prepared by property-liability insurance companies will be considered here:

1. The National Association of Insurance Commissioners (NAIC) Annual Statement (see Appendix A)
2. The NAIC Insurance Expense Exhibit (see Appendix B)
3. Reports to shareholders
4. Reports to stock exchanges
5. Reports to the SEC
6. Reports to policyholders

7. Federal income tax reports
8. Reports to company management

While the majority of these reports are financial accounting documents, others contain operating, management, and tax accounting information. Consequently, both statutory and GAAP accounting principles can be involved.

The NAIC Annual Statement

Insurance statutes in all states require that every insurance company authorized to transact business in the state prepare a comprehensive statement reporting its financial position, results of its operations and other supplementary financial data, verified under oath of a responsible officer of the company. The statement must be filed annually, and in some states quarterly, with the insurance department or other designated state authority. The annual filing presents a statement of the company's condition and affairs at December 31 of each year as required by the insurance regulatory authority. It must be filed on or before March 1 of the following year. Fines of up to $100 a day are imposed on delinquent companies unless a delay has been granted by the insurance regulatory authority for a later date. Once filed, these statements are public domain and available for general inspection by any interested party. Information contained in the reports is published in varying degrees of detail by a number of financial data services, such as *Best's Insurance Reports: Property-Liability*.

The regulatory reporting form, generally known as the "convention form of annual statement," "convention blank," or "Annual Statement," has existed for more than 100 years. The National Association of Insurance Commissioners (NAIC) (then known as the National Insurance Convention), was established in 1871, and the Convention's initial meeting assigned a permanent committee on blanks (financial statements) the duty of developing and revising uniform financial blanks for insurance companies. This committee has remained an important part of the NAIC to this day. Except where specific statutes of the various states conflict with the requirements of this form, all Annual Statements filed by insurance companies with state regulatory bodies must be on the current form recommended by the Blanks Committee and approved by the NAIC.

Preparation of the Annual Statement is governed by uniform accounting instructions and the examiners' manual, which are prepared and supervised by the Blanks Committee and the Examinations Oversight Task Force of the NAIC. These uniform instructions and the examiners' manual, in effect, represent a compilation of statutory insurance accounting principles.[7] They not only govern preparation of the Annual Statement but also define the basic accounting and record-keeping system used by insurance companies. Although there is no statutory provision or regulation that mandates companies to keep their records in any specific manner, the filing of required periodic statements of a prescribed form based on uniform principles and standards makes it impractical to maintain the records in any manner that does not facilitate the preparation of the Annual Statement.

In its current form, the Annual Statement is a document containing eighty-eight pages of financial statements, exhibits, and schedules. The cover identifies the document, contains the date, names the company and the state in which the form is filed, lists officers, directors, or trustees of the company, and shows the NAIC Company number and tax ID number and certain other information dealing with the company's location and history. The financial statements found within the first five pages roughly correspond to the summary financial statements of other businesses. The statutory balance sheet is contained on the second and third pages. The statement of underwriting and investment income and the statement of capital and surplus are on the fourth page. The statement of cash flow is on page 5. The fact that the Annual Statement continues for another eighty-three pages indicates the degree of financial disclosure required of insurance companies.

The summary financial statements are followed by a series of exhibits, supporting schedules, and a comprehensive questionnaire. These supporting materials break down the premium writings, the loss payments, unearned premium calculations, and loss reserve provisions in detail by line of coverage. They also show detailed calculation of special statutory loss and loss adjustment expense reserves and the development or maturation of loss reserves to indicate whether or not proper reserves have been carried by the company. The schedules that deal with assets itemize the investments and show their cost, market value, the income received, and similar data. The general interrogatories cover a variety of subjects; for example, one question asks the maximum retention of the insurer on any single exposure unit, other questions deal with the company's capitalization, and others inquire about reinsurance arrangements. The questionnaire discloses information that cannot conveniently be presented in financial exhibits and schedules.

In effect, the Annual Statement is a comprehensive set of working papers that enable the state insurance departments to study the financial position of the company and to obtain a fair idea of the authenticity and reliability of the figures presented without making annual field examinations. Careful study of the Annual Statement by a properly trained examiner can indicate the company's position and demonstrate whether or not further examination into the company's affairs and records is necessary.

The summary financial statements of insurance companies contained in the first five pages of the Annual Statement have a general structure and appearance the same as those found in the financial statements prepared by other commercial enterprises. This appearance disguises the fact that there are material differences between statutory accounting principles and the rules that underlie statements prepared on the basis of GAAP.

Some states and the Central Office of the NAIC now require that the Annual Statement also be submitted on a prescribed magnetic medium such as a computer diskette.

Balance Sheet. *Pages 2 and 3 of the Annual Statement present a balance sheet.* Because of the public nature of the insurance business, regulators impose a higher standard of financial solidity on insurance companies than is expected of other corporations. One way in which the higher standard is imposed is through restricting the assets that are eligible for inclusion on the statutory balance sheet.

Assets. There are two major divisions of assets on page 2 of the Annual Statement. The first seven lines show the various kinds of "invested" assets. These assets consist of bonds, preferred stock, common stock mortgages, real estate, collateral loans, cash (including bank deposits and short-term investments), and other invested assets. The distribution of assets among a large number of insurance companies for these investment categories was shown in Illustration 1-1. The percentages show the relative importance of each category to total assets as of the end of 1988 among 593 stock, 301 mutual, 38 reciprocal, and 8 Lloyds organizations. The industry total for these 940 property-casualty organizations is also given with the industry dollar volume and percent of assets compared to total assets given for major categories.[8] Chapter 2 discusses the nature and valuation of invested assets in detail.

Lines 8 through 20 of the Annual Statement list assets not normally considered investments. These items represent resources of value to the insurance companies even though, for the most part, they do not yield an investment return. The most important category among the noninvested assets is "Agents' Balances or Uncollected Premiums." This account represents insurance premiums due on policies written within ninety days prior to the statement date, net of agents' commissions and policyholder dividends, plus the net amount due on reinsurance assumed and less amounts for ceded reinsurance. An asset category closely related to agents' balances is entitled "Bills Receivable, Taken for Premiums." The amount shown on the balance sheet for this account is the aggregate value of promissory notes, signed by the insured, that are used to finance the installment purchase of insurance. Statutory rules dealing with the quality of the notes must be satisfied in order for a particular note to be included as an eligible asset in this category. Although not considered an investment, the notes bear interest.

Another important asset in this section of the balance sheet carries the title "Funds held by or deposited with reinsured companies." Values in this account represent amounts due, but not currently payable, from other insurance companies that are reinsuring part of their business with the insurer filing the statement.

Liabilities. Obligations resulting from past or current transactions that require a company to convey assets or perform services in the future are considered liabilities. This definition fits the obligations of insurance companies, but historically insurance accounting has used the word "reserves" to describe liabilities while general accounting terminology uses the word "reserve" to describe a portion of retained earnings earmarked for a specific purpose such as "Reserve for Unfunded Pension Obligations." Segregating in this manner implies that the noninsurance company may become obligated to convey assets or perform services at some time in the future because of a current or past transaction, but that this potential obligation is not definitely determinable at the statement date. The segregation of retained earnings by noninsurance companies thus creates an "in between" account, called a reserve, which is classified in the equity section of the balance sheet but, if more information were available, might more properly be considered a liability. Insurance reserves are not allocated retained earnings; they are true liabilities. Unfortunately, a few insurers, particularly mutual companies, use the term "reserve" to designate net worth. Such practices serve to confuse rather than clarify an understanding of insurance company financial statements. The customary insurance terminology which equates liabilities, estimated liabilities, and reserves is retained here.[9]

There are three general categories of property-liability insurance company reserves. The first category includes liabilities for losses and loss adjustment expenses. The second reflects an obligation of the insurer to provide coverage under insurance contracts for which premiums have been paid or are currently due but for which a portion of the coverage extends into the next accounting period. All other obligations are grouped into miscellaneous liabilities.

State insurance statutes require property-liability insurers to establish and maintain reserves for unpaid losses and loss adjustment expenses. Many insurance claims and the expenses that will be incurred to adjust them are difficult to evaluate prior to ultimate settlement. This is especially true of liability claims, the value of which may be influenced by such things as length of discovery period, economic conditions, inflation, legal jurisdiction, and other factors. Because values are not readily known for many losses at the balance sheet date, statistical techniques, actuarial concepts, and the judgment of claims personnel are employed to estimate loss and loss adjustment expense reserves. The resulting liability is called the insurer's loss and loss expense reserve.

Most policyholders pay for their insurance coverage in advance. Premiums collected in advance will be used to pay losses incurred before the policies expire or are canceled. Because property-liability insurers are liable for losses occurring after the accounting period's close and before expiration of the continuing policies' protection period, premiums are not recognized as being earned when collected. Any unexpired policy in force at the accounting period's end must have a proportionate share of its gross premium available to meet future costs associated with the unexpired protection as if all costs were incurred uniformly throughout the policy period. In the event of policy cancellation, any refund due offsets advance premium deposits. A corresponding liability, therefore, is shown on the insurers' balance sheet under the caption, "Reserve for Unearned Premium." Loss reserves show the insurer's liability for losses occurring before the accounting period ended; unearned premium reserves show the insurer's liability to provide coverage under continuing policies.

All liabilities found on a property-liability insurance company's balance sheet other than the loss and loss adjustment expense reserves and the unearned premium reserve are considered miscellaneous liabilities. Several liabilities in this category are peculiar to the insurance business, such as special statutory reserves for particular lines of liability insurance; others are in the nature of unpaid and accrued expenses and deferred costs similar to those shown on the balance sheets of many business organizations.

Illustration 1-15 shows the liabilities of property-liability insurance organizations at the end of 1988. The composition of a particular company's liabilities may differ from the averages for its particular segment. Nevertheless, the table indicates the relative significance of the liability categories that make up the obligations of property and liability insurance companies. The data also can be used to demonstrate the importance of accurate reserve estimation. Chapter 3 discusses the estimation of loss and loss adjustment expense reserves as well as the valuation of unearned premium reserves.

Illustration 1-15

Consolidated Liabilities and Capital and Surplus of Property-Liability Organizations (as of 12/31/88)

	Industry Total 940 Property-Casualty Organizations		Stock Company Total 593 Property-Casualty Organizations		Mutual Company Total 301 Property-Casualty Organizations		Reciprocal Total 38 Property-Casualty Organizations		Lloyds Total 8 Property-Casualty Organizations	
	(Mill. of $)	%	(Mill. of $)	%	(Mill. of $)	%	(Mill. of $)	%	(Mill. of $)	%
Losses	205,935	43.2	142,299	44.4	52,940	40.7	10,436	40.1	259.6	57.5
Loss Adjustment Expenses	35,758	7.5	23,743	7.4	9,122	7.0	2,823	10.8	69.4	15.4
Unearned Premium	76,831	16.1	51,757	16.2	20,434	15.7	4,615	17.7	25.6	5.7
Other Liabilities	40,211	8.4	30,407	9.5	8,522	6.5	1,269	4.9	13.3	2.9
Total Liabilities	358,735	75.2	248,206	77.5	91,018	69.9	19,142	73.5	367.8	81.4
Capital Paid-up	6,420	1.3	5,967	1.9	421	0.3	30	0.1	2.2	0.5
Guaranty Funds	290	0.1	31	0.0	245	0.2	12	0.0	1.7	0.4
Assigned Funds	53,822	11.3	40,356	12.6	12,731	9.8	724	2.8	11.7	2.6
Unassigned Funds	57,663	12.1	25,725	8.0	25,730	19.8	6,139	23.6	68.3	15.1
Policyholders' Surplus	118,195	24.8	72,079	22.5	39,127	30.1	6,906	26.5	83.9	18.6
Total	476,929	100.0	320,285	100.0	130,145	100.0	26,048	100.0	451.8	100.0

Based on data from *Best's Aggregates & Averages*, Property-Casualty, 1989.

Capital and Surplus. Conventional accounting terminology states that assets minus liabilities equals net worth. Using insurance accounting terminology, this relationship is expressed as admitted assets minus liabilities equals "policyholders' surplus," or simply surplus. The term policyholders' surplus is meant to convey the idea that total balance sheet assets are available primarily for the satisfaction of policyholder claims. In the case of stock insurance companies, the stockholders' claim on assets is subordinated to the claims of policyholders and other creditors. The use of the term policyholders' surplus for the company's net worth reflects the primacy given satisfaction of obligations to policyholders.

Several purposes are served by policyholders' surplus. Initial capitalization provides the resources needed by the insurer to begin business. After operations have commenced, policyholders' surplus furnishes a financial cushion to guard the insurer's solvency against fluctuating investment values and underwriting results. In any business, the growth of net worth is necessary for expansion. This is especially true for insurance companies because increases in premium volume depress statutory underwriting earnings and hence surplus during the current accounting period because prepaid expenses are not recognized. In addition to these general purposes, policyholders' surplus may also fulfill special functions; for instance, a portion of surplus may be set aside to comply with post-insolvency guarantee fund requirements.

The average size of policyholders surplus for the three primary types of insurance organizations is shown in Illustration 1-15. Stockholder-owned insurance companies, on the average, show a lower percentage of surplus to assets than mutuals or reciprocals. This should not be interpreted to mean that stock insurance companies are less financially strong than other insurers; nor does this mean that stock companies necessarily operate more efficiently than the others. Policyholders' surplus-to-asset ratios vary greatly among companies and over time. Chapter 5 addresses adequate policyholders' surplus in the establishment and maintenance of insurance company solvency.

Income Statement. A summary operating report entitled "Underwriting and Investment Exhibit Statement of Income" appears on page 4 of the Annual Statement. Three separate sources of income are shown. First, underwriting income is summarized as the excess of premiums earned over underwriting losses and expenses incurred. Not all net premiums written in a particular accounting period are recognized as revenue in that period. Revenue and expense recognition rules of accrual accounting apply to premium revenue and losses. Only the portion of premiums written in the current and prior accounting periods that corresponds to the protection services provided in the current period is recognized as earned. Losses and loss adjustment expenses paid during the year plus any increase in reserves for unpaid losses and loss expenses are allocated against the period's underwriting revenues. The treatment of other underwriting expenses resembles cash accounting practices. Expenses incurred in underwriting operations are treated as period expenses and recognized currently.

Two lines on the underwriting and investment exhibit summarize investment income. Net investment income earned for the period consists of interest, dividends, and real estate income collected and accrued less investment expenses and depreciation. Net capital gains or losses realized on the sale or maturity of assets are added to the investment income items. The sum of these two lines equals net gain or loss from investment activities for the year. Capital gains or losses on investments in stocks which remain unrealized at year end are not considered income (such annual changes are reflected as a direct adjustment to surplus).

The third section of the underwriting and investment exhibit shows revenue and expenses from sources other than underwriting and investment operations. There are several standard entries in this section and a variety of miscellaneous entries peculiar to individual company operations. For instance, one standard item—usually a negative figure—is entitled "Net Gain or Loss From Agents or Premium Balances Charged Off." This line is used to write off as a loss agent's or premium balances determined to be uncollectible. If amounts charged off in previous periods subsequently become collectible, an income entry for the amount recovered is made. A net gain is recorded as an increment to income for current period collections in excess of charge offs; a net loss is entered if the opposite relationship exists.

The sum of the net gains or losses from underwriting and investment operations plus total other income equals net income before policyholder dividends and income taxes. A deduction is taken for policyholder dividends incurred during the year. The dividend deduction includes dividends actually paid during the year less those incurred but unpaid at the beginning of the year plus dividends incurred but unpaid at year end. The income tax deduction includes federal and foreign income taxes incurred. The final entry in the underwriting and investment exhibit is statutory net income.

Capital and Surplus Account. The bottom section of page 4 of the Annual Statement contains a reconciliation of the policyholders' surplus account. This statement, entitled the "Capital and Surplus Account," corresponds to the statement of retained earnings found among the financial statements of other business organizations. The capital and surplus account presented in the Annual Statement appears to be an extension of the income statement. The final line in the underwriting and investment exhibit statement of income is line 16, net income. This total is brought forward to line 18 of the capital and surplus account. The first line in the capital and surplus account is line 17, policyholders' surplus at the beginning of the current period. Line 18 is the first change noted between capital and surplus at December 31 of the previous year (line 17) and surplus as regards policyholders, December 31 of the current year (line 32). Other changes in the capital and surplus account are reflected in line 19 to 31 and include such items as net unrealized capital gains or losses, and other gain or loss items resulting from operations that have not been reflected in income. A charge for the amortization of unfunded supplemental pension liabilities is an example of a cost that affects policyholders' surplus but does not flow through the income statement. Transactions involving capital accounts, such as declaration of a stock dividend or contributions of surplus by the company's founders are shown on lines 24 and 25. Stockholder cash dividends declared during the current years are deducted from surplus. Line 31 shows the year's change in surplus as regards policyholders. The closing policyholders' surplus figure on line 32 of the capital and surplus account must agree with the corresponding balance sheet entry on line 26, page 3 of the Annual Statement.

Statement of Cash Flow. A statement of cash flow appears on page 5 of the Annual Statement. This shows the sources and uses of funds within a property-liability insurance company. It serves two purposes: (1) it completes the disclosure of changes in financial position that cannot be fully determined by analyzing successive income statements and capital and surplus accounts and (2) it summarizes the financing and investing activities of the insurance company, including the extent to which it has generated funds from operations during the period. Page 5 lists funds provided from underwriting operations (subtotaled on line 5), funds provided from investments (line 6), and funds provided from disposition of investments (line 11). Other sources (uses) of funds listed include other income, dividends paid to policyholders, federal income taxes paid, and transactions involving capital and surplus accounts. Total funds provided are totaled on line 13.

The lower portion of this statement of cash flows shows how funds were applied. The cost of investments are detailed in six broad categories of invested assets. The sum of investments acquired and other applications of funds is subtracted from total funds provided. A positive difference in sources and applications of funds results in an increase in cash and short-term investments. The final two lines on the statement use the net change in funds to reconcile the year's beginning and ending cash and short-term investment balances.

Exhibits and Schedules. Detailed information supporting the summary financial statements appears immediately following the balance sheet, income statement, and capital and surplus account. The underwriting and investment exhibit on pages 6 through 11 itemizes resource and operating data that are presented summarily in the basic statements. Investment income, realized capital gains and losses, and unrealized capital gains and losses receive extended treatment on page 6, Part 1. The net income and the gain and loss items calculated here are transferred to the income statement and the capital and surplus account. Premiums—written, earned, and in force—are enumerated on pages 7 and 8, Part 2. The premium analysis provides information for the balance sheet (unearned premium reserve) and for the income statement (premiums earned). Losses and loss adjustment expenses paid and incurred during the year are listed on page 9, Part 3, by line of business. The total incurred loss figure is carried from page 9 to line 2 of the income statement on page 4. Unpaid losses, including IBNR claims, and loss adjustment expenses are displayed by line of business on page 10, Part 3A. Totals from this page are entered as loss and loss expense reserves in the liability section of the balance sheet on page 3. Page 11, Part 4 of the underwriting and investment exhibit gives a detailed presentation of loss adjustment expenses, other underwriting expenses, and expenses incurred in connection with investment operations. The first two expense categories shown here appear as deductions in the underwriting section on the income statement. Investment expenses are netted against investment income in Part 1 of the underwriting and investment exhibit on page 6; net investment income is then carried forward to the income statement.

Page 12 of the Annual Statement contains two exhibits: Exhibit 1, "Analysis of Assets"; and Exhibit 2, "Analysis of Nonadmitted Assets." It is sometimes said that the completion of the Annual Statement begins on page 12 because assets shown on the balance sheet are developed in Exhibit 1. Exhibit 2 analyzes any change in nonadmitted assets during the year.

Page 13, Exhibit 3, "Reconciliation of Ledger Assets," shows increases and decreases in the ledger accounts which together explain the year's change in ledger assets. Because nonledger accounts are not shown here, the exhibit may be considered an incomplete trial balance. It may seem strange that insurance companies publish what is essentially a cash basis trial balance as a supporting document to their financial statements. The usual explanation given for the practice is that the reconciliation of ledger assets is used in the examination process.

Page 14 (a separate page for each state) provides statistical detail of premiums written and earned, policyholder dividends, and losses paid, unpaid, and incurred, on direct business (excluding premiums for reinsurance accepted or ceded) by each line of business for which the insurer is licensed.

Pages 16 and 17 contain the regulatory questionnaire. Information provided on these pages should be reviewed carefully by anyone attempting to evaluate the company's financial condition and operations. Various interrogatories relating to the company's capitalization, reinsurance arrangements, affiliated companies, dealings with officers, employees, and stockholders, and the territory of its operations must be answered. An affirmation that reserves have been adequately provided also is required. The Annual Statement's remaining pages are devoted to analytical schedules. The content and purpose of the lettered schedules are summarized in Appendix C.

Five-Year Historical Data. A summary of financial data taken or developed from Annual Statements for the five most recent years appears on pages 21 and 22. This summary information facilitates analysis of trends in the insurer's recent operating performance and financial condition. The exhibit shows selected balance sheet and income statement items, traces changes in the composition of the insurer's cash and invested assets, and discloses investments in the securities of subsidiary and affiliated corporations during the five-year period. Loss reserve development data and selected financial ratios also are included. The exhibit contains all of the data needed to calculate the NAIC Insurance Regulatory Information System (IRIS) ratios. The IRIS ratios, which are key analytical yardsticks used in evaluating the status of an insurer, are described in Chapter 5.

Insurance Expense Exhibit

As a supplement to the Annual Statement, insurers are required to file the NAIC's "Insurance Expense Exhibit" (see Appendix B). It must be filed with the insurance department or other designated public authority of every state in which the insurer is licensed to transact business. The filing date is April 1 of the year following the calendar year covered by the exhibit. Several purposes are served by the document. It develops a complete statement of operating gain or loss before federal income taxes for each line of business. Operating results include statutory underwriting gain or loss, allocated investment income, and policyholder dividends. Results reported in the exhibit can be used to determine the company's profitability on each line of business. The report provides a uniform, detailed presentation of all expenses for each expense classification and each expense function by line of insurance. In addition, the exhibit furnishes aggregate expense data that may be used in ratemaking to determine appropriate expense levels by line and by function within each line.

The record keeping and reporting of expenses in an insurance company, as in other organizations, necessitate the use of a cost accounting system. Such a system records, classifies, and allocates expenses according to a predetermined underlying set of instructions. The NAIC originally established the underlying principles for a company's cost accounting system in a booklet entitled *Instructions for Uniform Classification of Expenses*. The purpose of the uniform instructions is to establish standards to be followed by all companies in classifying expenses. This uniformity facilitates meaningful comparisons among companies and over time. Standardized cost accounting instructions promote consistency among company accounting systems, Annual Statements, and supplementary reports such as the Insurance Expense Exhibit. Financial examinations conducted by insurance regulatory authorities also benefit from the uniform accounting procedures. The Insurance Expense Exhibit is discussed in Chapter 4.

Reports to Shareholders

All publicly owned stock property-liability insurance companies issue periodic reports to their owners. A company is considered "publicly owned" if it is subject to regulation by the SEC. The financial statements contained in these reports often require independent certification by a qualified accountant. Such certification usually involves development of financial data unavailable in the NAIC Annual Statement. Thus while these other financial statements may appear similar to the Annual Statement, they are intended to serve clearly distinct purposes and may be based on a separate set of accounting principles.

Reports to shareholders provide the owners with information on the company's current financial position and results of its operations during the most recent accounting period. Owners can use this information to evaluate for themselves the effectiveness of management's current policies.

Shareholder reports may include a comprehensive annual report and briefer quarterly reports. The content of these reports can be divided into two parts: a general communication to the owners by management and a set of formal financial statements. Although management's communication may contain some financial information, it typically concentrates on descriptive narratives. It allows management a chance to discuss events that have affected the company during the past accounting period and to comment on how past and future events are expected to impact on the company. For instance, the effects of natural disasters, political upheaval, or changing social mores may receive attention. These comments customarily are set forth in the president's letter to the shareholders. The letter often discusses the future of the insurance business and the economy and makes a statement regarding the company's future position in this developing environment. A comment on special problems within the business and how these problems relate to society at large has become typical. Although the textual portion of the report may be considered nonfinancial, it sets the stage for the formal financial statements.

Reports to Stock Exchanges

An insurance company whose stock is traded on an organized stock exchange must issue annual and quarterly reports to its shareholders and file a copy with the exchange. Failure to comply with this requirement results in termination of trading in the company's shares on the exchange. The financial statements contained in these shareholder reports must include a qualified accountant's certification that they comply with GAAP.

Reports to the SEC

In addition to the stock exchange requirements, all companies with publicly traded securities must comply with the disclosure requirements of the federal securities laws, primarily the Securities Act of 1933 and the Securities Exchange Act of 1934. Responsibility for enforcement of the federal securities laws rests with the SEC. The disclosure requirements of the 1934 Act apply to all companies with more than 500 shareholders and assets of $1 million or more. *Regulation S-X*, "Form and Content of Financial Statements," is the principal body of accounting rules and articles used by the SEC to administer the various federal securities laws. This body of regulations together with occasional "accounting series releases" promulgated by the SEC dictate the form and content of all financial statements and supporting materials filed with the Commission. Most documents filed with the SEC are available to shareholders and the general public upon request.

When any company first has its stock listed on a regulated stock exchange, or when it attains the minimum size and ownership limits, it must register with the SEC by filing Form 10. This form is used only once for the initial registration. In general, the financial statement requirements of Form 10 call for the filing of a certified balance sheet for the most current accounting period, an income statement, a statement of cash flow, and a retained earnings statement for the three previous years.

Financial statements of property-liability insurers filed with the SEC must accord with GAAP. The SEC's Form 10-K is the primary *annual* report of registered companies. Item 10 of Form 10-K contains financial statements of the registrant in comparative columnar form for the previous two years and a five-year summary of operations. It must be filed with the SEC within ninety days after the end of the registrant's fiscal year. Form 10-K actually may be of greater use to shareholders interested in making comparisons than the financial statements contained in the reports sent to shareholders because the SEC prescribes a uniform format and terminology to be used in completing the form. Also, Form 10-K contains more detail than normally is provided in the shareholder reports issued by most companies. A copy of Form 10-K can be obtained directly from the filing corporation or from the SEC.

A quarterly report on Form 10-Q also must be filed with the SEC for each of the first three quarters of the year. The fourth quarter information is contained in the annual 10-K report. Form 10-Q is due within forty-five days of the end of the quarter to which it applies. This form is briefer than Form 10-K and does not require certification. Although this form is not certified, it does require management to affirm that the information provided presents a fair statement of the results for the interim period.

Other Accounting and Statistical Reports

The reports discussed thus far primarily are intended for two groups: (1) the NAIC annual statement and the insurance expense exhibit satisfy state insurance department filing requirements and (2) the reports issued by stock insurers to their shareholders, to stock exchanges, and to the SEC satisfy disclosure requirements of publicly owned companies. Property-liability insurance companies prepare several additional reports for other users.

Policyholder Reports. Property-liability insurers that are not considered publicly owned also issue periodic financial reports to their owners. Nonpublicly owned companies include privately held stock companies, mutuals, reciprocals, American Lloyds associations, and captive insurers. Because these insurers do not solicit capital in the public financial markets, they are not required to comply with uniform reporting practices other than those imposed by state insurance regulation. Consequently, the nonregulatory reporting practices of these insurers tend to vary. It is customary, however, for nonpublicly owned insurers, especially mutuals, to distribute some form of annual financial report to their policyholders. Often they include a brief policyholder report along with premium billings. These reports present a synopsis of the company's current financial position and operating results during the most recent two-year period. Usually this information is taken from the Annual Statement and is not certified.

Several states now require insurance companies licensed in their state to have annual audits. A copy of the audit report must be filed with such states on or before June 30 of the following year. Nonpublic companies generally limit distribution of the audit opinion to their directors and regulatory authorities.

Reports to Statistical Agencies. Property-liability insurers file reports with statistical agents licensed by the states to collect and compile premium and loss experience for many lines of insurance. The requirement to file such data with an agency approved by the state may serve two purposes. States that require prior approval of rates for particular lines of insurance often allow insurers to establish loss costs collectively through a rate advisory organization or rating bureau. Rate advisory organizations such as the Insurance Services Office and the National Council on Compensation Insurance serve as both advisory organizations and statistical agents. In addition to the economy and efficiency of this coordinated effort in collecting data, combining premium and loss data from a number of companies increases the statistical credibility of the resulting pure premiums and expense margins. In states with so-called open competition rating, the statistical filing requirement provides a public record of the aggregate experience insurers have achieved. This record is of interest to insurers that develop their rates independently and the information also is available for regulatory and other public policy purposes.

Data for statistical reports are developed from the company's premium and loss records. The degree of detail and method of classifying this data on the statistical reports depends on the line of business and the procedures followed by a particular agency. Codes are assigned to identify general characteristics of insurance coverage. Additional coding is used to classify information pertaining to the line of insurance. It is the statistical agent's responsibility to verify that the premium and loss data supplied in the statistical reports it receives are in agreement with the company's Annual Statement. Specifically, the statistical data must correspond to the exhibit of premiums and losses and the state-by-state data in Schedule T. Ocean marine, aviation, and some inland marine lines of business are not included in reports to statistical agencies. Reinsurance assumed and ceded also is omitted from the reports.

Federal Income Tax Reports. The application of tax laws to any business enterprise is a highly complex subject that requires a thorough understanding of general accounting, the tax code, current court decisions relating to tax matters, and rulings and determinations of the Internal Revenue Service. In the case of regulated businesses like insurance, some understanding of accounting practices unique to the business is required. This discussion does not attempt to cover income taxation of property-liability insurance companies fully. It is merely an overview of some principles of income taxation as applied to nonlife insurers and their relationship to regulatory insurance accounting.

General Taxation Rules. Like most other business corporations, all property-liability insurance companies are subject to federal taxation in accordance with provisions of the current Internal Revenue Code (IRC). Basically, insurance companies are taxed as ordinary corporations.[10] In order to deal with the unique nature of insurance company operations, special sections of the IRC specifically treating insurers generally supersedes certain provisions of the general tax law. Nonetheless, computation of an insurance company's income tax obligation essentially involves the same types of calculations followed by other corporations.

Several aspects of the tax treatment afforded property and liability insurers are common to the taxation of all corporations:

- The requirement for filing a federal income tax return
- The application of graduated tax rates
- Certain administrative procedures involved with timely payment of taxes
- The availability of various tax credits
- Provision for carrying the tax losses and credits over to other tax years

These general rules are not discussed here.

Special Tax Rules. Determining an insurer's income tax obligation involves certain departures from the tax laws generally applied to corporations. These departures give recognition to the unique operating characteristics of insurance companies and to a large degree are made to accommodate accounting practices mandated by state insurance regulators.

Underwriting Income. Tax accounting principles recognize revenue only after the occurrence of a critical event which assures that the revenue will, in fact, be received. This event typically is the point of sale when the purchaser pays or becomes obligated to pay. Costs associated with a transaction are recognized as expenses when the costs are incurred or as they accrue. Thus, corporations use accrual accounting principles rather than cash-basis accounting to determine taxable income. The calculation matches recognized revenues and expenses rather than cash receipts and disbursements.

The normal tax rules of revenue and expense recognition are not used to calculate an insurer's taxable income. As premiums are received before the insurer fulfills its contractual obligations and regulatory insurance accounting requires that premium revenues be recognized as income proportionally over the contractual coverage period, tax rules are modified for insurers to agree in substance with revenue recognition principles inherent in the Annual Statement. As a result, most of the premium revenue flows into taxable income later than otherwise would be the case.

Similarly, the expense recognition rules used in the Annual Statement are incorporated in the tax law for insurance companies. Acquisition expenses for most organizations would be allocated against their corresponding revenues as that revenue was recognized into income. However, statutory accounting forces the immediate deduction of acquisition expenses when they are incurred. Revenues and expenses are "mismatched" by the annual statement recognition rules. Tax rules for insurers also allow this mismatching of revenues and expenses. This mismatching has the effect of reducing taxable income during periods of expanding sales because acquisition expenses are incurred and recognized in advance of the corresponding increase in premium revenues.

Another variance between general tax principles and the tax treatment afforded insurance companies relates to the recognition of losses. For an insurance company, claims settlement expenses are analogous to the cost of goods sold by a manufacturing or mercantile corporation. Noninsurance business organizations normally recognize costs only after the events creating them are completed and the amount of cost is fully determined. Unpaid losses and loss adjustment expenses in an insurance company are not fully determined at the close of the tax year; they at least partially must be estimated. Nevertheless, because reasonable estimates of aggregate loss and loss settlement expenses can be made, the estimated loss costs are recognized on a present value basis as deductions from revenue before their final value is fully known.

Underwriting income is determined as the difference between premiums earned on insurance contracts during the tax year and losses and expenses incurred. Each component of underwriting income is calculated in a way that parallels statutory rather than general accounting principles. Consider the accounts shown in Illustration 1-16. Premiums earned on insurance contracts during the current tax year are calculated in three steps: (1) direct premiums written and premiums or reinsurance assumed are added; (2) premiums returned for refunds and credits and premiums paid for reinsurance are deducted from gross premiums written; and (3) the change in unearned premiums between the end of the preceding and the current tax years reduced by 20 percent under the Tax Reform Act of 1986 is deducted from net premiums written. Losses incurred on insurance contracts are computed as: (1) losses paid during the tax year are added to reinsurance and salvage recoverable at the end of the preceding tax year; (2) from this amount, reinsurance and salvage recoverable at the end of the current year are subtracted; and (3) the change in the present value of unpaid losses during the current year is added. Expenses incurred during the current tax year equal the sum of expenses paid during the year plus (1) the change in loss adjustment expenses during the year and (2) the change in other unpaid expenses. A deduction also is allowed for dividends and similar distributions paid or declared to policyholders.

Reasonableness of Insurance Deductions. In 1975 the IRS issued revenue Procedure 75-56 as a guideline for ascertaining the reasonableness of estimated loss reserves. This guideline is intended for use by revenue agents examining property and liability tax returns. Unfortunately, the clarity of the Revenue Procedure has been questioned due to the subjective standard of reasonableness it imposes. When differences of opinion occur as to the reasonableness of loss reserve estimates, a challenge by the IRS can be expected.

Investment Income. An insurance company has two sources of investment income: (1) interest, dividends, rents and other investment earnings; and (2) realized capital gains and losses. Interest received by an insurance company on obligations of others, such as another corporation's bonds owned by the insurer, generally is fully includable as ordinary income to the insurer. Interest income on nontaxable municipal bonds is not entirely excludable from taxable income. The 1986 Act treats 15 percent of otherwise tax-exempt income as taxable if the underlying security was acquired after August 7, 1986. Interest income is reported on an accrual basis for both annual statement and income tax purposes. However, because of differences concerning the amortization of bond premiums and discounts, and due to the tax exemption of municipal bond interest, the amount of interest income subject to tax may substantially differ from that shown on the annual statement.

Generally speaking, for all corporations, 80 percent of the divi-

Illustration 1-16

Reconciliation of Annual Statement Net Income with Taxable Income

Annual Statement Net Income		$6,905,000
Adjustments for tax purposes:		
Difference between book/tax depreciation	(401,218)	
Fixed assets expensed	348,265	
PAL subtractions (mutuals only)	233,000	
Business meal exclusion	14,959	
Dividend received deduction	(311,847)	
Tax exempt interest	(2,037,765)	
Accrued dividends receivable	1,528	
15% tax-exempt interest and dividends		
after 8/7/86	112,751	
1/6 of 20% of 12/31/86 UEP†	598,488	
20% of UEP	314,806	
L & LAE discounting	394,873	
Premiums on officers life insurance	59,243	
Salvage & subrogation	50,351	
		622,566
Taxable income		6,282,434
Tax @ 34%		2,136,028
Environmental tax (from below)		6,936
Tax for the year		2,142,964
Taxable income from above		$6,282,434
Adjustments to arrive at adjusted		
current earnings (ACE):		
Add back:		
Tax exempt interest		2,037,765
Dividend received deduction		311,847
Subtotal		8,632,046
Less 15% of tax exempt interest		
interest and dividend received		
deduction after 8/7/86		112,751
Adjusted current earnings		8,519,295
Less tentative AMTI from above		6,282,434
Difference		2,236,861
AMT @ 75%		1,677,646
Tentative AMTI		6,282,434
Alternative minimum taxable income		7,960,080
AMT @ 20%		1,592,016
Environmental tax @ .12% of the modified		
AMTI for the year over $2,000,000		
($7,960,080 less $2,000,000 @ .0012 =)		7,152
Tax for the year		$1,599,168
Note: Alternative minimum not applicable since normal		
tax is a larger tax for the year.		

†The Tax Reform Act of 1986 included this "fresh start" provision to phase in the impact of the change in the tax treatment of the unearned premium reserve.

dends received on the common or preferred stock of another United States corporation is excluded from taxable income unless the stock was acquired after August 7, 1986. As with tax exempt interest income, these are subject to the 15 percent proration. This intercorporate dividend exemption is intended to reduce the multiple taxation of corporate income. The dividend exemption may encourage insurers to seek dividend income instead of interest income or to invest in stocks of corporations with high dividend payouts rather than companies that retain larger portions of their earnings and offer the possibility of capital gains.

Rents are included in taxable and Annual Statement income on an accrual basis. Prepaid rent is included in taxable income when received regardless of when it is considered earned. Insurance companies also have other miscellaneous sources of investment income such as the income earned by writing call options on stocks held in the company's investment portfolio.

Capital Gains and Losses. The sale of a capital asset at more or less than its cost basis for tax purposes gives rise to a gain or loss. At present (1989), capital gains tax rates are the same as ordinary income tax rates.

Tax rules normally only allow capital losses to be offset against capital gains. Under certain circumstances, however, property-liability insurers are allowed to offset capital losses against ordinary income. This so-called abnormal loss deduction arises in particularly adverse situations in which an insurer must sell assets to fund loss and dividend payments to policyholders. In order to qualify the capital loss for treatment as an abnormal loss deduction, the insurer's net premiums received plus gross investment income, exclusive of capital items, must be insufficient to fund loss, expense, and dividend payments.

Management Information. Other external reports begin with statutory accounting information and adjust it for the purposes to be served. To some extent the use of financial accounting data carries over into management accounting. The NAIC Annual Statement and stockholder financial reports are of use to management. Tax consequences, when material, should enter all management decisions. While these external reports enter into the management information system, they do not fully define it. Given the broader range of uses for accounting information within the company, some segments of the management information system are independent of the financial accounting process.

Contrasts to Financial Accounting. A company's internal accounting system differs from its financial accounting system in several respects. Management information is not expressed exclusively in terms of a monetary unit. Other units of measure provide useful information to management. For instance, activity in a particular service center might be measured in terms of the number of new policies, renewals, endorsements, cancellations, claims arising, claims closed, drafts issued, checks issued, and so forth. Such data can be used in performance evaluation and resource planning.

Management information often requires projection of data rather than analysis of historical results. Establishing budgets and making decisions involving alternative choices illustrate the need for projected information. Data used by management do not always come from within the company. Data supplied by insurance associations, institutions, and government agencies may be included in management reports. Outside data of this nature can be helpful in making comparative analysis.

Management information also differs from financial accounting in that it is more often used to influence the behavior of employees. This characteristic helps determine the format and use of internal accounting reports.

Use of Management Information. There are three broad uses of management information: communication, planning, and control. Each use can be subdivided and none is independent of the others.

Communication. Communication is vitally important in any business and becomes more formalized in larger organizations with diversified functions. Personal involvement of top management in operations is neither feasible nor desirable. Yet management must maintain familiarity with all aspects of operations if it hopes to avoid surprises involving negative results. To do this, management information must serve as an early warning system that detects problems quickly and reports dimensions of the problem accurately. Communication aspects of the information system also are used to inform personnel of operating policies and company goals. This information serves to facilitate daily activities and motivate employees in their work.

Planning. Planning involves setting goals for the company and mapping how these goals are to be achieved. For a stock property-liability company, the fundamental management objective might be expressed as long-run maximization of stockholder wealth. A mutual insurance company's management might state its primary objective to be minimization of policyholder cost. Other corollary objectives, such as maintenance or expansion of the company's market share, would be coordinated with the fundamental company objective. Management accounting data helps to set intermediate goals by which the firm's progress toward its objectives can be measured. The planning process requires communication and negotiation among managers at all organizational levels. In this way individual managers are given an opportunity to participate in planning the company's future and their own.

Control. There are several aspects to the management control process. Seeing that daily tasks are accomplished successfully is operational control. It is performed by front-line supervisory personnel and does not require the attention of senior management. The control process in which senior management does participate directly involves moving the company toward its operational goals. Frequently summary reports from predetermined responsibility centers that facilitate comparison of actual progress to planned performance are used for control purposes.

Management Reports. An executive of a large property-liability insurance company operating through independent agents stated that his company prepares 1,100 management reports each year.[11] The exact type and number of reports prepared for internal use varies greatly among insurance companies. A company's size, corporate affiliations, organizational structure, marketing system, the geographical scope of its operations, and other factors determine the types of management reports needed. A close-up view of an insurance company could easily give the impression that the huge volume of information being processed at any one time is uncontrolled. There seems to be a constant tendency for internal reports to multiply. Companies therefore find it necessary to continuously monitor their information systems in order to avoid meaningless proliferation and duplication of reports. In spite of the lack of uniformity among reports prepared for company management, the following examples illustrate the nature of these reports.

A great many reports contain operating data; five are major summary reports prepared for broad management purposes. In one company, an agency-based production report appears three times each year. The report shows premiums written and earned by line of business; these are matched with losses incurred, IBNR claims, and commission expenses. Data are set forth on a year-to-date basis with comparative information from the previous five years. The report provides sufficient detail for individual agency evaluation. This illustrates the type of performance report used to monitor agency profitability, loss development, and product mix. It highlights deviation of reported performance from projected standards in a timely fashion. Analysis of the report over several periods gives company management an indication of each agency's progress and growth potential. The report is distributed to all branches and agencies to provide each service unit with information on its own performance.

The insurer also prepares a monthly performance report that details company underwriting profitability for each responsibility center and line of business. Premiums written and earned, net of reinsurance, are matched with losses incurred, IBNR claims, and incurred expenses to determine statutory underwriting results for the year to date. These data are summarized in reported loss ratios, expense ratios, and combined ratios. The responsibility centers are defined by organizational category. For example, the company's personal property underwriting unit includes homeowners, dwelling, inland marine, and related lines. Data are aggregated from individual responsibility centers to the branch office level and then to the company level. Unit, branch, and company management thus are informed monthly on progress toward annual production and profit goals. Underwriting and ratemaking policy decisions can be reevaluated monthly using this performance information.

Performance reports are prepared periodically for investment operations. They detail recent acquisitions, show the current distribution of portfolio assets, and indicate current investment income. Average yields from the portfolio and from individual investment categories are shown along with rates of return on newly invested funds. Investment results are compared to the corresponding period in the previous year. In addition, the company's performance is compared to a broad-based market index, such as the Standard and Poor's Index of 500 Stocks.

Other management reports deal with resource utilization, cost allocation, and planning. Monitoring resource utilization often involves the use of nonmonetary data. For instance, the number of claims settled per employee-hour worked in the claims office can be a useful check on productivity. Count data on the volume of activity in a given service unit also can provide a base for allocating indirect (fixed) costs to the function. A fundamental planning report prepared monthly and at less frequent intervals is the cash budget. Cash budgeting facilitates synchronization of cash flows from premium revenues and investment returns, sales, and maturities with disbursements for loss settlements, expense payments, and investment acquisitions. Frequent comparisons of actual to budgeted cash utilization are required in coordinating underwriting and investment operations.

SUMMARY

This chapter described the principal types of accounting reports prepared by property-liability insurance companies. The form and content of the statutory Annual Statement is designed to facilitate regulatory purposes, especially solvency surveillance, the NAIC examination process, and premium tax collection. The Annual Statement's many exhibits and schedules contain detailed information useful in testing, evaluating, and otherwise amplifying the contents of its summary financial statements. Standards of accounting, referred to as statutory accounting principles, are imposed on property-liability insurers through the requirements for filing an Annual Statement, the Insurance Expense Exhibit, and other supplementary documents.

Mutual and reciprocal insurance companies prepare reports to their policyholders by extracting and summarizing information from their Annual Statement. Stock insurance companies also prepare external reports that are filed with the stock exchanges and the SEC. Reports to stockholders usually contain financial statements based on GAAP rather than statutory accounting rules. Material differences in these two sets of accounting standards can have a significant effect on the financial position and operating results reported by an insurer. Notes included in general purpose financial statements explain the basis of accounting used in their preparation and acknowledge the divergence from statutory accounting documents.

Both stock and mutual insurers prepare reports for internal use. Financial accounting data included in management reports is supplemented by other quantitative and nonquantitative information that enables control, planning, and decision making.

Chapter Notes

1. German Alliance Insurance Company v. Lewis, 233 U.S. 389 (1914).
2. Nebbis v. New York, 291 U.S. 502 (1934).
3. See Chapter 2 in *Audits of Fire and Casualty Insurance Companies* (New York: American Institute of Certified Public Accountants, 1966).
4. Eldon S. Hendricksen, *Accounting Theory*, revised ed. (Homewood, IL: Richard D. Irwin, 1970), pp. 57-59.
5. Committee on Auditing Procedure of the American Institute of Certified Public Accountants, *Auditing Standards and Procedures, Statement on Auditing Procedure No. 33* (New York: American Institute of Certified Public Accountants, 1963), pp. 70-71.
6. *Financial Reporting Trends, Fire and Casualty Insurance* (New York: Ernst & Ernst, 1974), pp. 13-19.
7. In 1980, the NAIC published a manual setting forth a compilation of current accounting practices and procedures prescribed or permitted by regulatory authorities. *Accounting Practices and Procedures Manual for Fire and Casualty Insurance Companies* (Milwaukee: National Association of Insurance Commissioners, 1980).
8. *Best's Aggregates & Averages: Property-Liability*, 50th annual edition (Morristown, NJ: A.M. Best Company, 1989), pp. 2, 4, 6, 8, 10.
9. Some authors use the term "estimated liabilities" for loss and loss adjustment expense reserves because the ultimate costs associated with these items are not known and must be estimated at the time financial statements are prepared. Other obligations of the insurer that can be evaluated more directly are called "liabilities." See, for example, Ruth Salzmann, "Estimated Liabilities for Losses and Loss Adjustment Expenses," in *Property-Liability Insurance Accounting*, 4th Ed., Robert W. Strain, editor (Durham, NC: Insurance Accounting and Systems Association, 1988), pp. 56-57.
10. Special tax provisions may apply to certain organizations established to provide medical malpractice insurance, to captive insurers, and to private investors participating in insurance exchange syndicates organized as "Subchapter S" corporations.
11. Carl B. Drake, Jr., "What an Insurance Executive Expects from Management Reports," *Best's Review*, Property-Liability Edition (May 1973), pp. 78-82.

CHAPTER 2

Valuation of Insurance Company Assets

This chapter is divided into three major sections. The first section describes the principal asset accounts of property-liability insurance companies. This nontechnical section introduces the necessary terminology and background material to understand property-liability insurance company balance sheets.

The second section of the chapter focuses on the impact of common stock and bond valuation on insurance company surplus. Discussion is limited to these two asset types because they represent the greatest portion of insurance company assets and the largest segments of assets over which management can exercise direct control.

The third section of the chapter examines the factors affecting investment policy and explains the concepts of insurance exposure and insurance leverage as they pertain to property-liability insurance companies. These concepts are necessary tools to provide a proper understanding of property-liability insurance company investment policy. This section addresses the role of underwriting results, product line mix, and risk/return attributes of common stocks and bonds in the formulation of an investment policy.

ASSETS OF PROPERTY-LIABILITY INSURANCE COMPANIES

The primary thrust of insurance company regulation is insurance company solvency. The insurance policy is a contract obligating the insurance company to make future financial settlements to, or on behalf of, insureds who incur economic loss. Statutory restrictions and

51

limitations on how insurance companies invest their assets ensure that they can meet their financial obligations to policyholders.

The states have enacted statutes and promulgated administrative regulations that seek to balance the interests of insureds, creditors, and the public without unduly limiting management initiative and judgment. For example, Wisconsin's insurance laws impose standards on investment of insurance assets which seek the following objectives:

(a) Safety of principal, and to the extent consistent therewith, maximum yield and growth;

(b) Stability of value, except where higher risk and possible fluctuations of value are compensated by a commensurate increase in yield and growth possibilities, and either special reserves or surplus is available in sufficient amount to cover reasonable foreseeable fluctuations in value;

(c) Sufficient liquidity to avoid the necessity in reasonably expected circumstances for selling assets at undue sacrifice;

(d) Reasonable diversification with respect to geographical area, industry, maturity, types of investment, individual investments and other relevant variables; and

(e) Reasonable relationship between liabilities and assets as to term and nature.[1]

These or similar standards apply in all states. One way regulators enforce them is to stipulate which assets are "admitted," or allowed to appear on the statutory balance sheet. Expenditures for nonadmitted assets flow through the surplus account and have the effect of decreasing policyholders' surplus.

The amounts shown for each class of assets entered on the balance sheet are calculated in the Annual Statement in "Exhibit 1—Analysis of Assets" found on page 12. This Annual Statement exhibit is the primary working paper used to determine the asset values that can be included in computing an insurer's net worth. In order to understand its function and importance, four asset classifications peculiar to the insurance business must be introduced: *ledger, nonledger, nonadmitted,* and *admitted.*

Ledger assets are assets recorded in the company's general ledger by way of the normal voucher-to-journal, journal-to-ledger, double-entry bookkeeping cycle. The assets discussed thus far normally are recorded in the company's general ledger and classified as ledger assets in Exhibit 1. In addition to the assets discussed, some insurers may carry other assets on their books. These are entered on blank lines provided in the Annual Statement. Some examples of miscellaneous ledger assets shown by some companies include the depreciated value of electronic data processing equipment, equity in assets of joint underwriting associations, and funds due from affiliated corporations.

Nonledger assets are not entered on the books of the insurer but instead are recorded directly in Exhibit 1 of the Annual Statement by way of a single-entry bookkeeping system. At the time of statement preparation, the values of nonledger assets are determined by itemizing the incompleted transactions from which these assets arise. The two most important nonledger assets are "Interest, Dividends, and Real Estate Income Due and Accrued" and the excess of market or amortized value over the book value of certain invested assets. Due and accrued investment income in the form of interest, dividends, and rent simply indicates the amounts receivable from invested assets at year end.

Nonadmitted assets may be excluded entirely from the balance sheet or may have a portion of their values eliminated as nonadmitted. For example, the value of furniture and equipment (other than large electronic data processing machines) is excluded in its entirety. Furniture and equipment are resources of significant value that will provide service during future accounting periods. Nevertheless, the restrictive rules of asset admissibility completely bar any statutory balance sheet value for these items. An asset whose value is only partially nonadmissible is illustrated by a stock whose ledger value exceeds the value determined in accordance with NAIC rules. The excess appears in column 3 of Exhibit 1 as a nonadmissible item and only the lower admitted value is carried forward to the balance sheet.

Admitted assets are the asset values actually shown on an insurer's balance sheet. These values are arrived at in Exhibit 1 by a formula.

Admitted Assets = Ledger Assets + Nonledger Assets − Nonadmitted Assets

The term *gross assets* sometimes is used to mean the sum of ledger and nonledger assets. Gross assets minus nonadmitted assets then are called *net* admitted assets. This latter term appears at the top of column 4 in Exhibit 1.

To illustrate the formula for admitted asset values, consider the following example. A particular insurer has recorded a total of $30 million as agents' balances due and payable. Of this amount, $5 million consists of balances outstanding beyond the ninetieth day. Because agents' balances are considered overdue and nonadmissible after ninety days, the ledger value for this asset must be reduced to its admitted value. The same insurer also has purchased common stock at a cost of

Illustration 2-1
Abbreviated Analysis of Assets

	(1) Ledger Assets	(2) Nonledger Assets	(3) Assets Not Admitted	(4) Net Admitted Assets
Common stocks	$50,000,000	$20,000,000	—	$70,000,000
Agents' balances	$30,000,000	—	$5,000,000	$25,000,000

$50 million and recorded this value for the securities in its ledger. During the accounting period, the stocks' market value has appreciated and equals $70 million at the statement date. The excess of market value over ledger value is a nonledger asset. Net admitted asset values for the agents' balances and common stock accounts are calculated in Exhibit 1 as shown in Illustration 2-1. The adjustment involving common stocks allows the insurer to include the securities on the balance sheet at their market value. Maintaining the ledger value at cost permits the comparison of historical and current values. When the securities are sold, the gain or loss will be determined by deducting the cost figure shown in the ledger from the proceeds of the sale. Reducing agents' balances by the amount overdue eliminates the portion of the ledger value considered to be illiquid.

The distinction between ledger and nonledger assets is not based on admissibility of the assets. Ledger and nonledger assets differ only in the way records of their values are kept. If, for some reason, a company wanted to convert a nonledger asset to a ledger asset, it could do so by making the appropriate journal entries and posting the journals to the ledgers. Some accounts treated as ledger assets by most insurance companies are treated as nonledger assets by others. The distinction between these two asset classifications does not imply a difference in quality.

On the other hand, nonadmitted assets *are* deemed to be of lower quality than assets admitted to the balance sheet. Although nonadmitted assets are resources of value that usually would be shown on the financial statements of other corporations, they do not meet the higher standards used by insurance regulators to judge financial solidity. Nonadmitted assets usually are excluded because they lack the liquidity deemed necessary by insurance regulators. An asset's liquidity is measured in two dimensions. First, the shorter the time necessary for conversion of the asset to cash, the more liquid the asset. Second, the higher the certainty of the amount of realization upon conversion to cash, the more liquid the asset. Uncertainties in regard to the time required or the amount realizable upon liquidation forces exclusion of certain assets from insurance company balance sheets. Significant assets such as automobiles, leasehold improvements, furniture, certain types of equipment, supplies, and others are nonadmitted because of their low liquidity characteristics.

Nonadmitted Assets

The principal asset categories generally considered to have some balance sheet value for noninsurance companies, but not admitted to an insurance company's statutory balance sheet are:

1. Investments other than those which are legal investments such as sums in excess of the maximum amount the company is permitted to invest in a particular security
2. All premiums due more than ninety days
3. Bills, notes, and accounts receivable not secured by collateral which would otherwise be a legal investment for an insurance company, such as notes from agents for premiums more than ninety days due
4. All prepaid expenses such as insurance premiums and agents' commissions
5. Office furniture, equipment, and supplies
6. Loans on personal security
7. Cash advances to, or in the hands of, officers or agents
8. Travel advances

Assets classified as nonadmitted items generally have one of two attributes: either they are (1) not legally allowed or (2) not liquid. Either attribute may disqualify an asset from being entered upon the insurer's statutory balance sheet. However, as discussed later, illiquidity does not necessarily disqualify an asset from being admitted.

Admitted Assets

There are many types of admitted assets owned by property-liability insurance companies. The different types of assets will be described in the following pages, along with an explanation of how they are recorded in the insurer's financial statements and how they are valued for statutory accounting purposes.

Bonds. Bonds are generally the largest single asset type for property-liability insurance companies. (Frequently, they may represent in excess of 50 percent of total admitted assets.) Bond investments can be divided into two categories: taxable and nontaxable. The interest on nontaxable bonds is partially exempt from federal income tax. Bonds are further categorized for statutory purposes according to the type of issuer:

1. Governments of the United States, Canada, or other countries
2. State territories, possessions, and political subdivisions thereof
3. Special revenue and special assessment obligations of government agencies
4. Railroads
5. Public utilities
6. Industrial and miscellaneous
7. Parents, subsidiaries, and affiliates

Schedule D of the Annual Statement provides a detailed listing of all bonds owned at year end and all bond transactions for the year.

State insurance regulations limit the amount an insurance company may invest in certain types of bonds. Although the limitations may vary by state, their general thrust is to prohibit an insurance company from investing more than a certain percentage of its assets into any one permitted category of bonds. Any investments in excess of these limitations are nonadmitted assets. The excess amount is charged to policyholders' surplus in any year in which such excess occurs.

Amortized cost (discussed later) usually is the statutory statement value of all bonds for which the NAIC permits such valuation. In its annual publication, *Valuation of Securities*, the NAIC lists nearly all bonds reported as owned by property liability insurance companies. The book of valuations indicates for each bond whether amortized cost valuation can be used. Certain short-term securities sold at a discount (such as U.S. Treasury Bills and commercial paper) and bonds in default with respect either to principal or interest generally are not eligible for amortization. They can be admitted on the insurer's balance sheet only at values determined by applying NAIC published market rates per thousand of par value to the par value of such securities owned. The difference between amortized cost and admitted asset market value of defaulted bonds is charged to policyholders' surplus in any year in which such difference occurs. If an insurance company owns state and municipal bonds which are not usually valued in the book, the insurer is permitted to list the bond at its amortized value as long as the bonds are not in default as to principal or interest.

Interest income from bond investments is recorded on an accrual basis. For example, a $100,000 par value bond with a 12 percent stated annual interest rate having interest payable on March 31 and September 30 would provide the bondholder with two semi-annual payments of $6,000. Because the bond interest earned from September 30 to December 31 is not received until March 31, the insurer can report as an admitted (nonledger) asset accrued interest earned. The accrual amount is obtained by dividing the accrual period, in this case one-quarter of a year, into the annual interest amount of $12,000, resulting in $3,000.

Common Stocks. Common stocks represent the second largest asset category for property-liability insurance companies (typically about one-eighth of a nonlife insurance company's admitted assets). Common stocks are categorized for statutory purposes into major groupings which reflect the primary business of the issuer such as railroads; public utilities; banks, trust and insurance companies; industrials and miscellaneous; and so forth. A detailed list of all stocks bought and sold during the year and owned at year end is presented in Schedule D of an insurer's statutory Annual Statement.

Most states have statutory rules and regulations that limit investments in common stocks. In general, these limitations restrict a property-liability insurance company from investing in stock of any one issuer an amount greater than a prescribed percentage of the insurance company's admitted assets. They may also limit the amount of stock ownership to a specified percentage of the issuer's outstanding stock. If an insurance company's investment exceeds these limitations, the excess is a nonadmitted asset and is charged to policyholders' surplus. These regulations have two purposes. First, they encourage portfolio diversification. Second, they discourage insurance companies from obtaining proprietary interests in noninsurance related activities.

The admitted asset value of common stocks is determined based on per share market values shown in the NAIC *Valuation of Securities* manual. Unlike bonds, the statutory statement value of common stocks is intended to reflect market variations in common stock prices. As common stock prices fluctuate, changes in market value are applied to policyholders' surplus as either losses or gains. Greater discussion of differences between bond and common stock valuations is presented in the next section.

Preferred Stocks. There are many different classes of preferred stocks owned by insurance companies, and some have unique characteristics. For admitted asset valuation purposes, such holdings are classed as either *Sinking Fund Preferred* or as *All Other Preferred.* Sinking fund preferred stock is valued at cost, and all other preferred at market value based on per share market rates reflected in the current year's NAIC *Valuation of Securities* manual.

Mortgage Loans. Property-liability insurance companies normally do not make substantial investments in mortgage loans. Generally, mortgage loans are long-term commitments, and until the recent advent of secondary mortgage markets, mortgage loans were difficult to convert to cash. Insurance companies limit their investments to first lien mortgage loans, since second mortgages are nonadmitted assets and are charged to policyholders' surplus when acquired.

An insurance company cannot carry, as an admitted asset in its financial statements, a mortgage loan in excess of the appraised value of the secured property. Any violation of these statutory regulations, which differ from state to state, will result in the amount of the difference being charged to the policyholders' surplus. Also, the statutory regulations of individual states stipulate limitations on the percentage of admitted assets an insurance company may have invested in mortgage loans.

The amount recorded as the initial investment in a mortgage loan is the amount of money given for the loan. If a mortgage loan is purchased the remaining amount of principal balance might not equal the consideration given for the loan because the interest rate on the purchased loan might not equal the rate currently charged for similar new mortgage loans. If there is a difference in rates, then the loan is acquired for a premium or discount (the difference between the consideration paid and the unpaid principal balance). The premium or discount will be amortized to income over the remaining life of the loan subject to certain time limits. The amortization will adjust the interest earned to equate the rate of return on the loan to the interest yield negotiated at time of purchase. Amortizing premiums or accruing discounts on mortgage loans is prescribed in the *Valuation of Securities* manual.

Mortgage loans in default, or those under foreclosure proceedings, continue to be classified as mortgage loans. Loans for which foreclosure proceedings have been completed, even to the extent of the court granting title to the mortgagee, temporarily retain their status as mortgage loans, since in some states the mortgagor still has the privilege of redeeming the mortgage during a stated redemption period. During this period, the loan remains classified as a mortgage loan until the insurance company obtains clear title; the asset is then transferred to the real estate account.

Interest on mortgage loans is recorded on a cash basis. Therefore, interest earned but not received is a nonledger asset and is treated similar to accrued bond interest. Interest due and accrued that is over one year past due is a nonadmitted asset.

Real Estate. Insurance companies own real estate either as investments or to provide office space for normal business activities. Real estate owned indirectly through joint ventures is reported as "Other Invested Assets" in the Annual Statement. Real estate is reflected in statutory financial statements at original cost, plus additions or improvements, less depreciation and encumbrances on the real estate. Cost includes the purchase price of the real estate acquired, plus the cost incurred to place the real estate asset in usable condition. Elements of cost include brokerage, legal fees, demolition, clearing, grading, fees for architects and engineers, and any additional expenditures for service equipment and fixtures made a permanent part of the structure. The purchase price is allocated between land and building since only the cost of the building will be depreciated over future periods. The costs of improvements and additions are added to the building account, unless these improvements have a useful life of less than one year when they are charged directly as a current period expense.

Insurance companies are permitted to depreciate buildings on either a straight-line or an accelerated depreciation basis, provided the method chosen is both systematic and rational. Since depreciation allocates the cost of the building to the periods benefiting from its use, the estimated useful life and the depreciation method used depend on the circumstances of each case. If an insurance company makes any leasehold improvements for the benefit of a lessee, the costs of the improvements are amortized over the lease period (ignoring any options to renew).

An insurance company that owns the building housing its own operating office space must charge itself rent expense for statutory financial statement purposes. This rental charge should be a fair and reasonable amount based on what the company normally would have to pay if it did not own its own buildings. Since the company offsets the rental charge to itself by corresponding rental income, there is no effect on net income. However, the accounting transaction allows the rental expense to be allocated among the three primary operating functions: loss adjustment, underwriting, and investment.

Collateral Loans. Similar to mortgage loans, collateral loans represent obligations backed by collateral. The insurance company retains the collateral to ensure the repayment of the loan in case of default. The loan is considered an admitted asset as long as (1) its unpaid balance does not exceed the market value of the collateral held and (2) the collateral itself is an authorized investment. Collateral loans are not common for property-liability insurance companies.

Cash. Insurance companies may maintain several bank accounts designated for specific purposes. These bank accounts may include a general operating account, investment account, payroll account, claim account, loss adjustment account, and so forth. In addition to bank accounts, insurance companies may have a portion of their cash in certificates of deposit, cash in transit, and petty cash.

An asset can be classified as cash on the Annual Statement if it is a medium of exchange that a bank will accept for deposit and immediately credit to the depositor's account. In addition, certain temporary investments—such as savings accounts in qualified depository institutions—are included in cash for statement purposes. There has been some confusion over whether shares in a money market mutual fund should be classified as cash. Technically, many states recognize as cash equivalents only cash on deposit with a member bank of the Federal Deposit Insurance Corporation or a qualified foreign bank. Money market fund shares are classified as common stock.

Short-Term Investments. Short-term investments generally are investments that when acquired will mature within one year such as U.S. Treasury Bills, commercial paper (GMAC Acceptance Notes, Ford Motor Credit, or similar instruments) and non-negotiable bank certificates of deposit, most of which are issued on a discounted basis. Valuation of such investments is based on market rates published in the NAIC valuation manual.

Other Invested Assets and *Aggregate Write-ins for Invested Assets* are residual categories for investments not falling within the foregoing classifications and are usually minor in amount. Valuation for such investments is often judgmental, and the burden of justifying their value rests with the company.

Agents' Balances. Agents' balances or uncollected premiums represent the sum of insurance premiums due from agents, policyholders, or other insurance companies. Most agency contracts stipulate the period of time an agent has to collect premiums and pay the insurance company—typically within thirty to forty-five days after the policy is recorded. Agents generally remit the premiums they collect net of commissions according to an established agency billing arrangement. Companies that directly bill policyholders also have uncollected premiums outstanding at year end. If an agent initially solicited the insurance, the company usually records the uncollected premium net of the commission or, if the commission is not netted, the company establishes a corresponding liability. When the company receives the policyholder's premium, it either issues a commission check or credits the agent's commission account and reduces any related liability for commissions payable. Amounts receivable for reinsurance assumed less amounts payable for reinsurance ceded also are classified as uncollected premiums.

The Annual Statement separates (1) premiums and agents' balances in the course of collection and (2) premiums, agents' balances, and installments booked but deferred and not yet due. No asset value can be shown for agents' balances or uncollected premiums over three months due. Amounts over three months due are nonadmitted assets and are charged to policyholders' surplus. However, under certain limited circumstances, amounts due from solvent insurance companies can be shown as being in the course of collection even though they are over three months due.

Funds Held by or Deposited with Ceding Reinsurers. Reinsurance is an integral part of the insurance business and involves the transfer of a portion of a loss exposure of the primary insurance company to another insurance company in return for a portion of the insurance premium. When the loss exposure is transferred, the company writing the original policy is referred to as the ceding company, and the company assuming a portion of the loss exposure is referred to as the assuming company. The terms of any reinsurance arrangement are stipulated in a reinsurance contract, which documents the agreement reached between the companies. Frequently, the reinsurance contract stipulates that the ceding company will withhold a portion of the premiums to which the assuming company is entitled in an amount equal to the unearned premium reserves and the loss reserves.

The funds held by or deposited with ceding reinsurers represent the amount owed by the ceding reinsurer to the assuming company but not currently payable. If the balance were currently payable, then it would be reflected in uncollected premiums, which is combined with balances due from agents.

Funds held by or deposited with ceding reinsurers are considered to be an admitted asset as long as the account is due from a solvent authorized insurance company. If the insurance company is insolvent or unauthorized, the balance due from that company must be treated as a nonadmitted asset and charged to policyholders' surplus.

Reinsurance Recoverable on Loss Payments. An insurance company transfers a portion of its loss exposure when it enters into a reinsurance contract. The assuming reinsurer receives a portion of the premium and, in return, promises to pay a proportionate share of the losses to which the ceding (direct) insurer is exposed. When a claim is settled and a draft is issued to pay damages incurred, the reinsurers are billed for their portion of the settlement. The receivable from reinsurers for their portion of the loss is recorded in an account called "reinsurance recoverable on loss payments." Reinsurance with an unauthorized company is included in this asset and offset by a liability to the extent required.

The records for reinsurance recoverable on paid losses are comparable to the records used in agents' balances. Effective follow-up and collection efforts are important, since disputes frequently arise over the interpretation of reinsurance contracts.

Because of problems in the timely collection of reinsurance balances, the NAIC recently promulgated new financial statement valuation rules applicable to reinsurance balances on both paid and unpaid losses and reinsurance credit on unearned premiums.

If reinsurance balances are more than 90 days due beyond the credit period specified in the reinsurance contract, these rules can require that 20 percent of all amounts due from that reinsurer be disallowed, with some exceptions pertaining to participations in mandatory pools or associations. In addition disputed amounts may be disallowed (non-admitted) in their entirety.

Bills Receivable Taken for Premium. In certain states, insurance premiums can be financed through a bill receivable. Bills receivable usually have an interest rate attached; therefore, accrued interest receivable must be calculated whenever financial statements are prepared. Bills receivable and any related accrued interest are considered admitted assets when the following conditions are met:

1. The note has been signed by the insured.
2. The unpaid balance of the note does not exceed the unearned premium on the policy for which it was accepted.
3. The note is not past due.

Federal Income Tax Recoverable. Property-liability insurance companies file tax returns in substance based on their statutory Annual Statement as adjusted by certain items specified in the Internal Revenue Code relating to part of loss, loss adjusting expenses, unearned premium reserves, and restoration of certain nonadmitted assets and statutory reserves relating to unauthorized reinsurance and Schedule P. Many of the corporate federal income tax rules apply to insurance companies. If an insurance company incurred a loss and was able to carry that loss back to the preceding three years to generate a federal income tax recovery, or if estimated tax payments made during the year exceed the tax liability, the recoverable amount is an admissible asset.

Electronic Data Processing Equipment. The furniture, equipment, and supplies owned by an insurance company are nonadmitted assets. In other words, all desks, filing cabinets, automobiles, office machines, stationery, printed forms, and so forth cannot be reflected on the balance sheet. Even though these assets are nonadmitted for statutory purposes, the company should maintain formalized accounting control over them because their value will appear in GAAP statements.

One exception to the admissibility of furniture and equipment in many states is major electronic equipment such as computers. This type of equipment generally represents a substantial investment. Recognizing this, many states permit insurance companies to admit the net book value of major electronic equipment if it exceeds a certain dollar amount. These rules generally pertain only to purchased computer hardware and not to the purchase of applications software or to the costs associated with developing software internally.

Authorized Investments in Affiliates. Insurance companies are often affiliated with other companies in order to expand the scope of their corporate activities. This may be accomplished through a direct ownership of subsidiary corporations or through a holding company structure. The financial relationship among affiliated companies frequently involves the insurance company investing in the bonds, preferred stock, and common stock of related corporations. Insurance regulators seek to monitor intercorporate investment activities, restrict the amount of insurer assets invested in affiliated companies, and influence the valuation of such investments. Individual state practices vary, but insurers generally are relatively free to invest in other insurance corporations and investment management companies. As the scope of the affiliated companies' activities becomes further removed from the business of insurance, more restrictive rules apply. Wisconsin, for example, places the following restrictions on domestic stock and mutual insurance companies:

(1) Insurance subsidiaries. An insurance corporation may form or acquire subsidiaries to do any lawful insurance business. There is no limit on the amount of investment in such subsidiaries except that for purposes of (minimum surplus) the total value of the outstanding shares of such a subsidiary shall be deemed to equal the amount of surplus possessed by the subsidiary in excess of its security surplus, as determined by the commissioner....

(2) Investment subsidiaries. An insurance corporation may form or acquire subsidiaries to hold or manage any assets that it might hold or manage directly. There is no limit on investment in such subsidiaries except that imposed by [valuation rules].

(3) Ancillary subsidiaries.

  (a) *Authorization.* An insurance corporation may form or acquire subsidiaries to perform functions or provide services that are ancillary to its insurance operations. It may have up to 10% of its assets invested in such subsidiaries.

(b) *Purposes.* Subsidiaries are ancillary subsidiaries if they are engaged principally in one or more of the following:

1. Acting as an insurance agent.
2. Investing, reinvesting or trading securities, or acting as a securities broker, dealer or marketing representative, for its own account or for the account of any affiliate.
3. Managing of investment companies registered under the federal investment company act of 1940, as amended, including related sales and services.
4. Providing investment advice and services.
5. Acting as administrative agent for a government instrumentality performing an insurance, public assistance or related function.
6. Providing services related to insurance operations including accounting, actuarial, appraisal, auditing, claims adjusting, collection, data processing, loss prevention, premium financing, safety engineering and underwriting services.
7. Holding or managing property used by the corporation alone or with its affiliates or the convenient transaction of its business.
8. Providing such other services or performing such other activities as the commissioner may declare ancillary by rule.
9. Owning corporations which would be authorized as subsidiaries under subsidy to 8 and under subs. (1) and (2).

(4) Other subsidiaries. An insurance corporation may form or acquire other subsidiaries than those under subs. (1) to (3). The investment in such subsidiaries may be counted toward satisfaction of the compulsory surplus requirement ... and the security surplus standard ... to the extent that the investment is a part of the leeway investments ... for the first $200,000,000 of assets or to the extent that the investment is within the limitations ... for other assets.[2]

For statutory purposes, if an insurance company "controls" another company (they are deemed to be in control with ownership of 10 percent or more of the common stock) the proportionate share of the controlled company's net worth is the value of the investment.

VALUATION OF BONDS, STOCKS, AND RELATED ITEMS

Bonds and common stocks represents the largest admitted asset accounts of property-liability insurance companies. Preferred stocks, loaned securities, dividends receivable, and interest due and accrued are closely related to these principal asset accounts. In combination, bonds, stocks, and related items represent in excess of 80 percent of an insurer's admitted assets. This section discusses rules used to value bonds, stocks, and related assets for presentation on the annual statement.

Bonds

Bonds entitle the bondholder to receive periodic payments; are generally traded in secondary markets which readily enable the bondholder to sell the bond prior to maturity; and bond valuation generally is determined by discounting to present value all future periodic payments and the face amount payable at maturity.

Definitions. There are some basic terms associated with bonds.

1. Coupon—The coupon is the stated and fixed return promised by its issuer. Generally, the coupon is expressed in either dollars or a percentage of the face amount of the bond. For example, a $90 coupon bond or 9 percent coupon rate bond are equivalent; this means a bond with a $1,000 face or par value paying a coupon of 9 percent of the face value is a $90 coupon bond.
2. Par Value—The face value amount which the issuing debtor promises to pay to the bondholder when the bond matures.
3. Premium—The amount paid by the purchaser in excess of the par value of the bond. Typically, a premium is paid when the coupon interest rate is greater than current interest rates for bonds of comparable maturity and risk.
4. Discount—The difference in the amount paid by the purchaser and the par value when the purchase price is less than the par value. Generally, bonds can be purchased at a discount when their coupon interest rate is lower than current interest rates for bonds of comparable maturity and risk.
5. Current Yield—This amount expressed as a percentage, is obtained by dividing the coupon amount in dollars by the current selling price of the bond. For example, a 14 percent coupon rate bond having a par value of $1,000 but selling for $1,250 has a current yield of 11.2 percent ($140 divided by $1,250). The current yield will equal the coupon yield only when the bond sells at par value.
6. Amortization of Premium or Discount—For both statutory and GAAP accounting purposes, bond premiums and discounts are prorated over the remaining years to the bond's maturity. The prorated amount is referred to as the amortization.
7. Amortized Cost—The cost at which insurance companies generally report their bond investments for statutory accounting purposes. Amortized cost equals the original purchase price

(including any commissions, taxes, and so on) plus or minus amortization since the date of acquisition.

8. Yield-To-Maturity—This figure is the interest rate necessary to equate the stream of future coupon payments, plus the return of principal at maturity, to the current price of the bond. By analogy to capital budgeting, the yield-to-maturity may be considered the bond's internal rate of return.

Determining Bond Values. In the most common situation, a bond is an investment security entitling the bondholder to receive a series of fixed periodic payments plus a return of principal at maturity. The periodic payments are referred to as coupons. The principal payoff is the face value of the bond. For example, a $10,000, five year, 8 percent bond purchased at issue entitles the bondholder to receive five annual coupons at $800 each plus a face value amount of $10,000 at the end of the fifth year.[3] Hence, the payment structure of the bond can be divided into two parts: one, the receipt of a stream of future coupon payments; and two, the receipt, in the future, of the face value amount.

The valuation of bonds is related to the present value of an annuity (the flow of interest from semi-annual coupon rates) plus the present value of a single sum (the par value of the bond to be received at the bond's maturity). The bond investor, in this case the insurance company, is attempting to value the bond so that any premium paid or discount received is amortized over the bond's remaining life in a manner that will reflect a fair and objectively stated asset value at December 31 of each year of the bond's remaining life and to adjust the income received from bond interest to reflect yield-to-maturity. This amortization of premiums or discounts is accomplished by either the *straight-line* or *annuity amortization* methods.

Straight-line Amortization. The straight-line method of amortization has the advantage of being easy to calculate and understand. Following the straight-line approach, the amount of premium (or discount) at purchase is divided by the number of years remaining until maturity, and the resulting amount is deducted (or added in the case of a discount) from the periodic coupon payments. Illustration 2-2 shows the straight-line amortization procedure for a $10,000, three year, 8 percent bond purchased for $10,534.60. The chief disadvantage of this method is that it results in an increasing rate of return on investment because the book value of the bond decreases as the net coupon payment remains constant. If a bond discount is being amortized, the straight-line method causes the rate of return on investment to decline from one period to the next.

Annuity Amortization. A more refined amortization method is called the annuity method because it results in the investor recognizing

Illustration 2-2

Straight-Line Amortization Schedule for a Bond Purchased
at a Premium

End of Year	Actual Coupon Payment	Amortized Premium	Effective Coupon Payment	Book Value	Effective Rate of Return[†]
0	—	—	—	$10,534.60	—
1	$ 800.00	$178.20	$621.80	10,356.40	5.95%
2	800.00	178.20	621.80	10,178.20	6.06
3	800.00	178.20	621.80	10,000.00	6.16
Totals	$2,400.00	$534.60	$1,865.40		
Average				$10,267.30	6.06%

[†]On average bond book value during the period.

a constant rate of return on the money invested in the bond. This rate of return equals the market rate of interest prevailing at the time the bond was purchased (6 percent in Illustration 2-2). Although the rate of return is constant, the amortization of the premium or discount increases each year. In reality, the market value of a bond is set so that the bond would yield 6 percent annually on the money invested in it. Therefore, at the end of the first year, the effective coupon return should be $10,534.60 × 0.06 = $632.08. But the investor actually receives $800.00; the $167.92 difference is part of the original principal being returned. Consequently, the book value of the bond is reduced to $10,366.68 ($10,534.60 − $167.92). Continuing the procedure throughout the years remaining to the bond's maturity produces the figures in Illustration 2-3.

Regardless of the procedure used, amortization of a bond premium reduces periodic investment income below the actual coupon payment. The straight-line method uses a constant charge against investment income to amortize the premium and thus produce a constantly increasing rate of return on the bond's book value. Some states require that the annuity method be used for annual statement purposes.

Illustrations 2-2 and 2-3 reflect the amortization of premiums paid on bonds purchased. The same amortization methods are used to handle discounts received on bonds purchased. In the case of discounts, the bond valuations are *increased* each year so that they will reflect par value at maturity, and interest income is adjusted upward each year to

Illustration 2-3

Amortization Schedule Based on the Annuity Method for a Bond Purchased at a Premium

End of Year	Book Value	Effective Coupon Payment at 6 Percent	Actual Coupon Payment	Amortized Premium
0	$10,534.60	—	—	—
1	10,366.68	$632.08	$ 800.00	$167.92
2	10,188.68	622.00	800.00	177.99
3	10,000.00	611.32	800.00	188.68
Totals	—	$1,865.40	$2,400.00	$534.59 [†]

[†]The one-cent error is due to the accumulation of rounding errors.

Illustration 2-4

Straight-Line Amortization Schedule for a Bond Purchased at a Discount

End of Year	Actual Coupon Payment	Amortized Discount	Effective Coupon Payment	Book Value	Effective Rate of Return[†]
0	—	—	—	$ 9,093.27	—
1	$ 800.00	$320.24	$1,120.24	9,359.51	12.18%
2	800.00	320.24	1,120.24	9,679.75	11.77
3	800.00	320.25	1,120.25	10,000.00	11.38
Totals	$2,400.00	$960.73	$3,360.73		
Averages				$ 9,519.64	11.77%

[†]Average book value during the period.

reflect the corresponding increase in bond valuation. The straight line and annuity methods of handling discounts received are depicted in Illustrations 2-3 and 2-4.

In Illustration 2-4, since the bond will be redeemed at its par value of $10,000, the discount is $960.73. This must be accumulated during the years in which the bond is held, or a capital gain will be experienced

Illustration 2-5
Amortization Schedule Based on the Annuity Method for a Bond
Purchased at a Discount

End of Year	Book Value	Effective Coupon Payment at 12 Percent	Actual Coupon Payment	Amortized Premium
0	$ 9,039.27	—	—	—
1	9,323.98	$1,084.71	$ 800.00	$284.71
2	9,642.86	1,118.88	800.00	318.88
3	10,000.00	1,157.14	800.00	357.14
Totals	—	$3,360.73	$2,400.00	$960.73

at the maturity date. Illustration 2-4 shows how the discount is accumulated using the straight-line method.

In this case the amortized discount accumulated each period is added to the coupon payment to produce the effective coupon payment. Dividing the effective coupon payment by the average book value of the bond results in a decreasing rate of return during the holding period. Once again, a constant return on investment will be realized if the annuity method of amortization is used. Illustration 2-5 shows the annuity amortization of the discount for this example.

Principles of Bond Valuation. Four principles explain the market value of a bond. First, bond values are inversely related to changes in market interest rates. That is, as market interest rates increase, bond values drop; alternatively, bond values rise as market interest rates decline. Second, bond values are more sensitive to interest rate changes as the maturity of the bonds increases. Third, "low" coupon bond values are more sensitive to interest rate changes than "high" coupon bonds, and fourth, as the level of the market interest rate increases, there is a greater change in bond values for a given percentage change in the interest rate.[4] These principles help to explain why the amortized cost valuation of bonds on an insurance company's financial statements usually does not represent the market value of the bonds. Whether bonds should continue to be valued at amortized cost rather than at their market value or at some modification of market value is a topic periodically reviewed by insurance regulators. The difference between amortized cost and market valuation is an important concept for insurance company managers to understand regardless of the statutory accounting treatment. For companies with cash flows sufficient to cover operating expenditures without liquidating bond investments, amortized cost valuation has the advantage of shielding policyholders' surplus from unnecessary fluctuations due to interim vagaries of the bond market. Companies unable to meet operating expenditures from current cash flow fail to disclose their hazardous financial condition by valuing bonds at amortized cost in excess of market value. Because the subject of valuation is so closely related to the adequacy of a company's cash flow, a later section of this chapter presents an analysis of insurance company cash flow and related subjects.

Common Stock

Common stocks on the statutory statement generally are valued at the "Association Values" (usually the same as market price for each stock) listed in the *Valuation of Securities* manual prepared by the NAIC's Securities Valuation Office (SVO). The published SVO's per share market rates enable insurance companies to calculate market values for each stock. It is usually the closing price quotation on the final business day of the year for publicly traded stocks. Insurance companies are required to submit information to the SVO that can be used to establish an association value of stocks for which a market price quotation is unavailable.

One distinction between admitted and nonadmitted assets is liquidity. Admitted assets ideally can be converted into cash without delay and without loss of value whereas nonadmitted assets may be illiquid. The valuation of common stocks at market value assures their liquidity at a relatively well-recognized market value amount.

State statutes may limit the amount invested in the common stock of a single corporation and its affiliates to a small percentage of admitted assets (for instance, 3 percent). Any excess investment in common stocks will be nonadmitted unless it can be included in other invested assets according to a leeway provision in the insurance code. A leeway provision permits investments in assets, not otherwise prohibited by statute, to a limited percentage of total assets. The purpose of such a leeway provision is to allow additional management discretion in the administration of an insurance company's investment program. Flexibility is especially important for common stock investments that might be partially excluded if the security's value appreciated to an amount in excess of the prescribed limit on investments in the stock of a single corporation.

Preferred Stock

Two valuation rules apply to preferred stocks. If the securities are in good standing (dividends are not in arrears) and are subject to a 100 percent mandatory sinking fund, they are valued at cost. Preferred stocks not subject to such a sinking fund arrangement are reported based on per share market rates listed for them in the NAIC manual. Because sinking fund preferreds are shown on the balance sheet at a constant value, they have a stabilizing effect on policyholders' surplus. Some insurance companies favor investments in sinking fund preferred stocks over preferred stocks whose values are carried at market because of the stable effect on surplus.

Stock-Related Valuation Situations

Two valuation situations for stocks occur when either the stock is valued ex-dividend (a dividend has been declared but not paid) or when an insurance company loans stock to authorized securities brokers or dealers.

Dividends. The balance sheet values of preferred and common stocks may or may not reflect the worth of the next regular dividend payment depending on whether or not the security is selling ex-dividend on the valuation date. Conceptually, the market price of stocks recognizes the property right the shareholder has to all future dividends that will be paid on the stock. However, the NAIC valuation of an ex-dividend stock includes no value for the dividend to be paid to the stockholder of record prior to the record date. Insurance companies that owned stocks in their portfolios on the dividend record date are permitted to include dividends receivable among admitted assets, if the stocks are ex-dividend at year end.

Loaned Securities. In some states, insurance laws or regulations permit domestic insurers to loan stock to authorized brokers or dealers in securities. The broker or dealer borrowing the stock places cash or cash equivalents in an escrow account to serve as collateral for the loan. The loaned stock continues to appear on the insurance company balance sheet as long as the amount of collateral is at least equal to the amount specified in the NAIC valuation manual. The admitted asset value is decreased by the amount of any deficiency in the collateral. In some states, bonds may be loaned and are treated in a manner similar to stocks.

PROPERTY-LIABILITY INSURANCE COMPANY INVESTMENT POLICY

A large number of factors influence the investment policy adopted by a particular property and liability insurance company. This section discusses three important determinants of the investment portfolio's size and composition. *Cash flow* from underwriting operations, *insurance leverage*, and *insurance exposure* have a major impact on the size and composition of the investment portfolio.

Cash Flow Analysis

Cash flow analysis examines the amount of cash retained by an insurance company generated from underwriting results, as well as investment income and portfolio turnover. This amount is termed *net cash flow from operations.*

Net cash flow from operations equals premium receipts and investment income minus payments for underwriting expenses, loss adjustment expenses, and losses.

Cash Inflows. A typical insurance company probably would experience a lag in premium receipts behind premiums written by about two months. For example, 15 percent of premiums might be received in the month policies are written, 75 percent in the succeeding month, and 10 percent in the following month. These percentages would vary from company to company and also by type of insurance written. In addition, some adjustments need to be made in anticipating the cash inflows.

Generally, each company might experience some seasonality in premiums written as well as anticipated investment income. Allowances should be made for the unevenness of these flows. The growth, equilibrium, and decline in cash inflows reflect the expansion, equilibrium, and contraction in written premiums, although usually with a slight lag.

Cash Outflows for Expenses. Payments for underwriting expenses include commissions, premium taxes, acquisition expenses, and all other nonloss-related expenses of the company. There are also lags in paying out these expenses. For example, premium taxes plus commissions plus one-half of other acquisition and nonloss-related expenses might be paid in the first month and the balance might be spread over the policy term. A company may determine that 80 percent of expenses occur in the first month, with the remainder evenly distributed over the lesser of either ten months or the policy term.

Expense payout patterns vary from company to company, but most nonloss-related expenses occur early in the policy term.

Cash Outflow for Loss and Loss Adjustment Expenses. The amount of cash payment for claims depends on the amount of losses incurred in the past and present and the distribution over time of the payments. Generally, projected loss payments are fairly constant from month to month, and the proportion of paid to incurred losses is independent of the absolute amount of total incurred losses for any one month. Each company may, however, determine its own seasonality depending on the type of coverage and the location of the majority of its policyholders. Incurred losses will weigh heavily on current cash outflows.

Net Underwriting Cash Flow. Net cash flow from underwriting is defined as premium receipts minus payments for underwriting expenses, loss expenses, and losses. Net cash flow from operations is the actual amount of cash retained by the company during each month. The cumulative net cash flow from operations represents the sum a company would have available for investment. The statutory underwriting result for any month is defined as earned premium minus loss and loss adjustment expenses incurred minus nonloss underwriting expenses incurred. Changes in the insurance company's reserves for loss and loss adjustment expenses are deducted as incurred. Nonloss underwriting expenses are deducted as incurred. Thus, the statutory underwriting profit formula ignores cash flow patterns and emphasizes immediate recognition of losses and expenses.

There are several important operating characteristics of property-liability insurance companies. First, property-liability insurance companies can very quickly accumulate relatively large pools of cash from their underwriting activities. The magnitude of the cash buildup depends on such factors as premium growth, loss ratio, and cash payout patterns. Second, as long as premiums are increasing, property-liability insurance companies are able to accumulate large cash holdings in spite of severe losses. However, if premium growth is not achieved and steady state occurs, then the net periodic addition to cash balances will equal the periodic statutory result. Further, if premium volume declines, then the final resulting accumulated net cash flow will equal the accumulated underwriting profit (or loss) for the entire period.

Cash flow analysis is useful in examining the impact of a line(s) of insurance premium receipt and loss and expense payout patterns on the accumulation of cash. Provided net cash flow from operations is positive, additional funds are being generated for investment. When net cash flow from operations is negative, investments must be converted to cash in order to meet the insurer's obligations. Depending on the mix of business among product lines and the length of the time horizon involved, cash flow analysis may produce results dissimilar to strict profit measures.

Cash flow analysis bears little relationship to either statutory or GAAP accounting results. For example, income taxes are levied on net income, but the substantial early accumulation of cash is invested and begins to generate returns before the end of the accounting period when taxes are computed. This delay permits the buildup of investment portfolios and the generation of investment income. In periods of high interest rates, investment income may increase to such an extent that it either exceeds underwriting income or, in periods of underwriting losses, exceeds the underwriting losses to such an extent that a profit is still earned for the year.

Insurance Leverage and Insurance Exposure

In addition to cash flow analysis, other tools helpful in examining an insurer's balance sheet include measurements of insurance leverage and insurance exposure. Unlike many other types of business, insurance companies normally do not use long-term debt as a source of financing; nor do insurers employ relatively large amounts of fixed assets in conducting their activities. This means that the financial structure and asset structure of insurers differ from noninsurance firms. Because of these operating characteristics, traditional measures of financial leverage and operating leverage are not useful for insurance companies.

Financial leverage involves the use of funds obtained at a fixed cost to increase returns to net worth. It is measured by the relative portion of assets financed by debt and equity. For the majority of insurance companies that do not directly include debt instruments in their capital structure, the traditional ratio of debt to equity offers little information. Insurers, however, substitute *insurance leverage* for financial leverage. This means that an insurer can in effect use its reserves (liabilities) to increase returns on capital. The two most important liabilities for insurance companies are the unearned premium reserve and loss reserves. The ratio of reserves (debt) to policyholders' surplus (equity) can be used as a measure of insurance leverage.

Operating leverage involves the employment of fixed assets for which the firm incurs a fixed cost (depreciation). The higher the degree of operating leverage, the more sensitive operating profits are to changes in sales. Although not a direct counterpart to operating leverage, the concept of insurance exposure relates to the amount of risk that policyholders' surplus can be exposed to, as measured by the amount of premiums written in relation to surplus. The ratio of premiums written (sales) to policyholders' surplus (equity) is used as a measure of insurance exposure.

Ratios of insurance leverage and insurance exposure focus on the liability-net worth portion of the balance sheet and on sales-net worth relationships. The primary issues to be addressed by investigating insurance leverage and exposure are (1) the extent to which a given amount of policyholders' surplus can support specific amounts of reserves or premiums and (2) the effects on underwriting and investment results that varying levels of insurance leverage and exposure can produce.

One significant impact of product line mix is insurance leverage as measured by the ratio of loss reserves to surplus. Certain *liability lines* of insurance can be characterized by the extended period of time during which loss reserves are outstanding. These lines are said to have a "long tail" with respect to loss payout. On the other hand, most *property lines* of insurance have reserve amounts from which full and final payments are made rather quickly. These lines are "short tail" with respect to loss payout.

For any line of insurance, given an assumed average loss ratio and a particular loss payout pattern, it is possible to estimate a reserve to premiums written ratio for that line. Similarly, for any given product mix, it is possible to compute the loss reserve-to-premiums written ratio.

The ratio of reserves to premiums written is important for two reasons: first, given a level of insurance exposure (the premiums written-to-policyholders' surplus ratio) it is possible to measure the resulting insurance leverage (reserves-to-surplus ratio) and second, having the ratio of reserves to premiums written by line of insurance, it is possible to measure the impact of product line mix not only on underwriting results but also on investment results for any given investment portfolio mix.

Insurance leverage is defined as the ratio of reserves to policyholders' surplus. Insurance exposure is defined as the ratio of premiums written to policyholders' surplus. The relation between these two concepts is:

$$\text{Insurance Leverage} = \text{Insurance Exposure} \times \frac{\text{Reserves}}{\text{Premiums Written}}$$

$$\frac{\text{Reserves}}{\text{Policyholders' Surplus}} = \frac{\text{Premiums Written}}{\text{Policyholders' Surplus}} \times \frac{\text{Reserves}}{\text{Premiums Written}}$$

For example, if a company determined that the reserves were $150 for every $100 of premiums written, and if the premiums written-to-policyholders' surplus ratio were, say, 3 to 1, then the resulting insurance leverage would be 4.5 to 1.

$$\frac{\text{Reserves}}{\text{Policyholders' Surplus}} = \frac{\text{Premiums Written}}{\text{Policyholders' Surplus}} \times \frac{\text{Reserves}}{\text{Premiums Written}}$$

$$= \frac{3}{1} \times \frac{150.00}{100.00}$$

$$= 4.5$$

On the other hand, if the company issued contracts having reserves that were only $50 for every $100 of premiums written and if the premiums written-to-policyholders' surplus ratio were again 3 to 1, then the resulting measure of insurance leverage would be only 1.50 to 1.

The first example is more typical of liability lines, while the second example is more typical of property lines. This is because liability losses tend to be paid over a longer period of time than property losses, resulting in larger loss reserves for liability lines at any given time. For a given value of the insurance exposure, a company that tends to emphasize liability lines of insurance can achieve greater insurance leverage than a company emphasizing property lines. This greater insurance leverage provides more funds for investment operations and may increase the company's earnings if underwriting and investment activities are profitable.

The greater insurance leverage associated with liability lines of insurance may encourage the sale of such insurance at rates that generate higher loss ratios than for property insurance lines. The increased insurance leverage from liability insurance may permit insurance companies to rely on the associated investment income to overcome the lower underwriting profits. However, in a competitive marketplace, and as money management techniques are refined and improved, the advantage that increased insurance leverage generates for liability lines will be compensated for by lower underwriting profits from these same lines. If this does occur, the product line mix will be less important in determining overall profitability for insurance companies. In the competitive insurance marketplace, product mix would have no impact on earnings.

Cash flow analysis highlights property-liability insurance companies' potential for accumulating cash for investment. Using the concepts of insurance exposure and leverage, it can be shown that product line mix has a significant impact upon the amount of funds available for investment. Instead of concentrating upon the asset side of the balance sheet as in the case of cash flow analysis, the concepts of insurance exposure and insurance leverage concentrate on the buildup of liability accounts relative to surplus. Cash flow analysis points to the use of funds generated from insurance operations, whereas leverage and exposure concepts point to the sources of these funds.

Insurance Company Objectives

Property-liability insurance companies must respond to the needs of at least two of their constituents: their policyholders and their stockholders. In the case of mutual insurance companies, there are only policyholders to be concerned with.

Focusing on what might be considered the foremost concern of each constituent group, it should be possible to specify insurance company objectives. Existing policyholders have as their primary concern the solvency of the insurance company. Having paid premiums to the insurer, the policyholders are concerned about the company's ability to meet its legal obligations to them. Stock insurers must be able to satisfy stockholder demands for profit. Additionally, stockholders may require that profits, or at least a portion of them, be distributed. Hence there exists a potential conflict of interest between policyholders and stockholders. At the extreme, management or regulatory practices overly responsive to the security interests of policyholders may deny stockholders an adequate return. Conversely, management practices which focus only on stockholder return considerations may prevent policyholders from ever receiving their contractual rights.

One way of specifying the needs of each constituency into a single objective for insurance company management to pursue would be to maximize profit subject to an acceptable level of risk. This objective addresses the needs of both policyholders and stockholders. The needs of policyholders are represented in the level of risk assumed. Once this has been determined, the interests of stockholders are represented through the maximization of profit.

Investment Portfolio Composition

This discussion of property-liability investment policy assumes that the only concerns are (1) the composition of the investment portfolio between common stocks and bonds, and (2) the maturity structure of the bond portfolio. By making these assumptions, at least seven aspects of investment policy are ignored. First, there is no discussion as to whether or not property-liability insurance companies should "buy and hold" or "actively trade" the securities in their investment portfolios. Second, there is no discussion as to how individual securities are selected, evaluated, purchased, or traded in a property-liability insurance company investment portfolio. Third, statutory minimum and maximum investment requirements are ignored. Fourth, tax implications such as tax-exempt versus nontax-exempt bonds and the 80 percent inter-corporate tax exclusion on dividends are ignored. Fifth, there is no discussion as to the mechanics of organizing, developing, and maintaining an investment department within a property-liability insurance company. Sixth, NAIC asset valuation as a determinant of investment strategy is ignored. And finally, there is no discussion as to the merit or difficulties of making the investment portfolio responsive to short-term deviations in long-run insurance underwriting profit expectations. While these omitted topics are important, emphasis here is placed on the interaction of investment objectives, asset valuation, insurance leverage, and insurance exposure.

To determine investment portfolio composition it is necessary to measure the return and risk parameters developed by the operating objective of the insurance company. Rational choices can be made among competing investment policies on the basis of their return and risk characteristics.

The total return available to the insurance company is the sum of underwriting returns and investment returns. The underwriting returns depend on the mix of business across lines of insurance as well as the profit margins for each line of insurance. The investment returns depend on investment portfolio composition and the return opportunities available from each type of investment.

The total "rate" of return on equity depends not only on the underwriting profit margin and investment return but also on insurance exposure and insurance leverage. The latter determinant is the result of product line mix. For example, assume these results:

Liability underwriting profit margin	1.00% (99.0 combined ratio)
Property underwriting profit margin	2.50% (97.5 combined ratio)
Liability reserves to premium	1.5 to 1
Property reserves to premium	0.5 to 1
Stock rate of return	6%
Bond rate of return	7%

If the mix between property and liability insurance were 50-50 and the insurance exposure (premiums written-to-policyholders' surplus ratio) were 3 to 1, then the pretax rate of return on equity from underwriting would be:

Underwriting return from property	+	Underwriting return from liability	=	Total underwriting return
$(3 \times 0.5 \times 2.5\%)$	+	$(3 \times 0.5 \times 1.0\%)$	=	5.25%

Further, if the investment portfolio composition were 50-50 as between stocks and bonds, then the rate of return would be 6.5 percent $(0.5 \times 6\%)$ + $(0.5 \times 7\%)$, and the pretax rate of return on equity from investment would be:

4.875	+	14.625	=	19.5
Investment return from property		Investment return from liability		Total investment return

$$(3 \times 0.5 \times 0.5 \times 6.5\%) + (3 \times 0.5 \times 1.5 \times 6.5\%) = 19.5\%$$

The total pretax rate of return from policyholder supplied funds is the sum of underwriting (5.25 percent) and investment (19.5 percent) returns, or 24.75 percent. A return of 24.75 percent of policyholders' surplus could be expected from investment of funds developed by the reserves and from underwriting profit. A further return of 6.5 percent of policyholders' surplus could be expected from investment of funds supplied by policyholders' surplus itself, resulting in a pretax return of 31.25 percent on policyholders' surplus.

As the example indicates, it is possible to increase total return several ways, provided the underlying sources of return are positive: first, increase insurance exposure, and second, increase investment in bonds (or whichever investment *currently* has the greatest returns). Note, however, that increasing insurance leverage may not offer a clear-cut opportunity to increase return. In the assumed data, the increase in insurance leverage accomplished by shifting from property to liability lines of insurance would be associated with a reduction in underwriting returns. The advantages gained by a shift from low-leveraged property insurance to high-leveraged liability insurance would depend on the underwriting profit margin of each line and the investment portfolio composition.

It would seem that the opportunity for increased leverage and the subsequent increased investment returns offset the reduction in underwriting profit resulting from the shift. Hence, at first blush, it is tempting to view the optimum policy from management's viewpoint to be an emphasis of liability insurance and increased investment in whichever assets offer the higher return.

Unfortunately, both underwriting and investment returns are subject to a degree of risk that varies according to the composition of the respective portfolios. Selling both property and liability insurance reduces overall risk, as does investing in both stocks and bonds. The least risky single product and single investment would be property insurance and bonds. The most risk with a single product and single investment would be liability insurance and stocks. Insurance company investment policy attempts to adjust the mix of stocks and bonds to strike the best balance of risk and return for the mix of business the company writes.

SUMMARY

The Annual Statement's balance sheet provides twenty categories for the classification of a property-liability insurance company's admitted assets. Eight of the categories are designated for cash and portfolio investments. The remaining categories list various receivables and other assets that qualify for presentation on the statutory balance sheet. This chapter has described the various asset categories and emphasized the valuation of stock and bond investments which comprise the majority of a typical nonlife insurer's admitted assets. For Annual Statement purposes stocks are shown at values prescribed by the NAIC; these values generally are the year-end market values of the stocks. Bonds generally are valued at amortized cost, and their statement value may differ significantly from their year-end market value.

The formulation of investment policy considers underwriting cash flow, insurance exposure, and insurance leverage. Typical underwriting cash flow patterns result in an accumulation of funds for investment by the insurance company. Funds accumulate more rapidly as the degree of insurance exposure, which is measured by the premiums written to policyholders' surplus, increases. The length of time required to settle losses also influences the amount of funds available for investment. Liability lines of insurance, which require the buildup of loss reserves, increase the amount of insurance leverage, as measured by the reserves-to-policyholders' surplus ratio, employed by an insurer and influence the returns to net worth and the riskiness of the insurer's operations.

Chapter Notes

---

1. §620.01, Insurance-Investments; Purpose and Scope, *Wisconsin Insurance Laws* (1980: National Insurance Law Service Publishing Company), pp. 263-264.
2. §611.26, Domestic Stock and Mutual Insurance Corporations; Subsidiaries, *Wisconsin Insurance Laws*, pp. 93-94.
3. It is common practice for bond interest to be paid semiannually rather than once a year. Therefore, a $1,000 par value bond that has semiannual coupons of $40 each is said to have a coupon rate of 8 percent because it pays $80 per year. In order to avoid the unnecessary refinement of using semiannual interest rates, all the illustrations in this chapter are based on annual coupon payments.
4. See Sydney Homer and Martin L. Leibowitz, *Inside the Yield Book* (Englewood Cliffs, NJ: Prentice-Hall, 1972), pp. 43-56.

CHAPTER 3

Liabilities and Policyholders' Surplus

The right side of a property-liability insurance company balance sheet contains the familiar categories, liabilities and owners' equity. However, the liabilities of a property-liability insurance company are different from those of a mercantile or manufacturing company. Liabilities of a nonlife insurer are composed predominantly of two accounts: loss reserves and the unearned premium reserve. These two liabilities arise from the unique nature of the business transacted. Insurance premiums are collected in the present in order to pay insured losses in the future. Exchanging present dollars for a future promise creates the unique obligations or liabilities for an insurer.

Loss reserves as of a certain date are, in theory, those amounts that would pay for all incurred and unsettled claims against the insurer. If losses were reported and paid immediately, no loss reserves would exist. Since delays occur between the time the loss is incurred and when it is finally settled, loss reserves are necessary to properly recognize the insurer's obligations. Reserves are established for losses that have been reported to the insurance company but have not yet been paid and for losses assumed to be incurred during the accounting period but not yet reported to the insurer. The liability for this second category of losses generally is referred to as the "incurred but not reported" (IBNR) reserve. Loss reserves are not established for losses expected to occur in the future.

The unearned premium reserve results from premiums collected at the beginning of the coverage period for which the insurer is obligated to fulfill its performance throughout the entire term of the policy. Although the premium has been received in full, it is not fully earned until the end of the coverage period. The total of all the unearned portions of premiums written by an insurer is represented by the unearned premium reserve. In *theory,* the unearned premium reserve represents the aggregate amount that an insurer would require in order to return to each insured the unearned portion of the premium in the event that the insurer decided to cancel all its contracts and retire from business.

A number of variables affect both loss reserves and unearned premium reserves. For example, the type of insurance written (product mix) significantly affects loss reserves, and length of the policy term influences the size of the unearned premium reserve. Both loss reserves and unearned premium reserves can be calculated by a number of different methods. Due to the variations brought on by estimation problems, methodology, and unplanned events, these reserves may not necessarily be an accurate representation of an insurer's liabilities. A substantial portion of this chapter will be devoted to a discussion of the variables that affect these two key liabilities.

All liabilities found on a property-liability insurance company's balance sheet other than the loss and loss expense reserves and the unearned premium reserve are considered miscellaneous liabilities. Normally, these obligations are a small part of total liabilities. However, one that has become increasingly significant and that receives further attention in this chapter is the liability for reinsurance transactions.

The owner's equity account of a property and liability insurance company is labeled "surplus as regards policyholders" and often is referred to as "policyholders' surplus." This term may seem to be a misnomer, since the account in many cases (for stock insurance companies) is a combination of capital stock contributed and earned surplus.

The policyholders' surplus account acts as a safety cushion for policyholders in the event an insurer suffers adverse results in the various aspects of its insurance business. If an insurer were to become insolvent and the loss and unearned premium reserves were insufficient to meet the insurer's contractual obligations, the policyholders and claimants can look to all assets of the insurer, even those funded by the owners. Therefore, the words "policyholders' surplus" are usually used in an insurance company for what other companies call "owners' equity."

LOSS RESERVES

Aggregate loss reserves generally are the largest and most important liability item on a property-liability insurer's balance sheet.

Loss reserves of an insurer are, in theory, those amounts that would liquidate all unsettled claims against the insurer. These include not only those claims of which the insurer has knowledge, but also unknown claims that have occurred and will be reported later.

Loss reserves are more important for some lines of insurance than others. In general, the so-called third-party lines produce larger loss reserves. These lines include auto bodily injury liability, workers compensation, medical malpractice, and other bodily injury liability (such as products, premises, and umbrella). These lines of insurance typically cover liability situations that tend to involve longer periods of time between the occurrence of a claim and its final disposition. Liability situations often involve bodily injuries. Property damages can be determined in reasonably short periods of time, but estimating various bodily injuries like permanent disabilities, long-term hospital confinements, and pain and suffering require relatively longer periods. Because of the extended time required before losses are ultimately settled, bodily injury liability lines of insurance commonly are referred to as "long-tail" lines. Insurance coverages that are relatively quick to settle are called "short-tail" lines.

Even though losses are settled relatively quickly, loss reserves are also established for first-party lines (such as fire, allied lines, home-owners, auto physical damage, burglary and theft, and marine) and property damage liability claims. With few exceptions, property losses are direct obligations of the insurer, with the claimant and insured being the same party. Even property damage liability claims are usually handled rapidly, as damages can be determined quickly and without complicating factors such as pain and suffering.

The financial strength of a property-liability insurer depends, to a great extent, on the status of its loss reserves. Serious under-reserving results in inadequate loss reserves which overstate the policyholders' surplus of an insurer and may lead to insolvency.

Capital and surplus may be severely distorted, and thus the financial solidity of an insurer materially misjudged, if liabilities are not estimated accurately. For example, assume a particular insurer's balance sheet shows total liabilities equal to 75 percent of assets, as shown in Illustration 3-1. Further assume that liabilities are understated by $10. As a result, the insurer's net worth has been overstated by almost 67 percent of its true value.

Moreover, because the changes in certain liabilities between the accounting period's endpoints are involved in calculation of under-writing results, incorrect reserve valuations also prevent meaningful analysis of the company's operating (income) statement.

State insurance statutes require property-liability insurers to establish liability accounts for unpaid losses and loss adjustment

Illustration 3-1

Net Worth Distortion Caused by Reserve Inadequacy

	Original Balance Sheet	Corrected Balance Sheet
Total assets	$100	$100
Liabilities	$ 75	$ 85
Capital and surplus	25	15
Total liabilities and net worth	$100	$100

$$\text{Overstatement} = \frac{\text{Change in Net Worth}}{\text{True Net Worth}} = \frac{\$10}{\$15} = 67\%$$

expenses. Many insurance claims and the expenses that will be incurred to adjust them are difficult to evaluate prior to ultimate settlement. This is especially true of liability claims, the value of which may be influenced by such things as length of discovery period, economic conditions, inflation, legal jurisdiction, and other factors. Because values are not readily known for many losses at the balance sheet date, statistical techniques, actuarial concepts, and the judgment of claims personnel are employed to estimate loss and loss adjustment expense reserves. The resulting liability is called the insurer's loss and loss expense reserve.

State insurance departments spend considerable effort in evaluating loss reserves in their periodic examinations of property-liability insurance companies. State regulatory officials focus on maintaining adequate loss reserves. Insurance commissioners would generally rather have the insurance company err on the side of over-reserving than under-reserving. Yet, this emphasis has limits, as excessive over-reserving may lead to unwarranted rate increases. In addition, tax authorities may become concerned and eventually assess penalties for over-reserving, since artificially high loss reserve levels have the effect of deferring income recognition and related income taxes.

Loss reserves are not cash or liquid asset funds. The aggregate loss reserve is a liability account—an accounting entry on the balance sheet—indicating a financial obligation of the insurance company. The ability to pay these liabilities depends on the liquidity of the assets offsetting the account entry. Thus, the proper valuation and stability of the insurer's assets are of critical importance, as discussed in the previous chapter.

Methods of establishing loss reserves are discussed later in this chapter. Estimation of loss reserves is not strictly a process whereby actuaries, adjusters, and accountants plug numbers into some predetermined formula. While various quantitative methods are employed, subjective elements are often present. Sometimes a difficult reserving situation requires an "educated guess." Top managerial input is usually included before a final figure for loss reserves is determined. The point is that the estimation of reserves is a difficult process in which quantitative techniques frequently have to be supplemented by subjective considerations and managerial judgment.

Whether or not loss reserves are properly estimated can only be determined over time. Comparing previous loss reserves for a certain set of claims with the actual dollars ultimately paid for those claims shows whether those reserves were adequate. It is impossible to say with certainty that the current loss reserves of an insurer represent the dollar amounts needed to settle the corresponding claims. The best indication of a company's current reserving proficiency is generally its record of past reserving. Various techniques, including schedules in the Annual Statement, can be used to measure past loss reserving performance. Some of the techniques will be discussed in later parts of this chapter.

Improper estimation of loss reserves, whether deliberate or by an error in methodology, eventually affects the future financial condition of an insurer. If loss reserves are underestimated in a particular year, underwriting profits for that year are overstated. As claims associated with these loss reserves are eventually settled, more money will be required than the estimate in the loss reserves. Consequently, the current under-reserving will depress future underwriting profits. Over-reserving produces the opposite effect. If loss reserves are overestimated, current underwriting profits are understated. As claims are settled, less money than estimated will be required, and future underwriting profits will be enhanced. Underwriting profits and losses are channeled (via account entries) into the policyholders' surplus account. Thus, the incorrect estimation of loss reserves directly affects policyholders' surplus and consequently the financial strength of the insurance organization.

Because of the leeway a company has in setting loss reserves, a company experiencing poor financial results may tend to under-reserve. Although this under-reserving may improve its current reported financial position, it will also lead to additional paid losses in the future. Alternatively, a company experiencing favorable financial results may tend to over-reserve. An insurer's estimation of loss reserves should in theory be totally independent of its financial performance, but it would be naive to assume that the relationship is totally ignored by the management of an insurance organization.

In the estimation process, loss reserves are established to cover (1) claims that have been reported and are in the process of adjustment, and (2) IBNR claims. The first area involves estimating the amount of dollars that may have to be paid. The second area requires estimating the number of claims as well as the dollar amount that may have to be paid for these claims.

Cost Accumulation Periods

Three different cost accounting periods—calendar-year, policy-year, and accident-year—are used by property-liability insurance companies.

Calendar-year. The calendar year—January 1 through December 31—is used in most businesses and is the basis required for reporting to insurance regulatory authorities (calendar year Annual Statement) and the Internal Revenue Service (Form 1120PC). The calendar-year period is used to accumulate data on premiums, investment income, expenses, and losses within a calendar year and is used in those financial reports that must be prepared shortly after the calendar year ends, such as statutory reports (due in March), tax returns (due April 15), published GAAP reports (generally issued by March 15), and agency profit-sharing reports. Because of these time restraints, the calendar-year method must include an estimate of IBNR in order to reflect the calendar-year's true loss statistics.

Policy-year. The policy-year period is unique to the insurance business. In this method, each transaction is related to the corresponding insurance policy. The aggregate transactions of all policies that become effective in a particular year determine the performance of these policies on a policy-year basis. The policy-year method is the only way an ultimate claims experience record can be obtained for a particular group of policies. This method is utilized by Lloyd's of London and other insurers domiciled in the United Kingdom. Such companies must also report their U.S. business on a calendar-year basis to U.S. regulatory authorities if they are authorized to transact insurance in the U.S.

Accident-year. The accident year is the calendar year in which the accident occurred. But accident-year data is used for a different purpose and at a later date than the calendar-year data. The accident-year period is used to accumulate loss results associated with a particular calendar year. For example, assume an insurer in its 19X1 calendar year estimated IBNR losses at $100 million for its various financial statements. In 19X2, some of the losses associated with that IBNR estimate are settled, some are reported and are in the process of adjustment, and some remain IBNR. Further assume that those 19X1 losses settled amount to $10 million, those reported and in the process of adjustment are estimated to have $35 million in ultimate associated loss payments, and the IBNR claims are now estimated at $60 million. In this case, the accident-year data for 19X1 prepared in 19X2 show the insurer under-reserved IBNR by $5 million in 19X1. The accident-year accumulation period accumulates the *loss costs* of 19X1 losses in years after 19X1, or 19X2 in the example. In each subsequent calendar-year, the associated loss costs for 19X1 are up-dated to reflect actual payments and new estimated reserves for the "accident-year" 19X1. In other words, an accident-year cost accumulation period "ages" the estimates of losses made in any given calendar year by up-dating loss information with actual payments and new reserve estimates until all losses associated with the given calendar year are extinguished. Accident-year information is used to test loss reserves in statutory statements through historical development of loss reserves. Accident-year information has other uses, such as merging it with calendar-year earned premium data to determine the adequacy of premiums for a line of insurance in a given year.

Cost Accumulation Periods Illustrated. To illustrate the application of the three cost accounting methods, suppose an insurer issued 200,000 one-year dwelling fire insurance, policies effective July 1, 19X5. During the coverage period, 6 percent of the insureds experienced an insured loss. Although losses occurred evenly throughout the year, there was a one-month delay between the occurrence of a fire and the time the insurance company recorded the loss in its statistical records. No other policies were issued in this line until July 1, 19X6, when 220,000 new fire policies were issued and became effective. The new contracts experienced the same loss and reporting pattern as the initial block of policies. Once again, no new policies were sold until July 1, 19X7, when 242,000 contracts were issued and became effective; the loss and reporting experience was identical to that of prior years. No new policies were issued in the dwelling fire line after July 1, 19X7. It is further assumed that the insurer consistently *understated* the number of IBNR claims in its calendar-year reports by 10 percent. Data for this example are shown in Illustration 3-2. These hypothetical numbers are claims counts, but they could be converted to dollar figures by multiplying by an assumed average claim value.

Calendar-year reported claims can be determined by summing the

Illustration 3-2
Hypothetical Claims Count Data

Policy Effective Date	Year Claim Is Reported				Policy Year Total
	19X5	19X6	19X7	19X8	
19X5	5,000	7,000	—	—	12,000
19X6	—	5,500	7,700	—	13,200
19X7	—		6,050	8,470	14,520
Calendar-year reported claims	5,000	12,500	13,750	8,470	39,720
Plus ending IBNR estimate	900	990	1,089	0	2,979
Minus beginning IBNR estimate	0	900	990	1,089	2,979
Calendar-year total reported claims	5,900	12,590	13,849	7,381	39,720

columns in Illustration 3-2. In 19X5, 5,000 claims were reported from policies issued during that year. The 12,500 claims reported for 19X6 were from 19X5 policies that continued into 19X6 and from new 19X7 policies. Similarly, 13,750 claims were reported in 19X7, and 8,470 claims reports were made in 19X8. In addition to calendar-year reported claims, the company would have to estimate the number of incurred but not reported claims in each calendar-year. The fact that the estimate may be incorrect (as assumed in this case) does not affect the method of allocating claims to cost accounting periods. Total claims incurred in a particular year equal reported claims, plus the number of IBNR claims at year-end, minus IBNR claims at the beginning of the year. Calendar-year total claims are shown in the last row of Illustration 3-2.

Policy-year claims can be determined from the table by summing across the first three rows. All claims attributable to policies that took effect in July 19X5 have been reported by the end of 19X6. Therefore, the claims count for the 19X5 policy year is 12,000; for 19X6, the policy-year claims count is 13,200; and for 19X7, the policy-year claims count is 14,520. Under this approach, claims developing in years subsequent to the effective date are assigned to the year in which the policy took effect. In this way, the total claims cost ultimately developed by a particular block of policies can be compared to the actual premium charged for these policies.

Accident-year claims are assigned to the year in which the accidents occur. Therefore, hindsight allows the 1,000 claims that occurred in 19X5 but were not recorded until 19X6 to be reassigned to the earlier period. The claims count for accident year 19X5 is 6,000, in the 19X6 accident year, 12,600 claims were incurred (6,000 from 19X5 policies and 6,600 from 19X6 policies); in the 19X7 accident year, 13,860 claims were incurred (6,600 from 19X6 policies and 7,260 from 19X7 policies), and in 19X8, 7,260 claims were incurred from policies effective July 1, 19X7. The inaccurate IBNR estimate that affected calendar-year loss data does not affect the ultimate accident-year claims count. Statistical data compiled on an accident-year basis are important because they aid in tracing trends in loss data such as changes in claims frequency, inflationary influences on settlement costs, and so forth.

Accident-year claims data are often compared to earned premiums calculated on a calendar-year basis. For example, in the illustration, the 12,600 claims that had an accident date of January 1, 19X6 through December 31, 19X6, would be related to premiums earned in calendar year 19X6. This procedure produces a calendar-accident-year data base for analyzing price adequacy.

Methods of Estimating Reserves for Reporting Losses

Loss reserves fall into two general categories. First, there are claims that have been adjusted or are in the loss adjustment process. Second, there are losses which have occurred prior to the cutoff date for balance sheet preparation but have not been reported to the insurer and recorded in the claims register.

Within the first category, several subdivisions exist: (1) claims approved for payment but not yet paid, (2) pending claims that require further adjustment, and (3) previously closed claims that will be reopened for additional payments.

The second category of loss reserves reflects the insurer's liability for losses incurred prior to the financial statement cutoff date but reported after that date. Losses in this category usually are called IBNR (incurred but not reported) claims or, simply, unreported claims. Losses reported after the close of the accounting period that are the result of accidents occurring on or before the accounting cutoff date properly are classified as debts owing at the balance sheet date. Company claims or statistical personnel study time lags between loss occurrence and loss reporting, and they incorporate knowledge of normal time lags with other information to estimate IBNR liabilities.

Insurance companies sometimes are restricted in the choice of reserving method used for certain lines of business; in other lines they are free to select from among the general methods discussed here or any others that produce accurate results. Reserving procedures need not be mathematically complex, but they should facilitate statistical treatment so that reasonable confidence can be achieved. The insurance company's true liability for unpaid losses is the same regardless of the method chosen; the company's statisticians must select reserve valuation procedures that consistently result in close approximations to the true liability.

There are four principal methods used to set the value of reserves for *known claims:* (1) individual estimate method (claim-file reserves), (2) average value method, (3) loss ratio method (formula reserves), and (4) tabular value method. Other methods exist, but these four approaches to reserve estimation, and combinations thereof, are the most generally applied procedures.

Individual Estimate Method. As a part of the claim settlement process, insurance companies typically establish claim files in which all records relating to claims are maintained. When a loss is reported to the insurer, a reserve is established by field or home office claims personnel and entered in the claim file as the amount estimated to be adequate for settlement of the claim. These individual estimates are aggregated in the statistical records of the company and continuously revised for changes in the estimated amount needed to pay the claim. Individual estimates are based upon the judgment of adjusters and claims department officials responsible for settling the loss. This method can be used for any line of insurance, but it is most effective in situations where the claim is definite, the number of claims for a particular line is too small for reliable averages, or the variation in the amount of claims is too great to permit the use of averages. The individual estimate or claim file method of estimating loss reserve values may be most appropriate for property insurance and suretyship. Reserves established in this manner are usually known as "case reserves."

Average Value Method. Aggregate reserves for a line of insurance can be based on the average value for claims of various types that have been, or may be, received by the insurer. This value usually is determined from the insurer's experience on closed claims of different ages and categories and modified as necessary by actuarial projections of future payments. For each category, this average is multiplied by the number of unsettled claims of the particular type on hand and the number estimated as IBNR. This method is used in varying degrees by insurance companies. Some use it for smaller claims only, while others use it for a certain line, such as automobile physical damage claims. Still other companies may average all claims for a given period of time, such as ninety days, and then individually estimate all claims remaining open after that time. The average value method is especially appropriate for estimating claim reserves for lines of business in which losses are settled quickly, claims are not subject to reopening, the number of outstanding claims is large, and the relative variation among loss amounts is small. If the frequency and severity of losses in a particular line are relatively stable or growing at a constant rate over time, the claims count and average costs can be stored and updated on computer files and aggregate reserve calculations generated automatically using data processing equipment. This method is also known as "bulk reserving" in some companies.

Loss Ratio Method. Ultimate losses for a particular line of insurance can be estimated by applying an assumed loss ratio to premiums earned during a selected period. Losses and loss adjustment expenses paid to date are deducted from the ultimate loss figure to derive the current loss reserve. This method, known as the loss ratio or formula method, is required for establishing minimum statutory loss reserves in certain lines of business. Specific steps taken to calculate loss ratio reserves are described later in this chapter.

The loss ratio method has the advantage of being simple to understand and easy to apply. However, this method is not widely used except by companies with a large volume of accident and health insurance because the formula approach results in inaccurate and arbitrary estimates of the true liability for losses. The assumed loss ratio often differs from the ratio of incurred losses to premiums earned by the insurer.

Tabular Value Method. This method applies to certain types of claims in which the amount payable depends on the duration of life, the remarriage of the beneficiary, or some other contingency. Tabular reserves are established for claims involving total permanent disability, partial permanent but nondismembering disability, survivorship benefits, and the like. Such reserves are called "tabular reserves" because probabilities of the contingencies upon which the length of benefit period depends are taken from mortality, morbidity, and remarriage tables.

Although this is the least used reserving method, its application is essential for setting reserves in those lines of insurance in which benefits are subject to tabular valuation. A specific table may be mandated in some states for use in determining certain reserves—for instance, the table of remarriage rates used to evaluate income benefits payable under workers compensation insurance to a surviving spouse until remarriage.

Methods of Estimating Incurred But Not Reported Loss Reserves

Insurance companies establish a liability for claims that have occurred but have not been reported. The estimation process for "incurred but not reported" reserves is more complicated than the reserving process for reported losses because both the number and amount of the unreported claims must be estimated. Since the loss is unreported, there is obviously no indication of the basic nature or facts of the claim. Any estimation process involving individual case estimates is not possible.

IBNR reserves are usually estimated on the basis of experience and modified for current conditions, such as increased exposure, changed claim processing cutoff dates, rising claim costs, severity and frequency of recent claims, and so on. In large companies, the total number of IBNR claims may be great enough to permit a statistical approach based on a formula modified for the aforementioned factors. The formula basis is ordinarily used for normal losses only. Catastrophe and other large losses are excluded from experience statistics and separate estimates made.

The IBNR estimate should take into account company claim reporting practices and the anticipated effect of present conditions on the company's activities. It is not practical for companies to review, evaluate, and record reserves for every claim reported through December 31. A consistent processing cutoff date between years makes IBNR reserve developments more meaningful and reliable. Many companies end processing for the year on December 15 and use the IBNR reserve to provide for two types of losses: (1) those reported but not recorded before year-end due to processing time limitations; and (2) those incurred but not reported as of December 31.

Normal reporting delays for each type of loss and transfer delays between branches and the home office affect the IBNR reserve development. Exposure by line of insurance is an important consideration. Third-party bodily injury claims tend to produce the most difficult reserve estimation challenges.

Since large IBNR cases occur sporadically, composition of the previous year's "reserve development" must be evaluated before it is used to predict the current reserve. Reserve development refers to changes in the estimated amount needed to settle incurred losses adjusted for loss payment. The term is quantified by adding reserves for losses incurred prior to the current year and still outstanding at the end of the current year, to payments made in the current year for losses incurred prior to the current year, and then subtracting the previous year's loss reserve estimate. To evaluate reserves set in prior years, it may be necessary, for example, to separate the catastrophe and noncatastrophe losses in order to get a true picture of the previous year's actual development.

Many insurers view IBNR reserves narrowly as simply a provision for the lag in reporting and recording of claims at the end of the accounting period. However, some actuaries advocate a broader use for IBNR reserves to include adverse developments on reported claims. Companies following this broader approach can estimate their IBNR reserve by working backwards. This procedure involves forming an estimate of ultimate expected losses, subtracting losses incurred as of the valuation date, and considering the difference to equal the IBNR reserve.

Present conditions play a significant part in establishing the IBNR loss reserves. The previous year's development should be modified to reflect:

- Change in amount of premiums in force or units of exposure by line,
- Change in composition of premiums in force,
- Claim severity during the last quarter,
- Accident frequency for the quarter, and
- Results of development over several previous years.

Experience, once modified, may then be used to compute percentages over some base that can be applied to the current year. The IBNR reserve can then be computed as a percentage of:

- Premiums written during the period,
- Premiums in force at the end of the period,
- Earned premiums during the period,
- Incurred losses, or
- Unpaid reported losses.

It can also be related to the number of claims reported in a recent period. The important considerations are that the base chosen has proven to be reliable and is used consistently.

There is little uniformity in IBNR reserve estimates among insurance companies. A study of the IBNR reserves established by ten different insurers found substantial variations among the ratios of their unreported claims to paid losses. Results of the study are shown in Illustration 3-3. Three of the six coverage groups show average reserves for unknown claims equal to almost 50 percent or more of paid losses. Clearly, IBNR reserves can have a significant impact on an insurance company's financial position and operating results.

Illustration 3-3
IBNR Reserves as a Percent of Paid Losses*

Coverage	Minimum	Maximum	Average
Fire	5%	19%	12%
Boiler and Machinery	0	255	48
Fidelity	35	109	76
General Liability (BI and PD)	44	148	85
Automobile Liability (BI and PD)	12	41	25
Workers Compensation	19	48	30

*Reprinted with permission from Warren, McVeigh, Griffin, "Risk Management Notes: IBNR Reserves by Line," *Business Insurance*, 17 April 1978, p. 30.

Evaluation of Loss Reserves

For balance sheet presentation, an insurer is required to determine the value at which its claims ultimately will be settled. The aggregate of these estimated costs establishes the value of the insurer's liabilities for unpaid losses as of the report date. Loss reserves generally are not discounted to their present value. Both statutory accounting practice and generally accepted accounting principles require that the insurer reserve a whole dollar for future payment of every dollar of unpaid losses. An exception is made for certain claims that are settled with periodic payments of specific amounts. Such losses are discounted with conservative interest assumptions and included in loss reserves at their present value.

Since loss reserves are estimated, it is necessary to evaluate the accuracy of the estimates periodically. Certain external variables, like inflation, can affect loss reserve development. In addition, the insurer might deliberately manipulate loss reserve levels to adjust its reported financial status.

Numerous parties may be interested in the evaluation process. State insurance regulators, through periodic examinations, analyze the adequacy of loss reserve levels. Their primary objective is to maintain insurer solvency, so they are most concerned with companies whose reserves are inadequate. Although of less importance, regulators are also concerned with excessive loss reserving which may lead to unwarranted rate increases.

Reinsurers, particularly when deciding whether to assume an existing block of business, are concerned with loss reserve adequacy. Company management is interested in the development of their own loss reserves. Even though management can influence loss reserve levels, it is interested in the effects of external variables as well as the ability of its technical people to estimate reserves accurately.

Accountants preparing independent audits of a property-liability insurance company test loss reserves. Tax authorities, concerned with deferred tax payments resulting from over-reserving, may examine loss reserves. Investors interested in the purchase of an insurer's common stock or control of the company might seek information on loss reserve practices. Finally, buyers of insurance, particularly sophisticated corporate buyers, may want data on loss reserve performance.

Evaluating the judgment of those who established loss reserves can be difficult. In the case of first-party claims, however, the evaluation is usually fairly simple. All policies for fire or similar types of loss provide that when the policyholder presents proper proof of loss, the company will pay, within a reasonable time, up to the amount that the policy provides. Courts have decided that sixty to ninety days is usually a reasonable period of time, but generally these cases are settled within a few days or weeks. Since first-party claims usually involve physical damage to property, the cost of settlement can be estimated in advance by comparing available repair estimates to the claim amount. As a result, the evaluation of these claim reserves usually does not pose a major problem.

A third-party liability claim is a different proposition. The insurance contract states that the insurance company will indemnify the claimants for damages for which the insured is legally liable under the terms of the policy. Two questions arise: (1) Is the insured liable? and (2) What is the amount of liability?

Unlike property damage, in which the extent of damage can be measured by a qualified adjuster, a precise estimate of the value of a bodily injury is not easily determined. This uncertainty as to whether or not liability attaches, together with the extent of damages, is part of the nature of liability claims. Furthermore, in injury cases, a period of time may elapse before an individual realizes the extent of an injury. For instance, the claimant may submit a claim for a broken rib and then find that more serious internal injuries have developed. Ultimately, the adequacy or inadequacy of claim reserves is determined by developing and analyzing the reserves.

Workpapers used by auditors or insurance company management to develop and analyze loss reserves are designed to indicate emerging trends. Analysis and interpretation of loss reserve developments require informed judgment. Understanding the company's overall operating philosophy with respect to claim reserving and payment practices is essential.

In evaluating loss reserve developments, some key indicators of the adequacy or inadequacy of loss reserves are:

- Consistent shortages or savings on prior years' developments
- Accident-year loss ratios that are higher or lower than the company's previous experience
- Average reported costs for an accident year higher or lower than the developed cost of prior accident-year reported claims

These indicators cannot be properly evaluated without first considering current trends and conditions such as:

- Changes in company policy or underwriting practices
- Expected inflationary trends
- Anticipated leniency in court settlements, or legislated limits on the amount of the claim
- Trends in average cost of settlement
- Trends in average settlement period
- Change in geographical exposure
- Change in reinsurance treaties

In small companies, statistical analysis of claim reserves is usually not reliable because of the small volume of cases; in new companies, historical data are not available. For these companies, the following actions are critical to the evaluation of reserve adequacy.

- Review of the method by which claim reserves are established.
- Study of the accident-year loss ratios to form an opinion on the expected loss ratio. Any major variance in loss ratio should be examined to determine the cause.
- Appraisal of the personnel involved in the overall management of the company. The claim department adjusters should be appraised for their ability to establish accurate loss reserves.
- Comparison of the company's experience with industry experience.

Whenever primary insurers experience reserve problems, reinsurers assuming business from them encounter the same problem, only at a later date, because of the lag in receiving claim information. Therefore, assumed reinsurance contracts should be reviewed for trends in the reserve and reserving levels. If a company is assuming large amounts from another company, an attempt should be made to obtain the same type of statistical data as used for preparing loss reserve developments on direct business.

Workpapers. A set of workpapers, such as those that follow, normally aids company management or outside parties in evaluating the adequacy of the loss reserves on the Annual Statement. There are many other excellent methods of appraising claim reserves; but in the absence of actuarial assistance, these workpapers will generally produce the desired results.

The statistical data necessary to develop these workpapers should be classified by coverage between direct and assumed business, net of applicable ceded insurance. Any change in the reinsurance program must be considered if the results are to be comparable from year to year.

General guidelines for completing the workpapers are:

- Losses paid should be segregated by reported year within the accident year.
- Salvage, subrogation, and reinsurance recoveries should be segregated for claims paid in prior years, indicating the date the claim was reported, the accident year, and the year the claim was paid. Recoveries on claims paid in the current year should be segregated the same as losses paid (by reported year within the accident year).
- Reported loss reserves at the end of the period must be processed the same as losses paid.
- Reported and IBNR claim reserves at the beginning of the period should be shown by accident year.
- Claim counts are required for loss reserves and for new claims reported during the year; they should be segregated by accident year.

Development of Reported Loss Reserves. Illustration 3-4 shows a worksheet for automobile bodily injury, general liability bodily injury, and workers compensation claims. These lines are grouped together because they generally take a long time to settle and require very careful analysis to ensure the adequacy of their loss reserves. However, this worksheet could be used for all lines of business.

This table is prepared for reported claims only to study the overall averages established at the end of each accident year and to follow the claims to their ultimate cost. The current provision for unpaid claims is evaluated by comparing the average developed cost to date for each accident year. The trends are then used to predict the ultimate cost for each accident year.

The six categories of data presented in Illustration 3-4 provide the following information:

Item 1a. The number of claims in reserve at the end of the accident year is the number of claims still pending from among the claims reported during an accident year.

Items 1b, c, d. The number of claims still pending one year after the end of the accident year, and so forth.

Item 2. The cumulative loss payments are the sum of the amounts paid during the years following the accident year.

Item 3. The claim reserves, Items 3a, 3b, 3c, 3d, and 3e, represent the reserves in dollars outstanding at the end of each of the years indicated, beginning with the end of the accident year on claims outstanding as of that date. These amounts represent the aggregate of the reserves pertaining to the number of claims shown in Items 1a, 1b, 1c, 1d, and 1e.

Item 4. Cost represents the total cost to date of all reported claims which had been pending at the end of the accident year. This total is arrived at by combining the respective lines of Items 2 and 3.

Item 5. The savings or loss on development of loss reserves is the difference between Item 3a, the claim reserve at the end of the accident year, and the developed cost, Item 4, at the end of the respective year of development. A positive number indicates that prior loss reserves were excessive. A negative number indicates that prior loss reserves were inadequate.

Item 6. Average cost represents the developed average cost of claims for the year-end outstanding claims and is obtained by dividing the totals on the respective lines in Item 4 by Item 1a.

Development of IBNR Reserves. The workpaper in Illustration 3-5, in addition to providing the amount of savings or loss in the provision for incurred but not reported claims, also shows the length of time required to receive notice of all claims. Some companies treat reopened claims as IBNR claims. Therefore, the evaluator should ascertain how the company treats such claims before interpreting the results derived from the analysis.

The developed cost data forms a basis for determining the IBNR claim provision. Data presented in Illustration 3-5 differ slightly from the information provided in Illustration 3-4. The following items are included in that analysis of IBNR reserve development:

Item 1. Total cumulative number of claims reported is the total count of all claims resulting from accidents during such

Illustration 3-4
Development of Reported Loss Reserves by Accident Year

Coverage: Auto Bodily Injury, General Liability Bodily Injury, and Workers Compensation					
	Accident Year				
Item	19X0	19X1	19X2	19X3	19X4
1. Number of claims in reserve at:					
a. End of accident year	151	154	160	189	211
b. One year later	113	108	101	114	
c. Two years later	69	59	76		
d. Three years later	51	43			
e. Four years later etc.	39				
2. Cumulative loss payments after:					
a. One year's development	$115,867	125,999	129,058	137,969	—
b. Two years' development	189,116	227,845	234,742		
c. Three years' development	256,324	271,883			
d. Four years' development etc.	299,978				
3. Claim reserves:					
a. At end of accident year	$241,298	249,172	261,836	309,674	346,251
b. One year later	146,420	151,355	132,778	299,871	
c. Two years later	136,893	133,439	114,829		
d. Three years later	97,167	89,555			
e. Four years later	56,777				
4. Cost:					
a. At end of accident year (3a)	$241,298	249,172	261,836	309,674	346,251
b. One year later (2a + 3b)	262,287	277,354	261,836	437,840	
c. Two years later (2b + 3c)	326,009	361,284	349,571		
d. Three years later (2c + 3d)	353,491	361,438			
e. Four years later (2d + 3e)	356,755				
5. Savings (loss):					
a. At end of one year (3a − 4b)	$(20,989)	(28,182)	—	(128,166)	—
b. At end of two years (3a − 4c)	(84,711)	(112,112)	(87,735)		
c. At end of three years (3a − 4d)	(112,193)	(112,266)			
d. At end of four years (3a − 4e)	(115,457)				
6. Average cost:					
a. At end of accident year (4a ÷ 1a)	$ 1,598	1,618	1,636	1,638	1,641
b. At end of one year (4b ÷ 1a)	1,737	1,801	1,636	2,317	
c. At end of two years (4c ÷ 1a)	2,159	2,346	2,185		
d. At end of three years (4d ÷ 1a)	2,341	2,347			
e. At end of four years (4e ÷ 1a)	2,363				

accident year and reported subsequent to the end of the year.

Item 2. Cumulative loss payments is the amount of payments on claims reported in Item 1.

Item 3. The loss reserves, Items 3a, 3b, 3c, 3d, and 3e, represent the reserves outstanding at the end of years indicated, beginning with the end of the accident year. In many cases, especially in the liability lines, losses are reported more than one year after the accident year. Therefore, the loss reserve in years subsequent to the accident year might include a provision for additional IBNR in addition to the claims already reported.

Item 4. Cost represents the total of the respective lines of Items 2 and 3.

Item 5. The savings or losses on loss reserves is the difference between Item 3a, the loss reserve at the end of the accident year, and the cost to date, Item 4, at the end of the respective year of development. Again this is the key item indicating the degree of over-reserving or under-reserving.

Analyzing reserve development along the lines illustrated in these work papers provides a retrospective test of an insurer's reserving practices. Because loss reserves typically are the largest liability on a property-liability insurance company's balance sheet, the accuracy with which these reserves are estimated is crucial to proper evaluation of the company. The Annual Statement contains a schedule that, although not identical, is similar to the working papers shown in Illustrations 3-4 and 3-5.

Annual Statement Development Schedule. Prior to the adoption of the 1989 blank, Annual Statements contained four schedules reflecting the development of loss, and in some instances, loss adjustment expense reserves. Those schedules were identified by the letters G, K, O, and P. G covered fidelity and surety lines of business; K, credit; O, pure property (short-tail lines); and P, liability and multiple peril (long-tail lines).

Effective with the 1989 Annual Statement, data previously presented in Schedules G, K, and O appear in Schedule P. This schedule effectively displays loss experience for all lines of business including nonproportional reinsurance assumed and ceded as separate lines of business. Earned premiums, losses incurred, and loss adjusting expense by earned/incurred year are displayed in Schedule P. Long-tail lines developed experience is reflected for each of the past ten years plus all prior years combined. Short-tail lines shows each of the past two

Illustration 3-5
Development of Incurred But Not Reported Loss Reserves
by Accident Year

	Coverage: Auto Bodily Injury, General Liability Bodily Injury, and Workers Compensation				
	Accident Year				
Item	19X0	19X1	19X2	19X3	19X4
1.Total cumulative number of claims reported:					
a. One year later	29	31	28	33	
b. Two years later	37	37	35		
c. Three years later etc.	41	42			
2. Cumulative loss payments:					
a. At end of one year	$ 19,750	27,300	28,600	29,100	
b. At end of two years	43,100	51,900	47,800		
c. At end of three years	74,600	77,700			
d. At end of four years	89,000				
3. Loss reserves:					
a. At end of accident year (initial IBNR)	$ 49,000	56,000	82,500	87,500	91,000
b. One year later	45,000	43,000	51,900	54,000	
c. Two years later	42,000	47,000	43,000		
d. Three years later	25,400	28,000			
e. Four years later	17,500				
4. Cost (2 + 3):					
a. At end of accident year (initial IBNR)	$ 49,000	56,000	82,500	87,500	91,000
b. One year later (2a + 3b)	64,750	70,300	80,500	83,100	
c. Two years later (2b + 3c)	85,100	98,900	90,800		
d. Three years later (2c + 3d)	100,000	105,700			
e. Four years later	106,500				
5. Savings (loss):					
a. At end of one year (3a – 4b)	$(15,750)	(14,300)	2,000	4,400	
b. At end of two years (3a – 4c)	(36,100)	(42,900)	(8,300)		
c. At end of three years (3a – 4d)	(51,000)	(49,700)			
d. At end of four years (3a – 4e)	(57,500)				

years and then all prior years. Provision is also made in subschedules to reflect separately the experience on a claims-incurred basis and claims-made basis.

Schedule P—Analysis of losses and loss expenses is the primary tool used by state insurance department officials in examining an insurer's loss reserve adequacy. Its various parts are detailed and require a laborious effort for proper analysis. This section highlights the more relevant portions of the schedule.

Schedule P is the most complex schedule included in the Annual Statement. The schedule develops the insurer's historical experience on reserves for loss and loss adjustment expenses. It assists in predicting loss reserve levels at various points in time by extrapolating from past loss experience. The schedule may require reserve provisions for certain lines of business that are in addition to reserves provided based on the judgment of management. If the compilation of schedule P indicates that additional reserves are required, a liability item appears on the balance sheet under the title "Excess of Statutory Reserves over Statement Reserves." Schedule P provisions do not affect underwriting results (shown on the income statement) for the year, since they are a direct charge to the surplus account.

Parts 1, 2, 3, 5, and 6 of the schedule consist of summaries of various subparts. (There is no part 4.) Schedule P, Part 1 appears in Illustration 3-6. The subparts of Part 1 are identified by letters from A to Q. Subparts A through H reflect earned premiums and loss and loss expense for lines of business that tend to generate long-tail claims. These subparts include multi-peril, auto liability and medical, workers compensation, medical malpractice, and other liability. Parts I through Q cover lines that tend to generate claims with shorter tails. These shorter-tail coverages include fire and allied, inland marine, earthquake, glass, burglary and theft, auto physical damage, fidelity, surety, financial guaranty, credit, accident and health, international, and reinsurance.

Subparts A to H (long-tail) show earned premiums for the current and nine prior years by the year in which the premiums were earned. The earned premiums reflected in the current year's financial statements include amounts pertaining to prior years. These prior amounts came from delayed recording of premiums, return premiums, and premium adjustments on retrospective rated policies or reporting form policies and other adjustments. Although the income statement reflects all such premiums as earned in the current year, Schedule P reallocates the earned premium to the proper earned year. If the Schedule P earned premiums from the previous year's Annual Statement are subtracted from the total Schedule P premiums of the current year, the difference should be equal to the earned premiums reflected in the current year income statement. Stated another way, earned premiums in Schedule P, Parts A to H are cumulative by earned year for ten one-year periods.

Illustration 3-6
Schedule P—Part 1—Summary (000 omitted)

1 Years in Which Premiums Were Earned and Losses Were Incurred	Premiums Earned			Loss and Loss Expense Payments						11 Total Net Paid (5−6+7 −8+10)	12 Number of Claims Reported— Direct and Assumed
	2 Direct and Assumed	3 Ceded	4 Net (2−3)	Loss Payments		Allocated Loss Expense Payments		9 Salvage and Subrogation Received	10 Uncollected Loss Expense Payments		
				5 Direct and Assumed	6 Ceded	7 Direct and Assumed	8 Ceded				
1. Prior	XXXX	XXXX	XXXX								XXXX
2. 1980											XXXX
3. 1981											XXXX
4. 1982											XXXX
5. 1983											XXXX
6. 1984											XXXX
7. 1985											XXXX
8. 1986											XXXX
9. 1987											XXXX
10. 1988											XXXX
11. 1989											XXXX
12. Totals	XXXX	XXXX	XXXX								XXXX

Note: For "prior," report amounts paid or received in current year only. Report cumulative amounts paid or received for specific years. Report loss payments net of salvage and subrogation received.

Years in Which Premiums Were Earned and Losses Were Incurred	Losses Unpaid				Allocated Loss Expenses Unpaid				21 Unallocated Loss Expenses Unpaid	22 Total Net Losses and Expenses Unpaid	23 Number of Claims Outstanding— Direct and Assumed
	Case Basis		Bulk + IBNR		Case Basis		Bulk + IBNR				
	13 Direct and Assumed	14 Ceded	15 Direct and Assumed	16 Ceded	17 Direct and Assumed	18 Ceded	19 Direct and Assumed	20 Ceded			
1. Prior											XXXX
2. 1980											XXXX
3. 1981											XXXX
4. 1982											XXXX
5. 1983											XXXX
6. 1984											XXXX
7. 1985											XXXX
8. 1986											XXXX
9. 1987											XXXX
10. 1988											XXXX
11. 1989											XXXX
12. Totals											XXXX

Years in Which Premiums Were Earned and Losses Were Incurred	Total Losses and Loss Expenses Incurred			Loss and Loss Expense Percentage (Incurred/Premiums Earned)			Discount for Time Value of Money		32 Inter-Company Pooling Participation Percentage	Net Balance Sheet Reserves After Discount	
	24 Direct and Assumed	25 Ceded	26 Net*	27 Direct and Assumed	28 Ceded	29 Net	30 Loss	31 Loss Expense		33 Losses Unpaid	34 Loss Expenses Unpaid
1. Prior	XXXX	XXXX	XXXX	XXXX	XXXX	XXXX			XXXX		XXXX
2. 1980											
3. 1981											
4. 1982											
5. 1983											
6. 1984											
7. 1985											
8. 1986											
9. 1987											
10. 1988											
11. 1989											
12. Totals	XXXX	XXXX	XXXX	XXXX	XXXX	XXXX			XXXX		

*Net = (24 − 25) = (11 + 22)

Subparts I to Q (short-tail) reflect earned premiums in the same manner but only for the current, last, and all prior years.

Loss and loss adjustment expenses (collectively hereafter described as losses) are reflected in subparts A through Q by the year in which the loss was incurred, for the same lines of business and periods in which the related premiums were displayed. Paid losses (and collected salvage and subrogation) and outstanding losses are shown separately as well as allocated and unallocated loss adjustment expenses. The number of claims reported is also shown for payments on certain lines and number of claims outstanding for reserve (unpaid) amounts. Other columns reflect the effect of discounting reserves to present values and intercompany pooling percentages. Statutory reserving and Annual Statement reporting generally do not permit discounting except for the indemnity portion of workers compensation and medical malpractice reserves. Discounts, if any, accordingly should be restored before reflecting loss data in Schedule P.

Parts 2, 3, 5 and 6 of Schedule P consist of several subparts identified by the same letters and corresponding lines of business as Part 1.

Illustration 3-7 shows Schedule P, Parts 2, 3, 5, and 6. Part 2 displays incurred losses and allocated loss expense to the nearest $1,000 (000 omitted) at each year end for the same periods (A to H ten years, I to Q two years, and both all prior years) as reflected in Part 1. The numbers reported for particular year ends generally change from year to year even if no additional losses were reported for a particular claim year. This situation arises from the fact that very few claims are settled for the exact amount of the reserve. The difference between the reserved amounts and the settlement amount changes the incurred dollars. In addition, closed without payment claims which had a reserve thereon, salvage and subrogation recoveries, increases or decreases in reserve values, and other factors affect incurred loss numbers.

Part 3 of Schedule P displays cumulative paid losses and allocated loss expenses for the same years and subparts as previously described. For those subparts, it also indicates by year the number of claims closed by payment and the number closed without payment.

Part 5 reflects data similar to that in Part 1 for policies issued on a claims-made basis under commercial multiple peril, medical malpractice, and other liability lines of business for 1987 and subsequent years.

Part 6 reflects by incurred loss year bulk and incurred but not reported loss reserves and allocated (loss adjustment) expense reserves at the end of each year for the applicable period.

An excess reserve for loss and loss adjustment expenses may or may not be necessary. Such reserves apply only to workers compensation, medical malpractice, other liability, and credit lines of business.

Illustration 3-7
Schedule P—Parts 2, 3, 5, and 6

SCHEDULE P—PART 2—SUMMARY

1 Years in Which Losses Were Incurred	INCURRED LOSSES AND ALLOCATED EXPENSES REPORTED AT YEAR END (000 OMITTED)										DEVELOPMENT**	
	2 1980	3 1981	4 1982	5 1983	6 1984	7 1985	8 1986	9 1987	10 1988	11 1989	12 One Year	13 Two Year
1. Prior	*											
2. 1980	XXXX											
3. 1981	XXXX	XXXX										
4. 1982	XXXX	XXXX	XXXX									
5. 1983	XXXX	XXXX	XXXX	XXXX								
6. 1984	XXXX	XXXX	XXXX	XXXX	XXXX							
7. 1985	XXXX	XXXX	XXXX	XXXX	XXXX	XXXX						
8. 1986	XXXX	XXXX	XXXX	XXXX	XXXX	XXXX	XXXX					
9. 1987	XXXX	XXXX	XXXX	XXXX	XXXX	XXXX	XXXX	XXXX				XXXX
10. 1988	XXXX	XXXX	XXXX	XXXX	XXXX	XXXX	XXXX	XXXX	XXXX			XXXX
11. 1989	XXXX	XXXX	XXXX	XXXX	XXXX	XXXX	XXXX	XXXX	XXXX	XXXX	XXXX	XXXX
12. Totals											XXXX	XXXX

*Reported reserves only. Subsequent development relates only to subsequent payments and reserves.
**Current year less first or second year, showing (redundant) or adverse.

SCHEDULE P—PART 3—SUMMARY

1 Years in Which Losses Were Incurred	CUMULATIVE PAID LOSSES AND ALLOCATED EXPENSES REPORTED AT YEAR END (000 OMITTED)										12 Number of Claims Closed With Loss Payment	13 Number of Claims Closed Without Loss Payment
	2 1980	3 1981	4 1982	5 1983	6 1984	7 1985	8 1986	9 1987	10 1988	11 1989		
1. Prior	*										XXXX	XXXX
2. 1980	XXXX										XXXX	XXXX
3. 1981	XXXX	XXXX									XXXX	XXXX
4. 1982	XXXX	XXXX	XXXX								XXXX	XXXX
5. 1983	XXXX	XXXX	XXXX	XXXX							XXXX	XXXX
6. 1984	XXXX	XXXX	XXXX	XXXX	XXXX						XXXX	XXXX
7. 1985	XXXX	XXXX	XXXX	XXXX	XXXX	XXXX					XXXX	XXXX
8. 1986	XXXX	XXXX	XXXX	XXXX	XXXX	XXXX	XXXX				XXXX	XXXX
9. 1987	XXXX	XXXX	XXXX	XXXX	XXXX	XXXX	XXXX	XXXX			XXXX	XXXX
10. 1988	XXXX	XXXX	XXXX	XXXX	XXXX	XXXX	XXXX	XXXX	XXXX		XXXX	XXXX
11. 1989	XXXX	XXXX	XXXX	XXXX	XXXX	XXXX	XXXX	XXXX	XXXX	XXXX	XXXX	XXXX

Note: Net of salvage and subrogation received.

SCHEDULE P—PART 5—CLAIMS-MADE
(000 omitted)

PART 5E—COMMERCIAL MULTIPLE PERIL

| 1 Years in Which Premiums Were Earned and Losses Were Incurred | 2 Premiums Earned | 3 Loss Payments | 3.1 Cumulative Number of Claims Closed with Payments | 3.2 Cumulative Number of Claims Closed Without Payments | (d) Loss Expense Payments | | | | 6 Loss and Loss Expense Payments (3+4+5) | 7 Percent 6÷2 | 8 Number of Claims Outstanding | 9 Losses Unpaid | 10 Loss Expense Unpaid | 11 Total Losses and Loss Expense Incurred (6+9+10) | 12 Percent 11÷2 |
					4 Allocated	4a Percent 4÷3	5 Unallocated	5a Percent 5÷3							
1. 1987															
2. 1988															
3. 1989															
4. Totals															

SCHEDULE P—PART 6—SUMMARY

BULK AND INCURRED BUT NOT REPORTED RESERVES AND ALLOCATED EXPENSES AT YEAR END (000 OMITTED)

1 Years in Which Losses Were Incurred	2 1980	3 1981	4 1982	5 1983	6 1984	7 1985	8 1986	9 1987	10 1988	11 1989
1. Prior										
2. 1980	XXXX									
3. 1981	XXXX	XXXX								
4. 1982	XXXX	XXXX	XXXX							
5. 1983	XXXX	XXXX	XXXX	XXXX						
6. 1984	XXXX	XXXX	XXXX	XXXX	XXXX					
7. 1985	XXXX	XXXX	XXXX	XXXX	XXXX	XXXX				
8. 1986	XXXX	XXXX	XXXX	XXXX	XXXX	XXXX	XXXX			
9. 1987	XXXX	XXXX	XXXX	XXXX	XXXX	XXXX	XXXX	XXXX		
10. 1988	XXXX	XXXX	XXXX	XXXX	XXXX	XXXX	XXXX	XXXX	XXXX	
11. 1989	XXXX	XXXX	XXXX	XXXX	XXXX	XXXX	XXXX	XXXX	XXXX	XXXX

To calculate the excess, a percentage minimum loss and expense ratio by year is determined, which is applied to the net earned premium by year. The results are then compared to the net loss and loss expenses incurred and any year with the minimum in excess of the incurred produces an excess reserve for the difference. This excess reserve allows no benefit of offset for years in excess of the minimum. Data used for the calculations appear in Parts 1 or 5 of Schedule P.

The minimum ratio can vary depending on premium volume on the individual lines mentioned above, each line standing on its own. If by line premiums earned exceed $1 million in three out of five years (other than credit), the lowest ratio for a qualifying year (over a million) can be used for the minimum ratio, subject to a cap of 75 percent. Companies with by line volume under one million dollars must use a minimum loss ratio of 60 percent for other liability and medical malpractice lines, 65 percent for workers compensation, and 50 percent for credit.

Loss Adjustment Expense Reserves

Reserves for unpaid losses usually provide only for loss payments and not for any associated loss adjustment expenses. In addition to the cost of the loss, significant expenses are incurred by insurers in investigating, processing, and paying losses. A reserve is established for anticipated future expense payments required to settle losses (whether reported or not) that occurred before the close of the current accounting period. This loss settlement expense reserve is included as a separate liability on the statutory balance sheet.

There are two types of loss adjustment expenses—allocated and unallocated. Allocated loss expenses are allocated to a specific claim, such as legal fees and outside claims adjusters' fees. Unallocated loss expenses are not allocated to a specific claim, such as salaries and rent. Different methods are used to set the reserves for allocated and unallocated loss adjustment expenses.

The relation of allocated to unallocated adjustment expense varies according to the company and its methods of adjusting. Some companies have few unallocated and mostly allocated expenses. For example, some do not allow anyone but their own salaried employees to adjust their claims unless absolutely unavoidable such as when an accident or loss is reported in some distant territory where it is cheaper to hire a local adjuster on a contract basis. Others adjust every claim through independent adjusters. This latter case generates greater allocated expenses.

Some companies still include allocated loss adjustment expenses in the estimates on the open claims. For instance, when they set up a reserve for a claim, they may estimate the claim will cost $1,000 plus $100 for the independent adjusting. Therefore, the reserve is set at $1,100.

The better practice, followed by most companies, is to keep claim reserves and adjustment expense reserves separate. Reserves for allocated and unallocated loss adjustment expenses also are usually determined separately. Allocated expense reserves might be determined on a case basis or by a study of the relationship of allocated loss expenses paid to losses paid. Unallocated loss expense reserves are usually based on time studies or on a relationship of unallocated loss expenses paid to losses paid.

Since allocated loss expense payments are chargeable to specific claims, individual payments can be recorded in the same detail as the claims themselves. The coverage, class of risk, accident date, reported date, state territory, and so forth can all be pinpointed. Any method used to establish or test loss reserves can also be used to establish or test allocated loss expense reserves.

Reserves for losses are more significant than reserves for loss adjustment expenses. In terms of aggregate amounts, reserves for loss adjustment expenses are a small percentage of total loss reserves (5 to 20 percent depending on the business mix). In addition, estimating amounts needed to pay loss adjustment expenses is generally easier than estimating amounts needed to pay losses. Different methods apply in estimating allocated and unallocated loss adjustment expense reserves.

Allocated Loss Adjustment Expense Reserves. Two ways are used to determine allocated loss adjustment expense reserves: the case basis and the formula basis. When using the case basis, the claims adjuster reviews the claims file and determines what the reserve for allocated loss expenses should be. Most companies, however, determine the reserves on a formula basis.

Over the years formula reserves have been calculated by a calendar-year "paid-to-paid" method. This approach involves calculating the ratio of allocated loss expenses paid to losses paid by line. Frequently, this ratio is averaged over a period of three years in order to reduce the impact of yearly fluctuations in the ratio. The ratio is then multiplied by the reserve for losses to obtain the reserve for allocated loss expenses. Frequently, the ratio is multiplied by the entire IBNR loss reserve and 50 percent of the reported loss reserves, using the theory that, on the average, one-half of the allocated loss expenses have already been paid on reported claims.

In the past few years the problem of computing adequate loss adjustment expense reserves has received attention. A review of state examiners' reports indicates a significant increase in the number of adjustments for deficiencies in such reserves. The calendar-year "paid-to-paid" method of calculating reserves generally results in an understatement, because the method assumes that each paid loss carries with it the same ratio of allocated adjustment expense regardless of how long it has remained unsettled. This constant ratio does not always occur, particularly on the long-tail lines of business which can incur expensive litigation costs over many years before all claims are settled.

Generally, a large number of claims are paid within one or two years of the accident, with little or no related attorneys' fees or costs. On the other hand, the insurance company may resist an unreasonable claim in court over a period of several years. If the company wins the case, it will pay no loss, but it will have paid substantial attorneys' fees and court costs. It is this type of settlement that causes the difficulty in estimating the loss adjustment expense reserves. The pending loss reserve tends to consist of proportionately more claims that involve costly loss adjustment expenses than the whole population of claims settled in a calendar year.

As the calendar-year paid-to-paid method of calculating allocated loss adjustment expense reserves is likely to result in an inadequate provision for this liability, the development of prior years' reserves should be closely reviewed as a check on the adequacy of the reserves. The need to review reserve developments of prior years' reserves is more significant for companies writing liability lines than for those writing primarily property lines. If a company establishes allocated loss expense reserves on a calendar-year paid-to-paid basis and a development of prior years' reserves shows this produces inadequate reserves, a change in method is appropriate and prudent.

Unallocated Loss Adjustment Expense Reserves. Unallocated loss adjustment expenses (ULAE) generally are defined as those expenses connected with the process of adjusting and recording of policy claims which are not charged to specific claims. Although a company's employees may do work that could be related to specific claims, the statutory rules require that salaries paid to employees involved in the claim function or related administration be treated as an unallocated loss adjustment expense. A reserve for unallocated loss adjustment expenses is required by both statutory accounting practices and generally accepted accounting principles.

A common method used to calculate the reserve for ULAE is to relate the paid ULAE to paid losses for a prior period or periods (often a three- or five-year average) and to apply the developed ratios to unpaid losses at the statement date. This method is based on two assumptions generally accepted in the insurance business:

1. The ratio of unallocated loss adjustment expenses paid to paid losses applies to any loss, regardless of how long it has been in the loss reserve. In other words, all claims carry with them a percentage of the unallocated adjustment expense, and this percentage is applicable to all claims. Thus, the calendar-year paid-to-paid ratio is applicable to all claims as far as unallocated loss expenses are concerned.
2. A substantial amount of the unallocated expenses for a particular claim is expended when the claim is first reported, and the remainder is expended when the claim is closed. Accordingly, the ratio developed is reduced by the estimated portion of ULAE expended when a claim file is opened. It is usually 50 percent when applied to unpaid reported losses, and the full ratio is applied to IBNR reserves.

While 50 percent is the most common estimate of the portion of ULAE incurred when a reserve is established, the actual percentage will vary by company and by line of business. For example, the unpaid ULAE for a workers compensation claim will probably be less than 50 percent, since a large reserve is often established for related monthly payments, which incur little ULAE.

The current ratio of paid ULAE to paid losses is usually sufficient for providing the ULAE reserve for reported losses for property insurance lines, which are usually settled in a relatively short period. The trend of the ratio, however, should be reviewed for the IBNR calculation and liability lines, since the ratio in future periods will be applied to all outstanding claims regardless of the incurred date or reported date of the claim. If the ratio of the paid ULAE to paid losses is increasing, the ULAE reserve based on the current ratio probably would not be adequate. This trend would have particular significance to IBNR claims, since the full ratio of future periods will be applied to such claims when reported.

While the ratio method is probably the most common method, other, more sophisticated methods are also used. One such method is the payment projection method, which is based on studies to determine (1) what percent of ULAE paid in a calendar year is applicable to a particular accident year and (2) what percent of the total ULAE to be paid for a particular accident year has been paid to date.

By definition, developments cannot be used to test the adequacy of unallocated loss adjustment expense reserves. The adequacy of the reserve for unallocated loss adjustment expenses depends primarily on the use of sound cost accounting and expense allocation methods, as well as the proper method of calculating the reserve.

Insurance companies classify their expenses in accordance with uniform procedures set forth in Regulation 30 of the New York Department of Insurance and adopted by other states. All expenses are classified into twenty-one major expense categories in Part 4 of the Underwriting and Investment Exhibit on page 11 of the Annual Statement. Expenses are broken down further on the Insurance Expense Exhibit into five functional areas: (1) investment expenses; (2) loss adjustment expenses; (3) acquisition, field supervision, and collection expenses; (4) taxes; and (5) general expenses.

Because the way a company allocates its expenses affects the calculation of the unallocated loss adjustment expense reserve, company management and auditors periodically review the basis of allocation. Questions such as the following assist the review of the expense allocation:

1. Who was responsible for developing the allocation methods?
2. When were these methods developed?
3. Has the company's mode of operation changed since the methods were developed?
4. Has the increase or decrease in volume been considered since the methods were developed?
5. Were interdepartmental services considered in arriving at total departmental cost?
6. How was company overhead allocated to departments?
7. Was officers' compensation distributed logically?
8. Were the bases used to distribute costs truly indicative of the operation?

The distribution of unallocated loss adjustment expenses by coverage must be accurate. The best way to distribute unallocated loss adjustment expenses to coverages is to determine the unit cost involved each time a claim file is reviewed. Ideally, time studies would determine the time spent in handling claims, although in practice such time studies are rare.

While the adequacy of the ULAE reserve cannot be tested retrospectively, it is included in the Schedule P development. The NAIC required certain measurement and allocation standards which companies meet in both statutory and GAAP reports.

The purpose of the ULAE reserve is to set aside a large enough amount to cover the costs of all services (other than those classified as allocated loss expenses) necessary for liquidating the company's entire liability associated with unsettled claims as of the statement date. While many methods can be used, it is essential that the established ULAE reserve be adequate.

Certification of Loss Reserves

In 1980, the NAIC adopted a loss reserve opinion rule which allows individual states to require that a loss reserve certification be filed as an amendment to the Annual Statement. Reserve certification is intended to assure regulators that loss and loss adjustment expense reserves are sufficient in the opinion of a competent loss reserve specialist. Only companies domiciled in states that have adopted the NAIC reserve opinion rule must file the certification. At least seven states—California, Illinois, Massachusetts, New Jersey, Texas, Florida, and New York—presently require that loss reserves be certified.

The certification rule requires a statement of opinion regarding sufficiency of the company's loss reserves and the fairness of the computational methods which derived the reserves. The opinion, which is similar to the opinion statement of an independent auditor, sets forth:

1. the relationship of the specialist to the insurance company;
2. the specialist's qualifications;
3. the annual statement items and amounts with respect to which the specialist is expressing an opinion;
4. the scope of the specialist's examination, including whether the specialist tested the underlying data for accuracy or relied on data prepared by the company; and,
5. an opinion paragraph concerning the sufficiency of the reserves.

Any individual competent in loss reserving is allowed to render the opinion. A "qualified loss reserve specialist" is defined to include members of the American Academy of Actuaries, consultants, company officers or employees who assert competency in loss reserve evaluation. The certification of reserves must accompany the Annual Statement filing in most states.

UNEARNED PREMIUM RESERVE

The unearned premium reserve typically is about one-quarter of the total liabilities in a property-liability insurance company's balance sheet. In primarily property insurance companies it can be the largest liability. This liability represents, at least in theory, the aggregate amount of the unearned portion of the premium an insurer would need to return to each policyholder should the insurer go out of business and cancel all outstanding policies as of a given date. Assuming policies are in force, the unearned premium may be thought of as that amount required to provide for losses and expenses during the unexpired term of the policy.

To illustrate the concept of unearned premium reserves, assume a one-year fire insurance policy was issued on July 1 at an annual premium of $200. If a set of financial statements were prepared at the close of the business day on which the policy was issued, the entire premium would be shown in the liability section of the balance sheet as unearned. This is true even though the insurance company had to use a portion of the premium revenue immediately to pay for the expenses associated with writing the coverage. The insurer's Annual Statement is dated December 31. At that time one-half of the protection period has elapsed. One-half of the policy's advance premium, $100, would be included in earned premiums for the year and the remaining half, $100, would remain in the unearned premium reserve. The remaining $100 is the maximum amount that would have to be returned to the policy-holder if the coverage were canceled by the insurance company. Another way to interpret the reserve is to consider it as the approximate amount an insurance company would have to pay a reinsurer to assume its obligation under the contract. This later view of the unearned premium reserve as the amount of premium necessary for portfolio reinsurance of a retiring insurance company's obligations explains why the liability sometimes is called the "reinsurance reserve."

Since for some companies it would be too expensive to compute the unearned premium of each policy as of the financial statement date, companies employ approximation methods that produce reasonably accurate aggregate reserves. The first step in calculating this liability is to develop the "premiums in force" figure which serves as the source for the computation. Premiums in force is a total of "original premiums" of all policies in force as of a certain date, since each new policy is automatically placed in premiums in force and remains there until it expires or is canceled. "Original premiums" are discussed in Chapter 4.

Every policy is segregated in the in-force record according to its term and expiration date. At any financial statement date, the in-force record is tabulated by policy term (six months, twelve months, eighteen months, two years, and so forth) and by month and year of expiration. This tabulation facilitates the application of fractions or percentages to the various group totals to determine the unearned portion. The sum of the group calculation represents the total liability for unearned premiums. The Underwriting and Investment Exhibit (Part 2) in the Annual Statement displays the summarized information and the final calculations for the total unearned premium reserve.

Pro Rata Methods of Calculating the Unearned Premium Reserve

A number of different methods are used in calculating the unearned premium reserve. Because so many transactions are involved, determining the exact amount of unearned premium on each policy in force can be costly and impractical. Insurers often use simplifying assumptions, therefore, to facilitate the calculation. Thus some insurers assume that policies are written evenly over a year or a month while other insurers calculate the unearned premium reserve on a daily basis.

Monthly Pro Rata Method. The monthly pro rata method assumes that the statistical average of a large number of policies that provide identical coverage yields an unearned premium not materially different from the combined results of individual computations. Many states now insist on the monthly pro rata method, since it is generally more accurate than the annual pro rata method, which assumes that all policies are written evenly throughout the year.

The monthly pro rata method of calculating unearned premiums assumes that, on the average, the same amount of business is written each day of the month. The year is divided into twenty-four half months because it is assumed that the effective date for the premiums written during the month will be the fifteenth day. At the end of the month, one twenty-fourth (1/24) of the month's writing will have been earned on policies written for a one-year term and twenty-three twenty-fourths (23/24) will be unearned. If the policy was written for a three-year term, one seventy-second (1/72) would be earned and the unearned premium would be seventy-one seventy-seconds (71/72) of the month's in-force premiums. If the policy was written for a six-month term, one-twelfth (1/12) would be earned and the unearned premium would be eleven-twelfths (11/12) of the month's in-force premiums. The longer the policy term, the greater the size of the unearned premium reserve at the end of the period in which the premiums were written. Illustration 3-8 shows the unearned premium reserves by the monthly pro rata method for three policies of different lengths at the end of one, six, and twelve months.

Daily Method. The daily method of calculating unearned premiums is based on the exact number of days the premium covers or in some instances on a 360-day year. This method requires greater computer capacity and also requires including the day of expiration in the premiums in force statistical data. The formula is the unexpired number of days remaining divided by the days in the period, multiplied by the premiums in force.

For a company writing personal lines, the difference in unearned

Illustration 3-8
Unearned Premium Reserve (UPR) by Monthly Pro Rata Method

		Unearned Premiums and Fractions Used at the End of					
		1 Month		6 Months		12 Months	
Policy Term	Premium	UPR	Fraction	UPR	Fraction	UPR	Fraction
1 year	$120	$115	23/24	$ 65	13/24	$ 5	1/24
2 years	$240	$235	47/48	$185	37/48	$125	25/48
3 years	$360	$355	71/72	$305	61/72	$245	49/72

premiums resulting from changing to a daily pro rata method from the monthly pro rata probably would not be significant, since these policies are usually written evenly throughout the month. However, for a company writing commercial lines policies, which are often effective the first of the month, the change could substantially reduce the unearned premiums.

Special Methods

Pro rata methods do not apply for certain types of premiums. These situations include retrospective premiums, installment premiums, audit premiums, and advance premiums.

Retrospective Premiums. The premium for a retrospectively rated insurance policy is adjusted at the end of the coverage period to reflect the insured's loss experience during the policy term. The current year's experience determines the year's premium within predetermined maximum and minimum limits. An initial premium is due at the beginning of the year, and the final cost is fixed after the policy term has expired. Retrospective rating is used for workers compensation, general liability, automobile liability, automobile physical damage, burglary, and glass insurance.

Retrospectively rated policies generally are written for an annual term; the premium deposit is fully earned by the end of the year. Since the deposit premium is not a final premium, the insurance company may make either an additional charge or a refund, depending on whether the actual cost proves to be more or less than the originally estimated cost. This additional charge or credit may take the form of either (1) an increase or reduction in the subsequent premium or (2) an actual invoice to the policyholder or a refund by the insurance company. Whichever form it takes, the refunds must be recognized by being included in the reserve for unearned premiums.

Statutory insurance accounting principles require the insurer to include in the unearned premium liability any rate credits or return premiums due the policyholder. Either of two methods may be used to compute this liability. The first method develops a ratio of retrospective return premiums to earned standard premiums by analyzing each line of insurance over past policy years. The standard premium is the premium based on the insured's experience rate, with allowance for the appropriate premium discount. This ratio of return-to-earned standard premiums is applied to the earned standard premiums currently in force for which the current year's retrospective calculation has not been made. This calculation results in the required unearned premium for liability return premiums in the particular line of insurance.

The second method used to determine unearned premium credits considers each retrospectively rated exposure separately. The basic premium, losses, loss conversion factor, and premium tax multiplier for each exposure are used to arrive at an estimate of the return premium due the insured. Although highly accurate estimates can be obtained by use of this method, it is impractical if more than a small number of policies are involved.

Not all retrospectively rated exposures receive rate credits at the end of the policy term; upward adjustments are made subject to predetermined maximum limits if the insured's loss experience during the term has been adverse. Insurance companies may not currently recognize any anticipated additional charge on in-force policies that are subject to retrospective rating. Any additional "retrospective charge," when made, will be a premium invoice on a policy that already has expired. This charge is not considered an admitted asset.

Installment Premiums. Installment premiums on policies with terms of more than one year are generally treated as successive one-year policies. Thus a three-year policy in equal annual installments is entered as if it were three one-year policies.

Audit Premiums. Audit premiums are obtained through an examination of the insured's books or other records to determine the premium due the insurance company for protection furnished. Since the protection has been furnished, such premiums are considered earned when recorded by the company. Workers compensation and certain general liability policies commonly require audits because the exposure base on many of these policies is not known at the time the policy is written. These policies usually include a deposit premium and provide for monthly, quarterly, or semi-annual audit premiums in addition to a final audit premium after the policy expires. Audit premiums are based on reports prepared by the insured and subject to audit by the insurance company.

Various methods are used to recognize how and when the deposit premium is earned. Care should be taken to select a method that does not result in overstating the earned premium. Such overstatement can occur when the deposit is not proportional to the period covered, as when a workers compensation policy with audits at six-month intervals requires a deposit of 75 percent of the estimated annual premium. Some methods in use are:

1. The deposit is earned over the period covered by the deposit. When the audit premium is received, the deposit premium is reversed and reinstated for the following period.
2. The full estimated annual premium is entered, and modified accordingly, when the audit premiums are received.
3. The deposit is earned pro rata over the life of the policy. The pro rata unearned deposit premium is then increased by some amount (often one-twelfth of the deposit premium) to prevent overstating the earned premium when the audit premium is received.

Advance Premiums. Advance premiums are premiums on policies that have been issued but do not become effective until after the date of the statement. This happens most often in companies that write renewals thirty to sixty days before expirations. These companies include as premiums written the premiums on advance business. However, the more common practice is to record the premiums as they become effective.

Conservative Statement of the Unearned Premium Reserve

The unearned premium reserve results from insurance premiums collected in advance for a service to be performed in the future. The calculation for this reserve assumes that premiums are spread evenly over the period of the policy. However, a disproportionate amount of expenses including commissions, underwriting costs, policy writing costs, and other acquisition expenses are incurred at the beginning of the policy period. Since premiums must be recognized as being earned evenly over the period although these initial expenses must be recorded immediately, a statutory underwriting loss occurs early in the period. This loss results in a drain on policyholders' surplus.

This underwriting loss is an "accounting" and not a cash loss. The account loss results from accruing revenues (premiums earned) evenly over the period while expenses are recognized immediately. The accounting losses and subsequent accounting drains on surplus can be particularly severe in the case of a newly organized, rapidly growing insurer. Coupled with large immediate outlays for organizational and operating expenses, a new insurer can expect to experience a considerable decrease in policyholders' surplus.

The statutory accounting method of calculating the unearned premium reserve portrays an insurer's financial position conservatively. The realization rule involved anticipates expenses prior to realizing the related revenues. The unearned premium reserve allows the insurer to pay for both losses and expenses as if they were incurred evenly throughout the term of coverage, but the disproportionately large initial expenses have already been recognized. Thus as the unearned premium reserve for policies already written diminishes over time, not all of the unearned premium reserve will be required. Because initial expenses have been recognized, the unearned premium reserve is overstated by approximately the amount of these initial expenses. This redundant amount appears only in statutory statements and is referred to as the "equity" in the unearned premium reserve. The amount of this equity varies, but it may range from 20 to 40 percent of the unearned premium reserve. Investors interested in purchasing property-liability company stock either rely on GAAP statements, which make adjustments for the equity, or adjust statutory statement data by adding a certain percent of the unearned premium reserve to the policyholders' surplus of the company.

If an insurer were to stop writing all new business, the equity in the unearned premium reserve would eventually flow to the surplus account. Since such an action is unrealistic, an insurer suffering substantial surplus drains often reinsures a portion of its business. Under the most typical arrangement, the reinsurer assumes the obligation for the unearned premium reserve and pays the ceding insurer a commission to reimburse it for expenses associated with originating the business. This transaction releases the equity in the unearned premium reserve for the reinsured business and leads to an immediate recognition of an increase in surplus on the insurer's financial statement.

The length of the policy period affects the magnitude of the unearned premium reserve. In general, the longer the policy period, the greater will be the unearned premium reserve. Companies that write predominantly longer term business like fire, homeowners, and fidelity bonds have a relatively higher unearned premium reserve. The problem of surplus drain is particularly severe for a new fast-growing company writing a substantial portion of longer term business. The trend of insurers toward shorter term policies mitigates the effects of statutory accounting's unearned premium reserving rules.

Finally, an important distinction should be made between a company's loss reserves and its unearned premium reserve. A considerable estimation or judgment component is present in the calculation of loss reserves. The unearned premium reserve is a straightforward arithmetical computation. Assuming the company is honest, the unearned premium reserve may be accepted as adequate. No need exists, as in loss reserves, to test for adequacy by using historical development schedules.

LIABILITIES FOR REINSURANCE TRANSACTIONS

When insurance companies compile their financial statement reserves for losses, loss adjustment expenses, and unearned premiums, credit is taken for reinsurance ceded (reserves reduced) to other companies (reinsurers). Authorized reinsurers are licensed in the state of the ceding company's domicile while unauthorized reinsurers are not so licensed. If a dispute arises between the ceding company and an unauthorized reinsurer, it can become difficult to litigate the matter and enforce collection of amounts due. Because of this cloud over transactions with unauthorized reinsurers, the regulators generally disallow the reinsurance credit taken, unless sufficient funds have been withheld from the reinsurer to cover the credit plus any amounts recoverable on paid claims. To avoid or reduce the statutory penalty, it is common for companies to remit reinsurance premiums to unauthorized reinsurers on an earned, rather than a written, basis. The excess of the written premium over the earned premiums is treated as "Funds Held or Retained by the Company for Account of Unauthorized Companies." In addition, funds may be deposited by the reinsurer with the ceding company, or a letter of credit may be arranged from an acceptable bank.

Reinsurance transactions are reflected in Schedule F of the Annual Statement and are summarized on page 3 (Liabilities), lines 13a through 13e. If a provision is required, it is charged against the Capital and Surplus Account on page 4 of the Annual Statement.

It was once common to say that the reinsurer "stood in the shoes of the primary company" or "that the fortunes of the reinsurer followed those of the ceding company." Reinsurers generally followed the judgment of the primary company as to questions of coverage and amount of loss and even permitted backdating of cessions. In the "Equity Funding" fraud, however, a life insurance company submitted nonexistent death claims to its reinsurers over a considerable period of time. More recently, reinsurance frauds involving the manager of a Lloyd's of London syndicate have been disclosed. Prior to those events, reinsurance balances due from authorized companies were considered admitted assets regardless of their age.

During the 1980s, problems with the collection of reinsurance balances, especially with alien reinsurers, made some balances outstanding for a year or more. In addition, many reinsurance contracts were subject to commutation due to financial problems of the reinsurers. Because of the emerging changes in the reinsurance environment, in 1989 the NAIC adopted new rules for valuing reinsurance balances.

Reinsurance contracts have settlement clauses that require the settlement of balances within a specified period of time, usually sixty days. If reinsurance balances remain uncollected ninety days after that due date, then 20 percent of the balance is considered overdue (a nonadmitted asset) for statutory purposes. A similar percentage of underdue amounts from the same reinsurer on losses and unearned premiums and any other balances is also nonadmitted. If experience indicates a higher percent is appropriate, the higher percent should be used. The overdue rules and penalties do not apply to balances arising from participation in mandatory insurance mechanisms such as assigned risk pools or FAIR Plans.

POLICYHOLDERS' SURPLUS

The total capital and surplus of an insurance company, according to statutory accounting terminology, is called "surplus as regards policyholders" or policyholders' surplus. It is the difference between an insurer's admitted assets and liabilities. Thus it represents the company's net worth on the statutory balance sheet.

Components of Policyholders' Surplus

On the Annual Statement, the policyholders' surplus section is subdivided into capital paid-up, gross paid-in and contributed surplus, unassigned funds, special surplus funds, and treasury stock. Several of these classifications require explanation; some are significant only to stock insurance companies.

Capital paid-up is the aggregate par or stated value of the company's capital stock outstanding. Although stock could be preferred or common, most states permit only common stock. The classes of stock authorized and issued by an insurance company, along with other details concerning the corporation's equity shares, are described in Item 4 of the general interrogatories found on page 16 of the Annual Statement. A stock insurer cannot obtain a license to operate unless all of its outstanding stock is issued for at least its par or stated value. This requirement encourages those organizing a new stock insurance company to set the per share par value of the company's stock relatively low to facilitate rapid sale and encourage wide distribution of the equity shares.

Gross paid-in and contributed surplus comes from the sale of stock for an amount in excess of the stock's par or stated value per share and by any subsequent contributions of funds from stockholders. Thus, if a $5.00 par value common share is issued for $7.50, $2.50 is credited to the gross paid-in and contributed surplus account. After the initial capitalization is completed, the corporation may need additional equity. This need commonly arises as sales volume increases and new lines of insurance are written. If the corporation has issued all of its authorized capital stock, it must seek state approval of a change in its charter before additional stock can be sold. This process can be time-consuming and costly. An alternative source of new equity is to procure contribution from existing stockholders. These contributions—which may be in the form of cash, donated assets other than cash, or forgiveness of indebtedness—also are credited to the gross paid-in and contributed surplus account.

Mutual insurance corporations, unincorporated mutual associations, and reciprocal or interinsurance exchanges do not issue capital stock and have no stockholders. Therefore, they show no entry for capital paid-up. Instead these organizations begin business with initial policyholder/subscriber contributions or *guarantee funds*.[1] This initial capitalization may be furnished by prospective policyholders wishing to purchase insurance from a cooperative organization they helped to establish, or the capital may be deposited by an interested party other than the policyholder/subscriber. The amount of guarantee fund contributions is shown on line 24c of the balance sheet's policyholders' surplus section. It is this initial guarantee fund which satisfies state capitalization requirements that must be met prior to commencement of underwriting operations. After the company has generated additional surplus through successful operations, the initial contributions may be paid back, usually with interest, to the company's founders. State laws regulate the permissibility and timing of such repayments.

Unassigned funds represent the retained earnings less dividends since the inception of the company. This account reflects all adjustments to surplus, such as the charge for unauthorized reinsurance, additional liability for Schedule P loss reserves, and unrealized capital gains or losses on investments. The amount of unassigned surplus sets a limit on the amount that can be distributed as nonliquidating dividends to policyholders or stockholders. A liquidating dividend is a return *of* the owner's investment in the company while a nonliquidating dividend is the return *on* the owner's investment. Because nonliquidating dividends can come only from unassigned surplus, this account is sometimes referred to as "free surplus."

Special surplus funds that have been authorized by the board of directors for a specific purpose are merely segregations of otherwise unassigned surplus. As an example, an insurance company writing lines of business that have widely fluctuating loss ratios may decide to establish a specially earmarked subdivision of policyholders' surplus and call it "reserve for extraordinary losses." This "reserve" is sometimes equal to the deductible amount in the company's catastrophe reinsurance contract. The use of the term "reserve" to classify a portion of surplus does not change this net worth account into a liability. Special surplus accounts often relate to underwriting loss and investment value fluctuations. A common segregation of surplus provides for assessments by post-insolvency insurance company guaranty funds (discussed in Chapter 5). Insurers might also assign portions of their surplus for potential income taxes on unrealized capital gains, policyholder dividends not yet declared, or other contingencies. Regardless of their intended purpose, earmarked surplus accounts restrict the amount of funds available for stockholder or policyholder dividends.

Treasury stock is a corporation's own stock, once issued and later reacquired by the company. The cost of treasury stock is deducted from otherwise available capital and surplus in order to arrive at the corporation's total net worth (surplus as regards policyholders).

State insurance codes specify the minimum amounts of capital paid-up and paid-in and the contributed surplus required to obtain a certificate of authority as well as the minimum amount of surplus as regards policyholders required to continue writing business. These required amounts vary according to the lines of business written by the company. The state insurance regulatory capitalization requirements are described in greater detail in Chapter 5.

Factors Affecting Policyholders' Surplus

Four factors principally affect policyholders' surplus of a property-liability company: (1) its underwriting results, (2) its investment performance, (3) developments in its loss reserves, and (4) its growth rate. Favorable results in any of these four areas produce an increase in the policyholders' surplus account. Hence, for a going concern, these four variables may be thought of as the primary sources of policyholders' surplus. Alternatively, unfavorable results in any of these four areas cause a decrease in policyholders' surplus. The purposes of policyholders' surplus may be thought of as providing a safety cushion to absorb such adverse results. Policyholders' surplus protects the policyholder as well as the company by maintaining the company's solvency during periods of unfavorable operating results.

A property-liability company is primarily in the business of writing insurance. When underwriting gains result, policyholders' surplus is increased by these gains minus any applicable taxes. While any business is subject to unprofitable years, the insurance business is particularly vulnerable to rapid economic or societal changes. Since losses and expenses must be estimated, failure to anticipate and respond to adverse future developments may produce underwriting losses. Delays in obtaining desired premium increases can also complicate an insurer's financial position. When underwriting losses do occur, policyholders' surplus must be sufficient to cover these losses.

The nature of the business also involves insurance companies in substantial investment operations. Policyholders' funds, rather than sitting idly until they are needed, are channeled into a wide variety of investments. Investment income (dividends, interest, and rents) consti-tutes a positive flow to surplus in virtually all situations. The sale of the stocks or bonds may produce realized gains or losses. Unrealized gains or losses on bonds, which are valued at amortized cost, do not affect surplus. However, since common stocks must be carried on the balance sheet at market value, unrealized gains and losses also result. In recent years, unrealized gains and losses have caused considerable fluctua-tions in insurance companies' policyholders' surplus accounts.

The effects of loss reserve developments on policyholders' surplus have been described in early portions of this chapter. Loss reserve developments are reflected in underwriting results and can cause considerable increases and decreases in policyholders' surplus.

The growth variable is an anomaly in the insurance business. Generally, growth of a business is a positive factor that can be assumed to increase the firm's net worth. In property-liability insurance, however, due to the surplus drain resulting from an increasing unearned premium reserve, rapid growth may appear detrimental to the company's financial position. Assuming that the new business is profitable, accounting funds will eventually flow to the surplus account as growth levels or moderates. In the long run, growth through writing profitable business can be expected to bolster policyholders' surplus. Yet during periods of rapid growth, an increasing unearned premium reserve drains surplus. This effect of growth is one of the principal reasons for minimum surplus requirements. Adjusting statutory finan-cial statements for general purpose use in conformity with GAAP removes the irregular impact that sales growth has on surplus.

SUMMARY

The principal liabilities of a property-liability insurance company are the loss and loss adjustment expense reserves and the unearned premium reserve. The aggregate loss and loss adjustment expense reserves that appear on an insurer's annual statement are supposed to disclose the amount needed to pay all unsettled claims that have occurred up to that date. Because estimates must be made in advance of ultimate settlement the ability to judge the accuracy of an insurer at setting loss reserve levels is important. Loss development schedules in the Annual Statement give insight into the over- or under-reserving tendencies of particular insurers.

Loss reserves do not represent liabilities for losses that have not yet occurred on policies that have been written. This is the function of the unearned premium reserve. The reserve for unearned premiums represents the proportionate premium revenue received or in the course of collection on policies that currently are in force. As the protection service afforded by the policies is provided, revenues are released from the unearned premium reserve and realized as a contribution to income. While realization of revenue is deferred through the unearned premium reserve, expenses associated with issuing the corresponding insurance are realized as incurred. This results in an "investment" of the company's surplus in the unearned premium reserve because expenses are charged off immediately while premium revenue is deferred.

Capital and surplus of a property-liability insurance company serves three functions. First, it provides the initial funds to establish the company and begin operations; second, it is a continuing source of funds for financing increased sales and expansion; third, it provides a safety cushion to absorb adverse underwriting and investment experience without loss to policyholders. Capitalization requirements imposed by state insurance regulations set minimum net worth requirements that must be complied with by insurers that remain in operation. Company management must be cognizant of the factors that impact on policyholders' surplus and must guard against losses that threaten the financial strength and continued existence of the insurer.

Chapter Note

1. Each insured in a reciprocal assumes a proportional share of all loss exposures transferred to the organization, other than his or her own. The term "subscriber" rather than "policyholder" therefore is used to signify the insured's unique relationship with the interinsurance exchange.

CHAPTER 4

Insurance Company Revenues and Expenses

When insurance in placed in force, an entry to record the sale is made in the insurance company's accounts. Usually, the entry debits accounts receivable and commissions paid and credits premiums written. As the premiums are collected, cash is debited and accounts receivable are credited. Out of these funds and other operating funds, the insurance company pays the agent's commission and operating expenses. The remaining money is available for the payment of claims, taxes, investment, in some cases for policyholder dividends, and for profit.

Losses may be reported to the insurer during the period of coverage or at some later date. In certain lines of insurance (glass insurance) claims are settled almost immediately; in other lines (medical malpractice on an occurrence basis) claims may be paid long after the policy has expired; and, in still other lines (workers compensation) loss settlement payments are made over a number of years.

Net funds received after payment of commissions and underwriting expenses are invested consistent with current loss payment cash needs, the insurer's investment objectives, and regulatory constraints.

This chapter examines the accounting treatment of revenues, losses, and expenses of an insurance company and their relation to the financial statements. It also considers the effects of reinsurance, investment income, and capital gains and losses.

The two principal revenue sources for an insurer are premiums written and investment income and gains. The Annual Statement reports premium revenue by line of business, such as automobile liability, workers compensation, fire, and accident and health. It shows the losses paid and incurred in the same way. Investment income and gains are shown in detail on the Annual Statement. The schedule of interest, dividend, and real estate income analyzes the investment income by type of investment.

State insurance regulators want to analyze the experience on each line of business sold. Consequently, the Insurance Expense Exhibit was developed to provide an analysis of the operations of the insurer by line of business. Premiums, losses, loss adjustment expenses, commissions, taxes, and other expenses are allocated by line. Investment income is allocated to individual lines of business in order to study each line's total contribution for ratemaking purposes.

PREMIUMS WRITTEN CYCLE

A premium is the consideration received from an insured in exchange for the insurance company's contractual obligation to insure the exposure against financial loss. The premium accounting cycle includes all phases of premium recognition by the insurance company— from policy inception to expiration. The functions involved in the premium cycle include:

- Sales and policy issue
- Underwriting
- Premium recording
- Premium collecting

Illustration 4-1 depicts a simplified picture of the typical premium cycle. In certain situations, these procedures may occur in a different sequence than the one shown. For example, within the limits of their authority, some agents may bind coverage and issue policies before the underwriting evaluation of the application. Regardless of the sequence, however, all of these activities are implicit in any premium transaction.

Sales and Policy Issue

As in any business, the premium or revenue cycle (premium written cycle in the insurance business) begins with a sales effort. Different insurance companies generate sales through general agents, local and regional agents, brokers, and direct marketing efforts.

Policy issue can take place at:

- The producer's office
- The company's branch office
- The company's home office

Illustration 4-1

The Premium Accounting Cycle

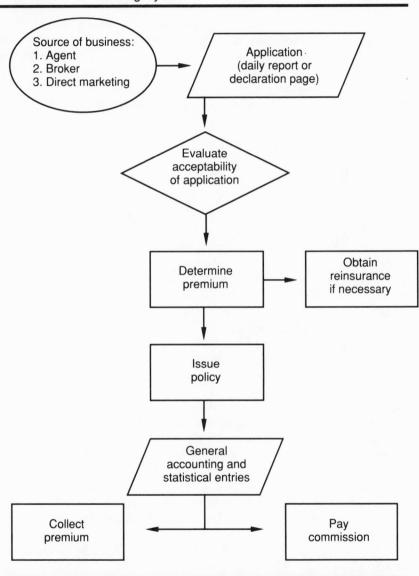

If a producer writes a policy, a daily report (a copy of the policy's declaration page), application and other supporting information go to the company underwriter. When the branch or home office writes a policy, the company underwrites from an application submitted by a producer. The application contains applicant underwriting information on which the company bases its decision to accept (continue coverage), accept with conditions or reject (flat cancellation) the opportunity to provide coverage.

The distribution of copies of the policy generally includes the policyholder and lienholder, if any, (for evidence of coverage), the producer (for confirmation of coverage and use in servicing policy-holders), the branch office (for use in servicing producers or policy-holders through decentralized loss and policy issue control), and the home office (for use by the accounting, statistical, audit, and inspection departments).

Underwriting

The underwriting function includes an evaluation of the acceptability of the loss exposure, a determination of the premium, a review of contract conditions and terms, and an evaluation of the company's capacity to assume the entire exposure (whether or not to reinsure). The first underwriting function—evaluation of the acceptability of the loss exposure—involves a recognition of hazards and potential losses based on a review of information submitted and coverage requested. In addition, underwriters investigate loss exposures according to company procedures, and state statutes where required. For example, applicants for automobile insurance may be checked against driving records issued by state departments of motor vehicles. Applications for other coverages may require an engineering survey, a fire hazard survey, or other information.

The underwriting function also calculates the premiums on policies written by the company, and checks the premiums on policies written by agents against appropriate rate filings. Of course, underwriting expertise plays a role in determining and reviewing rate levels and determining appropriate policy terms and conditions. An unacceptable or improperly priced submission can become acceptable through modification of contract provisions.

Reinsurance requirements are determined in accordance with company underwriting policy and expertise. Reinsurance may:

- Increase the insurer's capacity to accept business,
- Stabilize underwriting results,
- Finance a portion of the business being written, and
- Protect surplus from catastrophic losses.

Often, an agent can bind insurance coverage before the underwriting is completed and the application is accepted by the company. In such cases, the company reviews the coverage and records the daily. The company can record the policy before the ultimate underwriting decision is made, and if subsequently rejected, the exposure in the policy can then be canceled and any related accounting entries reversed.

Premium Recording

Premium recording includes the coding and processing of transactions evidenced by originating documents such as dailies and endorsements. This process produces the written premium and statistical premium data needed to calculate premiums in force and premiums earned. The exact nature of a particular company's premium recording process depends on whether the insured is billed by the agent or by the company.

The flow chart shown in Illustration 4-2 depicts the processing of a premium transaction in a situation in which the agency issues the policy and bills the insured. The agency then collects the premium from the insured and remits it to the insurer according to the agency or company account current records and the agency agreement. Although simplistic, the flow chart illustrates the essential steps in the policy issue and premium recording process.

A policy is written in the agent's office on policy forms supplied by the insurance company. A copy of the information contained in the policy declarations is made; and this daily report, along with any supporting documents, is submitted to the insurer. The agent may also collect a full or partial premium payment at this point or arrange for premium financing. Upon receipt of the daily and any accompanying documents, the company registers the policy identification number in order to maintain control of policy forms. The underwriting process then begins. If the loss exposure is unacceptable, the company issues a cancellation notice; otherwise, the company begins the process of recording the policy data in its accounting and statistical records.

Dailies and endorsements can be coded either during or after the underwriting process. Coding involves assigning an alphanumeric label to each transaction so that it can be stored according to an indexing system and rapidly retrieved. A major reason to code information is to facilitate compilation of data for the Annual Statement. For example, state codes are necessary to produce Schedule T (premium written by state), and insurance line codes are necessary to produce the Underwriting and Investment Exhibit.

Once policy data are recorded in the company's information system, various statistical reports can be prepared, such as premium tax schedules, rating bureau reports, experience rating reports, activity reports to management, and so forth. The data simultaneously are used

Illustration 4-2
Simplified Premium Transaction Processing

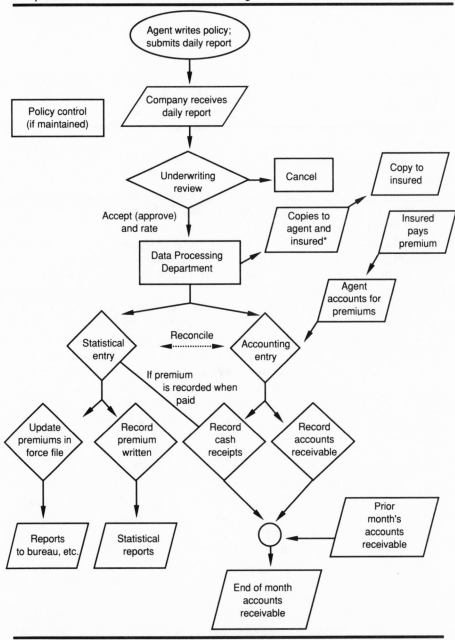

*Note: If the process involves the agent's submission of an application for coverage and the company's selection of its insureds prior to policy issue, the policy would be prepared at this point. A copy of the policy would be sent to the interests insured and a daily report sent to the agency.

as the source of accounting entries. For example, if premiums are recognized at policy issue, the initial accounting entry might be:

Accounts Receivable (debit) $160
Commission Expense (debit) $40
    Premiums Written (credit) $200

Within forty-five to sixty days, the agency remits its payment on its account current. At that time, the cash receipt is recorded and the account receivable balance eliminated.

Cash (debit) $160
    Accounts Receivable (credit) $160

These entries are posted to the company's ledger accounts monthly, or more frequently, and periodic receivables and receipt records are updated. Some companies may defer recognition of premiums written until cash receipts are recorded rather than at the time of policy issue. In many cases, both methods of premium recognition are used by the same company for different lines of insurance.

Premium processing creates a series of premium records or files. These files appear in a number of different forms and fulfill several purposes. An *accounting file* is used to maintain a record of agents' balances (accounts receivable) and to determine overdue agents' balances (which may be nonadmitted assets for statutory purposes). A *statistical file* is used to record, test, and verify data and to produce premiums in force and unearned, premium written registers, board and bureau reports, and producer performance reports. In addition, the statistical file may be used to control policy expirations, installment premium billings, timing of policy audits, and reinsurance ceded records. The statistical file is necessary to determine the two basic premium amounts:

- Premiums written—the amount of premiums billed less premiums returned to the insured. This figure is recorded to the general ledger as premium revenue.
- Original premiums—the amount of premiums for the full term of a policy for the current coverage at the latest premium rate shown in the policy or endorsement to the policy. This figure is used in compilation of in-force premiums and is the basis for calculating unearned premiums.

Illustration 4-3 shows an example of how the *original premium* differs from the *written premium*. Assume a company issues a policy with an annual term for a premium of $120. Six months later a coverage change doubles the annual premium. The company issues an endorsement for an additional premium for the six months (50 percent

Illustration 4-3
Original and Written Premiums

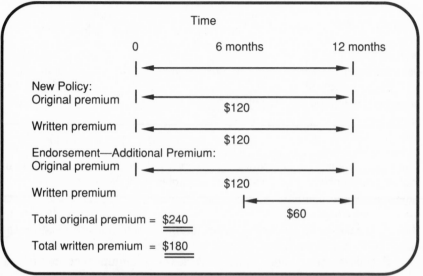

pro rata portion of $120). The *original premium* for this policy would be $240 and the written premium would be $180.

The original premium concept is the basis for determining the premiums in force, which is the aggregate of the original premiums from all policies that have been recorded but that have not expired or been canceled. Premiums in force are determined by updating the previous cumulative premiums in force by the periodic contribution to the premiums in force and deducting expirations and cancellations.

The statistical file input also produces the premiums written register. New policy and endorsement transactions are used to produce monthly premium registers simultaneously with or before the updating of the statistical file.

Statistical file premiums written input (gross premiums before agent's commissions) is then reconciled with accounting file input. After reconciliation, the accounting file can be maintained on a net of agents' commissions basis.

Premiums written is derived and recorded from the processing of the monthly transactions, but then must be converted to premiums earned. Premiums earned equals premiums written for the period, plus the unearned premium reserve at the beginning of the period, less the unearned premium reserve at the end of the period. This accounting entry by line of insurance is included in Part 2 of the Underwriting and Investment Exhibit in the Annual Statement. Barring premium rate changes, if an insurance company writes the same mix and the same amount of business each year, premiums written and premiums earned will be equal, as the unearned premium reserve will remain constant. A company that is growing will experience an increasing unearned premium reserve, causing the earned premiums figure to be less than written premiums. The opposite will occur in a company whose written premiums are declining.

Premiums written may be thought of as a cash measure of premium income. Recognition of premium income is deferred until service is delivered in the future. Premiums earned, on the other hand, may be thought of as an accrual measure. In a sense, premiums earned is the more important measure because it is used as the measure of revenue in the statement of income in the Annual Statement.

Statistical file data may be used for other premium-related controls, including:

- *Premium transactions.* These are coded by reinsurance agreement and summarized by reinsurer for payment.
- *Policy expiration notices.* Notices are prepared by comparing the expiration date of each policy with a control date. This procedure helps agents renew policies on time and controls removal of expired premiums from the in-force file.
- *Installment premium billings.* By use of special coding, these billings can also be controlled by a file designed to generate billings on the next due date.
- *Policies subject to periodic audit for the determination of premiums.* These policies require quarterly or other periodic premium billing based on payroll or gross receipts. The timing of premium audits is important for consistent premium recording. The audited premium is determined after the exposure period and is earned when billed and recorded.
- *Participating policies, loss experience, policy profitability and earned premium.* Participating policies provide for a partial return of premium (or dividend) to the policyholder, based on policy profitability. However, dividends are a company obligation only when they are declared. Statutes prohibit promising dividends, contractually or otherwise.
- *Accounting for reinsurance assumed and ceded.* This may be integrated with premium processing. Both premiums written and unearned premiums include reinsurance premiums, whether assumed or ceded.
- *Nonadmitted agents' balances.* These balances are determined by a simple comparison of dates in the accounting files of agents' balances remaining after ninety days.

Premium Collecting

The premium collecting function includes billing premiums, receiving cash, applying cash to agents' balances, and paying agents' commissions. Three basic methods are used for billing premiums: (1) agents agents are billed by the company, (2) accounts are rendered to the company by agents, and (3) policyholders are billed directly by the company.

Agents Billed by the Company. Some companies prepare monthly statements, called accounts-current, which are sent to their agents. The statements usually include policy number, name of the insured, effective date of the policy, gross premium, commission rate, and amount of commission for each policy. The company-prepared account-current shows how much the agent owes and the company expects to be paid. As agents respond to the account-current statements, premium transactions are added to, and remittances are removed from, the unpaid premium file.

Accounts Rendered to the Company by Agents. Many companies permit agents to pay on the basis of their own agency account-current. Under this method, agents send a monthly statement to the company listing individually all transactions for which the agent's records show a premium is due. For the most part, the company will have previously recorded these transactions as premium revenue and agents' balances from dailies received or issued.

The company compares the account submitted by the agent to the transactions it recorded earlier. Any differences are accumulated and classified as:

- Items included in agents' account currently but not yet recorded by the company
- Items recorded but not currently included in the account, or
- Discrepancy in amounts when an item is both reported by an agent and recorded by the company.

The company usually controls differences by treating the account rendered by the agent as a unit and establishing ledger control over differences.

Policyholders Billed Directly by the Company. Companies can have a direct bill operation whether or not they have agents. Those companies without agents generally use company-paid salespersons to sell their insurance coverages. In a direct bill operation, the premiums are billed directly to the policyholders by the insurance company.

The recording of direct bill premiums written is done in either of two ways. One method is to record premiums written when the policyholder is billed, usually thirty to sixty days in advance of the effective date of the policy. The other method is to record premiums written as the premiums are collected. Since the premiums are billed in advance, they should be collected prior to the effective date of the policy. If the premium is not collected by the effective date, the policy is canceled.

For companies paying commissions, a summary of the collections is prepared monthly, by producer, and the commission is paid on that basis. This procedure differs from an agency type of operation in which the agent collects from the policyholder and remits net of commission to the company.

LOSS CYCLE

The loss cycle includes five functions: loss processing, loss and loss expense estimates, loss recording, loss settlement, and loss reserve evaluation. These various functions are diagramed in Illustration 4-4.

Loss Processing

After a loss, the claimant sends a notice of the loss either to the company or to the policyholder's agent or broker. A claim notice is generally required from the claimant and includes (1) a brief summary of the loss or injury, (2) the time and date of the loss or injury, (3) how the loss or injury happened, and (4) the policyholder's name and policy number.

There is always a delay between the date of the loss or injury and the claim report date, although the length of the delay varies depending on the type of loss. When a loss report is received, the validity of the claim is first determined by comparing the loss notice to the daily report to establish that insurance coverage is in force. Next, a loss file is created and assigned an identifying number for use throughout processing. All documents on reporting, adjusting, recording, and settling the claim are kept in that file.

A loss abstract (often called a claim label or face sheet) prepared from information in the loss report, adjuster's report, and the daily, is used to record the new loss in subsidiary records. It is sometimes used as a summary of transactions for that loss file. The loss abstract contains coded information as outlined in Illustration 4-5.

Loss and Loss Expense Estimates

When insurance coverage has been verified, an adjuster is as-

Illustration 4-4
Simplified Claims Processing Cycle

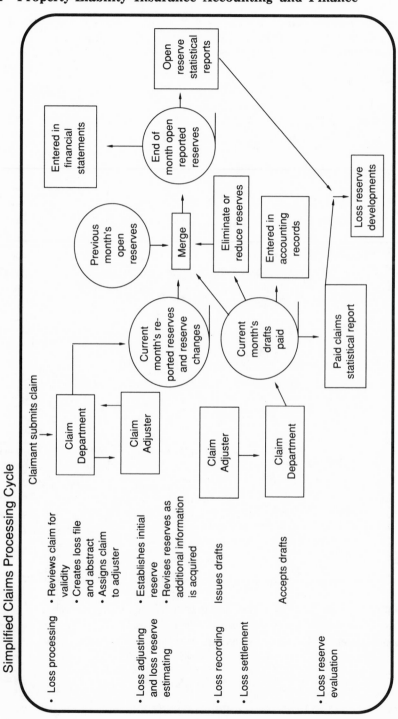

Illustration 4-5
Outline of Information in a Loss Abstract

I. Dates

    A. Accident occurrence date
    B. Accident report date
    C. Term and effective date

II. Loss Identification Data

    A. File number
    B. Cause and location of loss
    C. Type of loss or injury
    D. Claimant identification
    E. Catastrophe code

III. Policy Identification Data

    A. Policy number
    B. Agent or producer
    C. Lines and amounts of coverage
    D. Amount of deductibles to be absorbed by the insured
    E. Reinsurance arrangements, if any
    F. Coinsurance percent
    G. Lienholder

IV. Monetary Information

    A. Original estimate of the loss incurred value
    B. Loss expense and loss adjustment expense payments
    C. Reserve changes and amount of current reserve
       outstanding, and subrogation, salvage, and reinsurance
       receipts

signed. Depending on where the loss occurred, the type and amount of the loss, and the experience required, the adjuster may be an independent adjuster or the company's own employee or agent.

An adjuster investigates the loss to determine that it actually occurred, that coverage is in effect, and that the claim is otherwise valid. Sometimes, the determination of whether the loss is a covered loss, under the terms of the policy, is a difficult decision, and requires consultation among the adjuster, the underwriter, or the legal department. Photographs, surveillance reports, medical reports, and any other reports may be assembled to substantiate the loss. If the policy contains any special limiting provisions, a determination must be made as to the policyholder's adherence to these provisions.

The adjuster estimates the amount of the loss and loss adjustment expenses. For property losses, the approximate amount of salvage value is also reported to the company. The adjuster also finds out, if possible, if any subrogation rights are available.

The claims adjuster bases the original estimate of the amount of the loss on information available at the time of the original report. As additional information is acquired, the estimate is revised until the case is closed. The estimate made by the adjuster is reviewed by a company claims examiner or a supervisor to make sure the estimate is sound and consistent with company guidelines.

Loss Recording

The loss recording function accumulates data on loss costs and loss adjustment expenses incurred by claim. The loss cost incurred on a claim has two parts, the unpaid (loss reserve) portion and the paid portion.

Details on losses incurred are kept on the gross and net basis. The gross basis provides for the loss cost before reinsurance, subrogation, or salvage recoveries. The net basis provides for the amount of loss incurred by the company after reinsurance, subrogation, and salvage. Financial statements show losses on a net basis. In the Underwriting and Investments Exhibit of the Annual Statement, Parts 3 and 3A, a record of the composition of net losses incurred is shown.

Insurance companies do not reflect estimated amounts of subrogation and salvage recoverable in their statutory financial statements either as a reduction of outstanding loss reserves or as an estimated receivable. The amount of any subrogation or salvage receivable is not recorded until the cash is received.

Gross and net loss detail may be required for a claim, depending on the volume of transactions affected and the type of reinsurance treaties in force. These records may be kept manually, or they may be a part of the computerized master loss files.

Throughout the life of the claim, the cumulative paid portion and reserve portion are maintained separately for each claim. A record of loss adjustment expenses incurred, which are directly attributable to a specific claim (called allocated loss adjustment expenses), is sometimes maintained. Many companies do not keep allocated loss adjustment reserves on an individual case basis, but compute these reserves on an

Illustration 4-6

Accounting Effects of Selected Loss Transactions

	Effect on Loss Reserve (Nonledger)	Effect on Loss Paid (Ledger)	Effect on Incurred Loss
To record new claim	Increase	None	Increase
To increase the estimate of total cost of the loss	Increase	None	Increase
To decrease the estimate of total cost of the loss	Decrease	None	Decrease
To make partial payment in settlement	Decrease	Increase	None (if decrease and payment are equal)
To make final settlement payment at amount less than the loss reserve	Decrease to zero	Increase	Decrease (called a savings on reserve)
To make final settlement payment at amount greater than the loss reserve	Decrease to zero	Increase	Increase (called deficiency on reserve)
To receive subrogation or salvage	None	Decrease	Decrease
To close a loss file without payment	Decrease	None	Decrease

overall formula basis. All companies maintain a record of cumulative allocated loss expenses paid for each claim.

Illustration 4-6 summarizes some of the transactions that may be included in the loss records during the life of the claim. Subsidiary records support both ledger and nonledger accounts. Loss reserve totals may be reconciled from month to month by summarizing transactions for these categories.

The loss reserve, any related reinsurance recoverable, and loss adjustment expense reserve are added to the outstanding loss file tape or other subsidiary record. No entry is made in the general ledger at this time because these are all nonledger assets and liabilities. A ledger adjustment is made on December 31 for outstanding loss reserves, related reinsurance recoverable, and loss adjustment expense reserve. The adjuster or a claims supervisor makes reserve changes from a reevaluation of facts or evaluation of new facts. Changes are added to the subsidiary record from coded change notices.

Once the loss settlement is recorded, loss and loss adjustment payments are put on record. A payment affects both the general ledger (because paid losses must be charged and cash credited) and the subsidiary record of losses (because the loss reserve is decreased and the amount of loss paid increased). Payment of loss in excess of the company's retention results in reinsurance receivable and a bill to the reinsurer.

Subrogation or salvage recovered is coded and entered in the general ledger and subsidiary loss records. Once losses paid and salvage received have been recorded separately, they are combined in the records. They are listed separately because a record of the composition of net losses incurred is required in the Underwriting and Investment Exhibit of the Annual Statement. Total loss paid and salvage received are combined to determine the net total amount of loss incurred. Subrogation or salvage received reduces the total loss incurred.

Property-liability insurance companies compile and maintain detailed loss data in order to complete the Annual Statement and produce other reports for management. Detailed loss data appears in Parts 3 and 3A of the Underwriting and Investment Exhibit and in Schedule P of the Annual Statement. Examples of management reports containing extensive loss data include reports showing losses by producer; losses by line, location, or department; losses on reinsured business; loss experience for large loss exposures; loss experience on retrospectively rated policies; and analyses of unallocated loss adjustment expenses.

Loss Settlement

Loss settlement includes not only partial and final payment to the claimant for the loss liability but also payment of allocated loss adjustment expenses. Final settlement requires a release from the claimant as evidence that the claim has been settled satisfactorily. When the loss payment is made by check the claimant must sign a release, which is a separate proof of loss document. Draft loss payments have a release printed on the draft. The release is effective when the draft is endorsed.

After final payment is made to all claimants, the loss file is reviewed to make sure all necessary procedures have been followed. Final payments are approved and coded to remove the reserve from the outstanding loss records. All loss adjustment expense payments are verified, and any open loss adjustment expense reserve is removed from the company records. Paid loss records are checked to see that they contain the correct amount of loss and loss adjustment expense payments. Reinsurers are notified of their portion of loss and loss adjustment expenses, and the related receivable recorded. Any salvage and subrogation possibilities should be recorded and collection efforts followed. Policy records should be updated so that future underwriting will have loss information available. Coverage on property that no longer exists should be canceled. If all procedures have been followed properly, the loss file or loss pocket is stamped "closed" or "paid."

Loss Payments

Loss payments are made by draft or check. Checks are controlled and treated as outstanding when issued. Drafts are controlled, either on an issued or honored basis. Draft payments have advantages over checks because they are subject to company review before being honored. Draft-signing authority is sometimes delegated to a lower responsibility level than check-signing authority. In addition, use of drafts rather than checks allows more flexible management of insurance company cash balances.

When drafts are controlled as issued, they are recorded immediately as paid losses and credited to a liability account called outstanding loss drafts. The draft copy is input to reduce the loss reserve, to increase losses paid in the subsidiary loss records, and to record the paid loss in the general ledger. Drafts presented for payment by the bank and approved by the company are credited to cash and debited to the liability account—outstanding loss drafts. Insurance companies issuing large volumes of drafts usually record the drafts as issued.

When drafts are controlled as paid, they are recorded when honored. Drafts issued and not yet presented for payment have no effect on the financial statements since the amount of the unpaid loss remains in the loss reserve. This is a significant distinction between the two methods of accounting for loss payments made by draft. If drafts are recorded as issued, any over- or under-estimation of the loss reserve is recognized immediately. On the other hand, if the draft is not recorded until paid, any inaccuracy in loss reserves remains until payment of the draft.

The draft copy is used to record the loss payment after it is matched with the cleared draft. A system is needed to control both the original draft and the copy because either one can be received first by the company when independent or field adjusters have authority to issue drafts. Suspense accounts are normally used for this control. The account is debited when the draft is purchased from the bank and credited when the draft copy is received.

Any method of loss payment generates a payment voucher which may be outstanding for some time because it may require endorsement by several parties (claimant, loss payee, payee's attorney, and so forth). If the insurer pays with a check, it represents an immediate use of cash as the bank must have a balance on hand to cover all checks outstanding. The use of drafts, on the other hand, does not reduce the cash balance until the draft is presented to the bank and accepted by the insurer.

EXPENSES

Expenses incurred by a property-liability insurer arise out of the company's marketing, underwriting, policy servicing, claims administration, and investment operations. The degree to which the company can effectively perform these activities while limiting their costs determines the internal operating efficiency of the insurer. Other things equal, an insurance company that operates efficiently can offer lower premium rates and generate higher profits. Proper monitoring and control of expenses is an essential determinant of successful performance.

Part 4 of the Underwriting and Investment Exhibit of the Annual Statement is a schedule of expenses paid and incurred. Expenses are classified in the Exhibit horizontally into three functional expense groups: (1) loss adjustment expenses, (2) other underwriting expenses, and (3) investment expenses. They are also classified in the Exhibit vertically by object or purpose. Both the functional expense groups and the expense classifications are prescribed by the uniform accounting instructions (Regulation 30 of the State of New York). These instructions define the items going into each expense classification and the methods of allocating expenses by functional expense groups, as well as by major and minor lines of business. The allocation of expenses to lines of business is necessary to prepare the Insurance Expense Exhibit (IEE), an important supplement to the Annual Statement, that companies must file separately. This exhibit contains an analysis of premiums, losses, expenses, and net income by line of business before federal income taxes.

Uniform Accounting Instructions

The uniform expense allocation rules establish cost accounting within the insurance business and facilitate comparisons among companies for expense analysis and control purposes.

The objective of uniform accounting instructions is to allocate insurance company expenses uniformly within prescribed principal groupings. Expenses are allocated:

1. By companies, wherever more than one company is operated jointly
2. By nature of expense (major expense object)
3. By functions (such as investment, loss adjusting, other underwriting)
4. By lines of business (such as automobile liability, automobile physical damage, workers compensation, and so forth)

The uniform accounting instructions provide specific rules for the allocation of expenses to these various categories. Where a specific rule is not feasible, the instructions prescribe procedures and methods of determining the proper allocation.

The allocation of expenses as set forth by the uniform accounting instructions is based on four principles:

1. All direct expenses, or those expenses obviously incurred for specific companies or purposes whether by function, line of insurance, coverage or nature of expense, are to be allocated as incurred.
2. Other expenses not directly allocable but related to some direct expenses are allocated in the same proportion as the direct expenses to which they are related.
3. General expenses not related to any direct expenses are allocated on the basis of time studies (or other special studies that can help classify the expenses into categories consistent with their nature).
4. Those general expenses (such as general advertising) not subject to allocation based on time and special studies are to be allocated on the basis of premium volume.

All bases of allocation are compiled or calculated from the transactions or procedures for the period applicable to the expenses allocated unless the use of any other period is justified by investigation made during the applicable period. In most insurance companies, employee salaries constitute a major item of expense that is not always directly allocated. Once salaries are properly allocated, the bulk of the job is done. In fact, so many other general expenses bear such a close relationship to salaries that once salaries have been allocated, they serve as the basis for allocating other general expenses.

Under the uniform accounting instructions, all expenses are segregated and correspond precisely to those contained in Part 4 of the Underwriting and Investment Exhibit. Illustration 4-7 shows this exhibit from the 1988 Annual Statement filed by the Government Employees Insurance Company. Columns 1, 2, and 3 indicate the functional expense groupings, and rows 1 through 21 classify expenses according to the purpose for which they were incurred. For example, during 1988, Government Employees Insurance Company incurred legal and auditing expenses (line 17) that totaled $11,209,492. The loss adjustment function was responsible for $553,634; underwriting functions other than loss adjustment incurred $975,751; and investment operations accounted for $9,680,107 of the total audit and legal expense.

The twenty-one expense classifications are, in effect, general ledger expense accounts and include all expenses of the particular type incurred by the company during the year. It does not matter which department of the company or line of insurance may have been involved.

Insurance Expense Exhibit

The IEE is a supplement to the Annual Statement. This Exhibit contains an analysis of profitability by line of business, showing net income before federal income taxes. Like Part 4 of the Underwriting and Investment Exhibit in the Annual Statement, the IEE also contains an analysis of expenses by classification and function. Greater detail is given in the IEE by subdividing the "other underwriting (functional) expense" group listed in the annual statement into three sub-functions: (1) acquisition, field supervision, and collection expenses; (2) taxes, licenses, and fees; and (3) general expenses.

The IEE has three main purposes. First, it presents the company's expenses on a uniform basis for each account by function, and for each function by line of business. For example, total loss adjustment expenses incurred are shown on line 22, column 1, Part 4 of the Underwriting and Investment Exhibit of the Annual Statement (Illustration 4-7). These functional expenses are shown by object classification in column 1, Part I of the IEE (Illustration 4-8) and by line of insurance on line 4, Part II of the IEE (Illustration 4-9). Second, the IEE reports the operating gain or loss by line of business after consideration of the statutory underwriting result, the investment income assigned, and policyholders' dividends. Third, it furnishes aggregate expense data by line of insurance which can be used as a source data for expense loadings in ratemaking.

The Exhibit is made up of four separate parts. A description of the information contained in each part is given below. Each part is illustrated with an excerpt from the 1989 IEE.

Part I—Allocation to Expense Groups. Part I of the IEE is an expansion of Part 4 of the Underwriting and Investment Exhibit in the Annual Statement. As shown in Illustration 4-8, expenses are itemized in this section for three functional expense groups and the three subfunctional groups for "other underwriting expenses."

- Investment expenses
- Loss adjustment expenses
- Other underwriting expenses
  - acquisition, field supervision, and collection expenses
  - general expenses
  - taxes, licenses, and fees

Each line of incurred expense figures shown in Part I of the IEE correspond to its counterpart line in Part 4 of the Underwriting and Investment Exhibit.

Investment expenses comprise all expenses incurred, even those expenses only partly incurred in connection with investing funds and obtaining investment income. In addition, expenses and taxes on company-owned real estate are classified as investment expense.

Loss adjustment expenses comprise all expenses connected, in whole or in part, with the adjustment and recording of policy claims. Acquisition, field supervision, and collection expenses comprise all expenses incurred wholly or partially in soliciting and procuring business, writing policy contracts, receiving and paying premiums and commissions, and all related activities.

General expenses include underwriting expenses not specifically attributable to the acquisition of business. Taxes, licenses, and fees include state and local insurance taxes, insurance department licenses and fees, payroll taxes, and other similar expenses. Federal and foreign income taxes and real estate taxes are not included in this expense category.

Illustration 4-9 shows to which functional group of IEE each type of expense should be allocated or the basis to be used to allocate such expense. Because salaries comprise a major expense element in insurance companies, special instructions are provided for salary allocation. Some expenses—for example, director's fees and printing and stationery—may be distributed as an overhead item on the salaries of employees in a particular department or division of the company, or

Illustration 4-7

Underwriting and Investment Exhibit of the Government Employees Insurance Company—
Annual Statement for the Year Ended December 31, 1988

Underwriting and Investment Exhibit
Part 4 — Expenses

	1 Loss Adjustment Expenses	2 Other Underwriting Expenses	3 Investment Expenses	4 Total
1. Claim adjustment services:				
(a) Direct	57,461,741			57,461,741
(b) Reinsurance assumed	9,003,015			9,003,015
(c) Reinsurance ceded	4,800,407			4,800,407
(d) Net claim adjustment services (a + b − c)	61,664,349			61,664,349
2. Commission and brokerage:				
(a) Direct		15,439,726		15,439,726
(b) Reinsurance assumed		2,912,762		2,912,762
(c) Reinsurance ceded		3,930,633		3,930,633
(d) Contingent — net				
(e) Policy and membership fees				
(f) Net commission and brokerage (a + b − c + d + e)		14,421,855		14,421,855
3. Allowances to managers and agents				
4. Advertising		14,405,078		14,405,078
5. Boards, bureaus and associations		4,644,069		4,644,069
6. Surveys and underwriting reports		4,192,313		4,192,313
7. Audit of assureds' records				
8. Salaries	53,625,864	68,234,495		121,860,359
9. Employee relations and welfare	8,984,475	10,946,570		19,931,045

10.	Insurance	282,395		324,376	606,771
11.	Directors' fees				
12.	Travel and travel items	2,633,776		866,993	3,500,769
13.	Rent and rent items	6,342,178		9,254,359	15,596,537
14.	Equipment	5,202,932		10,405,700	15,608,632
15.	Printing and stationery	2,412,849		3,527,991	5,940,840
16.	Postage, telephone and telegraph, exchange and express	6,833,719		20,277,713	27,111,432
17.	Legal and auditing	553,634	9,680,107	975,751	11,209,492
17A.	Totals (Items 3 to 17)	86,871,822	9,680,107	148,055,409	244,607,337
18.	Taxes, licenses and fees:				
	(a) State and local insurance taxes			25,951,547	25,951,547
	(b) Insurance department licenses and fees			240,414	240,414
	(c) Payroll taxes	4,228,269		5,331,022	9,559,291
	(d) All other (excluding federal and foreign income and real estate)			9,197,154	9,197,154
	(e) Total taxes, licenses and fees (a + b + c + d)	4,228,269		40,720,137	44,948,406
19.	Real estate expenses				
20.	Real estate taxes				
20A.	Reimbursements by uninsured accident and health plans				
21.	Aggregate write-ins for miscellaneous expenses	263,234		(19,219,341)	(18,956,107)
22.	Total expenses incurred	153,027,674	9,680,107	183,978,059	346,685,840
23.	Less unpaid expenses — current year	147,292,511	52,439	22,539,774	169,884,724
24	Add unpaid expenses — previous year	128,005,214	133,930	27,280,540	155,419,684
25.	TOTAL EXPENSES PAID (Items 22 − 23 + 24)	133,740,377	9,761,598	188,718,825	332,220,800

Details of Write-Ins Aggregated at Item 21 for Miscellaneous Expenses

2101.	Contributions			734,683	734,683
2102.	Outside services	263,234		643,699	906,933
2103.	Fair and other plan expenses			106,881	106,881
2104.	Special service contracts			(386,390)	(386,390)
2105.	Expenses related to service charges			(20,318,213)	(20,318,213)
2198.	Summary of remaining write-ins for Item 21 from overflow page				
2199.	TOTALS (Items 2101 thru 2105 plus 2198) (Part 4, Item 21)	263,234		(19,219,341)	(18,956,107)

Illustration 4-8
Insurance Expense Exhibit for the Year Ended December 31, 1989

PART I—ALLOCATION TO EXPENSE GROUPS

| Operating Expense Classifications | 1 Loss Adjustment Expenses | Other Underwriting Expenses | | | 5 Investment Expenses | 6 Total Expenses |
		2 Acquisition, Field Supervision and Collection Expenses	3 General Expenses	4 Taxes Licenses and Fees		
1. Claim adjustment services:						
(a) Direct						
(b) Reinsurance assumed						
(c) Reinsurance ceded						
(d) Net claim adjustment services (a + b – c)						
2. Commission and brokerage:						
(a) Direct						
(b) Reinsurance assumed						
(c) Reinsurance ceded						
(d) Contingent — net						
(e) Policy and membership fees						
(f) Net commission and brokerage (a + b – c + d + e)						
3. Allowances to managers and agents						
4. Advertising						
5. Boards, bureaus and associations						
6. Surveys and underwriting reports						
7. Audit of assureds' records						
8. Salaries						
9. Employee relations and welfare						

10. Insurance					
11. Directors' fees					
12. Travel and travel items					
13. Rent and rent items					
14. Equipment					
15. Printing and stationery					
16. Postage, telephone and telegraph, exchange and express					
17. Legal and auditing					
17a. Totals (Items 3 to 17)					
18. Taxes, licenses and fees:					
a. State and local insurance taxes					
b. Insurance department licenses and fees					
c. Payroll taxes					
d. All other (excl. fed. and foreign income and real estate)					
e. Total taxes, licenses and fees (a + b + c + d)					
19. Real estate expenses					
20. Real estate taxes					
21. Aggregate write-ins for miscellaneous operating expenses					
22. TOTAL EXPENSES INCURRED					

Details of write-ins aggregated at Item 21
for miscellaneous operating expenses

2101
2102
2103
2104
2199 TOTALS (Line 21)

companywide. For operating expense classifications that allow overhead on salaries to be used as the basis for allocation, companies may adopt any other basis that yields more accurate results.

Part II—Allocation to Lines of Business. Part II is divided into two sections:

- Section A—Premiums, losses, expenses and net income, and ratios to earned premiums
- Section B—Adjusted direct premiums and expenses, and ratios to adjusted direct premiums written.

Underwriting expenses shown by function in Part I of the IEE are allocated to the principal lines of business in Part II. Profitability for individual lines of business is determined by analysis of the data shown in the annual statement. The following revenue and expense categories are included:

- Revenue
  - Net premiums written
  - Net premiums earned
  - Net investment gain or loss and other income
- Expense
  - Net losses incurred
  - Loss adjustment expenses incurred
  - Commission and brokerage incurred
  - Other acquisition, field supervision, and collection expenses incurred
  - General expenses incurred
  - Taxes, licenses, and fees incurred
  - Dividends to policyholders

Section A of Part II includes the effect of reinsurance assumed and ceded by the company. The presence of substantial reinsurance activities can distort many of the income and expense classifications if an adjustment is not made. To eliminate this distortion, Section B was developed to more clearly indicate the costs associated with writing direct business.

Section B is a better source for analyzing or determining expense loadings for rate-making purposes. Section B relates the expense classifications to direct premiums written whereas Section A shows the expense classifications to net premiums earned. It is generally agreed that expenses such as commissions, taxes, and other underwriting expenses bear a closer relationship to premiums written than to premiums earned.

Illustration 4-9

Expense Allocations

Type of Expense Incurred	Expense Function or Basis of Expense Allocation
(1) Claim adjustment services	
Direct	Loss adjustment expenses
Reinsurance assumed	Loss adjustment expenses
Reinsurance ceded	Loss adjustment expenses
(2) Commission and brokerage:	
Direct	See commission and allowances
Reinsurance assumed	Acquisition, field supervision, and collection expenses
Reinsurance ceded	Acquisition, field supervision, and collection expenses
Contingent — net	Acquisition, field supervision, and collection expenses
Policy and membership fees	Acquisition, field supervision, and collection expenses
(3) Allowances to managers and agents	See commission and allowances
(4) Advertising	Acquisition, field supervision, and collection expenses
(5) Boards, bureaus and associations	General expenses
(6) Surveys and underwriting reports	General expenses
(7) Audit of assureds' records	General expenses
(8) Salaries	See special instructions relating to the allocation of salaries and other expenses
(9) Employee relations and welfare	Overhead on salaries
(10) Insurance	Special studies
(11) Directors' fees	Overhead on salaries
(12) Travel and travel items	Special studies
(13) Rent and rent items	Overhead on salaries
(14) Equipment	Overhead on salaries
(15) Printing and stationery	Overhead on salaries
(16) Postage, telephone and telegraph, exchange and express, FAX	Overhead on salaries
(17) Legal and auditing	Special studies
(18) Taxes, licenses and fees	Taxes
(19) Real estate expenses	Investment expenses
(20) Real estate taxes	Investment expenses
(21) Miscellaneous	Special studies

Part III and IV—Summary of Workers Compensation Experience. Part III of the IEE produces a national workers compensation expense ratio on a standard premium basis.

Part IV of the IEE shows the earned premiums, losses incurred, and loss ratio, on a direct premiums written basis, for workers' compensation insurance by state. This part of the exhibit allows state insurance regulators to closely monitor experience in this politically sensitive social insurance line of business.

NET INVESTMENT INCOME

Investment income is an important part of an insurance company's total revenues. Since a large portion of assets are invested, substantial investment earnings result. In 1988, for instance, the net investment income of property and liability insurance companies amounted to $24.1 billion while underwriting operations produced a loss of $11.8 billion. This resulted in net operating income of $12.3 billion.[1]

Investment strategies vary from company to company. Some companies stress equity securities, thereby giving up some investment income for potential capital appreciation. Others invest their funds in debt issues to gain incremental current investment income.

Some state insurance departments consider investment income in developing premium rate structures for personal lines business. The IEE requires that investment income be allocated by lines of business, according to a formula prescribed by state insurance regulators. Since investment income is also derived from funds provided by policyholders' surplus (net worth), a separate category called "capital and surplus accounts" is included in Part II, Column 32 of the IEE to credit that account with its share of investment income.

Net investment income is the amount of investment income earned less the investment expenses. Interest and other income accruals are treated as nonledger assets. To determine the actual amount of interest earned, the interest collections for the year are added to or subtracted from the difference between the accruals at the beginning and at the end of the year. This computation gives the same result as if the interest accruals were recorded on the books throughout the year. An insurance company usually does not record these items on the books; it makes the computation for financial statement purposes only.

In many instances the purchase price of a bond is above or below the par value of the bond. Thus, if bonds are amortized, interest income includes the amortization and represents the effective rate of interest earned on the bonds. Some companies record these adjustments on the books monthly. Others compute them less frequently.

Dividends earned for the year are obtained by adding the dividend collected during the year to the dividends receivable at the end of the year less the dividends receivable at the beginning of the year.

Mortgage loan investment income earned is the gross amount collected during the year adjusted for any interest paid in advance and for the accrued interest at the beginning and end of the year. When the purchase price of a mortgage loan differs from the unpaid balance, statutory rules require amortization of the difference. This amortization is an adjustment to mortgage interest earned.

Real estate income usually consists of the amount charged for occupancy of an insurance company's own buildings plus any rents received from tenants. The amount charged for occupancy of its own buildings is investment income and, at the same time, rental expense to the various functional areas of operations. If the property is mortgaged, the interest payments are deducted from rental income.

Investment expenses are handled in the same manner as "other underwriting expenses." Certain items are charged directly to investment expense accounts; allocations are made from other expense accounts in accordance with uniform accounting instructions. In addition to investment expenses, other expenses such as depreciation of real estate and interest on borrowed funds are taken as deductions to arrive at net investment income.

Part 1 of the Underwriting and Investment Exhibit in the Annual Statement is a report on investment income collected and a calculation of investment income earned during the year. It is in itself a summary of figures that appear in Schedules A, B, C, D, N, BA, DA, and DB of the Annual Statement. These schedules are listings of assets owned:

- Schedule A, real estate;
- Schedule B, mortgages;
- Schedule C, collateral loans;
- Schedule D, bonds and stocks;
- Schedule N, bank accounts;
- Schedule BA, other invested assets;
- Schedule DA, short-term investments
- Schedule DB, financial options and futures

Totals of the interest, dividends, and other income collected; the interest, dividends and rentals paid in advance; and the accruals of interest and dividends at the end of the year, as shown in the various columns, are carried over into Part 1 of the Underwriting and Expense Exhibit. The items paid in advance and the accruals at the end of the previous year are carried over from Part 1 of the previous year's Annual Statement.

After these figures are included, the amount earned can be calculated.

ADD:	Amounts collected, current year
	Amounts received in advance, end of previous year
	Amounts accrued, end of current year
SUBTRACT:	Amounts received in advance, end of current year
	Amounts accrued, end of previous year
EQUALS:	Investment income, current year

The total of these items represents total interest, dividends, and real estate income earned. From this total of earned investment income is deducted the total investment expenses incurred (from Part 4 of the Underwriting and Investment Exhibit which shows the expenses incurred and the allocation of expenses between functional groups) and the depreciation of real estate for those companies that depreciate real estate annually on a formula basis. The difference between the total interest, dividends, real estate income, and total deductions is known as the *net investment income*. The net investment income is carried over to line 8 of the Underwriting and Investment Exhibit Statement of Income.

Part 1A of the Underwriting and Investment Exhibit reports the profits and losses on investments disposed of during the year and the gains and losses from changes in the admitted value of investments. The second column shows the profits on sales or maturity by types of investments: bonds, stocks, mortgage loans, real estate, collateral loans, cash and bank deposits, short-term investments, and other invested assets and options and futures. The third column shows the losses on sales or maturity. Columns 4 and 5 show the increases or decreases, by adjustment in book value, for the amortization of premiums or discounts on securities and for the depreciation on real estate. These adjustments are made here only in those cases where amortization of premiums or discounts are not included in interest income and depreciation on real estate is not shown as a reduction of real estate income in the preceding schedule.

The increases or decreases by adjustment in the book value of investments shown in columns 4 and 5 are supported by details in Schedules A and D. The Annual Statement blank allows companies to choose between reflecting amortization of premiums and discounts as adjustments to interest earned or as unrealized gains or losses. If they are reflected in interest earned, they are not included in Part 1A. Companies occasionally make adjustments in book values of real estate to reflect appraisals or write-downs of values authorized by the company's board of directors and appropriate committees of the board. Such adjustments are reflected in Part 1A.

Column 6 shows the changes resulting from market fluctuation or change in admitted value of securities. The figures are not contained in the company's ledger but are determined during preparation of the Annual Statement. They represent the change in the difference between the admitted value of each group of securities and their book value at the beginning and end of the year. The securities at the beginning and at the end may be entirely different since a 100 percent turnover during the year, although unlikely, is possible. In each case, the profits and losses on the liquidation or other disposition of securities will be shown in columns 2 and 3. Any adjustments in book value appear in columns 4 and 5. Column 6 shows the residual difference (in the value of each group of securities) resulting from revaluation (at the end of the year as compared to the beginning of the year) of the inventory of securities on hand.

After all these figures are calculated, the net difference, or the net gain or loss from all sources, is calculated. This total—the "total capital gain or loss for the year"—is then broken down on lines 11 and 12 to show two separate amounts (which together must equal the grand total on line 10), representing (1) the net realized capital gains and losses and (2) the net unrealized capital gains and losses. The realized gains or losses are normally the net of columns 2 and 3. The unrealized gains or losses are generally the net of columns 4, 5, and 6. This distribution is necessary because the net realized capital gains and losses are carried to the income statement. The unrealized capital gains and losses are reflected in the capital and surplus account.

OTHER INCOME

Items of income or expense not related to the underwriting or investment function are recorded in the Other Income section of the Statement of Income.

Agents' balances recovered or charged off consist of agents' balances written off during the period less the amounts recovered on balances previously charged off. As described in Chapter 1, agents' balances more than ninety days old are considered a nonadmitted asset and deducted from surplus. (Under generally accepted accounting principles, the company makes a provision for bad debts and charges the accounts written off against such provision).

Finance and service charges not included in premiums are used when a company charges policyholders a fee for paying their premiums on an installment plan. Other types of accounts included in this section are items such as outstanding checks charged off, sale of furniture and equipment, and interest expenses.

GAINS AND LOSSES IN SURPLUS

The year-to-year change in a property-liability insurance company's net worth is not fully explained by the current year's net income. The capital and surplus account shows gains and losses that, according to existing statutory accounting rules, do not flow through the income statement but are direct adjustments in surplus. This account is appended to the statutory Statement of Income and, together with the income statement, reconciles balance sheet surplus between the year's beginning and end. As an illustration, the capital and surplus account of Government Employees Insurance Company's (GEICO) 1988 Annual Statement appears in Illustration 4-10.

Net unrealized capital gains or losses result from reporting investments on the balance sheet at an admitted value different from book value. For example, stocks generally are shown at market value, which usually varies from cost or book value. Since property-liability insurance companies typically hold a significant portion of their assets in common stocks, market fluctuations can cause significant increases or decreases in surplus. Thus an entry must be made in the reconciliation of surplus to explain the change in value since the previous statement date. Column 6 of Part 1A of the Underwriting and Investment Exhibit summarizes net gains and losses arising from differences between book and admitted values of assets. For instance, in GEICO's 1988 Annual Statement, as shown in Illustration 4-11, bonds exempt from U.S. tax ($1,966,272) and bonds of affiliates ($756,146) were written-down in value and preferred stocks of affiliates ($26,400) and of unaffiliated firms ($25,451,315), and common stocks of affiliates ($59,841,105) and of unaffiliated firms ($12,920,294) were written-up in value. The net unrealized capital gain of $95,516,694 calculated in Part 1A of the Underwriting and Investment Exhibit is carried forward to line 19 of the capital and surplus account.

In statutory accounting practices, this "unrealized" gain or loss is reflected in the company's surplus. However, no provision is made for federal income taxes which would become payable if such income is realized; nor is any provision made for tax refunds for unrealized capital losses. The failure to consider these adjustments does not agree with SFAS No. 60, *Accounting and Reporting by Insurance Enterprises.* Therefore, this practice does not fully conform with GAAP, and an adjustment must be made when statutory financial statements are converted for general purpose use.[2]

Change in nonadmitted assets is the difference between the nonadmitted assets carried at the beginning of the accounting period and those carried at its end. This entry is necessary to reflect the gain or loss in surplus for the nonadmitted assets. Exhibit 2 in the Annual Statement is an inventory of the assets considered nonadmitted at the beginning and end of the year.

Change in the liability for unauthorized reinsurance records the change in the liability a company must set up when reinsurance is placed with a company not licensed in the state where the Annual Statement is being filed. Schedule F—Part 2 of the Annual Statement is an inventory of the unauthorized companies at balance sheet date. The appropriate columns of Part 2 are transferred to lines 13a thru 13e of the liabilities page in the balance sheet. The difference between years of line 13e is the amount charged or credited to surplus.

The change in foreign exchange adjustment applies when a company has assets and liabilities in a foreign country. These assets and liabilities must be converted to United States currency for financial statement purposes. Line 16 of the liabilities shows the change in the foreign exchange adjustment between financial statement dates, which is charged or credited directly to surplus.

Change in excess of statutory reserves over statement reserves (Schedule P) consists of the change between periods of the excess of the statutory reserve over the case basis reserve and the loss expense reserve for certain lines of business which is reflected on line 15 of the balance sheet. Changes in excess reserves affect surplus but not income.

Capital changes are segregated by source of increase or decrease. The items "paid in" and "transfers to and from surplus" record changes in capital stock during the year. Paid-in applies whenever capital stock is issued for cash. Transfers from surplus record the stock issued when a stock dividend has been declared. Transfers to surplus apply when the par value of the stock has been lowered but the number of shares outstanding has stayed the same.

Surplus adjustments relate to the capitalization of the company segregated by source of the increase or decrease. The captions "paid in" and "transfers to and from capital" record changes in gross paid-in

Illustration 4-10

Annual Statement for the Year 1988 of the Government Employees Insurance Company

CAPITAL AND SURPLUS ACCOUNT

	Current Year	Previous Year
17. Surplus as regards policyholders, December 31 previous year (Page 4, Column 2, Item 32)	537,706,556	650,305,852
GAINS AND (LOSSES) IN SURPLUS		
18. Net income (from Item16)	194,268,908	133,308,329
19. Net unrealized capital gains or (losses) (Part 1A, Item 12)	7,386,682	(108,509,007)
20. Change in non-admitted assets (Exhibit 2, Item 31, Col. 3)	(1,014,212)	(3,711,594)
21. Change in liability for unauthorized reinsurance (Page 3, Item 14, Col. 2 – 1)		
22. Change in foreign exchange adjustment		
23. Change in excess of statutory reserves over statement reserves (Page 3, Item 15, Col. 2 – 1)	(75,972)	(80,564)
24. Capital changes:		
(a) Paid in		
(b) Transferred from surplus (Stock Divd.)		
(c) Transferred to surplus		
25. Surplus adjustments:		
(a) Paid in		
(b) Transferred to capital (Stock Divd.)		
(c) Transferred from capital		
26. Net remittances from or (to) Home Office		
27. Dividends to stockholders (cash)	(92,100,000)	(133,550,000)
28. Change in treasury stock (Page 3, Item 25C (1) and (2), Col. 2 – 1)		
29. Extraordinary amounts of taxes for prior years	(5,505,564)	(56,459)
30. Aggregate write-ins for gains and losses in surplus		
31. Change in surplus as regards policyholders for the year (Item 18 thru 30)	102,959,842	(112,599,295)
32. Surplus as regards policyholders, December 31 current year (Items 17 + 31) (Page 3, Item 26)	640,666,399	537,706,556

DETAILS OF WRITE-INS AGGREGATED AT ITEM 5 FOR UNDERWRITING DEDUCTIONS

0501. LAD program income	(3,352,390)	(3,145,356)
0502.		
0503.		
0504.		
0505.		
0598. Summary of remaining write-ins for Item 5 from overflow page		
0599. TOTALS (Items 0501 thru 0505 plus 0598) (Page 4, Item 5)	(3,352,390)	(3,145,356)

DETAILS OF WRITE-INS AGGREGATED AT ITEM 12 FOR MISCELLANEOUS INCOMES

1201. Miscellaneous income or (expenses)	706,956	260,614
1202. Expenses related to service charges	(20,318,213)	(21,689,972)
1203.		
1204.		
1205.		
1298. Summary of remaining write-ins for Item12 from overflow page		
1299. TOTALS (Items 1201 thru 1205 plus 1298) (Page 4, Item 12)	(19,611,257)	(21,429,357)

DETAILS OF WRITE-INS AGGREGATED AT ITEM 30 FOR GAINS AND LOSSES IN SURPLUS

3001.		
3002.		
3003.		
3004.		
3005.		
3098. Summary of remaining write-ins for Item 30 from overflow page		
1299. TOTALS (Items 3001 thru 3005 plus 3098) (Page 4, Item 30)		

Illustration 4-11

Annual Statement for the Year 1988 of the Government Employees Insurance Company

Underwriting and Investment Exhibit: Part 1A—Capital Gains and (Losses) on Investments

1	2 Profit on Sales or Maturity	3 Loss on Sales or Maturity	4 Increases by Adjustment in Book Value	5 Decreases by Adjustment in Book Value	6 Net Gain or (Loss) from Change in Difference Between Book and Admitted Assets	7 Total (Net of Cols. 2 to 6 incl.) (2 − 3 + 4 − 5 + 6)
1. U.S. government bonds	892,051	189,840				702,212
1.1 Bonds exempt from U.S. tax	1,163,439	695,235			20,000	488,204
1.2 Other bonds (unaffiliated)	900,220	274,343				625,878
1.3 Bonds of affiliates						
2.1 Preferred stocks (unaffiliated)	2,194,748	503,170			2,223,461	3,915,039
2.11 Preferred stocks of affiliates	23,865					23,865
2.2 Common stocks (unaffiliated)	88,246,324	21,739,229			(2,267,671)	64,239,424
2.21 Common stocks of affiliates					(8,263,585)	(8,263,585)
3. Mortgage loans						
4. Real estate						
5. Collateral loans						
6.1 Cash on hand and on deposit						
6.2 Short-term investments						
7. Other invested assets						
8. Financial options and futures						
9. Aggregate write-ins for capital gains and (losses)					15,674,478	15,674,478
10. Totals	93,420,648	23,401,816			7,386,682	77,405,514

(Distribution of Item 10, Col. 7)

11. Net realized capital gains or (losses)* (Page 4, Item 9) (Col. 2 − 3, Item 10) — 70,018,831

12. Net unrealized capital gains or (losses)* (Page 4, Item 19) (Col. 4 − 5 + 6, Item 10) — 7,386,682

*Attach statement or memorandum explaining basis of division.   † Excluding depreciation on real estate included in Part 1, Item 12.

and contributed surplus. Paid-in reflects cash received in excess of par value when additional capital stock is issued for cash or for surplus contributions by existing stockholders. Transfers to and from capital reflect stock dividends and reduction of par value of outstanding stock, as described in the preceding paragraph.

Net remittances to or from home office are used to record transfers of cash between a United States branch of a foreign company and the foreign company's home office. Change in treasury stock reflects the change in ownership of treasury stock at cost.

In addition to the captioned items in the capital and surplus statement, some companies make a direct charge to surplus for such items as adjustments to prior years' income taxes, effects of changes in accounting method, and errors noted in prior years' financial statements. Also, some companies provide a reserve for taxes on unrealized capital gains and show the change in the reserve as a write-in item in the statement.

ACCOUNTING FOR REINSURANCE TRANSACTIONS

A detailed discussion of reinsurance can be found in CPCU 5. No attempt is made in this text to analyze the nature and purpose of reinsurance or the institutional characteristics associated with this area of company operations. This section reviews principal accounting aspects of reinsurance, especially from the viewpoint of a ceding insurance company.

Reinsurance is a contractual arrangement under which one insurer (the ceding company) buys insurance from another insurer (the reinsurer or assuming company) to cover some or all of the losses incurred by the ceding company under insurance contracts it has issued or will issue in the future. The original insured is not a party to the reinsurance contract, and the reinsurance company is usually not directly obligated to the insured. In all reinsurance contracts, both parties must be insurance companies, a risk must be transferred, and although a contractual relationship exists between the ceding company and the reinsurer, no contract exists between the insured and reinsurer.

Reinsurance may be categorized in two ways. The first major categorization is by the method used to purchase reinsurance coverage. In general, there are two basic methods—*facultative* and *treaty* reinsurance. Facultative reinsurance requires the ceding company to negotiate a separate reinsurance agreement for each policy or group of policies it wishes to reinsure. Treaty reinsurance is automatic. The ceding company agrees in advance to cede certain classes of business to the reinsurer in accordance with the terms and conditions of the treaty, and the reinsurer agrees to accept the business ceded. Several variations of these two reinsurance methods exist.

The second way of categorizing reinsurance is according to the method of spreading the loss between the ceding company and the reinsurer. Under a *pro rata* contract, both contracting parties share the loss from the first dollar in the same ratio as they shared the premium. Under the *excess of loss* contract, the primary insurer retains all the loss up to a stated amount, after which the reinsurer pays all loss (or 80 to 90 percent of the balance of the loss) up to the limit set in the contract. The reinsurer's limits and its percentage of participation are always stipulated.

A pro rata contract usually runs for the term of the underlying policies and, upon cancellation, normally requires a return of portfolio (unearned premiums). An excess of loss contract usually runs for a stated period of time.

One of the purposes served by reinsurance is to increase the premium capacity of the ceding insurer; that is, it permits the primary company to increase the aggregate premium volume it can write. Reinsurance to allow this increased premium capacity can be arranged prior to premium volume expansions or after the primary company's existing capacity becomes strained. In the latter circumstance, a type of cession known as *portfolio reinsurance* can be arranged. Portfolio reinsurance is not attached as business is written. Instead, a block of business already in force is ceded. This procedure may be followed when a company wishes to withdraw from a line, territory, or agency. Frequently the portfolio is reinsured 100 percent by the assuming company.

Reinsurance Premiums and Commissions

Cessions under a pro rata contract are made on the basis of the premium stated in the policy and usually involve a 30 to 45 percent commission to the ceding insurer. In most contracts this commission is provisional and may be adjusted up or down by about five or six points, depending on the loss ratio. For example, the reinsurance treaty might provide for a provisional commission of 35 percent, to be adjusted after the end of the year according to the commission rates and loss ratios shown in Illustration 4-12.

Excess of loss premiums usually are computed by using an agreed-upon percentage of the total premiums written or earned for the line. Contracts of this type rarely provide for a commission. The rate quoted is usually provisional, however, and is subject to adjustment based upon the loss ratio.

It is important to know whether the premiums are ceded on a

Illustration 4-12
Retrospective Ceding Commission Scale
Pro Rata Reinsurance

Actual Loss Ratio	Commission Rate
50% or more	35%
49% but less than 50%	35.5
48% but less than 49%	36
47% but less than 48%	36.5
46% but less than 47%	37
45% but less than 46%	37.5
44% but less than 45%	38
43% but less than 44%	38.5
42% but less than 43%	39
41% but less than 42%	39.5
40% but less than 41%	40
Less than 40%	41

written or earned basis. In other words, are the premiums due the reinsurer at the inception of the policy or as they are earned? This provision in the contract governs the amount of liability for reinsurance premiums payable. It also determines whether the ceding company can take credit in the unearned premium reserve for the premiums ceded. Since one of the principal reasons for using reinsurance is surplus aid, or more properly stated, the recovery of acquisition costs before the premium is earned (early release of equity in the unearned premium reserve), most contracts are on a written premium basis, with a provisional commission equal to the ceding company's acquisition costs on the portion of the premium ceded.

For example, consider the reduction in policyholders' surplus occasioned by writing business at an acquisition expense ratio of 30 percent.[3]

Insurance premium	$100
Acquisition expenses	30
Company receives	70
Unearned premium reserve	100
Beginning surplus of $1,000 reduces to	970

Policyholders' surplus declines by the amount of acquisition expenses paid by the insurer.

The policy is reinsured to the extent of 60 percent under a pro rata reinsurance treaty that allows the ceding insurer a commission of 30 percent. This transaction has the following effects:

Reinsurance premium	$60
Commission to ceding insurer	18
Ceding company pays reinsurer	42
Credit to unearned premium reserve	60
Increase in surplus	18

The amount of premium transferred to the reinsurer equals the unearned premium reserve obligation the reinsurer assumes. The commission to the ceding insurer reimburses it for prepaid acquisition expenses on that portion of the business reinsured. Policyholders' surplus increases by the amount of the reinsurance commission. After completion of the reinsurance transaction, the net impact on the primary insurer of writing and reinsuring this policy is as follows:

Net premium to primary company	$ 40
Net acquisition expense	12
Company receives	28
Net unearned premium reserve	40
Beginning surplus of $1,000 reduces to	988

The ratio of direct premiums written-to-policyholders' surplus is 0.103 to 1 ($100/$970) but decreases (improves) after reinsurance is completed to 0.040 to 1 ($40/$988).

Reinsurance contracts written on an earned premium basis usually are identified with excess of loss and catastrophe reinsurance. There is rarely a commission allowance. Since the premiums are earned when ceded, there is no surplus aid in this type of contract.

Reinsurance Losses

Loss recoveries are governed by the contract. In the case of pro rata coverages, losses are shared in the same proportion as the premiums. For other types of reinsurance, the proportion is stipulated in each contract.

Losses recoverable appear under two categories: recoverable on paid losses and recoverable on pending losses. The first is usually shown as an admitted asset; the second is a deduction from the loss reserve. In either case, however, if the amount recoverable is due from a nonadmitted company, the amounts shown may have to be offset by inclusion in the reserve for unauthorized reinsurance.

Reinsurance Recoverable

Upon receiving notice of a loss, the loss department determines whether there is any right of recovery under a reinsurance agreement. In the case of most pro rata reinsurance, the daily report, showing appropriate reinsurance information, is inspected. In the case of excess of loss reinsurance, the loss examiner bases the decision on the terms of the applicable reinsurance contract.

Recoveries under catastrophe reinsurance are usually determined on the basis of data compiled by the statistical department. Each catastrophe is assigned a code number, and a recovery is set when the total incurred losses for any one catastrophe exceed the company's retention.

When it has been determined that there will be reinsurance recoverable on a loss, the estimated amount is usually entered in the claim file and in the data processing records on a separate reinsurance recoverable loss reserve card. In most cases, notices of losses are sent to reinsurers only for losses reinsured on a facultative basis or for the larger losses on a reinsurance treaty.

The Annual Statement provides for reporting gross unpaid losses, related reinsurance recoverable, and net unpaid losses. Listings prepared from the data processing records at statement dates give the required information. The estimated amounts of unpaid losses recoverable from reinsurers are not recorded, except in very rare cases, on the general ledger. When losses and loss expenses are paid, however, most companies record the actual amount of reinsurance recoverable both in the general ledger and in subsidiary records. Some companies maintain a record of reinsurance recoverable on paid losses on a memorandum basis until collection is made.

Reinsurance recoverable must be divided into amounts recoverable from authorized companies and amounts recoverable from unauthorized companies. Insurance companies are required to provide a reserve for reinsurance recoverable from unauthorized companies in the amount that such receivables exceed the funds held by the ceding company for the account of unauthorized companies.

Reinsurance Accounting Records

In the case of facultative reinsurance, a monthly listing (or bordereau) detailing the particulars of each risk reinsured is the ceding company's standard method of reporting to the reinsurer. Treaty reinsurance is frequently handled in monthly or quarterly totals only.

When pooling arrangements are in effect, no reinsurance records are prepared until the direct writing records have been summarized and monthly or quarterly totals are complete. In other words, under a pooling arrangement, the only reinsurance entries required are prepared from totals of business written.

SUMMARY

This chapter traced revenue and expense flows through a property-liability insurance company. The premiums written cycle begins with the sale of insurance and includes premium recording and premium collecting. Companies using direct billing methods may differ in their premium accounting procedures from companies using agent billing. Many insurers make use of both billing methods for various lines of business. Direct billing is advantageous to the insurance company if the premium volume in a particular line is large enough to justify the personnel and EDP billing equipment to perform the collection function. Direct billing may also increase the velocity of premium payments by eliminating the credit period associated with the payment of agents' accounts current. Effective cash management requires close monitoring and control of premiums collections.

The loss paid cycle encompasses one of the most important operations of an insurance company. Careful monitoring and control of claims processing is necessary to assure equitable treatment of policyholders and third-party claimants and to synchronize the insurance company's cash flow. Loss records must be sufficiently detailed to permit in-depth management reports, to provide statistical data for rate-making purposes, and to facilitate preparation of financial accounting reports. In the Annual Statement, information on salvage and reinsurance recoveries is merged with loss payments on direct business and reinsurance assumed to determine net losses paid during the accounting period. Net payments plus changes in accrued losses equal the period's losses incurred.

Expenses of an insurance company represent a substantial portion of the premium dollar, and controlling these expenses is vital if a company is to be successful. Uniform expense classification and allocation rules have been developed for statutory reporting purposes. Uniformity allows comparisons to be made among companies for expense analysis purposes and also facilitates use of inter-company data in ratemaking. Statutory expense reporting usually is not adequate for management information needs. More frequent and detailed expense reports are prepared for internal analysis and control.

Investment income, a source of revenue to a property-liability insurance company, is comprised of interest, dividends, and real estate income. A periodic determination of investment income is made on an accrual accounting basis and reported in the Annual Statement. Sales and maturities of invested assets contribute additional cash flow to the insurer. Net realized gains and losses on investments are included in investment income during the year in which the asset matures or is sold. Net investment income for the year is arrived at by charging investment expenses incurred, real estate depreciation, and interest on borrowed funds against investment income plus net realized capital gains and losses.

Some items of income or expense are not properly classified as either underwriting income or investment income on the annual statement. These items are recorded under the caption "Other Income" and affect both net income and policyholders' surplus.

Certain changes in balance sheet asset and liability values are not reflected in the statutory measurement of periodic income. Instead, direct charges or credits are made to policyholders' surplus. Statutory accounting does not recognize the potential federal income tax effects related to unrealized capital gains and losses credited or charged to surplus in this manner.

Reinsurance may reduce a ceding insurance company's unearned premium, loss and loss adjustment expense reserve requirements, and lower the ceding company's net loss payments. Reinsurance also reduces the impact on surplus that would otherwise occur from a growth in sales with its resulting charge of acquisition expense to surplus. Whether or not these benefits are reflected in surplus is determined by the reinsurance company's authority to act as a reinsurer within a particular regulatory jurisdiction. The benefit to surplus of reinsurance placed with an unauthorized reinsurer may not be reflected on the ceding company's statutory report. Benefits to surplus of reinsurance placed with an authorized reinsurer are reflected on the ceding company's statutory report.

Chapter Notes

1. *Best's Aggregates & Averages: Property-Casualty, 1989* (Oldwick, NJ: A. M. Best Company, 1989), p. 3.
2. Section In 6, "Insurance Industry," *Accounting Standards* Vol. 2, Current Text as of June 1, 1982, Financial Accounting Standards Board (New York: McGraw-Hill Book Company, 1982), p. 58021.
3. This example is adapted from Robert J. Murphy, "Reinsurance Accounting," *Property-Liability Insurance Accounting,* ed. Robert W. Strain (Santa Monica, CA: The Merritt Co., 1976), pp. 267-268.

CHAPTER 5

Insurance Company Financial Analysis and Solvency Surveillance

Insurance is purchased to obtain a financial recovery in case a loss occurs. It is illogical, therefore, to buy insurance from a company of questionable financial strength in order to obtain a lower premium, more lenient underwriting conditions, broader coverage, or for any other reason. However, determining the financial strength of insurers is difficult. The price of insurance and the breadth of coverage do not automatically indicate an insurer's ability to honor its contractual promises. A company with lower premiums than its competitors may be just as strong financially as other insurers or it may be weaker. Similarly, a small, regional insurer may be as safe or safer than a widely known national company.

In addition to those parties whose interests are insured, insurance agents, brokers, risk managers, and insurance companies evaluate the financial condition of insurers. Agents and brokers have an obligation to place insurance with solvent and financially sound insurers. They also may have a fiduciary obligation to fund loss payments or return unearned premiums on insurance placed with an insurer that becomes insolvent. Often risk managers request the assistance of insurance producers in evaluating insurance companies. Ultimately, however, the risk manager is responsible for the companies selected. A ceding insurance company, desiring stabilization of underwriting results and protection from catastrophic losses, must evaluate the financial strength of the reinsurers it deals with.

Appraising the solvency and stability of insurance companies requires an understanding of insurance accounting and finance. Agents, brokers, risk managers, and insurance company personnel should have an understanding of insurance company financial statement trends and should be able to understand and evaluate the reports of Best's and of state insurance departments.

While it may be expected that insurance company top management would have a well-defined set of corporate objectives, researchers have found that management often is unable to state precisely what it wants the company to achieve. Discussions with top managers of several prominent insurers revealed multiple corporate objectives, including a desire to (1) maintain market share, (2) raise profits, (3) avoid insolvency, and (4) adhere to some notion of socially responsible conduct.[1]

Financial analysis assumes that the fundamental strategic objective of an insurance company's management is to maximize the rate of return on company equity for a given level of assumed risk, consistent with statutory solvency requirements. This is an important objective of most insurers, and it provides a direct criterion for operational decision making. Furthermore, this criterion reinforces the business's social goal. Insurance companies, like other business enterprises, can best serve society by providing efficient service at a profit. Whether or not they succeed in this regard can be ascertained from the financial reports of insurance companies. These reports contain a wealth of valuable information. Initial sections of this chapter develop tools of financial analysis that can be used to evaluate the progress of property-liability insurers toward meeting their fundamental objective.

Techniques used to establish and maintain the financial integrity of the insurance mechanism are discussed later in the chapter, as are arrangements that protect the public from loss once a default occurs. The chapter also notes alleged deficiencies of the current back-up system, which is based on state insurance guarantee funds, and reviews some alternative ways of providing protection against insurer insolvencies.

UNIQUE CHARACTERISTICS OF INSURANCE OPERATIONS

In many respects, financial analysis of insurance companies follows the same essential principles used to evaluate any corporation's financial stature. Concepts of liquidity, leverage, profitability, and growth are as appropriate in the insurance business as elsewhere. The unique characteristics of insurance operations, however, cause some modification of how these concepts are applied.

Other business enterprises usually can estimate their costs accurately before pricing their products. Insurance companies operate in a significantly different manner. Insurers must establish prices in advance of knowing the costs associated with the services they provide. Current prices must be established from forecasts of the ultimate costs expected to arise from exposures underwritten during the period in which the rates are used. This unique pricing environment affects the financial statements primarily through the loss reserves. Judging the accuracy with which reserves are established and maintained is fundamental to evaluation of a property-liability insurer.

The fact that insurance companies are financial intermediaries also affects analysis of their financial statements. Essentially, an insurer manages two risk portfolios that can be described in terms of expected returns and variances. An insurer raises funds by binding itself to selected insurance contracts. This creates its *underwriting portfolio*. The results achieved from insurance operations are unknown in advance and contingent upon ultimate loss settlement and expense experience. The other risk portfolio is the *investment portfolio*, which consists of securities expected to yield a return, but which may result in a loss, depending on the outcome of investment activities. As a financial intermediary, the insurer must simultaneously manage both portfolios in a manner that achieves corporate goals and complies with insurance regulatory requirements.

Insurers also have an unusual capital structural compared to other businesses. Capital structure refers to various forms of permanent financing as represented by long-term debt, preferred stock, and common equity. Traditionally, insurance companies have not included long-term debt or preferred stock in their capital structure. Instead, capital has been raised from owner supplied equity and retention of earnings. The absence of long-term debt from the capital structure causes many of the leverage ratios common to financial analysis to be inappropriate for insurers unless modified.

Regulatory insurance accounting practices greatly influence how insurance company financial statements can be analyzed. Chapter 1 listed a number of ways in which statutory insurance accounting differs from accounting practices used outside the insurance business. These differences make conventional methods of financial analysis difficult to apply to insurance companies.

Over the years a set of basic measurement statistics has been developed and used to analyze property-liability insurance companies. The statistics initially were based only on statutory financial data but gradually have been adjusted to make the relationships they measure more comparable to those of noninsurance enterprises. In the discussion that follows, financial ratios traditionally used with the property-liability insurance business are described. The set of financial ratios, or tests, that currently constitute the National Association of Insurance

Commissioners' (NAIC) Insurance Regulatory Information System (IRIS) are presented in the discussion of insurer solvency.

Basic Operating Statistics

Three sets of ratios are used to analyze the operating characteristics of property-liability insurance companies: (1) capacity ratios, (2) liquidity ratios, and (3) profitability ratios. These operating statistics are developed from the statutory income statement and balance sheet and in some instances require adjustment to make them more useful for comparative analysis.

Capacity Statistics. An insurance company's capacity primarily is determined by the amount of capital it can commit to underwriting a portfolio of loss exposures. Capacity therefore is considered to be a function of capitalization.[2] The adequacy of an insurer's capital relative to the volume of business is important both as an operating characteristic and as a solvency measurement.

Two factors constrain a company's ability to increase premium volume. First, the statutory accounting treatment of acquisition expenses causes a reduction in policyholders' surplus as new sales occur. This effect creates an absolute limit on a company's capacity to write new business because a required minimum policyholders' surplus must be maintained.

Company management imposes the second capacity constraint. Variability in underwriting and investment experience causes unexpected fluctuations in policyholders' surplus. These fluctuations could render the company technically insolvent unless an adequate surplus buffer has been maintained above the minimum statutory level. Management must decide what level of policyholders' surplus is adequate for a desired rate of growth in premium volume. This commonly is called the *capacity problem* although it actually involves the twin problems of capacity and capitalization.[3]

Several approaches may be used to estimate capital adequacy. One approach uses actuarial techniques to develop the theoretical aggregate loss distribution of an insurance company. Knowing the statistical properties of the loss distribution facilitates management decisions about the desired level of surplus.[4]

A simplistic approach to the capacity problem applies conventional rules-of-thumb. The most popular of these benchmarks are the so-called Kenney Rules. There are two major rules found in Roger Kenney's book, *Fundamentals of Fire and Casualty Insurance Strength.* One rule applies to insurers writing primarily property insurance. It states that the ratio of policyholders' surplus to the unearned premium reserve should be 1 to 1; that is, the insurance company should have one dollar's worth of policyholders' surplus for each dollar of unearned premium.

$$\frac{\text{Kenny Rule}}{\text{``Fire Ratio''}} = \frac{\text{Policyholders' Surplus}}{\text{Unearned Premium Reserve}} \geq 1.00$$

Strict application of this rule would require curtailment of new insurance sales as the unearned premium reserve approached the size of policyholders' surplus. Thus, it acts to limit an insurer's capacity to accept more business. The rationale behind this rule is that the principal liability for a property insurer is the unearned premium reserve; therefore, a 1 to 1 ratio means that the company has two dollars in assets for each dollar obligated to policyholders. Although Kenney offers little justification for this rule, it may have been derived from a belief that essentially all assets held by an insurance company are current assets and the unearned premium reserve is a current liability. The Kenney "Fire Ratio" of 1 to 1 would equate to a current ratio of 2 to 1 following this line of reasoning if it is assumed that the unearned premium reserve is the only current liability. If a 2 to 1 current ratio is desirable for noninsurance corporations then, by analogy, a ratio of one dollar in the unearned premium reserve for each dollar of policyholders' surplus is appropriate for property insurers.

A second Kenney Rule is applied to companies that write primarily casualty insurance. It states that the ratio of premiums written to policyholders' surplus should not exceed 2 to 1.

$$\frac{\text{Kenny Rule}}{\text{``Casualty Ratio''}} = \frac{\text{Premiums Written}}{\text{Policyholders' Surplus}} \leq 2.00$$

Here, premiums written are viewed as a source of future obligations to policyholders either in the form of premium refunds or loss payments. Premiums written to policyholders' surplus, therefore, is used as a substitute for the ratio of debt to owners' equity.[5]

Although the Kenney Rules are almost devoid of logical, theoretical, or empirical justification, they furnish a quick solution to the complicated problem of determining an insurance company's capital adequacy and capacity to underwrite new business. Over the years, state insurance regulators often have referred to these popular benchmarks in judging whether an insurance company is overextending its capital through rapid premium growth.

A slightly different rule-of-thumb approach for judging financial strength, called *cover ratios,* was developed in Great Britain and used by surplus lines associations in the United States. Once again, ratios are established that relate premiums written to various balance sheet accounts.

One rule recommends that loss reserves plus policyholders' surplus should "cover" net premiums written by 2.5 times or more:

$$\frac{\text{Loss Reserves} + \text{Policyholders' Surplus}}{\text{Premiums Written}} \geq 2.5$$

Another rule is used for workers compensation insurance. It holds that the company should at all times maintain loss reserves at least equal to the premium volume written during the year in this line of insurance:

$$\frac{\text{Loss Reserves for Workers Compensation}}{\text{Premiums Written in Workers Compensation}} \geq 1.0$$

The most general cover ratio (below) prescribes the proper relationship between admitted assets and net premiums written during the year in all lines of business. This ratio has a distinct advantage over the Kenney Rules in that it is independent of errors in the loss reserve estimates. Both ratios in the Kenney system incorporate policyholders' surplus, which is either overstated or understated if loss reserves are inadequate or excessive, respectively. Relating admitted assets to premium volume avoids the necessity of judging loss reserve adequacy. An assets-to-premiums ratio of at least 1.25 to 1 is considered desirable. Smaller ratios are interpreted as indicators of financial weakness:

$$\frac{\text{Admitted Assets}}{\text{Premiums Written}} \geq 1.25$$

Liquidity refers to the firm's ability to meet obligations as they come due. This ability depends upon cash flow, the relationship between assets and liabilities, and the nature of assets available to discharge debt. In judging the liquidity characteristics of particular assets, the time required to convert the asset to cash and the proportion of value expected upon conversion must be considered.

Almost all admitted assets of an insurer are readily marketable. The only inventories consist of furniture, equipment, and operating supplies, which are extremely illiquid (nonadmitted assets). Agents' balances or uncollected premiums less than ninety days due the insurer are analogous to net accounts receivable in a noninsurance company. These premium balances customarily are less than one-tenth of the company's assets. Due to the absence of significant investments in accounts receivable and inventories, traditional turnover ratios are not important for insurance company financial analysis.

An *insurer's liquidity* can be judged by comparing its cash and high-grade marketable securities to the total of the unearned premium and the loss reserves. If highly liquid assets equal or exceed liabilities to policyholders, the insurer's position is satisfactory. But if assets with relatively low liquidity characteristics would be needed to satisfy

Illustration 5-1
Government Employees Insurance Company—
1988 Balance Sheet (in millions of dollars)

	Statutory Values	Bonds at 75% Statutory Values
Assets		
Bonds	1,191	893
Other admitted assets	1,220	1,220
Total admitted assets	2,411	2,113
Liabilities and policyholders' surplus		
Liabilities	1,770	1,770
Policyholders' surplus	641	343
Total liabilities and policyholders' surplus	2,411	2,113

underwriting obligations, the insurer lacks sufficient liquidity. Poor liquidity exposes the insurer to investment losses in the event that liabilities have to be settled from the forced sale of assets below their carrying values. For example, at the end of 1988 the Government Employees Insurance Company (GEICO) had a bond portfolio of approximately $1,191 million valued at amortized cost and policy-holders' surplus equal to $641 million (Illustration 5-1).

If the total bond portfolio were liquidated at 75 percent of its statement value, policyholders' surplus would be only slightly over half ($343 million ÷ $641 million = 53.5 percent) of what it was before.

A measure of an insurer's balance sheet liquidity can be formed by relating cash and the current value of invested assets to the company's policyholder obligations:

$$\text{Liquidity Ratio} = \frac{\text{Cash + Invested Assets (Market Value)}}{\text{Unearned Premium Reserve + Loss and Loss Adjustment Expense Reserves}}$$

A calculated value of this ratio less than 1.00 indicates an undesirable situation. Ratio values greater than 1.00 show that the insurer could cover the balance sheet values of its obligations to policyholders by converting invested assets to cash at current prices. Market values for most securities are listed in Schedule D of the Annual Statement and may be included in notes to general purpose financial statements.

(Bonds generally are shown at amortized cost rather than market in Schedule D.)

Another aspect of liquidity is disclosed by analyzing cash flows to and from the insurance company. Underwriting and investment operations provide cash through premium writings, interest, dividends, rents, proceeds from the sale and maturity of investments, and the recapture of previously paid federal income taxes. Funds are applied to loss and expense payments, investment purchases, and dividends to policyholders and stockholders. Any remaining funds increase the company's cash position or are invested in short-term securities. A cash flow statement is contained in the NAIC Annual Statement. For several years, the NAIC has constructed three cash flow ratios from data contained in the statement of cash flow, the balance sheet, and Schedule D. The three cash flow ratios supplement the IRIS tests results discussed later. The cash flow tests measure the extent by which alternatively defined liquid resources cover any shortfall in operating cash flow. The ability of the cash flow ratios to help identify insurance companies headed for difficulties has not yet been determined, but negative operating cash flow calls for careful study of the insurer's financial condition. Construction of the cash flow ratios is shown in Appendix D.

Companies that prepare audited GAAP financial reports issue a statement which summarizes cash flows during the accounting period. The liquidity demands of underwriting operations can be discerned by comparing the sources and uses of funds as portrayed in this statement. For a growing insurance company, underwriting operations should make a substantial net contribution to the company's cash reservoir.

Profitability. Measuring profitability of an individual insurer and of the insurance business as a whole is an important, complex and, in some instances, controversial exercise. The ability to operate profitably ultimately determines whether or not a particular insurance company survives and grows. But an insurance company's relative profitability can be misinterpreted. Over a period of years, the aggregate profitability of insurers reflects competitive conditions within the insurance business and provides an indication of how insurers have fared relative to other business sectors. Profitability helps determine if conditions are sufficiently attractive to encourage capacity expanding capital flows to the insurance business.

Several measures of profitability are used for property-liability insurers. Perhaps the most commonly quoted figure is the *combined ratio*. Because the combined ratio frequently is used as a shorthand index of profitability, it is essential to understand its relationship to the statutory underwriting result. Other profit measurements are constructed by (1) combining underwriting and investment results; (2) relating profits to sales, assets, and net worth; and (3) expressing earnings on a per share of stock basis.

Combined Ratio. The determination of underwriting gain or loss is shown in Illustration 5-2. The calculation begins with *premiums earned.* This differs from the normal sales revenue figure found in most businesses' income statements. *Premiums written* are a more accurate indication of sales activity during the accounting period but, because revenue recognition is deferred, premiums written are not shown on the income statement. Instead, premiums earned during the year must be developed from written premiums and changes in the unearned premium reserve. This is done in Illustration 5-2 and in Part 2 of the Underwriting and Investment Exhibit on the NAIC Annual Statement. Three categories of deductions are shown: (1) losses incurred, (2) loss expenses incurred, and (3) other underwriting expenses incurred. Participating insurers might also deduct policyholder dividends at this point to arrive at a modified net underwriting figure.

Several important ratios can be constructed from the data in Illustration 5-2. The *pure loss ratio* measures the fundamental cost of underwriting operations. It expresses the relationship between losses and premiums in percentage terms. While there are several bases for expressing the loss ratio, the most useful basis for financial analysis purposes is to divide losses incurred during the year by premiums earned in the same period:

$$\text{Pure Loss Ratio} = \frac{\text{Losses Incurred}}{\text{Premiums Earned}} \times 100\%$$

The numerator of this ratio, losses incurred, includes changes in loss reserves for known and for IBNR claims. Because these reserves must be estimated, they have the potential to distort operating results if the reserves are inaccurately set. Nevertheless, the companywide ratio is readily determinable from the statutory income statement. It is widely used as a benchmark of financial results. Using premiums earned in the ratio's denominator instead of premiums written results in a better matching of losses with the more nearly related revenues in all instances when premium volume fluctuates between accounting periods.

The loss ratio may be calculated either with or without loss adjustment expenses in the numerator. Most analysts and independent reporting services, such as Best's, include loss adjustment expenses so that all costs associated with the losses are contained in one statistic,

Illustration 5-2

Government Employees Insurance Company—1988 Net
Underwriting Gain—Statutory Basis (in thousands of dollars)

Premiums earned (see below)		$1,353,359
Deductions		
Losses incurred (see below)	$ 964,190	
Loss adjustment expenses incurred	153,028	
Other underwriting expenses incurred, etc.	180,625	
Total underwriting deductions		1,297,843
Net Underwriting Gain (Loss)		$ 55,516
Development of Premiums Earned:		
Net premiums written		$1,140,916
Plus: Unearned premiums previous year		738,147
Minus: Unearned premiums current year		525,704
Premiums earned during current year		$1,353,359
Development of Losses Incurred:		
Loss payments (net of reinsurance and salvage)		$ 988,172
Plus: Net losses unpaid current year		985,269
Minus: Net losses unpaid previous year		881,359
Losses incurred current year		$1,092,082

which they call the net loss ratio. Using the data in Illustration 5-2, the net loss ratio is:

$$\text{Net Loss Ratio} = \frac{\text{Incurred Losses and Loss Adjustment Expenses}}{\text{Premiums Earned}}$$

$$= \frac{\$964,190 + \$153,028}{\$1,353,359} \times 100\% = 82.6\%$$

The premiums and losses shown in the statutory income statement and in Illustration 5-2 are net of reinsurance transactions. Unless otherwise defined, reference to the loss ratio means that losses incurred have been added to loss adjustment expenses and the sum has been divided by premiums earned with all figures net of reinsurance transactions.

A second important ratio developed from the statutory income statement is the *expense ratio*. It expresses the relationship between underwriting expenses and premiums. The numerator includes all the expenses shown in the Underwriting and Investment Exhibit, Part 4 under the caption Other Underwriting Expenses. Included are acquisition and premium collection and field supervision costs plus general expenses, taxes, licenses, and fees. Investment expenses are not included in calculation of underwriting gain or loss and therefore are not involved in computation of the expense ratio.

The denominator of the expense ratio can be either premiums written or premiums earned. A *trade basis* expense ratio is formed by dividing expenses incurred by premiums written. A *financial basis* expense ratio uses premiums earned rather than premiums written as the ratio's denominator. The ratios using data contained in Illustration 5-2 are:

$$\frac{\text{Expense Ratio}}{\text{(Trade Basis)}} = \frac{\text{Expenses Incurred}}{\text{Premiums Written}} = \frac{\$180,625}{\$1,140,916} \times 100\% = 15.8\%$$

$$\frac{\text{Expense Ratio}}{\text{(Financial Basis)}} = \frac{\text{Expenses Incurred}}{\text{Premiums Earned}} = \frac{\$180,625}{\$1,353,359} \times 100\% = 13.3\%$$

If premiums written and earned are substantially different, understanding the nature of their construction is helpful in reconciling financial ratios with the statutory underwriting result.

The *combined ratio* is formed by adding the loss ratio and the expense ratio. Assuming both the loss and expense ratio use premium earned as their denominator, a financial basis combined ratio is obtained. This form of the ratio is useful because the underwriting profit margin is equal to 100 percent minus the combined ratio.

$$\frac{\text{Combined Ratio}}{\text{(Financial Basis)}} = \text{Loss Ratio} + \frac{\text{Expense Ratio}}{\text{(Financial Basis)}}$$

$$= 82.6\% + 13.3\% = 95.9\%$$

$$\text{Underwriting gain} = 100\% - 95.9\% = 4.1\%$$

The most frequently used form of the combined ratio is constructed with the *trade basis expense ratio*. Combining a loss ratio based on premiums earned and an expense ratio based on premiums written produces a more meaningful measure of underwriting profit when premium volume is increasing or decreasing. The rationale of this approach lies in the fact that acquisition costs are a function of premiums written and, in compliance with statutory accounting rules, must be expensed as incurred. Financial reporting services such as Best's publish a trade basis combined ratio for individual insurance companies and company groups.

Consider the following financial information for a particular year:

Premiums Written	$200,000
Premiums Earned	100,000
Acquisition Expenses Incurred	80,000
Other Underwriting Expenses Incurred	5,000
Losses and Loss Adjustment Expenses Incurred	50,000

The combined ratio on the financial basis (which uses premiums earned as the denominator) relates losses and all expenses incurred to premiums earned:

$$\text{Combined Ratio (Financial Basis)} = \frac{\$50,000 + \$80,000 + \$5,000}{\$100,000} \times 100\% = 135\%$$

While the financial basis produces a combined ratio which, when subtracted from 100 percent, accurately reflecting the statutory percentage margin on premiums earned, it fails to indicate that significant acquisition expenses have been prepaid. Results of underwriting operations are unduly depressed following this approach.

On the trade basis, losses incurred once again are divided by premiums earned, but all expenses other than for loss adjustment are related to premiums written:

$$\text{Combined Ratio (Trade Basis)} = \left[\frac{\$50,000}{\$100,000} + \frac{\$80,000 + \$5,000}{\$200,000} \right] \times 100\% = 92.5\%$$

This calculation results in a combined ratio of less than 100 percent by relating acquisition expenses to the corresponding premiums. (Other Underwriting Expenses Incurred which are not a direct function of premiums written also are included in the numerator of the expense ratio.) Because these other expense items are small in comparison to acquisition costs, the distortion caused by lumping all expenses together is not great. Nonetheless, an underwriting gain of 7.5 percent (100 percent −92.5 percent) slightly overstates the true profit margin for this example. The combined ratio summarizes the overall underwriting performance of the insurer during an accounting period. It is useful for comparing results among various lines of insurance, among companies, and for comparing the result of a single insurer over several accounting periods. Its component parts are also significant. A company's loss ratio—overall and by the line of insurance—gives a general indication of the quality of business it writes and may give information on the adequacy of the company's premium rates. Operating efficiency and effectiveness are measured by the expense ratio. Comparisons of expense ratios among successive time periods offer an initial indication of overall expense trends and may flag the need for increased attention to cost control.

Investment Profit. Property-liability insurance companies tend to have a positive cash flow due to prepayment of insurance premiums. Net operating cash flow plus funds provided by policyholder surplus are invested to yield a profit in addition to any realized from underwriting operations. Investment income is an integral part of an insurance company's overall profitability. The importance of investment income can be seen in Illustration 5-3. Investment income as a percentage of average admitted assets is compared in the diagram to underwriting profit (loss) as a percentage of earned premiums for a large number of stock property-liability insurers. In thirty-seven of the forty-nine years from 1940 through 1988 the investment earnings rate of return exceeded the underwriting profit margin on premiums earned. In dollar amounts, investment income exceeded underwriting profit in forty-two of the forty-nine years. Income from investments exceeded underwriting profit on a percentage basis in each year since 1955 and on a dollar basis every year after 1955.

Two components of investment gain or loss are shown in the statutory income statement. Net investment income earned is the excess of interest, dividend, and real estate revenues over related investment department expenses. Net *realized* capital gains or losses arise from the sale of securities for amounts greater or less than their carrying values. *Unrealized* gains and losses in the investment portfolio are not included in investment income. Financial reports prepared to conform with GAAP generally follow the statutory approach of defining investment income exclusive of unrealized gains or losses. A separate disclosure of unrealized appreciation or depreciation in the value of securities is presented along with an adjustment to reflect deferred federal income taxes on unrealized changes in market values.

Investment income traditionally was considered separate from underwriting income within the property-liability insurance business. Returns from investment operations were considered to belong to the company and its owners rather than the policyholders in their role as consumers. It has been asserted that investment returns reimburse the insurance company for an advance credit given to the insured in the form of a premium discount. Stock insurance companies have used investment earnings as the source of dividend payments to stockholders and as a source of surplus growth. Two justifications for this viewpoint are offered. First, stockholders must be rewarded for using their capital to establish and maintain the company. A return on their investment commensurate with the opportunity cost of not employing these funds in an alternative enterprise of similar risk is deemed to be appropriate. Second, returns to equity are necessary to accumulate and attract new capital for expanded growth of the insurance business. As

Illustration 5-3

Stock Investment Income and Underwriting Results*

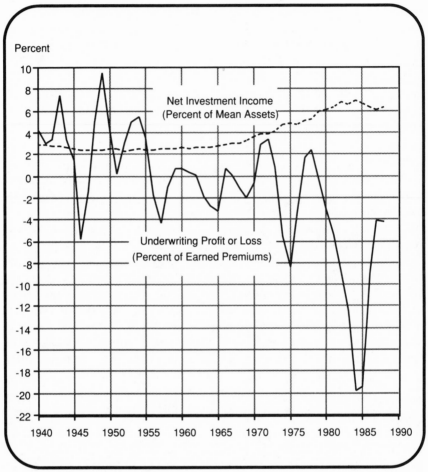

*Derived using data from *Best's Aggregates & Averages*, Property-Casualty, 1989, p. 93.

Illustration 5-3 shows, returns have not been forthcoming from underwriting activities and therefore must come from investments. A similar line of reasoning applies to mutual insurers. Investment income in a mutual serves either to reduce the cost of insurance for policyholder-owners or to increase the company's stability and capacity through additions to surplus.

In recent years, political and regulatory pressure has mounted against the traditional view of investment income. Explicit inclusion of investment income and realized capital gains in the ratemaking process has been advocated and adopted in many jurisdictions. Insurers have responded by reemphasizing the need for growth in underwriting capacity through capital formation. The fact that capital at times has been drained from property-liability insurers by holding companies desiring to employ funds at higher rates of return is offered as evidence that returns typically have been inadequate within the business. In addition, the dual impact inflicted on surplus by underwriting losses and depressed securities markets periodically highlights the need for increased earnings accumulations to provide stability. Company officials cite the need to expand underwriting capacity rapidly in order to keep pace with coverage needs heightened by economic growth and inflation.[6]

Two important relationships should be considered jointly when analyzing investment operations: (1) the degree of insurance exposure and (2) the proportion of assets invested in common stock. If both are high, there is a potential for disastrous results. The premiums written-to-policyholders' surplus ratio, therefore, should be inversely related to the proportionality of stock in the investment portfolio. Judgments in this area should incorporate knowledge of underwriting profitability. Heavy use of insurance leverage in a company which historically earns an underwriting profit may be consistent with substantial investments in common stock. On the other hand, a history of underwriting losses would not recommend a combination of an equity oriented investment portfolio and a high premiums written-to-policyholders' surplus ratio.

Profit Ratios. Four types of ratios are useful in analyzing property-liability insurance company profitability: (1) those showing profits in relation to revenues (premiums earned), (2) those showing profits in relation to investment, (3) those showing profits in relation to net worth, and (4) those showing profits in relation to the number of shares of common stock outstanding. The three sources of insurer profit—underwriting income, investment income, and capital gains—individually or in combination can be related to revenues (premiums earned), invested assets, or net worth. Because there is a multiplicity of profit measurements and ratios, it is easy to become confused when evaluating an individual insurance company's or the business's operating results. For the financial analyst to get an accurate idea of performance, a clear understanding of what each profit ratio measures is essential.

Underwriting Profit. The first profit ratio has been introduced; it is one minus the adjusted combined ratio:

$$\text{Underwriting Profit Ratio} = 1.00 - \text{Adjusted Combined Ratio}$$

This ratio is similar to the net profit margin for noninsurance business, but it differs from the net profit margin in that only a portion of the insurer's current operating income is included. No recognition is given to investment income or portfolio gains. The emphasis is on the efficiency of underwriting and not on overall profitability. Observation of trends in the underwriting profit ratio and comparisons of a particular company's ratio with averages for other insurers may be helpful in evaluating performance. Some analysts may further adjust the numerator of this ratio to reflect current and deferred income taxes.

Insurance Operating Profit. This index of profitability is similar to the underwriting profit ratio, but it also includes a portion of investment income. The estimated amount of investment income attributed to policyholder supplied funds is included in the ratio's numerator. Policyholder supplied funds are assumed to equal the reserves for unpaid losses and unpaid loss adjustment expenses and that portion of the unearned premium reserve (the excess over agents' balances and acquisition expenses) available for investment. The amount of investment income earned by policyholder supplied funds is estimated by applying the net investment yield earned by the insurer on invested assets other than stocks.

$$\frac{\text{Insurance Operating}}{\text{Profit Ratio}} = \frac{\text{Underwriting}}{\text{Profit Ratio}} + \frac{\left[\begin{array}{c}\text{Policyholder}\\\text{Supplied Funds}\end{array}\right] \times \left[\begin{array}{c}\text{Net Yield On}\\\text{Nonstock}\\\text{Investments}\end{array}\right]}{\text{Premiums Earned}}$$

The insurance operating profit ratio indicates the rate of return on premiums an insurer has earned from its insurance operations as distinguished from the earnings it has achieved by investing funds provided by capital and surplus.

Return on Invested Funds. Insurance reporting services use various measures for return on invested funds to monitor the investment performance of property-liability insurers. One ratio shows the relationship between net investment income and average admitted assets:

$$\text{Investment Earnings Ratio} = \frac{\text{Net Investment Income}}{\text{Average Admitted Assets}}$$

Investment income includes interest, dividends, and real estate income, less investment expenses, but before federal income taxes. This ratio gives a narrowly defined measure of investment earnings.

A broader rate of return figure for investment operations compares total *realized* investment profit or loss to average admitted assets:

$$\text{Investment Profit Ratio} = \frac{\text{Total Investment Profit (Loss)}}{\text{Average Admitted Assets}}$$

The numerator of this ratio adds realized capital gains (losses) to investment income and produces an overall index of investment performance. Care should be taken in comparing investment return ratios with the underwriting profit ratio, since the latter ratio relates underwriting results to premiums earned rather than assets. In other words, the two ratios are not meaningful when added together.

Another type of ratio for investable funds relates profits to the company's net worth (policyholders' surplus):

$$\text{Return On Net Worth} = \frac{\text{Net Profit}}{\text{Policyholders' Surplus}}$$

Either statutory accounting or GAAP data can be used. If statutory results are being measured, net profit includes underwriting gain (loss), investment income, and realized capital gains. Policyholders' surplus at the end of the current year normally is used as the base of this profitability ratio. When constructed in this fashion, the ratio is logically inconsistent. Unrealized investment gains and losses are included in policyholders' surplus but not in profit. A better measurement adjusts the statutory data to conform with GAAP. An adjusted profits-to-adjusted net worth relationship is formed:

$$\text{Adjusted Return On Net Worth} = \frac{\text{Adjusted Net Profit}}{\text{Adjusted Policyholders' Surplus}}$$

This ratio's denominator does not include all investable funds. Only capital and adjusted surplus are used here; other resources are not included.

The rate of return on net worth is appropriate for comparisons among insurance companies. It avoids problems caused by differences in premium volume, underwriting results, and investment gains by summarizing overall operating success relative to the firm's net resources. This ratio indicates the company's earning power and ability to grow.

Earnings per Share. Earnings per share (EPS) is a measure of net income available to common stockholders expressed on a per share of stock basis:

$$\text{EPS} = \frac{\text{Net Income Available to Common Stockholders}}{\substack{\text{Weighted Average Number of Common Shares} \\ \text{Outstanding During the Accounting Period}}}$$

Stock insurers may published EPS figures based on statutory net income as well as on GAAP income. Reporting both earnings ratios serves to highlight the fact that statutory accounting principles result in profit measurements significantly different from those based on GAAP.[7]

Several other per share statistics may be reported by stock insurers or calculated by the financial analyst and compared to EPS. The dividend paid per share of stock is of interest to investors who wish to estimate the future dividend yield available from ownership of the insurer's stock. A comparison of EPS to dividends per share may indicate the likelihood that the current dividend will be continued or increased in the future. Another figure helpful in this regard can be determined by dividing the insurance company's unassigned surplus by the number of common shares outstanding. Statutory unassigned surplus represents the maximum amount of accumulated earnings potentially available for distribution. Although most companies intend to retain unassigned surplus to support current obligations and to finance future growth, the ratio of statutory unassigned surplus per share indicates the insurer's ability to continue stockholder dividend payments even during a year when EPS falls below the company's historical dividend per share payment.

Summary of Financial Ratios

Financial ratios that may be used to analyze property-liability insurance companies are summarized in Illustration 5-4. Ratio values calculated for a particular insurer should be interpreted carefully. Such values have little inherent meaning. Generally they become meaningful only when compared to business norms and to values determined for the same company in prior years or forecasted for the future. Where appropriate, the traditional benchmarks are included in the table.

Calculating ratios of debt to equity gives an indication of the potential drain on policyholders' surplus associated with leverage. Whether or not an insurer will be able to meet its obligations to policyholders also depends on the payment schedule associated with claims in the process of settlement and on the revenues generated by underwriting and investment operations. In the short run the insurer's ability to remain solvent when faced by adversities rests upon the liquidity of its assets and the ability of cash flow to meet expenses and pay claims. Survival and growth over the long term is a function of profitability. How rapidly a company grows depends on the interaction of insurance leverage and profitability. Financial analysis, therefore, looks beyond ratios of debt-to-equity and evaluates the liquidity and profitability of the insurer as well.

Illustration 5-4
Summary of Financial Ratios

Ratio	Formulation	Acceptable Value
I. CAPACITY Kenney's "fire" auto	$\dfrac{\text{Policyholders' Surplus}}{\text{Unearned Premium Reserve}}$	$\geq 1{:}1$
Kenney's "casualty" ratio	$\dfrac{\text{Premiums Written}}{\text{Policyholders' Surplus}}$	$\leq 2{:}1$
Cover ratio "1"	$\dfrac{\text{Loss Reserves} + \text{Policyholders' Surplus}}{\text{Premiums Written}}$	$\geq 2.5{:}1$
Cover ratio "2"	$\dfrac{\text{Loss Reserves for Workers Compensation}}{\text{Premiums Written for Workers Compensation}}$	$\geq 1{:}1$
Cover ratio "3"	$\dfrac{\text{Admitted Assets}}{\text{Premiums Written}}$	$\geq 1.25{:}1$
II. LIQUIDITY Liquidity ratio	$\dfrac{\text{Cash} + \text{Invested Assets (Market Value)}}{\text{Unearned Premium} + \text{Loss Reserves}}$	$> 1{:}1$

III.PROFITABILITY

Underwriting profit
  (Financial basis) $= 1.00 - \text{Combined Ratio (Financial Basis)}$

$$= 1.00 - \left(\frac{\substack{\text{Losses and Loss Adjustment Expenses Incurred} \\ + \text{ Acquisition Expenses Incurred} \\ + \text{ Other Underwriting Expenses Incurred}}}{\text{Premiums Earned}} \right)$$

Underwriting Profit
  (Trade basis) $= 1.00 - \text{Combined Ratio (Trade Basis)}$

$$= 1.00 - \left[\left(\frac{\substack{\text{Losses and Loss} \\ \text{Adjustment} \\ \text{Expenses Incurred}}}{\text{Premiums Earned}} \right) + \left(\frac{\substack{\text{Acquisition Expenses Incurred} \\ + \text{ Other Underwriting} \\ \text{Expenses Incurred}}}{\text{Premiums Written}} \right) \right]$$

Underwriting profit
  ratio $= 1.00 - \text{Adjusted Combined Ratio}$

$$= 1.00 - \left[\left(\frac{\substack{\text{Losses and Loss Adjustment Expenses Incurred} \\ + \text{ Acquisition Expenses Incurred} \\ + \text{ Other Underwriting Expenses Incurred} \\ - \text{ Equity in Unearned Premium Reserve}}}{\text{Premiums Earned}} \right) \right]$$

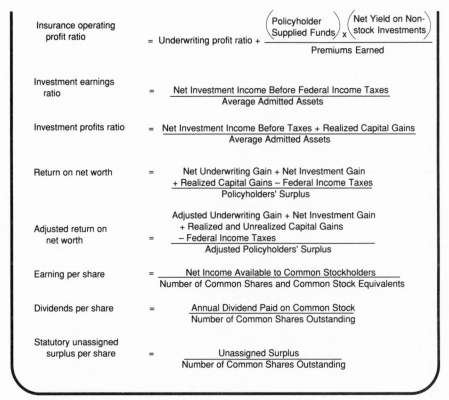

$$\text{Insurance operating profit ratio} = \text{Underwriting profit ratio} + \frac{\left(\begin{array}{c}\text{Policyholder}\\\text{Supplied Funds}\end{array}\right) \times \left(\begin{array}{c}\text{Net Yield on Non-}\\\text{stock Investments}\end{array}\right)}{\text{Premiums Earned}}$$

$$\text{Investment earnings ratio} = \frac{\text{Net Investment Income Before Federal Income Taxes}}{\text{Average Admitted Assets}}$$

$$\text{Investment profits ratio} = \frac{\text{Net Investment Income Before Taxes} + \text{Realized Capital Gains}}{\text{Average Admitted Assets}}$$

$$\text{Return on net worth} = \frac{\text{Net Underwriting Gain} + \text{Net Investment Gain} + \text{Realized Capital Gains} - \text{Federal Income Taxes}}{\text{Policyholders' Surplus}}$$

$$\text{Adjusted return on net worth} = \frac{\begin{array}{c}\text{Adjusted Underwriting Gain} + \text{Net Investment Gain}\\ + \text{Realized and Unrealized Capital Gains}\\ - \text{Federal Income Taxes}\end{array}}{\text{Adjusted Policyholders' Surplus}}$$

$$\text{Earning per share} = \frac{\text{Net Income Available to Common Stockholders}}{\text{Number of Common Shares and Common Stock Equivalents}}$$

$$\text{Dividends per share} = \frac{\text{Annual Dividend Paid on Common Stock}}{\text{Number of Common Shares Outstanding}}$$

$$\text{Statutory unassigned surplus per share} = \frac{\text{Unassigned Surplus}}{\text{Number of Common Shares Outstanding}}$$

The normal values of standard ratios should not be considered inviolate rules. For instance, aggregate data for property-liability insurers in 1988 revealed a premiums written-to-policyholders' surplus ratio of approximately 1.71 to 1, a value within the normally acceptable bound. Numerous individual insurers were operating at much larger writings-to-surplus ratios without threatening policyholder security. On the other hand, an insurer whose liquidity ratio dropped below 1 to 1 clearly would be in an undesirable situation. Additional care should be exercised in comparing profitability ratios. While comparisons of profit indexes among insurers may be meaningful, comparisons of insurance company rates of return with those of other types of businesses should not be made without an adjustment to reflect financial and operating risks in both sectors.

FINANCIAL RATINGS OF INSURANCE COMPANIES

Financial analysis of individual insurance companies can be a laborious, time-consuming, and costly procedure. For these and other reasons, persons seeking to appraise the financial condition of a particular insurance company may refer to the specialized financial evaluation provided by an insurance reporting service and expressed as a grade or rating. The predominant insurance company rating service in the United States is A.M. Best Company, which annually publishes ratings for life insurance and property-liability insurance companies. The rating system applied to nonlife insurers by Best is described here, based on *Best's Insurance Reports, Property-Casualty*, published annually.

The 1989 edition of *Best's Insurance Reports* presented financial information on 940 stock, mutual, reciprocal, and American Lloyds insurance organizations, encompassing 2,075 insurance companies that wrote more than 99 percent of domestic premiums.

Best's Evaluation Procedures

The rating system developed by the A.M. Best Company attempts to evaluate the factors that affect the financial performance of insurance companies in order to determine whether each company has the ability to meet the obligations of its contracts. Best's uses quantitative and qualitative evaluations in analyzing the ability of a company to perform its future obligations.

Best's Quantitative Measures. Financial tests have been established over the years by the A.M. Best Company. These quantitative measures have been developed to analyze operating performance and financial condition of a company.

Profitability Tests. Profit from operations is a measure of the ability of management to provide attractive insurance products and services to policyholders at competitive prices. At the same time the company must remain efficient and control costs in order to compare favorably with the competition. Profitability tests include the combined ratio, operating ratio, net operating income to net premium earned, yield on investments, change in policyholders surplus, and return on policyholders surplus.

Leverage Tests. Use of leverage increases returns on capital and increases the risk of variation of that return. Best's uses seven leverage tests: change in net premiums written, net premiums written to policyholders surplus, net liabilities to policyholders surplus, net leverage, ceded reinsurance leverage, gross leverage, and surplus aid to policyholders surplus.

Liquidity Tests. An insurer must meet its obligations in the short and long run. This can be done by holding cash and sound investments that are diversified yet can be readily converted to cash. With a high degree of liquidity, an insurer has the flexibility to withdraw from unprofitable lines and expand into more profitable ones. Best's liquidity tests include quick liquidity, current liquidity, agents' balances to policyholders surplus, and investment leverage.

Best's Qualitative Measures. Qualitative measures are judgments and not mathematical measures.

Spread of Risk. Best's analyzes the book of business on both a geographic and a by-line-of-business basis. Geographic location can have a great impact on the extent of exposure to various hazards such as hurricanes, tornadoes, earthquakes, and so forth.

Amount and Soundness of Reinsurance. Reinsurance is essential and plays an important role in risk spreading and financial security of insurers. Both the amount of reinsurance purchased and the quality of reinsurers are examined.

Quality and Estimated Market Value of Assets. Assets are reviewed to determine the potential impact on policyholders' surplus if the assets need to be sold quickly. The higher the liquidity or quality of the assets, or both, the more certainty there is on the value to be received on the sale of these assets. The market value of nonequity assets is impacted by the yield and maturity, particularly with bonds. For this reason, the impact on policyholders' surplus due to changes in interest rates on interest sensitive assets is estimated.

Adequacy of Reserves. Reserves are essential to evaluating profitability, leverage, and liquidity. Policyholders' surplus is what is available after reported reserves have been established. Reported net income is what remains after reported reserves have been subtracted.

Management. The integrity, competence, and experience of management, although difficult qualities to assess, are important factors for success in the insurance industry, where financial integrity and security are more critical than in many other types of business endeavors.

Best's Rating System

The 1989 Edition of *Best's Trend Report for Property-Casualty Insurance Companies* reported that of the 2,075 companies included in *Best's Insurance Reports*, approximately 66 percent were assigned a Best's Rating ranging from A+ (Superior) to C– (Fair). The remaining 34 percent were a "Not assigned" rating. Illustration 5-5 summarizes the distribution of ratings.

The assigned ratings are:

Illustration 5-5

Best's Property-Casualty Ratings Summary Table

Rating	Number of Companies	Percent of Companies
A+	428	20.6
A	350	16.9
A–	134	6.5
B+	130	6.3
B	41	2.0
B–	15	0.7
C+	6	0.3
C	5	0.2
C–	0	0.0
100% reinsured companies	197	9.5
NA-1—NA-5	702	33.8
NA-6—NA-10	67	3.2
Totals	2,075	100.0%

The ratings are combined into major categories, disregarding modifiers and placing at the NA-3 level those too young to rate except by using parent company ratings. Those companies which are 100 percent reinsured are isolated.

*Based on data from *Best's Online Insurance Management Reports,* Release No. 17, August 14, 1989.

A+	Superior
A and A–	Excellent
B+	Very good
B and B–	Good
C+	Fairly good
C and C–	Fair

These ratings are assigned according to Best's opinion of overall performance of the company compared to the norms of the property-liability insurance business. The A+ (superior) rating means that insurers generally have demonstrated their strongest ability to meet their respective policyholder and other contractual obligations. A rating of C– (fair) means that the company has demonstrated only a fair ability to meet its obligations.

Each of these companies may also be assigned a rating modifier to qualify the status of an assigned rating. The modifier appears as a lower-case suffix to the rating (for example, Ac, Be, or Cg). The rating modifiers are:

c - Contingent rating
e - Parent rating
g - Group rating
p - Pooled rating
q - Qualified rating
r - Reinsured rating
s - Consolidated rating
w - Watch list
x - Revised rating

Rating Modifications for Performance. Four rating modifiers are based on the performance of the company to which the modifier is assigned.

Contingent Rating. A contingent rating, "c," is temporarily assigned to a company when there has been decline in performance (profitability, leverage liquidity, or a combination of these). Although the decline may not be significant enough to warrant a reduction in the overall rating, unless correction action is taken, or more current adverse information becomes available, the rating may be reduced.

Qualified Rating. A qualified rating, "q," is assigned to a company that might be adversely affected by (1) pending state legislation that would mandate rate restrictions or (2) the possibility of payments due from mandated state residual market programs which are equal to, or in excess of, its policyholders' surplus.

Watch List. A watch list "w" assignment may be given due to a downward trend in performance based on profitability, leverage liquidity, or a combination of these. However, the trend may not be significant enough to deserve an actual reduction in the assigned rating.

Revised Rating. The revised rating, "x," is given when the assigned rating of the company was revised during the year in which the rating is shown.

Rating Modifications Based on Affiliations. Five rating modifiers may be assigned to a company whose rating is based on an affiliation with one or more other property-liability insurers in the industry.

Parent Rating. An "e" parent rating may be received by a subsidiary company if the parent ownership exceeds 50 percent. The rating is based on the consolidated performance of the parent and subsidiary.

Group Rating. A "g" group rating may be given to a group of companies if they are related by either common management or ownership. A pooling of a substantial portion of their net business and having only minor differences in their underwriting and operating performance would permit this group rating.

Pooled Rating. A "p" pooled rating is assigned to companies under common management or ownership that pool 100 percent of their net business. All premiums, expenses, and losses must be reasonably prorated in relationship to the policyholders' surplus of each member of the group.

Reinsured Rating. The "r" reinsured rating indicates that the rating and financial size category assigned to the company is that of an affiliated carrier which reinsures 100 percent of the written net business of the company.

Consolidated Rating. The "s" consolidated rating is assigned to a parent company and is based on the consolidated performance of the company and its domestic property-liability subsidiaries in which it holds a 50 percent or greater ownership interest.

Not Assigned Rating. Approximately 34 percent of companies appearing in the Property-Casualty Edition of *Best's Insurance Reports* receive a "not assigned" rating. This designation (abbreviated NA) is divided into ten different classifications to explain why a company is not eligible for a Best's Rating. They are as follows:

- NA-1 special data filing (assigned primarily to small mutuals)
- NA-2 less than minimum size
- NA-3 insufficient experience
- NA-4 rating procedure inapplicable (for example, companies writing primarily financial guaranty insurance)
- NA-5 significant change (This classification is assigned to a previously rated company that experiences a significant change in ownership, management, or book of business that alters the general trend of the operations of the company. Depending on the nature of the change, a one to five year period may be required before the company may qualify for a rating.)
- NA-6 reinsured by unrated reinsurer
- NA-7 below minimum standards (assigned to companies not meeting the minimum standards for a Best's rating of C— although meeting minimum size and experience requirements)
- NA-8 incomplete financial information

- NA-9 company request (Many captives operate in markets that do not require a rating, but cooperate with A.M. Best so that a report can be prepared. Companies not agreeing with their assigned rating or Best's procedure or both may receive this classification. After this classification is received, A.M. Best normally requires a minimum two year waiting period before the assignment of a rating.)
- NA-10 under state supervision (This classification is assigned when a company is under any form of supervision, restraint or control by state regulatory authorities, including but not limited to, receivership, conservatorship, or rehabilitation.)

Financial Size. Each rated insurer is also classified into a financial size category determined by Best's estimate of the company's adjusted surplus. Financial categories of alien insurers are based upon financial statements of the alien companies which include assets and liabilities of their United States branches.

Best's traditionally has used distinctive notation to differentiate the financial category and the policyholders' or general rating. The financial classification system currently used by Best is shown in Illustration 5-6.

An insurer's size is reflected only in the financial category to which it is assigned and does not influence the general rating assigned the company. Small insurers can be as safe as larger insurers. Best's explicitly acknowledges the desirability of insurance coverage from a small, prudently managed, and adequately financed insurer in preference to a larger insurance company operated less successfully.

Changes in an insurance company's rating and financial category should be interpreted as an indication of the direction in which the company is heading. A downward trend over the course of several years is a cause for concern. Best's assigns new ratings during the spring of each year. Occasionally, extraordinary developments discovered after ratings are published cause a change in the assigned rating. In such cases, subscribers to Best's reporting services receive notification of rating changes through its weekly or monthly publications.

ESTABLISHING INSURANCE COMPANY SOLVENCY

The insurance mechanism can reduce the uncertainty of economic loss only to the extent that the mechanism itself is secure. Unfortunate consequences occasioned by the collapse of the insurance company can be devastating to innocent members of the public unable to collect first- and third-party claims, and prepaid but unearned premiums. Likewise,

Illustration 5-6

Best's Financial Size Categories for Property and
Liability Insurance Companies

Financial Size Category	Adjusted Policyholders' Surplus		
	(thousands of dollars)		
Class I	Up	to	1,000
Class II	1,000	to	2,000
Class III	2,000	to	5,000
Class IV	5,000	to	10,000
Class V	10,000	to	25,000
Class VI	25,000	to	50,000
Class VII	50,000	to	100,000
Class VIII	100,000	to	250,000
Class IX	250,000	to	500,000
Class X	500,000	to	750,000
Class XI	750,000	to	1,000,000
Class XII	1,000,000	to	1,250,000
Class XIII	1,250,000	to	1,500,000
Class XIV	1,500,000	to	2,000,000
Class XV	2,000,000	or	more

Adapted with permission from *Best's Key Rating Guide*,
Property-Casualty Edition, 1989, p. XVI.

the adverse financial and public relations effects of an insurer insolvency reverberate throughout the entire insurance business. A major public policy goal of insurance regulation, therefore, is the establishment and maintenance of insurance company solvency. Proper solvency requirements set minimum operating standards that serve as constraints on unreasonable or irresponsible management actions.

The Meaning of Solvency

Solvency may be defined to mean that an insurance company maintains the ability to meet its obligations as they are due, even though some claims arising from current operations will be settled a number of years in the future. This definition emphasizes the need for continued liquidity, adequate loss reserves, and appropriate premium rates. However, this definition cannot fully explain solvency because it fails to acknowledge the legal requirement that an insurance company must maintain at least a prescribed level of net worth.

In a regulatory context, an insurance company is *technically solvent* if its admitted assets exceed liabilities by a margin at least equal to the minimum capital or minimum surplus required by law. It becomes impaired the moment capital or surplus drops below the minimum level. Realistically, such a situation probably would not be discovered until some time after capital had been impaired.

For insurance company management purposes, a practicable definition of solvency is obtained by combining the previous approaches. A solvent insurer (1) collects premiums that realistically can be expected to satisfy anticipated loss settlements and meet all operating expenses and (2) maintains admitted assets sufficient to cover its existing liabilities, with a remaining safety margin that is at least equal to statutory net worth requirements. This defines a *minimum* solvency standard for management. In most, if not all, cases insurance companies choose to operate with a larger net worth than prescribed by statutory minimums.

As long as admitted assets exceed liabilities the company is still solvent. However, if the excess is less than the capital and surplus required by regulatory authorities, it is considered that capital is "impaired." When this condition arises, a "cease and desist" order is issued. This order means that no new business can be written until the impairment is "cured." In some such instances the company continues to "run off its business," pay claims, or seek reinsurance.

While "technical" insolvency may exist, an insurance company is not "legally" insolvent until the appropriate court so concludes.

Minimum Net Worth Requirements

The minimum amount of initial net worth required in order for a company to obtain a license to transact a certain type of insurance business is governed by the respective state insurance laws. In addition to statutory minimums for initial capital and surplus, many states require that minimum levels of net worth be maintained so long as the company is a going concern. These continuing minimums are commonly lower than the initial standards.

Initial Minimums. One of several initial minimums applies to a particular insurance company depending on (1) the state in which the company is domiciled, (2) the lines of insurance which the company wishes to write, and (3) the company's legal form. There is little similarity among net worth requirements set by the various states. For example, a stock fire insurance company needs $900,000 of capital and

Illustration 5-7
New Company Balance Sheet

Assets		Liabilities and Net Worth	
		Capital Paid Up	$1,000,000
Cash	$1,500,000	Surplus Paid In	500,000
		Total Liabilities	
Total Assets	$1,500,000	and Net worth	$1,500,000

surplus to meet the initial requirements in Illinois but only $150,000 if it is organized in Pennsylvania.[8] If the company intends to transact inland marine insurance as well as fire insurance, Pennsylvania mandates that initial capital and surplus be increased to $300,000. On the other hand, if the insurer restricts its activities to fire insurance but it is organized as an assessment mutual in Pennsylvania, it must have an initial surplus of only $50,000. The property-liability insurance business consists predominantly of stock and mutual companies writing multiple lines of insurance, but other organizational forms (reciprocals and Lloyds associations) and other operating methods (monoline) do exist. The diverse initial net worth requirements among state laws sometimes are justified by this pluralism within the insurance marketplace.

A stock insurance company acquires its initial capitalization from the sale of the corporation's common stock to investors. Organizers of the corporation, most of whom become active in its management, usually set a price for its shares above the stock's par or stated value. Amounts paid in excess of par value establish the corporation's initial surplus.[9] For example, suppose the new company must have at least $1 million capital and $500,000 surplus in order to be licensed in its state of domicile. Ignoring costs incurred in marketing stock, the incorporators can arrange the necessary financing by selling 100,000 shares of common stock with a $10 par value per share at an issue price of $15 per share. After the stock is issued, the insurer's beginning balance sheet would appear as in Illustration 5-7.

Mutual and reciprocal insurers do not have capital stock. They obtain their original financing from or through organizers whose entire contribution becomes paid-in surplus. The company frequently pays interest on this initial contribution, which is referred to as guarantee capital, and it may repay the organizers' initial contribution out of earnings during subsequent years. Repayments can be made *only* out of earnings and generally require approval by regulatory authorities.

Some states allow the licensing of mutual and reciprocal insurers with lower paid-in surplus than the total capital and surplus required of a stock insurer. This seemingly illogical practice is explained in several ways. First, nonstock insurers that have only minimum surplus possess a limited power to assess their policyholders. Second, it is argued that application of higher initial net worth standards would effectively prohibit organizing an insurer as a mutual or reciprocal. Third, at least some nonstock insurers are truly cooperative ventures established to provide insurance at cost to a previously existing trade association or other well-defined sponsor. Because such "noncommercial" insurers usually do not incur the large start-up costs that commercial insurers must bear, a smaller initial capitalization may be justified.[10] Regardless of the merit, if any, in these assertions, a need for sufficient net worth applies equally to all insurance companies.

The amount of initial capital and surplus invested in new insurance organizations varies greatly among companies and from year to year. Although recent comparable data are not readily available, 339 new stock property-liability insurers from 1973 through 1982 began operations with an average capitalization of $2.77 million. Actual investments by individual insurers, however, vary widely. Illustration 5-8 shows new companies formed for the ten-year period from 1979 to 1988. During that period 517 new companies were formed and 280 were retired, resulting in net company additions of 237. On average, 52 companies were formed per year while 28 were retired, resulting in 24 additional companies per year over that ten year period.

Continuing Functions.   Capital and surplus in a stock insurance company serve distinctly separate functions. If the company fails, capital acts as a guarantee fund to protect policyholders from loss. Minimum capital therefore must be maintained at all times. Impairment renders the company technically insolvent even though admitted assets may substantially exceed liabilities. Paid-in surplus does not remain as cash after the company is formed. It provides funds for investment and to pay for organizational fees, development expenses, establishment of an agency force, and to meet loss settlement fluctuations. Substantial decreases in surplus may occur before the new company "turns the corner" and begins to replenish surplus from operating income. The company presumably may continue operations unless and until it exhausts its final dollar of surplus. For instance, a stock fire insurance company that has minimum initial capital of $100,000 and surplus of $50,000 can reduce its net worth to $100,000 without becoming technically insolvent.

Like stock companies, mutuals and reciprocals also are allowed to invade initial surplus. However, since surplus for these insurers must

Illustration 5-8
New Property–Liability Insurance Organizations

Year	New Companies Formed	Retired Companies[†]	Net Company Additions
1979	51	22	29
1980	50	16	34
1981	26	10	16
1982	38	9	29
1983	47	27	20
1984	72	43	29
1985	58	46	12
1986	37	37	0
1987	66	28	38
1988	72	41	30
1979 to 1988	517	280	237

[†]For a more detailed breakdown of retired companies by voluntary retirements, mergers, and involuntary retirements, see Illustration 5-11.

Derived from data in *Best's Review*, Property-Causalty, vol. 89, no. 11, March 1989, p. 32.

function as both a guarantee fund and as a source of working capital, surplus cannot be depleted below a prescribed level. This minimum surplus typically is the same as the smallest amount of capital allowed for a comparable stock insurance company. The insurance code of Pennsylvania, for instance, requires a mutual insurer writing nonassessable policies to maintain unimpaired surplus equal to the minimum required capital of a stock company authorized to transact the same class or classes of business. An assessment mutual must maintain unimpaired surplus of at least 50 percent of its initially required surplus.[11]

Capital and Surplus Expansion

The legal minimum capital and surplus levels required for new insurance companies also apply to seasoned insurers even though the premium volume, operating complexity, and management competency have increased and improved since operations began. Company management and state insurance regulating authorities nevertheless expect net worth to grow as the company becomes larger. The relationship of premiums written to policyholders' surplus is used as a guide for

Illustration 5-9
Premiums–to–Surplus Ratio

Ratio of Net Premiums Written to Policyholders' Surplus			
Company	1988	1986	1984
Aetna Casualty & Surety Co.	2.1	2.0	2.5
Ohio Indemnity Company	0.9	1.3	1.4
St. Paul Fire and Marine	1.8	2.6	2.8
The Travelers Indemnity Company	1.9	2.2	2.3
United Fire & Casualty Company	1.4	1.8	3.1
United States Fidelity & Guaranty	2.5	2.9	3.5
All insurers	1.71	1.88	1.86

judging whether capital and surplus are adequate in an expanding company. Illustration 5-9 demonstrates that the relationship is, at best, a sliding scale.[12] Even larger premiums written-to-policyholders' surplus ratios than those exhibited by these companies have been shown by smaller insurers experiencing enlarged sales after suffering surplus losses due to cyclical earnings patterns. During periods of rapid sales expansion or when a company wishes to increase its market share, existing surplus may prove insufficient to support the desired growth. When this occurs, the insurer may need to alter its financial structure by increasing its equity base. This can be accomplished in several ways.

Traditionally, property-liability insurers have relied on internally generated profits for growth. However, retained earnings may be inadequate to sustain rapid upturns in premium volume caused by property value increases, higher liability coverages, and upward adjustments in premium rates. When internally generated funds are insufficient, the company must seek infusions of capital from existing owners or from the capital markets. A new issue of common stock is the most straightforward way to raise external equity capital, but its cost may be relatively high when compared to other alternatives and the potential for earnings and ownership dilution may displease existing stockholders. Many other financial instruments, commonly used by noninsurance companies, also may be employed by insurers. Preferred stock, debentures, and other fixed income instruments may be issued directly by an insurer and the resulting funds can be included in policyholders' surplus accompanied by a footnote explanation. Alternatively, a holding company parent of an insurer can issue bonds or other senior instruments and funnel the proceeds to the insurer by purchasing more of its common stock.[13] Recent tax code changes have encouraged rapid expansion of premium volume by property-liability insurance company subsidiaries that can operate at a tax loss and provide their industrial company parent with a tax shelter. Therefore, the public financial markets may be more receptive to the idea of providing capital to an insurer that is posting significant underwriting losses on rapid sales gains if the securities are issued by a noninsurance holding company and funds are passed through to the insurer. The exact arrangements used by a particular company depend on many factors, but it can be assumed that management attempts to minimize the corporation's weighted average cost of capital while simultaneously providing the capital infusion necessary for desired growth. The ability of the parent corporation to supply funds to a subsidiary insurance company should not be confused with the legal obligation to do so. The parent is not required to rescue a subsidiary in danger of financial collapse, although this outcome often occurs.

METHODS OF MAINTAINING SOLVENCY

State legislatures and insurance regulators attempt to assure solvency of insurance companies by several methods. These methods include, in addition to capital and surplus requirements, rate regulation, investment regulation, statutory accounting rules, financial reporting requirements, periodic examinations of insurance companies, and application of diagnostic tests to company financial data. Solvency surveillance through field examinations and the NAIC regulatory tests are described in this section.

Insurance Department Examinations

Insurance statutes of the various states require or permit the state's insurance commissioner to conduct periodic field examinations into the financial affairs and market conduct of all insurance companies authorized to do business in the state. The commissioner usually is required to examine all domestic insurers at least once every three to five years and may initiate an examination whenever it is deemed expedient. Authorized foreign and alien insurers also are examined periodically in conformance with the NAIC zone examinations described later in this section.

Purpose of Examinations. State insurance department financial examinations serve several purposes. First, the examination strives to identify as early as possible those insurers experiencing financial trouble or engaging in unlawful and improper activities. Second, the examination seeks to develop information needed for appropriate regulatory action.[14] Examinations also confirm that the subject companies are operating and reporting in accordance with the uniform accounting instructions promulgated by the NAIC for use in completing the Annual Statement. The tangible product of an examination is the report on examination prepared by insurance department examiners. Some states, notably New York, require that the report on examination or a summary thereof be read at the first meeting of the insurer's board of directors following receipt of the report. A copy of the report on examination also must be furnished to each member of the board of directors. This requirement is intended to notify board members, including outside directors, of the company's activities and financial condition. The examination therefore may be helpful to the company as well as serving its regulatory purpose. Company directors and regulators can use the examination to safeguard the interests of policyholders and stockholders.

Examination Procedures. State insurance department examiners are employees of the regulatory agency and typically are included in the state's civil service program. Some states employ only a few examiners, but in the major insurance jurisdictions over 100 examiners may be included in the department's staff. It has been estimated that over one-fourth of all insurance department personnel are examiners.[15]

Although they are state employees, or employees of private auditing firms, examiners conduct most of their work in insurance company home and branch offices. The subject insurer furnishes facilities and supplies for the on-site examination. In most states, all expenses associated with the examination are paid by the insurer. The manner in which an examiner receives his or her salary varies among the states, but the state usually bills the company examined for charges associated with the examination. These charges include the examiner's salary plus a "loading factor" to cover employee benefit costs and insurance department overhead.

An insurance company scheduled for examination often is requested to furnish selected information in advance of the examiners' visit. This information may include working papers from internal audits, reports from the company's independent public accountants, or other management information. Review of this material prior to company visitation allows the examination to focus on potential problem areas and thus reduces the time and cost involved. Examinations of large property-liability insurers may last as long as one year. Thus large insurers domiciled in states that require triennial examinations have examiners on their premises about one-third of the time. Close cooperation between insurance company employees and the examiners is essential to expedite the progress of the examination and hold down the cost.

NAIC Zone Examinations. To prevent duplication of examinations by the numerous insurance departments, the NAIC has divided the fifty-four separate regulatory jurisdictions into four zones. Jurisdictions assigned to each zone are shown in Illustration 5-10. One insurance commissioner in each zone is designated as the zone chairman. For all companies licensed in more than one zone or in more than three states in a single zone, the NAIC recommends an "Association" type of examination. This phrase means that the examination follows the uniform procedures and reporting requirements outlined by the *NAIC Financial Condition Examiners' Handbook*. Such examinations apply to nearly all insurance companies.

Whether a particular company is examined by one state or more than one state depends upon the geographical scope of its operations and the volume of business done in each jurisdiction. If an insurer has annual direct premiums written of $1 million or more in a zone or if at least 20 percent of its writing, regardless of dollar amount, are in a zone, a representative from that zone is invited to participate in the examination. The insurance department of the company's state of domicile notifies the NAIC secretary when it proposes to examine a company. The NAIC secretary checks the premium volume shown in the company's most recent Annual Statement and notifies the chairman of each zone eligible for participation. The zone chairman designates one of the states within the zone to appoint an examiner as the zone representative on the examination team. If all states within the zone waive participation, the zone waives participation and is not represented. The examination team is headed by an examiner-in-charge from the domiciliary state and assisted by his own staff and examiners representing each participating zone. The examiner-in-charge is responsible for outlining the examination program following the provisions of the *Examiners' Handbook*. Zone representatives may request investigation into specific areas of special interest to their state or members of their zone. Results are included in the report on examination.

The report on examination is prepared before the close of the examination and presented to the insurance company's officers for review and discussion. It contains summary financial statements from the most current Annual Statement along with an analysis of any specific changes resulting from the examination. Also included are a discussion of adverse findings, material changes in the financial statements, and other important regulatory information disclosed by the examination. In its current form, content of the report is predominantly critical in nature.

Illustration 5-10
NAIC Examination Zones

	Population (1988) (in 000s)	Examiners† (1988)	Total Ins. Dept. Staff	Property-Liability Companies Domiciled (1988)	Percentage of Property-Liability Direct Written Premiums (1988)
Northeastern = Zone I					
Connecticut	3,235	18	77	63	2.1
Delaware	649	33	41	90	0.3
District of Columbia	617	6	46	13	0.3
Maine	1,193	19	61	10	0.5
Maryland	4,599	36	160	43	2.0
Massachusetts	5,849	43	159	55	3.5
New Hampshire	1,088	19	43	29	0.6
New Jersey	7,756	51	420	65	3.6
New York	17,755	242	790	200	8.5
Pennsylvania	11,860	45	253	199	5.2
Rhode Island	989	14	40	22	0.5
Vermont	552	10	32	13	0.2
Virgin Islands	106	—	—	—	0.0
TOTAL	56,248	536	2,122	802	27.3
Southeastern = Zone II					
Alabama	4,119	14	56	30	1.3
Arkansas	2,400	12	68	13	0.8
Florida	12,249	110	714	93	5.1
Georgia	6,384	1	56	46	2.6
Kentucky	3,738	21	86	39	1.1
Louisiana	4,507	26	132	53	1.5
Mississippi	2,661	6	55	16	0.8
North Carolina	6,512	46	342	37	2.0
Puerto Rico	3,292	16	79	26	0.2
South Carolina	3,464	18	114	32	1.1
Tennessee	4,891	13	87	18	1.6
Virginia	5,977	43	148	19	2.1
West Virginia	1,886	6	50	18	0.5
TOTAL	62,080	332	1,987	440	20.8

Midwestern = Zone III				
Illinois	11,584	80	295	293	4.8
Indiana	5,531	26	92	121	1.8
Iowa	2,803	35	89	61	0.9
Kansas	2,477	13	149	33	0.9
Michigan	9,231	40	135	57	3.7
Minnesota	4,271	10	78	59	1.8
Missouri	5,132	53	132	80	1.9
Nebraska	1,593	15	61	49	0.5
North Dakota	669	4	26	13	0.2
Ohio	10,779	51	152	102	3.3
Oklahoma	3,288	23	98	52	1.0
South Dakota	707	8	22	52	0.2
Wisconsin	4,797	39	112	93	1.7
TOTAL	62,862	397	1,441	1,065	22.7

Western = Zone IV				
Alaska	554	12	25	12	0.3
American Samoa	38	0	2	4	0.0
Arizona	3,542	43	69	52	1.3
California	28,074	92	516	158	14.8
Colorado	3,350	21	70	23	1.2
Guam	130	4	4	4	0.0
Hawaii	1,101	7	35	14	0.5
Idaho	1,009	14	48	10	0.3
Montana	811	8	25	3	0.3
Nevada	1,021	21	39	8	0.4
New Mexico	1,557	1	59	12	0.5
Oregon	2,733	17	79	15	1.0
Texas	17,192	104	1,178	288	6.6
Utah	1,722	13	46	12	0.4
Washington	4,564	20	111	25	1.5
Wyoming	505	6	23	5	0.1
TOTAL	67,903	383	2,329	645	29.2

†Includes financial analysts, financial examiners, and market conduct examiners employed the insurance departments or supplied by other agencies.

Based on data from NAIC Proceedings, 1989, Statistical Abstract of the United States, and 1988 NAIC Insurance Department Survey

Critique of the Examination System. In recent years insurance regulators have reevaluated the procedures followed and purposes served by field examinations of insurance companies and the resulting report. The degree of overlap with examinations performed by inside auditors, independent public accountants, other state agencies, and the Internal Revenue Service has been recognized and attempts made to use these other examinations to help focus the attention of the financial condition examination. It has been suggested that every insurer required to complete an Annual Statement should be required to submit such statement to audit by an independent public accountant satisfactory to the commissioner of insurance.[16] Several states, such as Illinois and Massachusetts, have adopted rules requiring certain insurers to file annual audit reports prepared by independent certified public accountants. This practice permits the insurance departments to spend less time on financial verification and to target examination efforts on aspects of company operations that have the greatest impact on policyholders' surplus. The format of the report on examination has been changed to discourage ritualistic duplication of previous years' reports and to encourage disclosure of current company difficulties or unlawful and improper activities. Increased reliance on independent audits of insurance company financial statements represents a restructuring of regulatory procedures. Company examinations remain one of the most important phases of insurance supervision and solvency maintenance.

NAIC Regulatory Tests

In 1971, the NAIC developed a set of financial relationships or "tests" to provide diagnostic tools for the evaluation of insurance company strength. The tests were based on research conducted by several state insurance departments, especially in the California, Illinois, and Michigan departments. Initially, more than two dozen diagnostic tests were suggested, but this number was reduced during subsequent years because of disagreements over the significance of some relationships and because of insufficient staffing within many insurance regulatory departments. During the first few years of the tests' development and use they were called "solidity" or "solvency" tests and collectively known as the Early Warning System. However, because a direct measure of solvency was not provided by the diagnostic tools, a more general terminology has evolved. Since 1975 the two sets of separate but similar tests designed for property-liability insurance companies and life and health insurance companies have been called regulatory tests. A description of the tests, called IRIS, applied to nonlife insurers is presented in this section. It is based on the NAIC publication, "NAIC Insurance Regulatory Information System, Property-Liability Ratio Results 1988."

Purposes of the Tests. The primary purpose of the IRIS tests is early identification of companies which may require close surveillance by insurance regulatory authorities. The tests signal the need for more thorough inquiry into the company's status and operations. They also may be helpful in suggesting what specific areas are in need of most immediate attention. Scheduling priorities for special on-site examinations can be based on the tests' results.

The regulatory tests are not a substitute for a field examination or a timely audit of the Annual Statement. They only supplement traditional forms of financial surveillance. The NAIC admonishes its members not to use results of the IRIS tests as the sole basis for key decisions—such as issuing or renewing a company's certificate of authority to conduct insurance operations within the state. In addition, it is recommended that test results be interpreted by knowledgeable and experienced examiners who have familiarized themselves with the company's Annual Statements. Despite these admonitions, 70 percent of the state insurance departments responding to a survey said the tests are used to determine whether companies should be granted authority to write insurance.[17]

Critics of the present solvency surveillance system have pointed out that use of the regulatory tests implies a failure on the part of state insurance departments to perform their traditional financial surveillance functions properly. The regulatory tests are simply manipulations of data readily available in the Annual Statements filed with each state. The tests do not furnish additional raw data; nor do they change the regulator's ability to exercise administrative powers. Therefore, this approach to improving financial surveillance is criticized as an added layer of regulation on a solvency maintenance system that is fundamentally deficient. Nevertheless, because the regulatory tests furnish a quick indication of the companies in need of more detailed examination, they have become the backbone of the NAIC information system. They also are helpful in directing the attention of examiners to specific areas of inquiry.

Mechanics of the System. Each insurance company is requested or required to file its Annual Statement with the NAIC Support and Services Office to process the financial data and perform the regulatory tests. Exemptions from the filing requirement are granted to some insurers with geographically limited operations (single state companies, county mutuals, and so on). The filing company pays the NAIC a fee to cover costs of the IRIS program. In 1989, the fee ranged from $225 to

$2,313 per company, depending on premium volume. Reinsurers with zero direct written premiums were required to pay the minimum fee of $225. Results are reported to the insurance departments of each state in which the company operates.

Establishing criteria for test values is the heart of this system. The ability of the regulatory tests to discriminate between companies that can receive normal supervision and those that require immediate careful scrutiny rests on the definition of normal and exceptional values. An unsatisfactory test result *(exceptional value)* occurs whenever the value calculated for a particular company's data falls outside the "usual range" for that statistic. The usual range is defined in such a way as to include results expected from the majority of companies during a normal year. Because standards are set relative to operating results of all insurers under normal conditions, greater numbers of companies are expected to fall outside the usual range in years marked by aberrant economic forces. Each insurer with four or more test results outside the usual range is classified as a priority company. For companies with some statistics outside the usual range but less than four exceptional values, the tests identify specific areas that should be investigated further during the normal examination process.

Since 1978, IRIS has consisted of two phases. In the initial or "statistical" phase, financial ratios and related data are developed for all companies and groups in the system. Results of the statistical phase are fed into the second or "analytical" phase for review by experienced financial examiners. All companies that receive four or more test scores outside the usual range of values, and all companies that required immediate regulatory attention in the previous year, are scrutinized. Based on analysis of the IRIS test results and other information, some companies are designated as requiring immediate regulatory attention or targeted attention. Commentaries explaining the need for priority surveillance are prepared by the examiners and distributed to the state insurance department in the company's domiciliary state. A copy of the examiner team's commentary is sent to the subject company at the same time it is sent to the state of domicile. It is sent to all remaining state insurance departments at least two weeks later. If companies with four or more test results outside the usual range are not identified as requiring immediate or targeted regulatory attention in the analytical phase of IRIS, the commentaries explain the examiners' reasoning.

Nature and Interpretation of the Tests. The 1988 IRIS tests for property-liability insurers include eleven financial tests classified into four groups:

1. Overall Tests
   - Premium-to-surplus ratio
   - Change in writings
   - Surplus aid-to-surplus ratio
2. Profitability Tests
   - Two-year overall operating ratio
   - Investment yield
   - Change in surplus
3. Liquidity Tests
   - Liabilities-to-liquid assets ratio
   - Agents' balances-to-surplus ratio
4. Reserve Tests
   - One-year reserve development-to-surplus ratio
   - Two-year reserve development-to-surplus ratio
   - Estimated current reserve deficiency-to-surplus ratio

The calculation of each test is described below and the exceptional value criterion given. Illustration 5-11 summarizes results of the NAIC IRIS tests applied to property-liability insurers for the years 1988 and 1987.

Overall Tests. There are three overall tests.

Premium to Surplus. The ratio of premium to surplus is considered a gauge of the company's insurance exposure; that is, as more insurance is written, surplus is exposed to greater chance of variations. This ratio shows the relationship between written premiums and unadjusted statutory net worth. A calculated value greater than 3 to 1 is considered unfavorable; that is, in order for an insurer's premiums-to-surplus ratio to be acceptable, the calculated value should be less than or equal to ($\leq$) 300 percent:

$$\frac{\text{Net Premium Written}}{\text{Policyholders' Surplus}} \times 100\% \leq 300\%$$

For this test, if policyholders' surplus is zero or negative, a value of 999 is assigned to the ratio. If policyholders' surplus is positive but net premiums written are negative, a value of zero is assigned. Negative net premiums written could result for an insurance company that cedes more business than it writes either directly or as a reinsurer. Using these rules for calculating test values, all test scores fall within the range of zero to 999.

As this ratio's value approaches the 3 to 1 bench mark, regulators become interested in any mitigating relationships. For example, a high test value for this ratio may be interpreted less severely in the presence of the following:

Illustration 5-11

NAIC Consolidated Property–Liability IRIS Ratios for 1988 and 1987

IRIS Ratio		1988 (208 Groups)		1987 (211 Groups)	
		Simple Mean	Median	Simple Mean	Median
OVERALL TESTS					
1. Premium to Surplus	(A)	19?.4	184	200.3	204
	(E)	182.4	184	196.5	204
2. Change in Writings	(A)	14.3	4	58.6	8
	(E)	5.3	4	6.9	6
3. Surplus Aid to	(A)	3.8	1	8.2	1
Surplus	(E)	3.8	1	3.5	1
PROFITABILITY TESTS					
4.Two-Year Overall	(A)	90.9	90	97.3	92
Operating Ratio	(E)	90.9	90	97.3	92
5. Investment Yield	(A)	7.6	7.3	7.5	7.2
	(E)	7.6	7.3	7.5	7.2
6. Change in Surplus	(A)	22.6	12	50.0	11
	(E)	13.1	12	13.1	10
LIQUIDITY TESTS					
7. Liabilities to	(A)	84.1	84	86.1	85
Liquid Assets	(E)	84.1	84	86.1	85
8. Agents' Balances	(A)	18.9	16	21.5	18
to Surplus	(E)	18.9	16	21.5	18
RESERVE TESTS					
9. One-Year Reserve	(A)	7.2	0	32.4	4
Development to Surplus	(E)	2.4	0	9.0	4
10. Two-Year Reserve	(A)	22.4	5	71.6	15
Development to Surplus	(E)	13.4	4	25.4	12
11. Estimated Current	(A)	−9.6	−7	11.5	0
Reserve Deficiency to Surplus	(E)	−6.5	−7	10.5	0

(A) All company ratio results included in statistical calculations.
(E) −99 and 999 ratio values are excluded from statistical calculations.

Based on data from NAIC Insurance Regulatory Information System Ratio Results for 1988 and 1987.

1. A lower premium to surplus ratio for the group of affiliated insurance companies
2. Steadily increasing profits
3. A low concentration of business in liability lines of insurance
4. Adequate excess reinsurance
5. A conservative and properly valued investment portfolio
6. An adjustment for available surplus aid reinsurance (see discussion below)

The adequacy of surplus to absorb unexpected underwriting losses is evaluated more correctly by recognizing the interaction of these variables with the relationship between premiums and surplus. Illustration 5-11 shows the premium to surplus ratio *has a simple mean of* 182.4 for 1988 and 200.3 for 1987.

Change in Writings. This ratio measures the rate of change in written premium between the current year and the preceding year. The formula is:

$$\frac{\substack{\text{Net premium written,} \\ \text{current year}} - \substack{\text{Net premium written,} \\ \text{prior year}}}{\substack{\text{Net premium written,} \\ \text{prior year}}} \times 100\% \leq \pm 33\%$$

Fluctuations in written premium of more than ± 33 percent signal a need for closer examination of the causes. These causes may include expansion of operations on profitable lines, addition of new lines, new geographical areas, economic upturn, or additions to the agency force, but it might also include expansion of written premium by a lowering of underwriting standards in order to increase cash flow to an insurer that is in financial difficulty. Downward fluctuations greater than −33 percent likewise may reveal an insurer having financial difficulties and reducing operations sharply.

Illustration 5-11 shows the change in writings ratio has a simple mean of 14.3 for 1988 and 58.6 for 1987. The median ratio for change in writings, however, was 4 for 1988 and 8 for 1987. A relatively high frequency of abnormal results for this ratio indicates that other related financial ratios should be analyzed. A relatively low premium to surplus ratio (ratio 1), profitable operations (ratio 4), adequate reserves (ratios 9, 10, and 11), and a fairly stable product mix, generally permit an insurer to operate safely even with an exceptional change in writings.

Surplus Aid to Surplus. Many types of reinsurance treaties provide surplus aid by allowing the primary insurer to transfer all or a portion of its unearned premium reserve requirement to the reinsurance company. In order for this type of surplus aid to be available, the reinsurer must be legally licensed to transact reinsurance in the state under consideration; that is, it must be an *admitted* (authorized) reinsurance company. The reinsurer pays a commission to the ceding company to compensate it for acquisition expenses incurred. For purposes of this regulatory test, *surplus aid* is defined to consist of commissions on reinsurance ceded to nonaffiliated companies. Reinsurance transactions among affiliated companies are excluded so that the test will not be biased against members of fleets or groups participating in reinsurance pooling arrangements.

To form the test ratio, surplus aid is divided by policyholders' surplus and expressed on a percentage basis. Values below 25 percent are interpreted as acceptable:

$$\frac{\text{Surplus Aid}}{\text{Surplus}} \times 100\% < 25\%$$

Surplus aid is not specifically reported in the Annual Statement. Therefore, the numerator of this ratio must be estimated from available data. The following procedure is used:

$$\text{Surplus Aid} =$$

$$\left(\begin{array}{c}\text{Estimated Reinsurance} \\ \text{Commission Rate}\end{array}\right) \times \left(\begin{array}{c}\text{Unearned Premiums on} \\ \text{Reinsurance Ceded to Nonaffiliated}\end{array}\right)$$

The surplus aid-to-surplus ratio is an especially important regulatory test. Exceptionally large amounts of surplus aid are interpreted as an indication that the company's capitalization is not sufficient for the amount of direct insurance being written. The existence of significant surplus aid in the presence of inadequate surplus can distort results determined for some of the other regulatory tests. Consequently, several of the tests that include surplus in the calculation are recomputed with surplus adjusted to remove surplus aid whenever an exceptional value is determined for this ratio. The surplus-aid-to-surplus ratio shown in Illustration 5-11 indicates that the simple mean was 3.8 for the year 1988 and 8.2 for 1987.

Profitability Tests. There are three NAIC profitability tests.

Two-Year Overall Operating Ratio. This regulatory test is similar to the operating profit ratio of noninsurance companies in that it combines results from continuing normal operations, both underwriting and investment. The test is a measure of the ratio of underwriting losses and expenses reduced by investment returns. A ratio of less than 100 percent indicates a profitable operation.

Rather than being based on a single year's data, the current and prior years are considered together to mitigate fluctuations caused by interperiod revenue and cost allocations. The test value is calculated by combining two ratios:

$$\text{Two Year Overall Operating Ratio} = \left[\begin{array}{c}\text{Combined Ratio (trade basis)}\\ -\text{Investment Income Ratio}\end{array}\right] \times 100\% < 100\%$$

The definition of the trade basis combined ratio was given earlier. The investment income ratio is developed for this test and is determined by dividing interest, dividend, and real estate income net of expenses by *net premiums earned*. Subtracting the investment income ratio from the trade basis combined ratio and setting the critical value at 100 percent allows companies to allocate all of their investment income to support underwriting operations before recording an abnormal test result.

Setting the critical value at 100 percent does not imply that insurance companies are expected to operate over long periods of time without underwriting profit. The regulatory tests are not designed to suggest or impose long-term operating objectives but rather to signal acute disorders that require immediate correction. In the absence of capital gains (which are not recognized in this ratio), exceptional values for this test indicate that surplus is being depleted by continuing operations. Analysis of the test ratio's three components, loss ratio, expense ratio, and investment income ratio, assists in identifying where corrective measures are most appropriate—loss control, expense control, investment earnings, or some combinations of these elements.

Because under- or over-reserving can distort operating results, the company's true underwriting position is not fully described by the two-year overall operating ratio. Values determined for this test should be related to the reserve development tests discussed later in this section. Exceptional values for the reserve development tests recommend a recalculation of this test after adjustment of the prior year's reserve development. Illustration 5-11 shows the simple mean of the Two-Year Overall Operating Ratio to be 90.9 in 1988 and 97.3 in 1987.

Investment Yield. Investment earnings reflect the profitability and general quality of the company's investment portfolio. The investment yield ratio expresses net investment income as a percentage of the average amount of investment during the year. Calculated investment yields greater than 6.0 percent are considered to be within the usual range.

$$\text{Investment Yield} = \frac{\text{Net Investment Income}}{\text{Average Invested Assets}} \times 100\% > 6.0\%$$

Net investment income includes interest, dividends, and real estate income, but not capital gains or losses whether realized or unrealized. The ratio's numerator therefore can be taken directly from the Annual Statement. On the other hand, the denominator must be calculated from Annual Statement data for the current and prior years. Invested assets are defined to be cash and other invested assets listed on the first eight lines of the statutory balance sheet plus accrued investment income minus borrowed money. The ratio's denominator is computed by adding invested assets at the end of the prior year to invested assets at the end of the current, year, subtracting investment income for the current year, and dividing the net sum by two.

An investment yield of less than 6 percent may be symptomatic of serious problems in investment operations. For instance, unduly optimistic reliance on capital gains from speculative investments may be sacrificing current yield for potential appreciation. Low yields may be associated with investments made in securities of affiliated corporations or business ventures controlled by the insurance company's managers or owners. Imprudently large investments in home office facilities or other real estate may cause low current investment return and sacrifice liquidity as well. The types of invested assets owned by the insurance company can be determined from the Annual Statement. A study of the yield characteristics of each investment category pinpoints unfavorable holdings and helps shape a corrective strategy. Illustration 5-11 shows a simple mean of 7.6 in 1988 and 7.5 for 1987 for the investment yield.

Change in Surplus. This test provides an overall measure of how much better or worse off the company is at the end of the current accounting period compared to the previous year-end. The general form of the test and the usual range of test values are:

$$\frac{\text{Change in}}{\text{Surplus Ratio}} = \frac{\text{Change in Adjusted Surplus}}{\text{Adjusted Surplus Prior Year}} \times 100\% > -10\% < 50\%$$

The test is misnamed. Rather than being a ratio of the change in policyholders' surplus as listed in the Annual Statement, the test actually is based on *adjusted* surplus. An adjustment is made in the current and prior years' surplus for acquisition expenses. Although this adds some small degree of complexity to the calculation, it greatly increases the test's ability to discriminate between strong and weak companies.

Statutory surplus is adjusted for acquisition expenses subject to deferral under GAAP. Expenses included in the adjustment are agent's commissions, taxes, licenses and fees, and other underwriting costs associated with policy issue. The amount of expense adjustment is determined as:

$$\text{Expense Adjustment} =$$

$$\left(\frac{\text{Unearned Premium}}{\text{Reserve}}\right) \times \left(\frac{\text{Acquisition Expenses}}{\text{Net Premiums Written}}\right)$$

Policyholders' surplus plus the expense adjustment for the prior year is subtracted from policyholders' surplus plus the expense adjustment for the current year. This difference equals the change in adjusted surplus that appears in the test ratio's numerator:

$$\begin{matrix} \text{Changes in} \\ \text{Adjusted Surplus} \end{matrix} = \left(\begin{matrix} \text{Current Year's} \\ \text{Surplus} \\ + \\ \text{Expense Adjustment} \end{matrix} \right) - \left(\begin{matrix} \text{Prior Year's} \\ \text{Surplus} \\ + \\ \text{Expense Adjustment} \end{matrix} \right)$$

An increase in adjusted surplus greater than 50 percent would be very unusual for a company in sound financial condition. Although a growth in adjusted surplus of this magnitude may be possible for relatively small insurers, such a spectacular increase is interpreted as a sign of instability that may foreshadow insolvency. Large surplus increases also may be associated with changes in company management, control, or ownership. Further investigation is warranted when this ratio shows an excessive addition to adjusted surplus.

If the calculated ratio shows a decrease in adjusted surplus of more than 10 percent, additional analysis of operation results is advised. Such declines in surplus most often are accompanied by poor underwriting or investment results. The two-year overall operating ratio and the investment yield test help identify the reason or reasons for surplus declines related to normal operations. Other factors, such as capital gains and losses, capital transactions, dividends to stockholders, changes in nonadmitted assets, changes in surplus aid from reinsurance, change in utilization of unauthorized reinsurance, and changes in adjustments for foreign exchange also may explain an extraordinary drop in surplus. Illustration 5-11 shows the simple mean for the change in surplus to be 22.6 for 1988 and 50.0 for 1987. If those property-liability groups with abnormal experience for the year are excluded, the change in surplus for 1988 is 13.1 and is also 13.1 for 1987.

Liquidity Tests. There are just two NAIC liquidity tests.

Liabilities to Liquid Assets. This test shows liabilities as a percentage of liquid assets and defines the acceptable relationship to be:

$$\frac{\text{Liabilities to}}{\text{Liquid Assets}} = \frac{\text{Stated Liabilities}}{\text{Liquid Assets}} \times 100\% < 105\%$$

The primary rationale behind this test is that a number of insurers that became insolvent experienced increasing liabilities-to-liquid assets ratios in years immediately prior to their ultimate demise. Therefore, test results should be observed over several years as well as compared to the exceptional value criterion.

Several aspects of the ratio make it only a rough approximation of the insurer's ability to meet its obligation in a timely fashion. A portion of what is defined to be included in liquid assets may be less than totally realized in the short-term. Liquid assets are defined for this test to include cash, invested assets, and accrued investment income minus investments in affiliated companies and excluding real estate investments in excess of 5 percent of liabilities. Because bonds are included in invested assets at amortized cost rather than at current market value, liquidity may be overstated.

Questions may also be raised concerning the time required to convert real estate to cash and whether the balance sheet values will be realized upon conversion. The liquidity ratio does not deal with portfolio composition. Consequently, an insurer conceivably could hold all its assets in cash and be judged less liquid than another company with a large bond portfolio that currently could not be liquidated at its full Annual Statement value. This possibility results in an overstatement of liquidity for companies with assets at admitted values higher than market values. On the other hand, companies that have large deposits with ceding reinsurers cannot include these funds in invested assets even though the related liability must be shown in the test ratio's numerator. This exclusion results in an understatement of liquidity for companies with substantial reinsurance commitments. In all cases, the accuracy of loss reserve estimates is directly related to the ratio's ability to assess liquidity correctly. Illustration 5-11 shows the simple mean for liabilities to liquid assets to be 84.1 for 1988 and 86.1 for 1987.

Agents' Balances to Surplus. A high ratio of agents' balances to policyholders' surplus often has been a harbinger of financial distress. Agents' balances frequently prove uncollectible in the event the company is liquidated. The ratio gives an indication of how dependent surplus is on assets of questionable liquidity.

Data for this test can be taken directly from the Annual Statement. The calculation involves dividing agents' balances in the course of collection by surplus. Values less than 40 percent are considered to be within the acceptable range.

$$\text{Ratio of Agents'} \atop \text{Balances to Surplus} = \frac{\text{Agents' Balances in Course of Collection}}{\text{Surplus}} \times 100\% < 40\%$$

Illustration 5-11 shows agents' balances to surplus of 18.9 in 1988 and 21.5 in 1987.

Reserve Tests. There are three NAIC reserve tests.

One-Year Reserve Development to Surplus. One of the best ways to examine a company's loss reserving practices is to compare the development of claims costs with the original liability for losses. As claims pass from an unpaid to paid status, the accuracy with which reserves were originally established can be gauged. The one-year reserve development-to-surplus ratio does this with the most recent data available.

Adequacy of reserves outstanding at the end of a year can be measured by comparing those reserves with the total payments made on them during the current year plus reserves still outstanding on them at the end of the current year. The difference represents one-year reserve development. For example, assume reserves of $10,000 established on December 31, 19X0. During 19X1 payments on those reserves totaling $6,000 are made. On December 31, 19X1 reserves of $5,000 still exist on the 19X0 losses. This means that on reserves of $10,000, $6,000 has been paid and $5,000 is still reserved—a total of $11,000 reserved and paid on an original estimate of $10,000—resulting in a reserve deficiency of $1,000 for the one-year period.

The test ratio is constructed by dividing reserve development by the prior year's surplus. The resulting percentage indicates the extent by which the previous year's surplus was under-or over-stated through inaccurate reserve estimation given the benefit of one year's retrospective vision. Test values of less than 25 percent are considered to fall within the acceptable range:

$$\text{One-Year Reserve Development to Surplus Ratio} = \frac{\text{One-Year Reserve Development}}{\text{Prior Year's Surplus}} \times 100\% < 25\%$$

Illustration 5-11 shows the single mean for one-year reserve development to surplus to be 7.2 in 1988 for property-liability insurance groups and 32.4 in 1987. If, however, those groups with abnormal experience are excluded, the single means are 2.4 and 9.0 for 1988 and 1987, respectively.

Two-Year Reserve Development to Surplus. To calculate the two-year reserve development, the loss reserves at December 31 of the second preceding year are compared with the total payments made on them during the prior year and the current year plus any reserve balance still outstanding on them at December 31 of the current year. In the earlier example, if additional payments of $3,000 on the 19X0 losses were paid in 19X2 and a reserve of $3,000 still exists on the 19X0 losses, the two-year reserve deficiency would be $2,000.

The extent to which prior reserve estimates missed the mark is shown relative to surplus at the end of the second prior year:

$$\begin{array}{c}\text{Two-Year Reserve} \\ \text{Development to Surplus} \\ \text{Ratio}\end{array} = \frac{\text{Two-Year Reserve Development}}{\text{Second Prior Year's Surplus}} \times 100\% < 25\%$$

The acceptable range for this ratio is the same as for the one-year reserve development test. Any significant positive score recommends additional examination of reserve adequacy.

One- and two-year reserve development tests can be used to determine whether intentional understatement of loss reserves has been used to exaggerate surplus. Trends in the two reserve development ratios can be observed and the scores can be compared to one another. Illustration 5-11 indicates that the median ratio for the two-year reserve development to surplus was 5 for 1988 and 15 for 1987.

Estimated Current Reserve Deficiency to Surplus. Reserve development tests analyze how reserves established in prior years compare to payments actually made for losses plus current estimates of the remaining obligations. Although reserve development deals with how accurately claims liabilities were estimated during prior years, it also can be used to estimate the current adequacy of loss reserves and the related effect on surplus. The final NAIC regulatory test expresses the current estimated reserve deficiency or redundancy as a percentage of the current year's surplus. The estimated current reserve deficiency-to-surplus ratio is derived from results obtained in the two reserve development tests and is more difficult to describe than previous tests. The basic relationship and critical value are:

$$\begin{array}{c}\text{Estimated Current Reserve} \\ \text{Deficiency-to-Surplus Ratio}\end{array} = \frac{\text{Estimated Reserve Deficiency}}{\text{Surplus}} \times 100\% < 25\%$$

The denominator of the ratio is taken directly from the current Annual Statement, but the numerator must be derived from Annual Statement data and the reserve development tests. A series of five sequential mathematical relationships generates the estimated reserve deficiency. Due to the technical nature of the calculations, they are not discussed here.

The IRIS reserve tests have proven to be important solvency monitoring and diagnostic tools. Aggregate reserve development data for all insurers included in the IRIS program generally show reserve inadequacies. Although the current IRIS tests are limited to reserve developments through one or two years, the final reserve run-off and settlement of losses for many liability lines of insurance require a longer time period. The ultimate inadequacy may be greater than the current estimate. Because there frequently has been a history of reserve inadequacy among financially troubled insurers, regulators have focused three of the eleven IRIS ratios on estimated loss reserve levels.

If the reserve development tests or the current estimated reserve deficiency indicates that surplus is significantly overstated, some of the regulatory tests described earlier should be recalculated using an adjusted surplus figure. For example, suppose an insurer's current Annual Statement reports surplus to be $1 million, but the reserve development tests show that the company regularly underestimates loss reserves by 25 percent of surplus. Furthermore, the estimated current reserve deficiency-to-surplus ratio is 30 percent of surplus. All the earlier tests that included reported surplus would be performed again using an adjusted reserve figure of $700,000. In addition, the two-year adjusted underwriting ratio would be recalculated after the prior year's reserve development has been deducted from losses incurred. An insurer that would not be classified as a priority company on the basis of its original test scores might well be reclassified as a problem company after adjusting surplus for reserve inadequacies.

INSURANCE GUARANTY MECHANISMS

Insurance guaranty associations designed to provide reparations to policyholders and third-party claimants of insolvent property-liability insurers have been established in all fifty states, the District of Columbia, and Puerto Rico.[18] These funds do not directly guarantee the solvency of insurance companies. Rather, the guaranty associations reimburse entities with a justifiable loss against an *insolvent* insurance company. The amount of reimbursement usually is subject to both a deductible and a maximum limit of liability. Not all insurers licensed in a particular jurisdiction have their obligations guaranteed by the association. Generally, the associations respond to insolvencies of insurers that write all direct lines of property and liability insurance but not to insolvencies involving insurance companies that write life and disability income insurance, annuities, fidelity and surety bonds, credit, mortgage guaranty, and ocean marine insurance. A handful of states have formed separate guaranty associations for life insurance companies. With a few notable exceptions, the state insurance guaranty associations were created in the early 1970s in an effort to forestall federal intervention in this area of state insurance regulation.

State Guaranty Laws

Prior to 1969, only three states had enacted insurance company guaranty laws—New York in 1947, New Jersey in 1952, and Maryland in 1965. Today all fifty states have such legislation. Many of the laws are patterned after the model legislation, but significant variations are found in the various statutes. For example, some states place the assessment limit at 1½ percent or 1 percent of premiums written or do not state a maximum percentage limit. While most guaranty laws obligate the association to return unused resources to contributing insurers, nine state laws do not provide for such a refund. New York's guaranty plan, the earliest in existence, continues on a pre-insolvency funded basis although subsequent plans were either established on a post-insolvency assessment basis or were converted from pre- to post-funding. Coverage limits also vary among the separate associations. A deductible of $100 per claim is applied in the majority of states; but at least one state has a $50 deductible, another state imposes a $200 deductible, and ten plans do not involve deductible provisions. The single most common maximum coverage limit per claim is $300,000. Lower limits exist in some states, and at least one state, California, places a ceiling per claim at $500,000 (except for workers compensation claims, which are paid in full). In some states, notably New York, premiums collected but not earned at the time the insurer becomes insolvent do not become an obligation of guaranty fund.

Guaranty funds, sometimes known as insolvency funds (in Massachusetts and Rhode Island) are created by statute as nonprofit, quasi-governmental agencies. Members of their boards of directors are usually selected from representatives of the insurance industry. In addition to differences in the guaranty laws themselves, there are variations in related state statutes that affect how the plans operate. A few states have enacted so-called *early access* and *advanced priority* measures. Early access allows the guaranty association to gain immediate control of a delinquent insurance company's assets thereby protecting policyholders and others from the transfer of valuable resources to outside interests. By allowing the guaranty association quick access, the defunct company's assets can be used for the purpose intended—settlement of claims against the insurer. Advanced priority gives the plan a higher claim on an insolvent insurer's assets in liquidation than it would otherwise possess in the status of a general creditor. This priority should increase the likelihood that the association can return unused resources to contributing member companies after an insolvency case is settled.

Another operating characteristic that varies among the state plans arises from a basic public policy decision concerning who should bear the cost of insurance company insolvencies. Several states have enacted laws that grant insurers an offset against premium taxes for assessments paid to the guaranty fund. Premium tax offset provisions are justified on the basis that the guaranty of insurance obligations benefits members of the general public as well as policyholders. Therefore, it is reasoned, public funds are the proper source of reparation payments. Moreover, the tax offset arrangements might promote prevention of delinquencies because public funds are at stake. In effect, a state that allows a licensed insurance company to operate while in a hazardous financial condition is penalized through the loss of tax revenues if an insolvency results. Guaranty associations in states that grant tax offsets are not purely private sector mechanisms but are quasi-public solutions to the problems of insurance company insolvencies.

In most states, guaranty associations cover only specified lines of direct business (not reinsurance) and generally coverage is not extended to insurance written on an excess or surplus lines basis. At least one state, Illinois, has enacted a statute that attempts to minimize losses resulting from an insolvency by requiring insurers to maintain "policyholder security accounts." The law (Section 155.09 Illinois Insurance Code) seeks to prevent undue investment in assets which may prove of little value if forced liquidation becomes necessary. Essentially this requirement compels companies to cover their policy-holder liabilities—unearned premium, loss, and loss adjustment expense reserves—with investments in marketable securities. A segregation of insurance company assets into policyholder security or custodial accounts has been suggested several times as an amendment to the guaranty association model bill but, as yet, has not been adopted by the NAIC.

The state solvency guaranty laws form a patchwork of legislation that overall has produced a checkered record of operational effectiveness. Generally favorable results are reported for promptness and adequacy of claims settlement. It is estimated that between 60 and 70 percent of all claims against delinquent companies are discharged within nine months after the insurer has become insolvent. Consumers have received payments from the association that are approximately equal to their full economic loss whereas, prior to creation of these guaranty plans, reimbursements were ten to twenty cents on the dollar.[19] In terms of administrative efficiency, the overall record appears favorable. When an insolvency occurs, a member insurance company typically acts as the servicing agent for the guaranty association. This service involves claims investigation, loss settlement, and a report to the plan on the final discharge of its obligations related to the liquidated insurer. Over the twenty year period from 1969 to 1988, guaranty plans collected $2.48 billion through assessments from member companies and used more than 99 percent for insolvency reparations with less than one percent absorbed by administrative expense assessments.

In spite of this overall record of performance, a number of deficiencies exist in the present system. Criticism of the plans center around three major issues: (1) the associations' failure to have significant impact on reducing the number of insolvencies; (2) the plans' suspected inability to handle a major company default; and (3) difficulties arising from the use of single-state guaranty plans for multiple-state insurance operations.

Future of the Solvency Guaranty Mechanism

Pronouncements within the insurance business indicate that there is less than complete satisfaction with the current approach to guarantee insurance company financial performance. Significant problems continue to exist in regard to the operating effectiveness and capacity of state plans. Although record levels of investment income may have lessened the perceived urgency of dealing with solvency maintenance, guaranteeing the financial ability of insurance company performance will be an integral part of the evolving insurance environment. Even as far back as 1974, the New York Insurance Department, in declaring that it was taking a new approach to the combined issues of competitive rating and financial stability, stated that:

> The legitimate need for improved market performance by insurers also make(s) it increasingly less appropriate to regard preservation of strong financial condition and prevention of insolvency as absolute goals of insurance regulation. Instead, our objectives with respect to financial condition must increasingly be balanced against their impact on other goals of insurance regulation.[20]

If there is to be a trade-off between pricing flexibility and solvency maintenance, an efficient, effective, and equitable guaranty mechanism should be in place. The report to the Illinois Insurance Department on a 1982 insolvency emphasized the need for guaranty fund protection during periods of intense price competition:

> It was no surprise ... that the company was declared insolvent. It was just another situation where competition had pushed the commission rates too high and premiums too low to the point where bond portfolios were being liquidated to meet the daily cash flow requirements, resulting in the recognition of the loss of book value which ... exists in most, if not every, insurance company.[21]

As we go into the 1990s and beyond, the challenge of solvency guaranty mechanisms will continue and will likely continue to grow.

THE SOLVENCY RECORD

The ability to calculate precisely an optimal capital and surplus level for new and continuing insurance companies would be beneficial to all concerned with their operation. Actuarial science and modern financial management provide some guidance for setting net worth levels and making decisions involving alternative capital structures, but these management tools have limitations. Not even the shrewdest management can guarantee that unforeseeable contingencies will not destroy or severely reduce the financial capacity of the insurance company that it directs. Nor can government regulation prevent the occurrence of insurance company insolvencies. In the great majority of cases involving distressed insurers, efforts of regulatory agencies and the collective action taken by other members of the industry have averted significant economic losses to policyholders. Nevertheless, the delays, uncertainty, and psychological trauma inflicted by failure of insurers recommend thoughtful considerations of insurance company financial strength.

Economic Impact of Insolvencies

Constructing an accurate record of solvency for the property-liability insurance business is difficult. Some data sources group together voluntary retirements, mergers, involuntary receiverships, rehabilitations, conservatorships, and liquidations. A diary of corporate changes is published annually by A.M. Best Company. Illustration 5-12 shows a twenty-year summary of information on companies that exited the property-liability insurance business. The illustration shows that 234 property-liability insurers have departed involuntarily from the marketplace during the twenty-year period from 1969 to 1988. Undoubtedly a number of the corporate changes listed as mergers also involved companies that could not sustain operations as independent entities. This continued incidence of company failures is disquieting to policyholders, insurance company management, and governmental bodies that oversee the business of insurance.

A formalized mechanism for monitoring and reporting the economic impact of insolvencies has been established through creation of the National Committee on Insurance Guaranty Funds (NCIGF). The number of insolvencies reported by the NCIGF are listed by year in Illustration 5-13. According to the NCIGF, 169 property-liability insurance company insolvencies were recorded from 1969 through 1988.[22] These figures include only those companies whose demise resulted in a response from the guaranty funds. Twenty two insolven-

Illustration 5-12

Analysis of Property–Liability Company Retirements*

	Liquidated, Receivership, Rehabilitation, Conservatorship, Restraining Order, etc.	Mergers	Voluntary Retirements	Total
1969	4	11	16	31
1970	13	27	6	46
1971	13	23	3	39
1972	6	21	10	37
1973	6	13	6	25
1974	5	21	9	35
1975	28	21	5	54
1976	3	15	8	26
1977	6	5	7	18
1978	8	14	5	27
1979	9	9	4	22
1980	6	7	3	16
1981	2	6	2	10
1982	3	5	1	9
1983	7	13	7	27
1984	27	9	7	43
1985	26	3	12	41
1986	26	10	1	37
1987	15	8	5	28
1988	21	10	11	42
1969 through 1978	92	171	75	338
1979 through 1988	142	80	53	275
1969 through 1988	234	251	128	613

*Adapted with permission from "Corporate Changes—1982," *Best's Review*, Property-Casualty Edition, March 1983, p. 12 and "Corporate Changes—1988," *Best's Review*, Property-Casualty Edition, March 1989, p. 30.

cies occurred in 1985, the worst annual number of insolvencies experienced by the guaranty funds.

Amounts collected by post insolvency guaranty associations are listed by state in Illustration 5-14. California, the nation's most populous and largest insurance premium producing state, has levied the largest assessment for the guarantying benefits owed by insolvent insurers. The $2.48 billion net assessments paid by ongoing insurers from 1969 to 1988 was $1.36 per $1,000 of net premiums written by

Illustration 5-13
NCIGF Record of Insurance Company Insolvencies

Year	Number of Companies	Year	Number of Companies
1969	1	1979	2
1970	4	1980	4
1971	8	1981	6
1972	2	1982	9
1973	2	1983	4
1974	5	1984	19
1975	20	1985	22
1976	4	1986	17
1977	6	1987	12
1978	6	1988	16
1969 to 1978	58	1979 to 1988	111
		1969 to 1988	169

property-liability insurers countrywide. During the period from 1969 to 1982 only about fifty cents out of each $1,000 was used to support the solvency guarantee system. In 1988, the net insolvency assessments were $2.24 per $1,000 of insurance written. During 1988 there were $452 million of net insolvency assessments compared to property-liability industry net premiums of $202 billion. Most of the insurance company failures have been concentrated among small insurers. There should be concern, however, for the increasing amounts per $1,000 of net premiums written necessary to meet the insolvency assessments in the property-casualty industry.

Factors Leading to Insolvency

A variety of factors that precede delinquency proceedings have been identified through studies of insurance company failures. Some of the broadly defined causes are:

- Improper underwriting, reserving, and claims handling
- Financial condition of reinsurer
- Inadequate expense controls
- Questionable investment practices
- Management dishonesty
- Abnormal transactions with agents, brokers, or reinsurers
- Excessive commissions or management allowances

Illustration 5-14
Net Insolvency Assessments by State Guaranty Associations
1969–1988 (thousands of dollars)*

State	Amount	State	Amount
Alabama	$ 27,264	Nebraska	8,197
Alaska	9,343	Nevada	17,431
Arizona	41,243	New Hampshire	9,024
Arkansas	14,799	New Jersey	11,419
California	625,632	New Mexico	8,377
Colorado	28,301	New York	*
Connecticut	61,110	North Carolina	14,369
Delaware	16,359	North Dakota	4,320
D.C.	5,197	Ohio	47,032
Florida	354,719	Oklahoma	44,786
Georgia	53,492	Oregon	22,841
Hawaii	34,751	Pennsylvania	113,274
Idaho	6,091	Puerto Rico	31,780
Illinois	156,037	Rhode Island	7,973
Indiana	10,133	South Carolina	14,165
Iowa	26,053	South Dakota	5,307
Kansas	16,998	Tennessee	12,706
Kentucky	18,164	Texas	91,673
Louisiana	47,358	Utah	7,174
Maine	8,396	Vermont	4,379
Maryland	27,571	Virginia	14,041
Massachusetts	33,472	Washington	28,325
Michigan	114,095	West Virginia	14,102
Minnesota	115,333	Wisconsin	24,855
Mississippi	14,122	Wyoming	2,103
Missouri	27,735		
Montana	25,105	TOTAL	$2,478,522

*New York has a pre-insolvency, rather than a post-insolvency,
assessment guaranty fund.

*Based on data from National Committee on Insurance Guaranty Funds.

These factors and others have been found repeatedly by researchers analyzing delinquent insurers. Management dishonesty, as manifested in questionable agency balances and possible falsification of cash and investments, was almost universally present in a group of defunct Texas insurers studied by Douglas G. Olson.[23] In a subsequent study of eight Pennsylvania companies that became insolvent, Professor Olson stated "the history of most of the companies reflected intentional management ineptness, bordering on fraudulent behavior, rather than impersonal market forces."[24] Low underwriting standards and questionable investments highlight the profile of substandard automobile insurance company failures developed by Campbell K. Evans.[25]

SUMMARY

Several groups have an interest in evaluating the financial condition of insurance companies. Insureds, investors, insurance producers, insurance regulators, and others may be concerned with the solvency, liquidity, and profitability of one or more insurance companies. Most persons, however, have little knowledge of insurance accounting and are unable to evaluate insurance company finance. Individuals who have chosen insurance as their profession can be expected to be familiar with a subject others may consider to be complex, obscure, and arcane. Some basic tools for financial analysis of property-liability insurers have been presented in this chapter.

The list of ratios discussed here does not constitute an exhaustive treatment of the subject. It is necessary to go beyond calculation of financial ratios; statistics developed for a particular insurer should be compared to standard averages within the business and trends should be studied over several accounting periods. Rates of growth in a company's premiums, profits, and surplus should be balanced against the underwriting and investment risks taken by the insurer. Financial reporting services are a valuable source of financial information on individual insurers and of data for comparisons. Care must be taken to direct the analysis toward the future rather than allowing it to be only a compilation of past performance.

Security offered to policyholders through insurance products is based on the financial health and vigor of the insurance company that provides coverage. Managers of insurance companies have the first-line responsibility for solvency maintenance and must operate the company in a manner that is consistent with achieving this objective. Company management is supported in this area by insurance regulation that traditionally has identified preservation of solvency as a central regulatory purpose. Techniques or regulatory tools designed to help assure the continued ability of insurance company financial performance include:

- Minimum Capitalization Standards

- Uniform Annual Statements
- NAIC Zone Examinations
- NAIC Insurance Regulatory Information System Ratios
- Investment Portfolio Limitations
- State Insurance Department Surveillance
- State Insurance Department Conservation and Rehabilitation Efforts

In the event that a company does become insolvent, guaranty funds have been established to avoid losses to insureds and third parties that have a claim against an insolvent insurer.

The amount of capital and surplus relative to the volume of premiums written clearly has an effect on the probability that an insurer will be able to keep its promises. However, an insurance company's optimal operating position cannot be reduced to a simple ratio of premiums written-to-policyholders' surplus. Many other factors—including underwriting and investment profitability, diversification of the investment portfolio, and adequacy of loss reserve estimates— are interrelated with the impact that volume and capitalization have on an insurer's probability of continued solvency.

The recent history of property-liability insurance company failures does not project the image of financial solidity that ought to be desired by the insurance business and its regulators. Consistent failure of several companies each year creates a specter that haunts the insurance business whenever it attempts to gain operating flexibility— in pricing, for instance. Management and regulation for solvency are neither trivial endeavors nor easily accomplished tasks but some progress is being made toward improving the solvency record.

More than two hundred years ago, Adam Smith, in observing the insurance companies of his time, noted the need for adequate capitalization:

> The trade of insurance gives great security to the fortunes of private people, and by dividing among a great many that loss which would ruin an individual, makes it fall light and easy upon the whole society. In order to give this security, however, it is necessary that the insurers should have a very large capital. Before the establishment of the two joint stock companies for insurance in London, a list, it is said, was laid before the attorney-general, of one hundred and fifty private insurers who had failed in the course of a few year.[26]

Contemporary insurance regulation continues to rely on capital and surplus requirements as a standard that must be met if a particular insurance company is to be admitted or allowed to remain in the marketplace. The concept of maintaining solvency has been extended by establishing guaranty associations that have substantially reduced monetary losses to policyholders and third-party claimants. Improvements in the guaranty mechanism are being considered by insurance groups and governmental agencies. Because deductibles, limits placed on recoveries, and indirect costs of insolvencies force reparations to be less than complete, the guaranty mechanism should be considered a less than optimal solution. The preferred answer is to prevent insolvencies in the first place.

Chapter Notes

1. John L. Markle and A. E. Hofflander, "A Quadratic Programming Model of the Non-Life Insurer," *The Journal of Risk and Insurance*, Vol. 43, No. 1 (March 1976), pp. 99-120.
2. A less conventional line of reasoning that capacity is more usefully viewed as a problem in operating stability rather than capitalization is developed by James M. Stone, "A Theory of Capacity and the Insurance of Catastrophe Risks," *The Journal of Risk and Insurance*, Vol. XL, Nos. 2 and 3 (June and September, 1973), pp. 231-243 and pp. 339-355.
3. In actuarial literature, a more technical name is associated with the capacity/capitalization problem. It is called the "ruin problem" because it deals with how large liabilities can grow for a given amount of equity without the probability of the company being ruined (becoming insolvent) increasing beyond a selected small value. For example, if the ratio of liabilities to policyholders' surplus increases to 6 to 1 during a given time interval, say, three years, will the probability of ruin be greater than 0.001?
4. Theoretical and empirical papers have proposed the use of quadratic or chance-constrained programming models as aids to insurance company operational decision making. Leading articles in this area include: Yehuda Kahane and David Nye, "A Portfolio Approach to the Property-Liability Insurance Industry," *The Journal of Risk and Insurance*, Vol. 42, No. 4 (December 1975), pp. 579-598; Clement G. Krouse, "Portfolio Balancing Corporate Assets and Liabilities with Special Application to Insurance Management," *Journal of Financial and Quantitative Analysis*, Vol. 6 (September 14, 1971), pp. 77-104; John L. Markle and A. E. Hofflander, "A Quadratic Programming Model of the Non-Life Insurer," *The Journal of Risk and Insurance*, Vol. 43, No. 1 (March 1976), pp. 99-120; Tapan S. Roy and Robert Charles Witt, "Leverage, Exposure Ratios and the Optimal Rate of Return on Capital for the Insurer," *The Journal of Risk and Insurance*, Vol. 43, No. 1 (March 1976), pp. 53-72; and Howard E. Thompson, John P. Matthews, and Bob C. L. Li, "Insurance Exposure and Investment Risks: An Analysis Using Chance-Constrained Programming," *Operations Research*, Vol. 22 (September-October 1974), pp. 991-1007.
5. In Chapter 2 of this text, the concepts of *insurance exposure* and *insurance leverage* were defined. Insurance exposure is measured by the ratio of premiums written-to-policyholders' surplus. Insurance leverage is measured by the ratio of reserves-to-policyholders' surplus. Obviously the two concepts are closely related; increases in net premiums written result in increased reserves relative to surplus. When the ratio of premiums-to-surplus is used as a surrogate debt-equity ratio, the two concepts are combined and the terminology insurance leverage seems most appropriate.
6. Galen R. Barnes, "Financial Needs of a Mutual Insurance Company," *NAII 27th Annual Workshop Proceedings* (1981), pp. 11-18.

7. The determination of EPS in accordance with FASB requirements can be complicated for a firm with a complex capital structure. Readers interested in pursuing this topic further are referred to the discussion and illustrations contained in Leopold A. Bernstein, *Financial Statement Analysis: Theory, Application, and Interpretation*, rev. ed. (Homewood, IL: Richard D. Irwin, 1978), pp. 330-353; and Financial Accounting Standards Board, *Accounting Standards*, Vol. 2 (New York: McGraw-Hill Book Co., 1982), pp. 14127-14254.

8. *Illinois Insurance Code* § 13 [§ 625], p.15; and *Pennsylvania Insurance Laws* § 40-5-106, p. 55 (NILS Publishing Company, 1989).

9. General accounting uses the term "capital-surplus" to refer to capital paid in excess of par value. Because the annual statement caption is "surplus paid-in," this terminology is used here. The two terms are synonymous.

10. The initial surplus requirements for reciprocal insurers are discussed in detail by Dennis F. Feinmuth, *The Regulation of Reciprocal Insurance Exchanges* (Homewood, IL: Richard D. Irwin, Inc., 1967).

11. *Pennsylvania Insurance Laws and Related Statutes*, Ch. 2, Sec. 205.

12. *Best's Key Rating Guide, Property-Casualty* 1989 (Oldwick, New Jersey: A. M. Best Co., 1989).

13. Several alternative approaches can be used to convey additional funds to an insurance company that operates within a conglomerate or cogeneric. For example, International Telephone & Telegraph Corporation, parent of the Hartford Insurance Group, increased paid-in surplus of the insurance company group by contributing $100 million of assets to the insurers during 1977 and 1978. Assets transferred to the Hartford included various ITT properties and securities.

14. *Financial Condition Examiners Handbook* (Milwaukee, WI: National Association of Insurance Commissioners, 1976).

15. Robert A. Zelten, "Solvency Surveillance: The Problem and a Solution," *The Journal of Risk and Insurance*, Vol. XXXIX, No. 4 (December 1972), p. 576.

16. Robert A. Zelten, p. 586.

17. "50% of States Say NAIC Solvency Tests Primary Lead to Problem Cos.," *The National Underwriter*, Property/Casualty Insurance Edition, 17 June 1977, p. 32.

18. National Committee on Insurance Guaranty Funds, "Annual Insolvency Assessment Report, calendar-year 1988."

19. Harold C. Krogh, "Insurer Postinsolvency Funds: An Analysis of Operations," unpublished manuscript presented to the American Risk and Insurance Association (August 1977), p. 6.

20. "Regulation of Financial Condition of Insurance Companies," New York Insurance Department (1974), p. 74.

21. William Allen, "Kenilworth Insurance Company: A Case Study," (December 1982), p. 1.

22. National Committee on Insurance Guaranty Funds, "Annual Insolvency Assessment Report, calendar-year 1988."

23. Douglas G. Olson, "Insolvencies Among High-Risk Automobile Insurance

Companies" (unpublished Ph.D. dissertation, University of Pennsylvania, 1968).

24. U.S. Department of Transportation, *Insolvencies Among Automobile Insurers*, by Douglas G. Olson, Department of Transportation Automobile Insurance and Compensation Study (Washington, DC: Government Printing Office, 1970), p. 43.

25. Campbell K. Evans, "Basic Financial Differences of Substandard Automobile Insurers," *The Journal of Risk and Insurance*, Vol. 35, No. 4 (December 1968), pp. 489-513.

26. Adam Smith, *An Inquiry into the Nature and Causes of the Wealth of Nations*, Book V, Chapter I, Part III, Modern Library edition (New York: Random House, 1937), p. 715.

Bibliography

Accounting Practices and Procedures Manual for Fire and Casualty Insurance Companies. Milwaukee: National Association of Insurance Commissioners, 1980.

"Annual Insolvency Assessment Report, calendar-year 1988." National Committee on Insurance Guaranty Funds.

Auditing Standards and Procedures, Statement on Auditing Procedure No. 33. New York: American Institute of Certified Public Accountants, 1963.

Audits of Fire and Casualty Insurance Companies. New York: American Institute of Certified Public Accountants, 1966.

Barnes, Galen R. "Financial Needs of a Mutual Insurance Company." *NAII 27th Annual Workshop Proceedings,* 1981, pp. 11-18.

Bernstein, Leopold A. *Financial Statement Analysis: Theory, Application, and Interpretation.* Rev. ed. Homewood, IL: Richard D. Irwin, 1978.

Best's Aggregates & Averages: Property-Casualty, 1989. Oldwick, NJ: A.M. Best Company, 1989.

Best's Aggregates & Averages: Property-Liability. 50th annual edition. Morristown, NJ: A.M. Best Company, 1989.

Best's Key Rating Guide, Property-Casualty, 1989. Oldwick, NJ: A.M. Best Co., 1989.

Drake, Carl B., Jr. "What an Insurance Executive Expects from Management Reports." *Best's Review.* Property-Liability Edition, May 1973, pp. 78-82.

Evans, Campbell K. "Basic Financial Differences of Substandard Automobile Insurers." *The Journal of Risk and Insurance.* Vol. 35, No. 4. December 1968, pp. 489-513.

Feinmuth, Dennis F. *The Regulation of Reciprocal Insurance Exchanges.* Homewood, IL: Richard D. Irwin, Inc., 1967.

"50% of States Say NAIC Solvency Tests Primary Lead to Problem Cos." *The National Underwriter,* Property/Casualty Insurance Edition, 17 June 1977, p. 32.

Financial Condition Examiners Handbook. Milwaukee, WI: National Association of Insurance Commissioners, 1976.

Financial Reporting Trends, Fire and Casualty Insurance. New York: Ernst & Ernst, 1974.

Hendricksen, Eldon S. *Accounting Theory.* Rev. ed. Homewood, IL: Richard D. Irwin, 1970.

Homer, Sydney and Leibowitz, Martin L. *Inside the Yield Book.* Englewood Cliffs, NJ: Prentice-Hall, 1972.

"Insurance Industry." *Accounting Standards Vol. 2.* New York: McGraw-Hill Book Company, 1982.

Kahane, Yehuda and Nye, David. "A Portfolio Approach to the Property-Liability Insurance Industry." *The Journal of Risk and Insurance*, Vol. 42, No. 4, December 1975, pp. 579-598.

Krogh, Harold C. "Insurer Postinsolvency Funds: An Analysis of Operations." Presented to the American Risk and Insurance Association, August 1977.

Krouse, Clement G. "Portfolio Balancing Corporate Assets and Liabilities with Special Application to Insurance Management." *Journal of Financial and Quantitative Analysis*, Vol. 6, 14 September 1971, pp. 77-104.

Markle, John L. and Hofflander, A.E. "A Quadratic Programming Model of the Non-Life Insurer." *The Journal of Risk and Insurance*. Vol. 43, No. 1, March 1976, pp. 99-120.

Murphy, Robert J. "Reinsurance Accounting." *Property-Liability Insurance Accounting*. Edited by Robert W. Strain. Santa Monica, CA: The Merritt Co., 1976.

Olson, Douglas G. *Insolvencies Among Automobile Insurers*. Department of Transportation Automobile Insurance and Compensation Study. Washington, DC: Government Printing Office, 1970.

_____. "Insolvencies Among High-Risk Automobile Insurance Companies." Unpublished Ph.D. dissertation, University of Pennsylvania, 1968.

Pennsylvania Insurance Laws and Related Statutes, Ch. 2, Sec. 205.

"Regulation of Financial Condition of Insurance Companies." New York Insurance Department, 1974.

Roy, Tapan S. and Witt, Robert Charles. "Leverage, Exposure Ratios and the Optimal Rate of Return on Capital for the Insurer." *The Journal of Risk and Insurance*, Vol. 43, No. 1, March 1976, pp. 53-72.

Salzmann, Ruth. "Estimated Liabilities for Losses and Loss Adjustment Expenses." *Property-Liability Insurance Accounting*. 4th ed. Edited by Robert W. Strain. Durham, NC: Insurance Accounting and Systems Association, 1988.

Smith, Adam. *An Inquiry into the Nature and Causes of the Wealth of Nations*. Book V, Chapter I, Part III. Modern Library edition. New York: Random House, 1937.

Stone, James M. "A Theory of Capacity and the Insurance of Catastrophe Risks." *The Journal of Risk and Insurance*, Vol. XL, Nos. 2 and 3, June and September, 1973, pp. 231-243 and 339-355.

Thompson, Howard E.; Matthews, John P.; and Li, Bob C.L. "Insurance Exposure and Investment Risks: An Analysis Using Chance-Constrained Programming." *Operations Research*, Vol. 22, September-October 1974, pp. 991-1007.

Zelten, Robert A. "Solvency Surveillance: The Problem and a Solution." *The Journal of Risk and Insurance*, Vol. 39, No. 4. December 1972, pp. 576, 586.

Index

M

N

O

P

Appendix A

Annual Statement
of the
Fire and Casualty
Companies

FIRE AND CASUALTY COMPANIES—ASSOCIATION EDITION

Note: In the case of reciprocal exchanges and other types of insurers using special terminology, the printed items and references in this blank, if not appropriately changed, shall be construed to apply to such insurers in respect to corresponding data and information as the context may require.

ANNUAL STATEMENT
For the Year Ended December 31, 1989
OF THE CONDITION AND AFFAIRS OF THE

NAIC Group Code_____ NAIC Company Code_____ Employer's ID Number_____

Organized under the Laws of the State of_____, made to the

INSURANCE DEPARTMENT OF THE STATE OF

PURSUANT TO THE LAWS THEREOF

Incorporated _____Commenced Business _____

Statutory Home Office _____ , _____
(Street and Number)   (City or Town, State and Zip Code)

Mail Address_____ , _____
(Street and Number or P.O. Box)   (City or Town, State and Zip Code)

Main Administrative Office_____ _____
(Area Code)   (Telephone Number)

Primary Location of Books and Records _____ ,
(Street and Number)

_____ _____
(City or Town, State and Zip Code)   (Area Code)   (Telephone Number)

Annual Statement Contact Person and Phone Number_____

OFFICERS

President_____

Secretary_____   Vice Presidents {

Treasurer_____

DIRECTORS OR TRUSTEES

State of .... } ss
County of ....

.... President, ... Secretary, ... Treasurer

of the .... being duly sworn, each for himself deposes and says that they are the above described officers of the said insurer, and that on the thirty-first day of December last, all of the herein described assets were the absolute property of the said insurer, free and clear from any liens or claims thereon, except as herein stated, and that this annual statement, together with related exhibits, schedules and explanations therein contained, annexed or referred to are a full and true statement of all the assets and liabilities and of the condition and affairs of the said insurer as of the thirty-first day of December last, and of its income and deductions therefrom for the year ended on that date, according to the best of their information, knowledge and belief respectively.

Subscribed and sworn to before me this

.....................day of 1990   ....President

....Secretary

....Treasurer

ANNUAL STATEMENT FOR THE YEAR 1989 OF THE ....
                                                                                            (Name)

ASSETS	1 Current Year	2 Previous Year
1. Bonds (less $.................liability for asset transfers with put options)		
2. Stocks:		
2.1 Preferred stocks		
2.2 Common stocks		
3. Mortgage loans on real estate		
4. Real estate:		
4.1 Properties occupied by the company (less $.................encumbrances)		
4.2 Other properties (less $.................encumbrances)		
5. Collateral loans		
6.1 Cash on hand and on deposit		
6.2 Short-term investments		
7. Other invested assets		
8. Aggregate write-ins for invested assets		
8a. Subtotals, cash and invested assets (Items 1 to 8)		
9. Agents' balances or uncollected premiums:		
9.1 Premiums and agents' balances in course of collection		
9.2 Premiums, agents' balances and installments booked but deferred and not yet due		
9.3 Accrued retrospective premiums		
10. Funds held by or deposited with reinsured companies		
11. Bills receivable, taken for premiums		
12. Reinsurance recoverable on loss payments		
13. Federal income tax recoverable		
14. Electronic data processing equipment		
15. Interest, dividends and real estate income due and accrued		
16. Receivable from parent, subsidiaries and affiliates		
17. Equities and deposits in pools and associations		
18. Amounts receivable relating to uninsured accident and health plans		
20. Aggregate write-ins for other than invested assets		
21. TOTALS (Items 8a through 20)		

DETAILS OF WRITE-INS AGGREGATED AT ITEM 8 FOR INVESTED ASSETS

0801.		
0802.		
0803.		
0804.		
0805.		
0898. Summary of remaining write-ins for Item 8 from overflow page		
0899. TOTALS (Items 0801 thru 0805 plus 0898) (Page 2, Item 8)		

DETAILS OF WRITE-INS AGGREGATED AT ITEM 20 FOR OTHER THAN INVESTED ASSETS

2001.		
2002.		
2003.		
2004.		
2005.		
2098. Summary of remaining write-ins for Item 20 from overflow page		
2099. TOTALS (Items 2001 thru 2005 plus 2098) (Page 2, Item 20)		

NOTE: The items on this page to agree with Exhibit 1, Col. 4.
The Notes to Financial Statements are an integral part of this statement.

ANNUAL STATEMENT FOR THE YEAR **1989** OF THE ....
(Name)

		1 Current Year	2 Previous Year
	LIABILITIES, SURPLUS AND OTHER FUNDS		
1.	Losses (Part 3A, Column 5, Item 32)		
1A.	Reinsurance payable on paid losses (Schedule F, Part 1A, Section 2, Column 1)		
2.	Loss adjustment expenses (Part 3A, Column 6, Item 32)		
3.	Contingent commissions and other similar charges		
4.	Other expenses (excluding taxes, licenses and fees)		
5.	Taxes, licenses and fees (excluding federal and foreign income taxes)		
6.	Federal and foreign income taxes (excluding deferred taxes)		
7.	Borrowed money		
8.	Interest, including $ .... on borrowed money		
9.	Unearned premiums (Part 2A, Column 5, Item 34)		
10.	Dividends declared and unpaid:		
	(a) Stockholders		
	(b) Policyholders		
11.	Funds held by company under reinsurance treaties		
12.	Amounts withheld or retained by company for account of others		
13a.	Unearned premiums on reinsurance in unauthorized companies .... $		
13b.	Reinsurance on paid losses $ .... and on unpaid reported losses $		
	and on incurred but not reported losses $ .... recoverable from unauthorized		
	companies $		
13c.	Paid and unpaid allocated loss adjustment expenses recoverable from unauthorized companies $		
13d.	Less funds held or retained by company for account of such		
	unauthorized companies as per Schedule F, Part 2, Column 6 $		
13e.	Provision for overdue authorized reinsurance as per Schedule F, Part 2B, Section 2 $		
14.	Provision for reinsurance (Items 13a + 13b + 13c + 13e − 13d)		
15.	Excess of statutory reserves over statement reserves (Schedule P Interrogatories)		
16.	Net adjustments in assets and liabilities due to foreign exchange rates		
17.	Drafts outstanding		
18.	Payable to parent, subsidiaries and affiliates		
19.	Payable for securities		
20.	Liability for amounts held under uninsured accident and health plans		
21.	Aggregate write-ins for liabilities		
22.	Total liabilities (Items 1 through 21)		
23.	Aggregate write-ins for special surplus funds		
24A.	Common capital stock		
24B.	Preferred capital stock		
24C.	Aggregate write-ins for other than special surplus funds		
25A.	Gross paid in and contributed surplus		
25B.	Unassigned funds (surplus)		
25C.	Less treasury stock, at cost:		
	(1) .... shares common (value included in Item 24 A $ ....)		
	(2) .... shares preferred (value included in Item 24 B $ ....)		
26.	Surplus as regards policyholders (Items 23 to 25B, less 25C) (Page 4, Item 32)		
27.	TOTALS (Page 2, Item 21)		

DETAILS OF WRITE-INS AGGREGATED AT ITEM 21 FOR LIABILITIES

2101.			
2102.			
2103.			
2104.			
2105.			
2198.	Summary of remaining write-ins for Item 21 from overflow page		
2199.	TOTALS (Items 2101 thru 2105 plus 2198) (Page 3, Item 21)		

DETAILS OF WRITE-INS AGGREGATED AT ITEM 23 FOR SPECIAL SURPLUS FUNDS

2301.			
2302.			
2303.			
2304.			
2305.			
2398.	Summary of remaining write-ins for Item 23 from overflow page		
2399.	TOTALS (Items 2301 thru 2305 plus 2398) (Page 3, Item 23)		

DETAILS OF WRITE-INS AGGREGATED AT ITEM 24C FOR OTHER THAN SPECIAL SURPLUS FUNDS

24C01.			
24C02.			
24C03.			
24C04.			
24C05.			
24C98.	Summary of remaining write-ins for Item 24C from overflow page		
24C99.	TOTALS (Items 24C01 thru 24C05 plus 24C98) (Page 3, Item 24C)		

ANNUAL STATEMENT FOR THE YEAR 1989 OF THE ....
(Name)

		1 Current Year	2 Previous Year
UNDERWRITING AND INVESTMENT EXHIBIT			
STATEMENT OF INCOME			
UNDERWRITING INCOME			
1.	Premiums earned (Part 2, Column 4, Item 32)		
	DEDUCTIONS		
2.	Losses incurred (Part 3, Column 7, Item 32)		
3.	Loss expenses incurred (Part 4, Column 1, Item 22)		
4.	Other underwriting expenses incurred (Part 4, Column 2, Item 22)		
5.	Aggregate write-ins for underwriting deductions		
6.	Total underwriting deductions (Items 2 through 5)		
7.	Net underwriting gain or (loss) (Item 1 minus 6)		
INVESTMENT INCOME			
8.	Net investment income earned (Part 1, Item 15)		
9.	Net realized capital gains or (losses) (Part 1A, Item 11)		
9A.	Net investment gain or (loss) (Items 8 + 9)		
OTHER INCOME			
10.	Net gain or (loss) from agents' or premium balances charged off		
	(amount recovered $ .... amount charged off $ ....)		
11.	Finance and service charges not included in premiums (Schedule T, Column 8 total)		
12.	Aggregate write-ins for miscellaneous income		
13.	Total other income (Items 10 through 12)		
14.	Net income before dividends to policyholders and before federal and foreign income taxes (Items 7 + 9A + 13)		
14A.	Dividends to policyholders (Exhibit 3, Item 16, plus Page 3, Item 10b, Column 1 minus 2)		
14B.	Net income, after dividends to policyholders but before federal and foreign income taxes (Item 14 minus 14A)		
15.	Federal and foreign income taxes incurred		
16.	Net income (Item 14B minus 15) (to Item 18)		
CAPITAL AND SURPLUS ACCOUNT			
17.	Surplus as regards policyholders, December 31 previous year (Page 4, Column 2, Item 32)		
GAINS AND (LOSSES) IN SURPLUS			
18.	Net income (from Item 16)		
19.	Net unrealized capital gains or losses (Part 1A, Item 12)		
20.	Change in non-admitted assets (Exhibit 2, Item 31, Col. 3)		
21.	Change in liability for reinsurance (Page 3, Item 14, Column 2 minus 1)		
22.	Change in foreign exchange adjustment		
23.	Change in excess of statutory reserves over statement reserves (Page 3, Item 15, Column 2 minus 1)		
24.	Capital changes:		
	(a) Paid in (Exhibit 3, Item 6)		
	(b) Transferred from surplus (Stock Divd.)		
	(c) Transferred to surplus		
25.	Surplus adjustments:		
	(a) Paid in (Exhibit 3, Item 7)		
	(b) Transferred to capital (Stock Divd.)		
	(c) Transferred from capital		
26.	Net remittances from or (to) Home Office (Exhibit 3, Items 4b minus 12b)		
27.	Dividends to stockholders (cash)		
28.	Change in treasury stock (Page 3, Item 25C (1) and (2), Column 2 minus 1)		
29.	Extraordinary amounts of taxes for prior years		
30.	Aggregate write-ins for gains and losses in surplus		
31.	Change in surplus as regards policyholders for the year (Items 18 through 30)		
32.	Surplus as regards policyholders, December 31 current year (Items 17 plus 31) (Page 3, Item 26)		

DETAILS OF WRITE-INS AGGREGATED AT ITEM 5 FOR UNDERWRITING DEDUCTIONS

0501.			
0502.			
0503.			
0504.			
0505.			
0598.	Summary of remaining write-ins for Item 5 from overflow page		
0599.	TOTALS (Items 0501 thru 0505 plus 0598) (Page 4, Item 5)		

DETAILS OF WRITE-INS AGGREGATED AT ITEM 12 FOR MISCELLANEOUS INCOME

1201.			
1202.			
1203.			
1204.			
1205.			
1298.	Summary of remaining write-ins for Item 12 from overflow page		
1299.	TOTALS (Items 1201 thru 1205 plus 1298) (Page 4, Item 12)		

DETAILS OF WRITE-INS AGGREGATED AT ITEM 30 FOR GAINS AND LOSSES IN SURPLUS

3001.			
3002.			
3003.			
3004.			
3005.			
3098.	Summary of remaining write-ins for Item 30 from overflow page		
3099.	TOTALS (Items 3001 thru 3005 plus 3098) (Page 4, Item 30)		

ANNUAL STATEMENT FOR THE YEAR 1989 OF THE ....
(Name)

	1 Current Year	2 Previous Year
CASH FLOW		
1. Premiums collected net of reinsurance		
2. Loss and loss adjustment expenses paid (net of salvage and subrogation)		
3. Underwriting expenses paid		
4. Other underwriting income (expenses)		
5. Cash from underwriting (Item 1 minus item 2 minus item 3 plus item 4)		
6. Investment income (net of investment expense)		
7. Other income (expenses)		
8. Dividends to policyholders paid		
9. Federal income taxes (paid) recovered		
10. Net cash from operations (Item 5 plus item 6 plus item 7 minus item 8 plus item 9)		
11. Proceeds from investments sold, matured or repaid:		
11.1 Bonds		
11.2 Stocks		
11.3 Mortgage loans		
11.4 Real estate		
11.5 Collateral loans		
11.6 Other invested assets		
11.7 Net gains or (losses) on cash and short-term investments		
11.8 Miscellaneous proceeds		
11.9 Total investment proceeds (Items 11.1 thru 11.8)		
12. Other cash provided:		
12.1 Net transfers from affiliates		
12.2 Borrowed funds received		
12.3 Capital paid in		
12.4 Surplus paid in		
12.5 Other sources		
12.6 Total other cash provided (Items 12.1 thru 12.5)		
13. Total (Item 10 plus item 11.9 plus item 12.6)		
14. Cost of investments acquired (long-term only):		
14.1 Bonds		
14.2 Stocks		
14.3 Mortgage loans		
14.4 Real estate		
14.5 Collateral loans		
14.6 Other invested assets		
14.7 Miscellaneous applications		
14.8 Total investments acquired (Items 14.1 thru 14.7)		
15. Other cash applied:		
15.1 Dividends to stockholders paid		
15.2 Net transfers to affiliates		
15.3 Borrowed funds repaid		
15.4 Other applications		
15.5 Total other cash applied (Items 15.1 thru 15.4)		
16. Total (Item 14.8 plus item 15.5)		
17. Net change in cash and short-term investments (Item 13 minus item 16)		
RECONCILIATION		
18. Cash and short-term investments:		
18.1 Beginning of year		
18.2 End of year (Item 17 plus item 18.1)		

ANNUAL STATEMENT FOR THE YEAR 1989 OF THE ....
(Name)

UNDERWRITING AND INVESTMENT EXHIBIT
PART 1 — INTEREST, DIVIDENDS AND REAL ESTATE INCOME

1	2 Schedule	3 Collected During Year Less Paid For Accrued On Purchases	Paid in Advance		Due and Accrued‡		8 Earned During Year 3 + 5 + 6 − 4 − 7
			4 Current Year	5 Previous Year	6 Current Year	7 Previous Year	
1. U.S. government bonds	D*						
1.1 Bonds exempt from U.S. tax	D*						
1.2 Other bonds (unaffiliated)	D*						
1.3 Bonds of affiliates	D*						
2.1 Preferred stocks (unaffiliated)	D						
2.11 Preferred stocks of affiliates	D						
2.2 Common stocks (unaffiliated)	D						
2.21 Common stocks of affiliates	D						
3. Mortgage loans	B†						
4. Real estate	A§						
5. Collateral loans	C						
6.1 Cash on hand and on deposit	N						
6.2 Short-term investments	DA**						
7. Other invested assets	BA						
8. Financial options and futures	DB						
9. Aggregate write-ins for investment income							
10. TOTALS		#					#

DEDUCTIONS

11. Total investment expenses incurred (Part 4, Col. 3. Item 22)	
12. Depreciation on real estate (for companies which depreciate annually on a formula basis)	
13. Aggregate write-ins for deductions from investment income	
14. Total deductions (Items 11 to 13)	
15. Net Investment Income Earned (Item 10 minus Item 14—to Page 4, Item 8)	

*Includes $ .... accrual of discount less $ .... amortization of premium. **Includes $ .... accrual of discount less $ .... amortization of premium. ‡Admitted items only. State basis of exclusions
†Includes $ .... accrual of discount less $ .... amortization of premium. ‡Admitted items only. State basis of exclusions
§Includes $ .... for company's occupancy of its own buildings   #Includes for asset transfers with put options accounted for as financing arrangements. $ .... Column 3, $ .... Column 8.

DETAILS OF WRITE-INS AGGREGATED AT ITEM 9 OF PART 1

1	2	3	4	5	6	7	8
0901.							
0902.							
0903.							
0904.							
0905.							
0998. Summary of remaining write-ins for Item 9 from overflow page							
0999. TOTALS (Items 0901 thru 0905 plus 0998) (Part 1, Item 9)							

DETAILS OF WRITE-INS AGGREGATED AT ITEM 13 OF PART 1

DEDUCTIONS

1		
1301.		
1302.		
1303.		
1304.		
1305.		
1398. Summary of remaining write-ins for Item 13 from overflow page		
1399. TOTALS (Items 1301 thru 1305 plus 1398) (Part 1, Item 13)		

PART 1A—CAPITAL GAINS AND (LOSSES) ON INVESTMENTS

1	2 Profit on Sales or Maturity	3 Loss on Sales or Maturity	4 Increases by Adjustment in Book Value	5 Decreases by Adjustment in Book Value	6 Net Gain or (Loss) from Change in Difference Between Book and Admitted Values	7 Total (Net of Cols. 2 to 6 incl.) (2 − 3 + 4 − 5 + 6)
1. U.S. government bonds						
1.1 Bonds exempt from U.S. tax						
1.2 Other bonds (unaffiliated)						
1.3 Bonds of affiliates						
2.1 Preferred stocks (unaffiliated)						
2.11 Preferred stocks of affiliates						
2.2 Common stocks (unaffiliated)						
2.21 Common stocks of affiliates						
3. Mortgage loans						
4. Real estate				‡		
5. Collateral loans						
6.1 Cash on hand and on deposit						
6.2 Short-term investments						
7. Other invested assets						
8. Financial options and futures						
9. Aggregate write-ins for capital gains and (losses)						
10. TOTALS						

(Distribution of Item 10, Col. 7)	
11. Net realized capital gains or (losses)* (Page 4, Item 9) (Col. 2-3, Item 10)	
12. Net unrealized capital gains or (losses)* (Page 4, Item 19) (Col. 4 − 5 + 6, Item 10)	

*Attach statement or memorandum explaining basis of division.   ‡Excluding $ .... depreciation on real estate included in Part 1, Item 12.

DETAILS OF WRITE-INS AGGREGATED AT ITEM 9 OF PART 1A

1	2	3	4	5	6	7
0901.						
0902.						
0903.						
0904.						
0905.						
0998. Summary of remaining write-ins for Item 9 from overflow page						
0999. TOTALS (Items 0901 thru 0905 plus 0998) (Part 1A, Item 9)						

ANNUAL STATEMENT FOR THE YEAR 1989 OF THE ....
                                                                    (Name)

UNDERWRITING AND INVESTMENT EXHIBIT

PART 2 — PREMIUMS EARNED

Line of Business	1 Net Premiums Written Per Column 4, Part 2B	2 Unearned Premiums Dec. 31 Previous Year — per Col. 3 Last Year's Part 2	3 Unearned Premiums Dec. 31 Current Year — per Col. 5 Part 2A	4 Premiums Earned During Year Cols. 1 + 2 − 3
1. Fire				
2. Allied lines				
3. Farmowners multiple peril				
4. Homeowners multiple peril				
5. Commercial multiple peril				
8. Ocean marine				
9. Inland marine				
10. Financial guaranty				
11. Medical malpractice				
12. Earthquake				
13. Group accident and health				
14. Credit accident and health (group and individual)				
15. Other accident and health				
16. Workers' compensation				
17. Other liability				
19. Auto liability				
21. Auto phys. damage				
22. Aircraft (all perils)				
23. Fidelity				
24. Surety				
25. Glass				
26. Burglary and theft				
27. Boiler and machinery				
28. Credit				
29. International				
30A. Reinsurance*				
30B. Reinsurance*				
30C. Reinsurance*				
30D. Reinsurance*				
31. Aggregate write-ins for other lines of business				
32. TOTALS				

DETAILS OF WRITE-INS AGGREGATED AT ITEM 31

3101.				
3102.				
3103.				
3104.				
3105.				
3198. Summary of remaining write-ins for Item 31 from overflow page				
3199. TOTALS (Items 3101 thru 3105 plus 3198) (Item 31)				

*See Line 30 Instructions

Form 2

8

ANNUAL STATEMENT FOR THE YEAR 1989 OF THE .... (Name)

UNDERWRITING AND INVESTMENT EXHIBIT

PART 2A — RECAPITULATION OF ALL PREMIUMS

†Gross premiums (less reinsurance) and unearned premiums on all unexpired risks and reserve for return premiums under rate credit or retrospective rating plans based upon experience, viz:

Line of Business	1 Amount Unearned* (Running One Year or Less from Date of Policy)	2 Amount Unearned* (Running More than One Year from Date of Policy)	3 Advance Premiums (100%)	4 Reserve for Rate Credits and Retrospective Adjustments Based on Experience	5 Total Reserve for Unearned Premiums 1 + 2 + 3 + 4
1. Fire					1.
2. Allied lines					2.
3. Farmowners multiple peril					3.
4. Homeowners multiple peril					4.
5. Commercial multiple peril					5.
8. Ocean marine					8.
9. Inland marine					9.
10. Financial guaranty					10.
11. Medical malpractice					11.
12. Earthquake					12.
13. Group accident and health				(b)	13.
14. Credit accident and health (group and individual)**					14.
15. Other accident and health				(b)	15.
16. Workers' compensation					16.
17. Other liability					17.
18. Auto liability					18.
19. Auto phys. damage					19.
22. Aircraft (all perils)					22.
23. Fidelity					23.
24. Surety					24.
25. Glass					25.
26. Burglary and theft					26.
27. Boiler and machinery					27.
28. Credit					28.
29. International					29.
30A. Reinsurance***					30A.
30B. Reinsurance***					30B.
30C. Reinsurance***					30C.
30D. Reinsurance***					30D.
31. Aggregate write-ins for other lines of business					31.
32. TOTALS					32.

33. Accrued retrospective premiums based on experience

34. Balance (Line 32 plus line 33)

DETAILS OF WRITE-INS AGGREGATED AT ITEM 31

3101					01
3102					02
3103					03
3104					04
3105					05
3198 Summary of remaining write-ins for Item 31 from overflow page					98
3199 TOTALS (Items 3101 thru 3105 plus 3198) (Item 31)					99

†by gross premiums is meant the aggregate of all the premiums written in the policies or renewals in force.
Are they so returned in this statement? Answer: .... (b) Including $ .... reserved for deferred maternity and other similar benefits.
*State here basis of computation used in each case.
**Business not exceeding 120 months duration.
***See Line 30 instructions.

PART 2B — PREMIUMS WRITTEN

	1 Direct Business	Gross Premiums (Less Return Premiums), Including Policy and Membership Fees Written and Renewed During Year					4 Net Premiums Written 1 + 2a + 2b − 3a − 3b
		Reinsurance Assumed		Reinsurance Ceded			
		2a From Affiliates	2b From Non-Affiliates	3a To Affiliates	3b To Non-Affiliates		
1.							1.
2.							2.
3.							3.
4.							4.
5.							5.
8.							8.
9.							9.
10.							10.
11.							11.
12.							12.
13.							13.
14.							14.
15.							15.
16.							16.
17.							17.
18.							18.
19.							19.
22.							22.
23.							23.
24.							24.
25.							25.
26.							26.
27.							27.
28.							28.
29.							29.
30A.	XXXX						30A.
30B.	XXXX						30B.
30C.	XXXX						30C.
30D.	XXXX						30D.
31.							31.
32.							32.

01	01
02	02
03	03
04	04
05	05
98	98
99	99

Form 2

UNDERWRITING AND INVESTMENT EXHIBIT
PART 3 — LOSSES PAID AND INCURRED

Line of Business	Losses Paid Loss Salvage				5 Net Losses Unpaid Current Year (Part 3A, Col. 5)	6 Net Losses Unpaid Previous Year	7 Losses Incurred Current Year 4 + 5 − 6	8 Percentage of Losses Incurred (Col. 7, Part 3) to Premiums Earned (Col. 4, Part 2)	
	1 Direct Business	2 Reinsurance Assumed	3 Reinsurance Recovered	4 Net Payments 1 + 2 − 3					
1. Fire									1.
2. Allied lines									2.
3. Farmowners multiple peril									3.
4. Homeowners multiple peril									4.
5. Commercial multiple peril									5.
8. Ocean marine									8.
9. Inland marine									9.
10. Financial guaranty									10.
11. Medical malpractice									11.
12. Earthquake									12.
13. Group accident and health									13.
14. Credit accident and health (group and individual)*									14.
15. Other accident and health									15.
16. Workers' compensation									16.
17. Other liability									17.
19. Auto liability									19.
21. Auto phys. damage									21.
22. Aircraft (all perils)									22.
23. Fidelity									23.
24. Surety									24.
25. Glass									25.
26. Burglary and theft									26.
27. Boiler and machinery									27.
28. Credit									28.
29. International									29.
30A. Reinsurance**	XXX								30A.
30B. Reinsurance**	XXX								30B.
30C. Reinsurance**	XXX								30C.
30D. Reinsurance**	XXX								30D.
31. Aggregate write-ins for other lines of business									31.
32. TOTALS									32.

DETAILS OF WRITE-INS AGGREGATED AT ITEMS 31

3101.									01.
3102.									02.
3103.									03.
3104.									04.
3105.									05.
3198. Summary of remaining write-ins for item 31 from overflow page									98.
3199. TOTALS (Items 3101 thru 3105 plus 3198) (Item 31)									99.

*Business not exceeding 120 months duration
**See Line 30 Instructions

Form 2

ANNUAL STATEMENT FOR THE YEAR 1989 OF THE

_____ (Name) _____

UNDERWRITING AND INVESTMENT EXHIBIT

PART 3A — UNPAID LOSSES AND LOSS ADJUSTMENT EXPENSES

Line of Business	Adjusted or in Process of Adjustment		2 Deduct Reinsurance Recoverable from Authorized and Unauthorized Companies per Schedule F, Part 1A, Sec. 1, Col. 2	3 Net Losses Excl. Incurred But Not Reported 1a + 1b − 2	Incurred But Not Reported			5 Net Losses Unpaid Excluding Loss Adjustment Expenses 3 + 4a + 4b − 4c	6 Unpaid Loss Adjustment Expenses	
	1a Direct	1b Reinsurance Assumed Schedule F, Part 1A, Sec. 2, Col. 2			4a Direct	4b Reinsurance Assumed	4c Reinsurance Ceded			
1. Fire										1.
2. Allied lines										2.
3. Farmowners multiple peril										3.
4. Homeowners multiple peril										4.
5. Commercial multiple peril										5.
8. Ocean marine										8.
9. Inland marine										9.
10. Financial guaranty										10.
11. Medical malpractice										11.
12. Earthquake										12.
13. Group accident and health								(a)		13.
14. Credit accident and health (group and individual)**										14.
15. Other accident and health								(a)		15.
16. Workers' compensation										16.
17. Other liability										17.
19. Auto liability										19.
21. Auto phys. damage										21.
22. Aircraft (all perils)										22.
23. Fidelity										23.
24. Surety										24.
25. Glass										25.
26. Burglary and theft										26.
27. Boiler and machinery										27.
28. Credit										28.
29. International										29.
30A. Reinsurance***	XXX				XXX					30A.
30B. Reinsurance***	XXX				XXX					30B.
30C. Reinsurance***	XXX				XXX					30C.
30D. Reinsurance***	XXX				XXX					30D.
31. Aggregate write-ins for other lines of business										31.
32. TOTALS										32.

DETAILS OF WRITE-INS AGGREGATED AT ITEM 31

3101.						01
3102.						02
3103.						03
3104.						04
3105.						05
3198. Summary of remaining write-ins for item 31 from overflow page						98
3199. TOTALS (Items 3101 thru 3105 plus 3198) (Item 31)						99

**Business not exceeding 120 months duration.

***See Line 30 Instructions

(a) Including $ _____ for present value of life indemnity claims and $ _____ reserved for deferred maternity and other similar benefits.

ANNUAL STATEMENT FOR THE YEAR 1989 OF THE ....
(Name)

UNDERWRITING AND INVESTMENT EXHIBIT

PART 4 — EXPENSES

	1 Loss Adjustment Expenses	2 Other Underwriting Expenses	3 Investment Expenses	4 Total
1. Claim adjustment services:				
(a) Direct				
(b) Reinsurance assumed				
(c) Reinsurance ceded				
(d) Net claim adjustment services (a + b − c)				
2. Commission and brokerage:				
(a) Direct				
(b) Reinsurance assumed				
(c) Reinsurance ceded				
(d) Contingent — net				
(e) Policy and membership fees				
(f) Net commission and brokerage (a + b − c + d + e)				
3. Allowances to managers and agents				
4. Advertising				
5. Boards, bureaus and associations				
6. Surveys and underwriting reports				
7. Audit of assureds' records				
8. Salaries				
9. Employee relations and welfare				
10. Insurance				
11. Directors' fees				
12. Travel and travel items				
13. Rent and rent items				
14. Equipment				
15. Printing and stationery				
16. Postage, telephone and telegraph, exchange and express				
17. Legal and auditing				
17A. Totals (Items 3 to 17)				
18. Taxes, licenses and fees:				
(a) State and local insurance taxes				
(b) Insurance department licenses and fees				
(c) Payroll taxes				
(d) All other (excluding federal and foreign income and real estate)				
(e) Total taxes, licenses and fees (a + b + c + d)				
19. Real estate expenses				
20. Real estate taxes				
20A. Reimbursements by uninsured accident and health plans				
21. Aggregate write-ins for miscellaneous expenses				
22. Total expenses incurred				
23. Less unpaid expenses — current year				
24. Add unpaid expenses — previous year				
25. TOTAL EXPENSES PAID (Items 22 − 23 + 24)				

DETAILS OF WRITE-INS AGGREGATED AT ITEM 21 FOR MISCELLANEOUS EXPENSES

2101.				
2102.				
2103.				
2104.				
2105.				
2198. Summary of remaining write-ins for Item 21 from overflow page				
2199. Totals (Items 2101 thru 2105 plus 2198) (Part 4, Item 21)				

ANNUAL STATEMENT FOR THE YEAR 1989 OF THE ....
(Name)

EXHIBIT 1—ANALYSIS OF ASSETS

		1 Ledger Assets	2 Non-Ledger Including Excess of Market (or Amortized) Over Book Values	3 Assets Not Admitted Including Excess of Book Over Market (or Amortized) Values	4 Net Admitted Assets (Cols. 1 + 2 − 3)
1.	Bonds (Schedule D)				
2.	Stocks (Schedule D):				
	2.1 Preferred stocks				
	2.2 Common stocks				
3.	Mortgage loans on real estate (Schedule B):				
	(a) First liens				
	(b) Other than first liens				
4.	Real estate (Schedule A):				
	4.1 Properties occupied by the company (less $_____ encumbrances)				
	4.2 Other properties (less $_____ encumbrances)				
5.	Collateral loans (Schedule C)				
6.1	Cash on hand and on deposit:				
	(a) Cash in company's office				
	(b) Cash on deposit (Schedule N)				
6.2	Short-term investments (Schedule DA)				
7.	Other invested assets (Schedule BA)				
8.	Aggregate write-ins for invested assets				
9.	Agents' balances or uncollected premiums (net as to commissions and dividends):				
	9.1 Premiums and agents' balances in course of collection (after deducting ceded reinsurance balances payable of $_____)				
	9.2 Premiums, agents' balances and installments booked but deferred and not yet due (after deducting ceded reinsurance balances payable of $_____)				
	9.3 Accrued retrospective premiums				
10.	Funds held by or deposited with reinsured companies				
11.	Bills receivable, taken for premiums				
12.	Reinsurance recoverable on loss payments (Schedule F, Part 1A, Col. 1)				
13.	Federal income tax recoverable				
14.	Electronic data processing equipment				
15.	Interest, dividends and real estate income due and accrued				
16.	Receivable from parent, subsidiaries and affiliates				
17.	Equities and deposits in pools and associations				
18.	Amounts receivable relating to uninsured accident and health plans				
19.	Other assets:				
	19.1 Equipment, furniture and supplies				XXXXXX
	19.2 Bills receivable, not taken for premiums				XXXXXX
	19.3 Loans on personal security, endorsed or not				XXXXXX
20.	Aggregate write-ins for other than invested assets				
21.	TOTALS				

DETAILS OF WRITE-INS AGGREGATED AT ITEM 8 FOR INVESTED ASSETS

0801.					
0802.					
0803.					
0804.					
0805.					
0898.	Summary of remaining write-ins for Item 8 from overflow page				
0899.	TOTALS (Items 0801 thru 0805 plus 0898) (Page 12, Item 8)				

DETAILS OF WRITE-INS AGGREGATED AT ITEM 20 FOR OTHER THAN INVESTED ASSETS

2001.					
2002.					
2003.					
2004.					
2005.					
2098.	Summary of remaining write-ins for Item 20 from overflow page				
2099.	TOTALS (Items 2001 thru 2005 plus 2098) (Page 12, Item 20)				

EXHIBIT 2—ANALYSIS OF NON-ADMITTED ASSETS

Excluding Excess of Book over Market (or Amortized) Values and Item 15, Col. 3, Exhibit 1

		1 End of Previous Year	2 End of Current Year	3 Change for Year (Increase) or Decrease (Col. 1 − 2)
22.	Loans on company's stock			
23.	Deposits in suspended depositories, less estimated amount recoverable			
24.	Agents' balances or uncollected premiums over three months due:			
	24.1 Premiums and agents' balances in course of collection			
	24.2 Premiums, agents' balances and installments booked but deferred and not yet due			
	24.3 Accrued retrospective premiums			
25.	Bills receivable, past due, taken for premiums			
26.	Excess of bills receivable, not past due, taken for risks over the unearned premiums thereon			
27.	Equipment, furniture and supplies			
28.	Bills receivable, not taken for premiums			
29.	Loans on personal security, endorsed or not			
30.	Aggregate write-ins for assets not admitted			
31.	Total change (Col. 3) (Carry to Item 20, Page 4)	XXXXXX	XXXXXX	

DETAILS OF WRITE-INS AGGREGATED AT ITEM 30 FOR ASSETS NOT ADMITTED

3001.				
3002.				
3003.				
3004.				
3005.				
3098.	Summary of remaining write-ins for Item 30 from overflow page			
3099.	TOTALS (Items 3001 thru 3005 plus 3098) (Page 13, Item 30)			

EXHIBIT 3 — RECONCILIATION OF LEDGER ASSETS

INCREASE IN LEDGER ASSETS

1. Net premiums written (Part 2, Col. 1, Item 32) ....

2. Interest, dividends and real estate income received (Part 1, Item 10, Col. 3) ....

3. From sale or maturity of ledger assets (Part 1A, Col. 2, Item 10) ....

4. Other income items or increases, viz:

    (a) Agents' balances previously charged off ....

    (b) Remittances from home office to U.S. branch (gross) ....

    (c) Funds held under reinsurance treaties (net) ....

    (d) Borrowed money (gross) ....

    (e) Amounts withheld or retained for account of others (net) ....

    (f) Aggregate write-ins for increases in ledger assets ....

5. Adjustment in book value of ledger assets (Part 1A, Item 10, Col. 4) ....

6. Capital paid in (Page 4, Item 24a) ....

7. Surplus paid in (Page 4, Item 25a) ....

8.   Total (Items 1 to 7) ....

DECREASE IN LEDGER ASSETS

9. Net losses paid (Part 3, Col. 4, Item 32) ....

10. Expenses paid (Part 4, Item 25, Col. 4) ....

11. From sale or maturity of ledger assets (Part 1A, Col. 3, Item 10) ....

12. Other disbursement items or decreases, viz:

    (a) Agents' balances charged off ....

    (b) Remittances to home office from U.S. branch (gross) ....

    (c) Funds held under reinsurance treaties (net) ....

    (d) Borrowed money (gross) ....

    (e) Amounts withheld or retained for account of others (net) ....

    (f) Aggregate write-ins for decreases in ledger assets ....

13. Adjustment in book value of ledger assets (Part 1A, Item 10, Col. 5) and depreciation (Item 12, Part 1) ....

14. Federal and foreign income taxes paid ....

15. Dividends paid stockholders ....

16. Dividends to policyholders on direct business, less $.................... dividends on reinsurance assumed or ceded (net) ....

17   Total (Items 9 to 16) ....

RECONCILIATION BETWEEN YEARS

18. Amount of ledger assets as per balance December 31 of previous year ....

19. Increase or (decrease) in ledger assets during the year (Item 8 minus Item 17) ....

20.   Balance = ledger assets December 31 of current year ....

DETAILS OF WRITE-INS AGGREGATED AT ITEM 4(f) FOR INCREASES IN LEDGER ASSETS

04101. ....

04102. ....

04103. ....

04104. ....

04105. ....

04198. Summary of remaining write-ins for item 4f from overflow page ....

04199   TOTAL (Items 04101 thru 04105 plus 04198) (Page 13, Item 4(f)) ....

DETAILS OF WRITE-INS AGGREGATED AT ITEM 12(f) FOR DECREASES IN LEDGER ASSETS

12101. ....

12102. ....

12103. ....

12104. ....

12105. ....

12198. Summary of remaining write-ins for item 12f from overflow page ....

12199   TOTAL (Items 12101 thru 12105 plus 12198) (Page 13, Item 12(f)) ....

ANNUAL STATEMENT FOR THE YEAR 1989 OF THE ....
(Name)

NAIC Group Code ....
NAIC Company Code ....

EXHIBIT OF PREMIUMS AND LOSSES

BUSINESS IN THE STATE OF   **DURING THE YEAR**

1 Line of Business	Gross Premiums, Including Policy and Membership Fees, Less Return Premiums and Premiums on Policies Not Taken		4 Dividends Paid or Credited to Policyholders on Direct Business	5 Direct Unearned Premium Reserves	6 Direct Losses Paid (deducting salvage)	7 Direct Losses Incurred	8 Direct Losses Unpaid
	2 Direct Premiums Written	3 Direct Premiums Earned*					
1. Fire							
2. Allied lines							
3. Farmowners multiple peril							
4. Homeowners multiple peril							
5. Commerical multiple peril							
8. Ocean marine							
9. Inland marine							
10. Financial guaranty							
11. Medical malpractice							
12. Earthquake							
13. Group accident and health							
14. Credit A & H (Group and Individual)							
15.1 Collectively renewable A & H							
15.2 Non-cancellable A & H							
15.3 Guaranteed renewable A & H							
15.4 Non-renewable for stated reasons only							
15.5 Other accident only							
15.6 All other A & H							
16. Workers' compensation							
17. Other liability							
19.1 Private passenger auto no-fault (personal injury protection)							
19.2 Other private passenger auto liability							
19.3 Commercial auto no-fault (personal injury protection)							
19.4 Other commercial auto liability							
21.1 Private passenger auto physical damage							
21.2 Commercial auto physical damage							
22. Aircraft (all perils)							
23. Fidelity							
24. Surety							
25. Glass							
26. Burglary and theft							
27. Boiler and machinery							
28. Credit							
31. Aggregate write-ins for other lines of business							
32. TOTALS							

DETAILS OF WRITE-INS AGGREGATED AT ITEM 31 FOR OTHER LINES OF BUSINESS

3101.							
3102.							
3103.							
3104.							
3105.							
3198. Summary of remaining write-ins for Line 31 from overflow page							
3199. TOTALS (Items 3101 thru 3105 plus 3198) (Line 31)							

Finance and service charges not included in Lines 1 to 32 $ ....
*Direct premiums earned may be estimated by formula on the basis of country-wide ratios for the respective lines of business except where adjustments are required to recognize special situations.

ANNUAL STATEMENT FOR THE YEAR 1989 OF THE ....
(Name)

MEDICARE SUPPLEMENT INSURANCE EXPERIENCE EXHIBIT

FOR THE STATE OF ....

ADDRESS (City, State and Zip Code) ....

NAIC Group Code .... NAIC Company Code ....

PERSON COMPLETING THIS EXHIBIT ....

TO BE FILED BY JUNE 30 FOLLOWING THE ANNUAL STATEMENT FILING

1 Classification	2 Premiums Earned	Incurred Claims	
		3 Amount	4 Percent of Premiums Earned
A. Experience on individual policies			
1. Policies issued through 19........			
a. Reporting State			
b. Nationwide			
2. Policies issued after 19........			
a. Reporting State			
b. Nationwide			
B. Experience on group policies			
1. Policies issued through 19........			
a. Reporting State			
b. Nationwide			
2. Policies issued after 19........			
a. Reporting State			
b. Nationwide			

The undersigned officer hereby certifies that the company named above has complied with the requirements contained in the federal Omnibus Budget Reconciliation Act of 1987, Section 4081.

_____
Signature

_____
Title and Name (Please type)

ANNUAL STATEMENT FOR THE YEAR 1989 OF THE ....

(Name)

Form 2

GENERAL INTERROGATORIES

1. (a) Does the company issue both participating and non-participating policies? — Yes [ ] No [ ]
   (b) If yes. state the amount of net premiums in force on:
       (i) Participating policies. — $ _____
       (ii) Non-participating policies. — $ _____
2. For Mutual Companies and Reciprocal Exchanges Only:
   (a) Does company issue assessable policies? — Yes [ ] No [ ] N A [ ]
   (b) Does company issue nonassessable policies? — Yes [ ] No [ ] N A [ ]
   (c) If assessable policies are issued. what is the extent of the contingent liability of the policyholders? — _____ %
   (d) Total amount of assessments laid or ordered to be laid during the year on deposit notes or contingent premiums — $ _____
3. For Reciprocal Exchanges Only:
   (a) Does the Exchange appoint local agents? — Yes [ ] No [ ] N A [ ]
   (b) If yes. is the commission paid:
       (i) out of Attorney's in-fact compensation? — Yes [ ] No [ ] N A [ ]
       (ii) as a direct expense of the Exchange? — Yes [ ] No [ ] N A [ ]
   (c) What expenses of the Exchange are not paid out of the compensation of the Attorney-in-fact?

   _____

   (d) Has any Attorney-in-fact compensation. contingent on fulfillment of certain conditions. been deferred? — Yes [ ] No [ ] N A [ ]
   (e) If yes. give full information _____

4.

CAPITAL STOCK OF THIS COMPANY

1 Class	2 Number Shares Authorized	3 Number Shares Outstanding	4 Par Value Per Share	5 Redemption Price if Callable	6 IS DIVIDEND RATE LIMITED?		7 ARE DIVIDENDS CUMULATIVE?	
					Yes [ ]	No [ ]	Yes [ ]	No [ ]
Preferred								
Common				XXXX	XXX	XXX	XXX	XXX

5. (a) Does the company own any securities of a real estate holding company or otherwise hold real estate indirectly? — Yes [ ] No [ ]
   (b) If yes. (i) explain _____
       (ii) Name of real estate holding company _____
       (iii) Number of parcels involved? — _____
       (iv) Total book value — $ _____
6. (a) Is the company a member of an insurance Holding Company System consisting of two or more affiliated persons. one or more of which is an insurer? — Yes [ ] No [ ]
   (b) If yes, did the company register and file with its domiciliary State Insurance Commissioner. Director. or Superintendent. or with such regulatory official of the State of domicile of the principal insurer in the Holding Company System. a registration statement providing disclosure substantially similar to the standards adopted by the National Association of Insurance Commissioners in its Model Holding Company System Regulatory Act and model regulations pertaining thereto. or is the company subject to standards and disclosure requirements substantially similar to those required by such Act and regulations? — Yes [ ] No [ ] N/A [ ]
   (c) State regulating — _____
7. (a) Total amount loaned during the year:
       (i) to directors or other officers — $ _____
       (ii) to stockholders not officers — $ _____
   (b) Total amount of loans outstanding at end of year:
       (i) to directors or other officers — $ _____
       (ii) to stockholders not officers — $ _____
8. (a) Did any person while an officer, director or trustee of the company receive directly or indirectly, during the period covered by this statement, any commission on the business transactions of the company? — Yes [ ] No [ ]
   (b) Did any person while an officer, director, trustee or employee receive directly or indirectly, during the period covered by this statement, any compensation in addition to his regular compensation on account of the reinsurance transactions of the company? — Yes [ ] No [ ]
   (c) Has the company an established procedure for disclosure to its board of directors or trustees of any material interest or affiliation on the part of any of its officers, directors, trustees, or responsible employees which is in or is likely to conflict with the official duties of such person? — Yes [ ] No [ ]
   (d) Except for retirement plans generally applicable to its staff employees and agents and contracts with its agents for the payment of commissions, has the company any agreement with a person whereby it agrees that for any service rendered or to be rendered, he shall receive directly or indirectly any salary, compensation or emolument that will extend beyond a period of 12 months from the date of the agreement? — Yes [ ] No [ ]
9. What amount of installment notes is owned and now held by the company? — $ _____
10. (a) Have any of these notes been hypothecated, sold or used in any manner as security for money loaned within the past year? — Yes [ ] No [ ]
    (b) If y:t, what amount? — $ _____
11. Largest net aggregate amount insured in any one risk (excluding workers' compensation). — $ _____
12. What provision has this company made to protect itself from an excessive loss in the event of a catastrophe under a workers' compensation contract issued without limit of loss?

13. (a) Has this company guaranteed any financed premium accounts? — Yes [ ] No [ ]
    (b) If so, give full information _____

14. Has this company reinsured any risk with any other company and agreed to release such company from liability, in whole or in part, from any loss that may occur on the risk, or portion thereof, reinsured? — Yes [ ] No [ ]
    (b) If so, give full information _____

15. If the company has assumed risks from another company, there should be charged on account of such reinsurances a reserve equal to that which the original company would have been required to charge had it retained the risks. Has this been done? — Yes [ ] No [ ]
16. (a) Has this company guaranteed policies issued by any other company and now in force? — Yes [ ] No [ ]
    (b) If yes, give full information _____

17. (a) Were all the stocks, bonds and other securities owned December 31 of current year, over which the company has exclusive control in the actual possession of the company on said date, except as shown by the schedules of special and other deposits? — Yes [ ] No [ ]
    (b) If no, give full and complete information relating thereto: _____

18. (a) Have all private placement investments which were the subject of renegotiation or modification of their terms during the year been disclosed to the Valuation of Securities office of the NAIC, with full details as to the provisions renegotiated or modified? — Yes [ ] No [ ]
    (b) Have filings been made with the Valuation of Securities office of the NAIC in connection with acquisition and disposition of securities as required by Section 8 of the Valuation Procedures and Instructions for Bonds and Stocks? — Yes [ ] No [ ]
19. (a) Were any of the stocks, bonds or other assets of the company owned at December 31 of the current year not exclusively under the control of the company, or has the company sold or transferred any assets subject to a put option contract that is currently in force? — Yes [ ] No [ ]
    (b) If yes, state the amount thereof at December 31 of the current year:
        (i) loaned to others — $ _____
        (ii) subject to reverse repurchase agreements — $ _____
        (iii) subject to dollar repurchase agreements — $ _____
        (iv) subject to reverse dollar repurchase agreements — $ _____
        (v) pledged as collateral — $ _____
        (vi) placed under option agreements — $ _____
        (vii) letter stock or other securities restricted as to sale — $ _____
        (viii) other — $ _____
    (c) For each category above, if any of these assets are held by others, identify by whom held.
        (i) _____
        (ii) _____
        (iii) _____
        (iv) _____
        (v) _____
        (vi) _____
        (vii) _____
        (viii) _____
    (d) For categories (b)(i) and (ii) above, and for any other securities that were made available for use by another person during the year covered by this statement, attach a schedule as shown in the instructions to the annual statement.
    (e) For category (b)(vi) above, do any of the option agreements involve asset transfers with put options? — Yes [ ] No [ ]
    If yes, disclose in the Notes to Financial Statements the information specified in the instructions to the annual statement.

ANNUAL STATEMENT FOR THE YEAR 1989 OF THE .... (Name)

GENERAL INTERROGATORIES (Continued)

20. (a) State as of what date the latest financial examination of the company was made or is being made: ______
(b) By what department or departments? ______

21. (a) Has any change been made during the year of this statement in the charter, by-laws, articles of incorporation, or deed of settlement of the company? Yes [ ] No [ ]
(b) If yes, date of change: ______
If not previously filed, furnish herewith a certified copy of the instrument as amended.

22. (a) Has any direct new business been solicited or written in any state where the company was not licensed? Yes [ ] No [ ]
(b) If yes, explain ______

23. Is the purchase or sale of all investments of the company passed upon either by the board of directors or a subordinate committee thereof? Yes [ ] No [ ]

24. Does the company keep a complete permanent record of the proceedings of its board of directors and all subordinate committees thereof? Yes [ ] No [ ]

25. Have the instructions for completing the blank required by this department been followed in every detail? Yes [ ] No [ ]

ONLY UNITED STATES BRANCHES OF FOREIGN COMPANIES NEED ANSWER INTERROGATORIES 26 and 27:

26. What changes have been made during the year in the United States manager or the United States trustees of the company? ______

27. Does this statement contain all business transacted for the company through its United States branch, on risks wherever located? Yes [ ] No [ ] N/A [ ]

28. (a) During the period covered by this statement, did any agent, general agent, broker, sales representative, non-affiliated sales/service organization or any combination thereof under common control (other than salaried employees of the company), receive credit or commissions for or control a substantial part (more than 20 percent of any major line of business measured on direct premiums) of:
(i) sales of new business? Yes [ ] No [ ]
(ii) renewals? Yes [ ] No [ ]
(b) During the period covered by this statement, did any sales/service organization owned in whole or in part by the company or an affiliate, receive credit or commissions for or control a substantial part (more than 20 percent of any major line of business measured on direct premiums) of:
(i) sales of new business? Yes [ ] No [ ]
(ii) renewals? Yes [ ] No [ ]

29. (a) If the company recorded accrued retrospective premiums on insurance contracts on line 9.3 of the asset schedule, page 2, state the amount of corresponding liabilities recorded for:
(i) Unpaid losses: $______
(ii) Unpaid underwriting expenses (including loss adjustment expenses) $______
(b) Of the amount on line 9.3 of the asset schedule, page 2, state the amount which is secured by letters of credit, collateral and other funds? $______
(c) If the company underwrites commercial insurance risks, such as workers' compensation, are premium or promissory notes accepted from its insureds covering unpaid premiums and/or unpaid losses? Yes [ ] No [ ]
(d) If yes, provide the range of interest rates charged under such notes during the period covered by this statement?
(i) From ______%
(ii) To ______%
(e) Are letters of credit or collateral and other funds received from insureds being utilized by the company to secure premium or promissory notes taken by the company, or to secure any of the company's reported direct unpaid loss reserves, including unpaid losses under loss deductible features of commercial policies? Yes [ ] No [ ]
(f) If yes, state the amount thereof at December 31 of the current year:
(i) Letters of Credit $______
(ii) Collateral and other funds $______

30. What interest, direct or indirect, has this company in the capital stock of any other insurance company?

31. (a) Has this company written any Medicare supplement insurance business? Yes [ ] No [ ]
(b) If yes, indicate total premium volume $______

Ceded Reinsurance Report — Section 1. Annual Report of Reinsurance Transactions (including facultative and pooling transactions)

32. What is the maximum amount of return commission which would have been due reinsurers if they or you had cancelled all of your company's reinsurance or if you or a receiver had cancelled all of your company's direct business and reinsurance assumed as of the end of the period covered by this Annual Statement with the return of the unearned premium reserve? For:
(a) Intercompany pooling agreement: $______
(b) All other reinsurance: $______
(c) Total: $______

33. What would be the amount of the reduction in surplus as shown on this Annual Statement if adjustments were made to reflect the full amount described in Question 32?
(a) Intercompany pooling agreement: $______
(b) All other reinsurance: $______
(c) Total: $______

34. (a) On the basis of loss experience to date, have you accrued earned additional premiums which would be payable or return reinsurance commissions which would be refundable in the future if the reinsurer or you cancelled all of your company's reinsurance as of the end of the period covered by this Annual Statement? Yes [ ] No [ ]
(b) If you have not so accrued, what would be the amount of such additional premium or return commission?
(i) Intercompany pooling agreement: $______
(ii) All other reinsurance: $______
(iii) Total: $______

35. What would be the amount of the reduction in surplus as of the end of the period covered by this Annual Statement if adjustments were made to reflect the full amount described in Question 34?
(a) Intercompany pooling agreement: $______
(b) All other reinsurance: $______
(c) Total: $______

36. What would be the percentage reduction in surplus as of the end of the period covered by this Annual Statement from the combined effects of the amounts described in Questions 33 and 35?
(a) Intercompany pooling agreement: ______%
(b) All other reinsurance: ______%
(c) Total: ______%

37. What is the amount of additional reinsurance premiums, computed at the maximum level provided by the reinsurance contracts, in excess of amounts previously paid and presently accrued (including as accrued the amount shown in response to Question 34) on retrospective adjustment periods covering the most recent three years?
(a) Intercompany pooling agreement: $______
(b) All other reinsurance: $______
(c) Total: $______

38. What is the amount of return reinsurance commission, computed at the minimum level provided by the reinsurance contracts, in excess of amounts previously paid and presently accrued (including as accrued the amount shown in response to Question 34) on retrospective adjustment periods covering the most recent three years?
(a) Intercompany pooling agreement: $______
(b) All other reinsurance: $______
(c) Total: $______

39. What would be the percentage reduction in surplus as of the end of the period covered by this Annual Statement from the combined effects of the amounts described in Questions 37 and 38?
(a) Intercompany pooling agreement: ______%
(b) All other reinsurance: ______%
(c) Total: ______%

40. What would be the percentage reduction in surplus as of the end of the period covered by this Annual Statement from the combined effects of the amounts described in Questions 33, 35, 37 and 38?
(a) Intercompany pooling agreement: ______%
(b) All other reinsurance: ______%
(c) Total: ______%

18

Form 2

ANNUAL STATEMENT FOR THE YEAR 1989 OF THE ....
(Name)

NOTES TO FINANCIAL STATEMENTS

Form 2

ANNUAL STATEMENT FOR THE YEAR 1989 OF THE ....
(Name)

Note: In case the following schedules do not afford sufficient space, companies may furnish them on separate forms, provided the same are upon paper of like size and arrangements and contain the information asked for herein and have the name of the Company printed or stamped at the top thereof.

SPECIAL DEPOSIT SCHEDULE

Showing all deposits or investments NOT held for the protection of ALL the policyholders of the Company

1 Where Deposited	2 Description and Purpose of Deposit (Indicating literal form of registration of Securities)	3 Par Value	4 Statement Value	5 Market Value
999999	TOTALS			

ANNUAL STATEMENT FOR THE YEAR 1989 OF THE ....
(Name)

SCHEDULE OF ALL OTHER DEPOSITS

Showing all deposits made with any Government, Province, State, District, County, Municipality, Corporation, firm or
individual, except those shown in Schedule N, and those shown in "Special Deposit Schedule"

1 Where Deposited	2 Description and Purpose of Deposit (Indicating literal form of registration of Securities)	3 Par Value	4 Statement Value	5 Market Value
999999	TOTALS			

ANNUAL STATEMENT FOR THE YEAR 1989 OF THE ....
                                                                                        (Name)

FIVE-YEAR HISTORICAL DATA

All Figures Taken From or Developed From Annual Statements of Corresponding Years

Show amounts in whole dollars only, no cents; show percentages to one decimal place, i.e. 17.6.

	1 1989	2 1988	3 1987	4 1986	5 1985
Gross Premiums Written (Page 8, Part 2B [2C prior to 1988], Cols. 1 & 2)					
1. Liability Lines (Items 11, 16, 17 & 19)					
2. Property Lines (Items, 1, 2, 9, 12, 21, 25 & 26)					
3. Property and Liability Combined Lines (Items 3, 4, 5, 8, 22 & 27)					
4A. All Other Lines (Items 10, 13, 14, 15, 23, 24, 28, 29 & 30 [and 30D, 1988 and after] [and Item 31, 1986 and after])					
4B. Non-proportional Reinsurance Lines (Items 30A, 30B and 30C)					
5. Total (Item 31 [Item 32, 1986 and after])					
Net Premiums Written (Page 8, Part 2B [2C prior to 1988] Col. 4)					
6. Liability Lines (Items 11, 16, 17 & 19)					
7. Property Lines (Items, 1, 2, 9, 12, 21, 25 & 26)					
8. Property and Liability Combined Lines (Items 3, 4, 5, 8, 22 & 27)					
9A. All Other Lines (Items 10, 13, 14, 15, 23, 24, 28, 29 & 30 [and 30D, 1988 and after] [and Item 31, 1986 and after])					
9B. Non-proportional Reinsurance Lines (Items 30A, 30B and 30C)					
10. Total (Item 31 [Item 32, 1986 and after])					
Statement of Income (Page 4)					
11. Net Underwriting Gain or (Loss) (Item 7)					
12. Net Investment Gain or (Loss) (Item 9A)					
13. Total Other Income (Item 17 [Item 13, 1986 and after])					
14. Dividends to Policyholders (Item 18A [Item 14A, 1986 and after])					
15. Federal and Foreign Income Taxes Incurred (Item 19 [Item 15, 1986 and after])					
16. Net Income (Item 20 [Item 16, 1986 and after])					
Balance Sheet Items (Pages 2 and 3)					
17. Total Admitted Assets (Page 2, Item 22 [Item 21, 1986 and after])					
18. Agents' Balances or Uncollected Premiums (Page 2):					
18.1 In Course of Collection (Item 8.1 [Item 9.1, 1986 and after])					
18.2 Deferred and Not Yet Due (Item 8.2 [Item 9.2, 1986 and after])					
19. Total Liabilities (Page 3, Item 23 [Item 22, 1986 and after])					
20. Losses (Page 3, Item 1 [and item 1A, 1988 and after])					
21. Loss Adjustment Expenses (Page 3, Item 2)					
22. Unearned Premiums (Page 3, Item 10 [Item 9, 1986 and after])					
23. Capital Paid Up (Page 3, Items 25A and 25B [Items 24A and 24B, 1986 and after])					
24. Surplus as Regards Policyholders (Page 3, Item 27 [Item 26, 1986 and after])					
Percentage Distribution of Cash and Invested Assets					
(Page 2) (Item divided by Page 2, Item 7a [Item 8a, 1986 and after]) x 100.0					
25. Bonds (Item 1)					
26. Stocks (Items 2.1 and 2.2)					
27. Mortgage Loans on Real Estate (Item 3)					
28. Real Estate (Items 4.1 and 4.2)					
29. Collateral Loans (Item 5)					
30. Cash and short-term investments (Items 6.1 and 6.2)					
31. Other Invested Assets (Item 7)					
31A. Aggregate write-ins for invested assets (Item 8)					
32. Cash and Invested Assets (Item 7a [Item 8a, 1986 and after])	100.0	100.0	100.0	100.0	100.0
Investment in Parent, Subsidiaries and Affiliates					
33. Affiliated Bonds (Item 29, Col. 6, Sch. D Summary)					
34. Affiliated Preferred Stocks (Item 47, Col. 3, Sch. D Summary)					
35. Affiliated Common Stocks (Item 65, Col. 3, Sch. D Summary)					
36. Affiliated Short-Term Investments (Subtotals included in Schedule DA, Part 1, Col. 10)					
36A. Affiliated Mortgage Loans on Real Estate					
36B. All Other Affiliated					
37. Total of above Items 33, 34, 35, 36, 36A and 36B					
38. Percentage of Investments in Parent, Subsidiaries and Affiliates to Surplus as Regards Policyholders (Item 37 above divided by Page 3, Col. 1, Item 27 [Item 26, 1986 and after] x 100.0)					

ANNUAL STATEMENT FOR THE YEAR 1989 OF THE ....
(Name)

FIVE-YEAR HISTORICAL DATA
(Continued)

		1 1989	2 1988	3 1987	4 1986	5 1985
	Capital and Surplus Accounts (Page 4)					
39	Net Unrealized Capital Gains or (Losses) (Item 23 [Item 19. 1986 and after;)					
40	Dividends to Stockholders (Cash) (Item 3; [Item 27. 1986 and after])					
41	Change in Surplus as Regards Policyholders for the Year (Item 39 [Item 31. 1986 and after])					
	Gross Losses Paid (Page 9. Part 3 Cols 1 & 2)					
42	Liability Lines (Items 11. 16. 17 & 19)					
43	Property Lines (Items 1. 2. 9. 12. 21. 25 & 26)					
44	Property and Liability Combined Lines (Items 3. 4. 5. 8. 22 & 27)					
45A	All Other Lines (Items 10. 13. 14. 15. 23. 24. 28. 29 & 30 [and 30D. 1988 and after] [& Item 31. 1986 and after])					
45B	Non-Proportional Reinsurance Lines (Items 30A. 30B and 30C)					
46	Total (Item 31 [Item 32. 1986 and after])					
	Net Losses Paid (Page 9. Part 3. Col. 4)					
47	Liability Lines (Items 11. 16. 17 & 19)					
48	Property Lines (Items 1. 2. 9. 12. 21. 25 & 26)					
49	Property and Liability Combined Lines (Items 3. 4. 5. 8. 22 & 27)					
50A	All Other Lines (Items 10. 13. 14. 15. 23. 24. 28. 29 & 30 [and 30D. 1988 and after] [& Item 31. 1986 and after])					
50B	Non-Proportional Reinsurance Lines (Items 30A. 30B and 30C)					
51	Total (Item 31 [Item 32. 1986 and after])					
	Operating Percentages (Page 4) (Item divided by Page 4. Item 1) x 100.0					
52	Premiums Earned (Item 1)	100.0	100.0	100.0	100.0	100.0
53	Losses Incurred (Item 2)					
54	Loss Expenses Incurred (Item 3)					
55	Other Underwriting Expenses Incurred (Item 4)					
56	Net Underwriting Gain or (Loss) (Item 7)					
	Other Percentages					
57	Other Underwriting Expenses to Net Premiums Written (Page 4. Items 4 + 5 − 17 [Item 13. 1986 and after] divided by Page 8. Part 2B [2C prior to 1988] Col. 4. Item 31 [Item 32. 1986 and after] × 100.0)					
58	Losses and Loss Expenses Incurred to Premiums Earned (Page 4. Items 2 + 3 divided by Page 4. Item 1 × 100.0)					
59	Net Premiums Written to Policyholders' Surplus (Page 8. [Part 2B [2C prior to 1988] Col. 4. Item 31. [Item 32. 1986 and after] divided by Page 3. Item 27. [Item 26. 1986 and after] Col. 1 × 100.0)					
	One Year Loss Development (000 omitted) Schedule "P" [Schedule O and P. prior to 1989]					
60	Development in estimated losses and loss expenses incurred prior to current year (Part 2. Item 11. Col. 7 less Col. 6: Part 2-Summary; One Year Total. 1989 and after)					
61	Percent of development of loss and loss expenses incurred to policyholders' surplus of previous year end (Item 60 [Item 63 prior to 1989) divided by Page 4. Item 21 [Item 17. 1986 and after] Col. 1 × 100.0)					
	Two Year Loss Development (000 omitted)					
	Schedule "P" [Schedule O and P. prior to 1989]					
62	Development in estimated losses and loss expenses incurred 2 years before the current year and prior (Part 2. Item 9. Col. 7 less Col. 5: Part 2-Summary. Two Year Total. 1989 and after)					
63	Percent of development of loss and loss expenses incurred to reported policyholders' surplus of second previous year end (Item 62 [Item 68 prior to 1989] divided by Page 4. Item 21. [Item 17. 1986 and after] Col. 2 x 100.0)					

Form 2

ANNUAL STATEMENT FOR THE YEAR 1989 OF THE ....

(Name)

SCHEDULE A—PART 1

Showing all Real Estate OWNED December 31 of Current Year, the Cost, Book and Market Value thereof, the Nature and Amount of all Liens and Encumbrances thereon, including Interest Due and Accrued, etc.

No.	1 Quantity, Dimensions and Location of Lands, Size and Description of Buildings (Nature of encumbrances, if any, including interest due and accrued)	2 Date Acquired	3 Name of Vendor	4 Amount of Encumbrances	5 *Actual Cost	6 Book Value Less Encumbrances	7 †Market Value Less Encumbrances	8 Increase by Adjustment In Book Value During Year	9 Decrease by Adjustment in Book Value During Year	10 Gross Income Less Interest on Encumbrances	11 Expended for Taxes, Repairs and Expenses	12 Net Income	Rental Value of Space Occupied by		15 Year of Last Appraisal
													13 Company	14 Parent, Subsidiaries and Affiliates	
999999 TOTALS															X X X

*Including cost of acquiring title, and, if the property was acquired by foreclosure, such cost shall include the amounts expended for taxes, repairs and improvements prior to the date on which the company acquired title.
†State basis on which market value was determined

CLASSIFICATION

Showing the total amount of Real Estate owned in each State and Foreign Country

1 State	2 Market Value	1 State	2 Market Value	1 State	2 Market Value	3 Foreign Country	4 Market Value
					999999 TOTALS	X X X	

23

Form 2

ANNUAL STATEMENT FOR THE YEAR 1989 OF THE ....
.... (Name)

SCHEDULE A—PART 2

Showing all Real Estate **ACQUIRED** During the Year and Showing also Amounts Expended for Additions and Permanent Improvements Made During said Year to **ALL** Real Estate

No.	1 Quantity, Dimensions and Location of Lands; Size and Description of Buildings (or) Nature of Additions and Permanent Improvements made During the Year (Nature of encumbrances, if any)	2 Date Acquired	3 How Acquired	4 Name of Vendor	5 Cost to Company During the Year	6 Amount Expended for Additions and Permanent Improvements During the Year	7 Book Value December 31 of Current Year Less Encumbrances
9999999	TOTALS						

SCHEDULE A—PART 3

Showing all Real Estate **SOLD** or Otherwise Disposed of During the Year Including Payments During the Year on "Sales under Contract"

No.	1 Quantity, Dimensions and Location of Lands; Size and Description of Buildings (Nature of encumbrances, if any)	2 Date Sold	3 Name of Purchaser	4 †Cost to Company	5 Increase by Adjustment in Book Value During the Year	6 Decrease by Adjustment in Book Value During the Year	7 †Book Value at Date of Sale Less Encumbrances	8 ‡Amount Received Including Payments on Sales Under Contract	9 Profit on Sale	10 Loss on Sale	11 Gross Income During the Year Less Interest on Encumbrances	12 Expended for Taxes, Repairs and Expenses During Year
9999999	TOTALS											

† Including cost of acquiring title, and, if the property was acquired by foreclosure, such cost shall include the amounts expended for taxes, repairs, and improvements prior to the date on which the company acquired title. In reporting sales under contract, include payments received during the current year only
‡ Indicate payments on "Sales under Contracts" in Part 3 by inserting the letter "P" after the number of the parcel.
†† In case of sales under contract, include payments received during current year only, until book value per Part 1 is exhausted.

SCHEDULE A—Verification Between Years

1. Book value, December 31, previous year (Item 4, Col 1, Exhibit 1, prior year statement) ....
2. Increase by adjustment:
   (a) Totals, Part 1, Col 8 ....
   (b) Totals, Part 3, Col 6 ....
3. Cost of acquired, Part 2, Col 5 ....
4. Cost of additions and permanent improvements, Part 2, Col 6 ....
5. Profit on sales, Part 3, Col 9 ....
6. Total ....

7. Decrease by adjustment:
   (a) Totals, Part 1, Col 9 ....
   (b) Totals, Part 3, Col 5 ....
8. Received on sales, Part 3, Col 8 ....
9. Loss on sales, Part 3, Col 10 ....
10. Book value, December 31, current year (Item 4, Col 1, Exhibit 1) ....

Form 2

ANNUAL STATEMENT FOR THE YEAR 1989 OF THE .... (Name)

SCHEDULE B

Showing all Long-Term MORTGAGES OWNED December 31 of Current Year, and all Mortgage Loans Made, Increased, Discharged, Reduced or Disposed of During the Year

Indicate by symbols FHA and VA if loans are so insured. All such FHA and VA insured loans not in process of foreclosure may be summarized by year and state of issue and combined values may be shown for land and buildings.

1 Number	Record of Mortgage					Principal				Interest								Location and Description
	Date			4 State	5 Country	6 Book Value Dec. 31 of Previous Year	7 Amount Loaned During Year (A)	8 Amount Paid on Account or in Full During Year (B)	9 Increase or (Decrease) in Book Value	10 Book Value Dec. 31 of Current Year 6 + 7 - 8 + 9	11 Date Due	12 Rate of	13 Amount Past Due Dec. 31 of Current Year	14 Am't Accrued Dec. 31 of Current Year	15 Gross Am't Rec'd During Year	16 Paid for Accrued Interest on Mortgages Acquired During Year	17 Value of Lands Mortgaged	18 Value of Buildings	19 Amount of Fire Insurance Held by Company on the Buildings	20 (State if this mortgage is being foreclosed, or if there are any prior liens. State name of mortgagor if mortgagor is a parent, subsidiary, affiliate, officer or director.)
	2 Year Given	3 Year Due																		
999999	TOTALS										XXXX	XXXX					XXXX	XXXX	XXXX	XXXX

(A) Including all mortgages "purchased" or otherwise acquired during the year and all increases during the year on loans outstanding December 31 of previous year.
(B) Including mortgages under which Company has secured title and possession by foreclosure.

CLASSIFICATION

Showing the Total Amount of Long-Term Mortgage Loans on Real Estate in Each State and Foreign Country

1 State	2 Amount	1 State	2 Amount	1 State	2 Amount	3 Foreign Country	4 Amount
				999999 TOTALS		XXXX	

NOTE: Any casualty company having a majority of its premium volume derived from non-cancellable accident and health policies, may report on Schedule B forms of the Life Blank in lieu of this schedule.

25

ANNUAL STATEMENT FOR THE YEAR 1989 OF THE ....

(Name)

SCHEDULE B A—PART 1

Showing Other Long-Term Invested Assets OWNED December 31, Current Year

1 Number of Units and Description*	2 Year Acquired	3 Lessee or Location	4 Amount of Encumbrances	5 Cost to Company	6 Book Value at December 31, Less Encumbrances	7 Statement Value at December 31	8 Market or Investment Value at December 31, Less Encumbrances	9 Additions to or (Reductions) in Investment	10 (Decrease) or Increase by Adjustment in Book Value During Year‡	11 Gross Income Received During Year	12 Net Income Received During Year §	13 Amounts Accrued at December 31 §§	14 Amounts Past Due at December 31 §§
079999 Totals													

*Give detail description of investment and underlying security (Footnotes may be used to describe leases for each class in the aggregate). Indicate statutory category of investment, i.e. real estate, mortgage, security, or other. Include in this Schedule, showing subtotals by class and grand total for all classes: (1) All loans on or investments in oil and gas production payments except those listed on Schedule D, Part 1 or Schedule DA, (2) All Transportation Equipment, (3) Timber Deeds, (4) Mineral Rights carried as admitted assets, (5) Motor Vehicle Trust Certificates, (6) Any other class of admitted investment not clearly includable in other statement schedules.

‡Include additional investments made, or portion of investment repaid. ‡Include depreciation on real estate and transportation equipment, etc.; amortization of premium and accrual of discount if applicable. §After appropriate reduction for interest paid to manufacturer during year and depletion and amortization of mineral rights. §§After appropriate reduction for due and accrued interest payable to manufacturers.

SCHEDULE B A—VERIFICATION BETWEEN YEARS

1. Book value of other invested assets (Exhibit 1, Item 7, prior year annual statement) ....

2. Cost of acquisitions during year:
  (a) Column 5, Part 2 ....
  (b) Column 9, Part 1 ....
  (c) Column 7, Part 3 ....

3. Increase by adjustment during year:
  (a) Column 10, Part 1 ....
  (b) Column 8, Part 3 ....

4. Profit on disposition, Column 9, Part 3 ....

5. Total ....

6. Deduct consideration on disposition, Column 5, Part 3 ....

7. Reductions in investment during year:◊
  (a) Column 9, Part 1 ....
  (b) Column 7, Part 3 ....

8. Decrease by adjustment during year:
  (a) Column 10, Part 1 ....
  (b) Column 8, Part 3 ....

9. Loss on disposition, Column 10, Part 3 ....

10. Book value of other invested assets, Exhibit 1, Item 7, Current year ....

◊Cash payments on account of capital, e.g., depletion and amortization of Mineral Rights.

Form 2

ANNUAL STATEMENT FOR THE YEAR 1989 OF THE ....
(Name)

SCHEDULE B A—PART 2
Showing Other Long-Term Invested Assets ACQUIRED During Current Year

1 Number of Units and Description*	2 Date Acquired	3 Lessee or Location	4 Cost to Company	5 Consideration Paid During Current Year	6 Name of Vendor
TOTALS					
079999					XXX

SCHEDULE B A—PART 3
Showing Other Long-Term Invested Assets DISPOSED of During Current Year

1 Number of Units and Description*	2 Date Disposed of	3 Lessee or Location	4 Name of Purchaser or Nature of Disposition	5 Consideration	6 Book Value at Date of Sale	7 Additions to or (Reductions) in Investment	8 (Decrease) or Increase by Adjustment in Book Value During Year	9 Profit on Sale	10 Loss on Sale	11 Net Income
TOTALS										
079999										

*Include in this Schedule, showing subtotals by class and grand total for all classes: (1) All loans on or investments in oil and gas production payments except those listed in Schedule D, Part I, or Schedule DA. (2) All Transportation Equipment. (3) Timber Deeds. (4) Mineral Rights carried as admitted assets. (5) Motor Vehicle Trust Certificates. (6) Any other class of admitted investment not clearly includable in other statement schedules.

Form 2

28

ANNUAL STATEMENT FOR THE YEAR 1989 OF THE _____ (Name)

SCHEDULE C—PART 1

Showing all Long-Term Collateral Loans **IN FORCE** December 31 of Current Year

1 No.	2 Description of Securities Held as Collateral December 31 of Current Year (Give in this column the number of shares of each block of stock and rate of interest and year of maturity of each bond held as collateral)	3 Par Value	4 Rate Used to Obtain Market Value	5 Market Value Dec. 31 of Current Year	6 Amount Loaned Thereon	7 Date of Loan	8 Maturity of Loan	9 Rate on Loan	Interest			13 Name of Actual Borrower (State if the borrower is a parent, subsidiary, affiliate, officer or director)
									10 Amount Paid Due Dec. 31 of Current Year	11 Amount Accrued Dec. 31 of Current Year	12 Amount Received During Year	
9999999 TOTALS					XXXX	XXXX	XXXX	XXXX				XXXX

SCHEDULE C—PART 2

Showing all Long-Term Collateral Loans **MADE** During the Year

1 No.	2 Description of Security Accepted as Collateral When Loan was Made	3 Par Value	4 Rate Used to Obtain Market Value	5 Market Value at Date of Loan	6 Amount Loaned Thereon	7 Date of Loan	8 Maturity of Loan	9 Rate of Interest on Loan	10 Name of Actual Borrower (State if the borrower is a parent, subsidiary, affiliate, officer or director)
9999999 TOTALS						XXXX	XXXX	XXXX	XXXX

Form 2

ANNUAL STATEMENT FOR THE YEAR 1989 OF THE _____ (Name)

SCHEDULE C — PART 3

Showing all Long-Term Collateral Loans **DISCHARGED** in Whole or in Part During the Year

1 No. Indicate Partial Payments by the Letter "P"	2 Description of Collateral Released When Loan Was Discharged. (In case of partial payments enter collateral release only)	3 Par Value	4 Rate Used to Obtain Market Value	5 Market Value at Date of Discharge	6 Amount of Loan Repaid	7 Date of Loan	8 Date of Repayment	Interest		11 Name of Actual Borrower (State if the borrower is a parent, subsidiary affiliate, officer or director)
								9 Rate on Loan	10 Amount Received During Year	
999999 Totals						XXXX	XXXX	XXXX	XXXX	XXXX

SCHEDULE C — PART 4

Showing All Substitutions of Collateral During the Year

1 No. (To Correspond with No. Shown in Parts 1, 2 and 3)	2 Amount of Loan Col. 6 of Parts 1, 2 or 3	Collateral Substituted				Collateral Released			
		3 Description	4 Date	5 Par Value	6 Market Value	7 Description	8 Date	9 Par Value	10 Market Value
999999 TOTALS		XXXX	XXXX	XXXX		XXXX	XXXX	XXXX	XXXX

29

ANNUAL STATEMENT FOR THE YEAR 1989 OF THE ....
(Name)

SCHEDULE D — SUMMARY BY COUNTRY

Long-Term Bonds and Stocks **OWNED** December 31 of Current Year

1 Description		2 Book Value	3 †Market Value (Excluding accrued interest)	4 Actual Cost (Excluding accrued interest)	5 Par Value of Bonds	6 *Amortized or Investment Value
BONDS Governments (Including all obligations guaranteed by governments)	1. United States					
	2. Canada					
	3. Other Countries					
	4. Totals					
States, Territories and Possessions (Direct and guaranteed)	5. United States					
	6. Canada					
	7. Other Countries					
	8. Totals					
Political Subdivisions of States, Territories and Possessions (Direct and guaranteed)	9. United States					
	10. Canada					
	11. Other Countries					
	12. Totals					
Special revenue and special assessment obligations and all non-guaranteed obligations of agencies and authorities of governments and their political subdivisions	13. United States					
	14. Canada					
	15. Other Countries					
	16. Totals					
Railroads (unaffiliated)	17. United States					
	18. Canada					
	19. Other Countries					
	20. Totals					
Public Utilities (unaffiliated)	21. United States					
	22. Canada					
	23. Other Countries					
	24. Totals					
Industrial and Miscellaneous (unaffiliated)	25. United States					
	26. Canada					
	27. Other Countries					
	28. Totals					
Parent, Subsidiaries, and Affiliates	29. Totals					
	30. Total Bonds					
PREFERRED STOCKS Railroads (unaffiliated)	31. United States					
	32. Canada					
	33. Other Countries					
	34. Totals					
Public Utilities (unaffiliated)	35. United States					
	36. Canada					
	37. Other Countries					
	38. Totals					
Banks, Trust and Insurance Companies (unaffiliated)	39. United States					
	40. Canada					
	41. Other Countries					
	42. Totals					
Industrial and Miscellaneous (unaffiliated)	43. United States					
	44. Canada					
	45. Other Countries					
	46. Totals					
Parent, Subsidiaries, and Affiliates	47. Totals					
	48. Total Preferred Stocks					
COMMON STOCKS Railroads (unaffiliated)	49. United States					
	50. Canada					
	51. Other Countries					
	52. Totals					
Public Utilities (unaffiliated)	53. United States					
	54. Canada					
	55. Other Countries					
	56. Totals					
Banks, Trust and Insurance Companies (unaffiliated)	57. United States					
	58. Canada					
	59. Other Countries					
	60. Totals					
Industrial and Miscellaneous (unaffiliated)	61. United States					
	62. Canada					
	63. Other Countries					
	64. Totals					
Parent, Subsidiaries, and Affiliates	65. Totals					
	66. Total Common Stocks					
	67. Total Stocks					
	68. Total Bonds and Stocks					

†Statement value for preferred stocks. For certain bonds, values other than actual market may appear in this column (See Schedule D, Part 1, for details).
The aggregate value of bonds which are valued at other than actual market is $................................
*Companies, societies, and associations which do not amortize their bonds should leave this column blank.

SCHEDULE D — VERIFICATION BETWEEN YEARS

1. Book value of bonds and stocks, per Items 1 and 2, Col. 1, Exhibit 1, previous year .... _____

2. Cost of bonds and stocks acquired, Col. 5, Part 3 .... _____

3. Increase by adjustment in book value:
   (a) Col. 10, Part 1 ..... _____
   (b) Col. 9, Part 2, Sec. 1 _____
   (c) Col. 8, Part 2, Sec. 2 _____
   (d) Col. 9, Part 4 _____

4. Profit on disposal of bonds and stocks, Col. 11, Part 4 .... _____

5. Total .... _____

6. Deduct consideration for bonds and stocks disposed of, Col. 5, Part 4 .... _____

7. Decrease by adjustment in book value:
   (a) Col. 11, Part 1 ..... _____
   (b) Col. 10, Part 2, Sec. 1 _____
   (c) Col. 9, Part 2, Sec. 2 _____
   (d) Col. 10, Part 4 ..... _____

8. Loss on disposal of bonds and stocks, Col. 12, Part 4 .... _____

9. Book value of bonds and stocks, per Items 1 and 2, Col. 1, Exhibit 1, current year .... _____

Form 2

(Name)

SCHEDULE D—PART 1A

Quality Distribution of All* Bonds Owned December 31, Current Year At Statement Values and By Major Types of Issues

1 Quality Rating Per The NAIC Designation	2 1 Year or Less	3 Over 1 Year Through 5 Years	4 Over 5 Years Through 10 Years	5 Over 10 Years Through 20 Years	6 Over 20 Years	7 Total Current Year	8 Col. 7 as a % of Line 5.5 Col 7	9 Totals From Col 7 Prior Year	10 % From Col 8 Prior Year
Section 1 Governments Schedule D (Group 1)									
1.1 YES X, YES C									
1.2 NO* NO* C									
1.3 NO** NO* C									
1.4 NO									
1.5 TOTAL									
Section 2 Political Subdivisions, Governmental Agencies and Authorities (Groups 2, 3 and 4)									
2.1 YES X, YES C									
2.2 NO* NO* C									
2.3 NO** NO** C									
2.4 NO									
2.5 TOTAL									
Section 3 Other (Unaffiliated) (Groups 5, 6 and 7)									
3.1 YES X, YES C									
3.2 NO* NO* C									
3.3 NO** NO* C									
3.4 NO									
3.5 TOTAL									
Section 4 Parent, Subsidiaries and Affiliates (Group 8)									
4.1 YES X, YES C									
4.2 NO* NO* C									
4.3 NO** NO** C									
4.4 NO									
4.5 TOTAL									
Section 5 Total Bonds									
5.1 YES X, YES C									
5.2 NO* NO* C									
5.3 NO** NO* C									
5.4 NO									
5.5 TOTAL									

† Includes aggregate statement value of all bonds shown in Schedules D and DA .... prior year of bonds with 2 designations.
* Includes $ .... current year. $ ....

NAIC Designation Definitions:
YES — Investment Grade
NO* — Non Investment Grade — Average Quality
NO** — Non Investment Grade — Below Average Quality
NO — Bonds in or near default on principal or interest payments

NOTE: The letter "C" following a designation indicates a demand or perpetual obligation valued at original cost. The letter "X" following a designation indicates the obligation is rated in the top four categories by a recognized rating organization. The letter "Z" indicates an obligation whose NAIC designation was not approved by the Securities Valuation Office at the date of statement.

31

Form 2

ANNUAL STATEMENT FOR THE YEAR 1989 OF THE ....

(Name)

SCHEDULE D — PART 1

Showing all Long-Term BONDS Owned December 31 of Current Year

Bonds to be grouped in the following manner and each group arranged alphabetically (The listing in Groups 2, 3 and 4 should be alphabetical by State.) Show sub-totals for each group.

1. Governments (including all obligations guaranteed by governments).
2. States, Territories and Possessions (direct and guaranteed).
3. Political Subdivisions of States, Territories and Possessions (direct and guaranteed).
4. Special revenue and special assessment obligations and all non-guaranteed obligations of agencies and authorities of governments and their political subdivisions.
5. Railroads. (unaffiliated)
6. Public Utilities. (unaffiliated)
7. Industrial and Miscellaneous. (unaffiliated)
8. Parent, Subsidiaries and Affiliates.

1		2		3				4	5	6	7	8	Interest			Supplemental columns for data concerning Amortization								See Note	
CUSIP Identification***	**Description	Interest		Date of				Book Value	Par Value	Rate Used to Obtain Market Value	§§Market Value (excluding accrued interest)	Actual Cost (including accrued interest)	9.1 Amount Due and Accrued Dec. 31 of Current Year on Bonds not in default	9.2 Gross Am't Received During Year	10 Increase by Adjustment in Book Value During Year	11 Decrease by Adjustment in Book Value During Year	12 Amount of Interest due and accrued Dec. 31, current year on bonds in default as to principal or interest	13 §NAIC Designation	14 Year Acquired	15 Effective Rate of Interest at Which Purchase Was Made	16 †Amortized or Investment Value Dec. 31 of Current Year	17 ‡Increase in Amortized Value During Year	18 ‡Decrease in Amortized Value During Year
	Give complete and accurate description of all bonds owned, including the location of all street railway and miscellaneous companies. If bonds are "serial" issues give amount maturing each year.	Rate of	*How Paid	Maturity		††Option																	
				Year	Month	Year	Call Price																	
0999999 TOTALS										XXX									XXX	XXX	XXX			

*Insert initial letters of months in which interest is payable.

**Where a bond is payable in a foreign currency the par value and purchase price in that currency should be included as part of the description.
†Perpetual bonds, bonds in default as to principal or interest and bonds not amply secured, are to be entered in this column at market value.
‡Companies which use "Amortized Values" as "Book Values" may omit entering figures in these columns, and provide the following footnote: "The increases and decreases in amortized values are the same as those shown in the columns for 'Increase and Decrease by Adjustment in Book Value', excepting as otherwise indicated."
§Insert the NAIC designation for such security printed in the NAIC Valuations of Securities manual.

NOTE.— This supplemental information, required of all Companies which amortize their bonds, is not to be used as a substitute for the information required in preceding columns, but in addition thereto.
††Show year and call price pertaining to option. If any, on which amortization is based. On bonds purchased at a premium, the maturity date or call feature producing lowest amortized value should be used.
§§Where a market value is published in the NAIC Valuation of Securities Manual, it must be entered in Column 7. Where amortized value or any other value is used, insert a symbol alongside of the amount reported.
***CUSIP numbers entered are to conform to these provided and published by the Securities Valuation Office. See Annual Statement Instructions.

Form 2

(Name)

SCHEDULE D—PART 2—SECTION 1

Showing all **PREFERRED STOCKS** Owned December 31 of Current Year

Stocks to be grouped in following order and each group arranged alphabetically, showing sub-totals for each group:

Railroads. (unaffiliated) Industrial and Miscellaneous. (unaffiliated)

Public Utilities. (unaffiliated) Parent, Subsidiaries and Affiliates.

Banks, Trust and Insurance Companies. (unaffiliated)

CUSIP Identification***	1 Description Give complete and accurate description of all preferred stocks owned including redeemable options, if any, and location of all street railway, bank, trust and miscellaneous companies.	2 No. of Shares	3 Par Value Per Share	4 Book Value	5 *Rate Per Share	6 Statement Value	6A Rate Per Share Used In Obtain Market Value	6B Market Value	7 Actual Cost	Dividends 8.1 Declared but Unpaid	Dividends 8.2 Amount Received During Year	9 Increase by Adjustment in Book Value During Year	10 Decrease by Adjustment in Book Value During Year	11 NAIC Desig- nation	12 Year Acquired
0659999	Total Preferred Stocks	XXXX			XXX		XXXX							XXX	XXXX

*Insert the word 'cost' for preferred stocks eligible for stabilization under Section 3 (II) (d) of the N.A.I.C. Valuation Procedures. Insert the market value rate for preferred stocks not eligible for stabilization.

***CUSIP numbers entered are to conform to those as provided and published by the Securities Valuation Office. See Annual Statement instructions.

§Insert the NAIC designation for such security printed in the NAIC Valuations of Securities manual.

33

Form 2

ANNUAL STATEMENT FOR THE YEAR 1999 OF THE .... (Name)

SCHEDULE D — PART 2 — SECTION 2

Showing all COMMON STOCKS Owned December 31 of Current Year

Stocks to be grouped in following order and each group arranged alphabetically, showing sub-totals for each group
Railroads, (unaffiliated)
Public Utilities, (unaffiliated)
Banks, Trust and Insurance Companies, (unaffiliated)
Industrial and Miscellaneous, (unaffiliated)
Parent, Subsidiaries and Affiliates

| 1 | | 2 | 3 | 4 | 5 | 6 | Dividends | | 8 | 9 | 10 | 11 |
| | | | | | | | 7.1 | 7.2 | | | | |
CUSIP Identi-fication***	Description	No. of Shares	Book Value	Rate Per Share Used to Obtain Market Value	Market Value	Actual Cost	Declared but Unpaid	Amount Received During Year	Increase by Adjustment in Book Value During Year	Decrease by Adjustment in Book Value During Year	§NAIC Desig-nation	Year Acquired
	Give complete and accurate description of all common stocks owned, including redeemable options, if any and addresses (City and State of all Street railway, banks, trust and insurance companies, savings and loan or Building and loan associations and miscellaneous companies.											
069999	Total Common Stocks			XXXX							XXX	XXXX
079999	Total Preferred and Common Stocks			XXXX							XXX	XXXX

NOTES: Complete information must be furnished in connection with any holding of preferred or common stock on the statement date which is optioned or restricted in any way as to its sale by the issuer.
Identify all such securities by the symbol "R" to be inserted beside the figure shown as the rate per share to obtain market value.
Transferable shares only of Savings and Loan or Building and Loan Associations to be reported herein.
***CUSIP numbers entered are to conform to those as provided and published by the Securities Valuation Office. See Annual Statement instructions.
§Insert the NAIC designation for such security printed in the NAIC Valuations of Securities manual. For all common stocks bearing the NAIC designation "U" provide the number of such issues .... the total $ value of all such issues ....

ANNUAL STATEMENT FOR THE YEAR 1989 OF THE ....
.... (Name)

SCHEDULE D—PART 3
Showing all Long-Term Bonds and Stocks ACQUIRED During Year

Bonds, preferred stocks and common stocks to be grouped separately
showing sub-totals for each group.

CUSIP Identification***	1 Description§ Give complete and accurate description of each bond and stock††	2 Date Acquired*	3 Name of Vendor*	4 No. of Shares of Stock	5 Actual Cost (Excluding Accrued Interest and Dividends)	6 Par Value of Bonds	7 Paid for Accrued Interest and Dividends
269999	TOTALS						

§Enter as separate summary items the totals of Columns 6, 7 and 15 of Part 5 for bonds, preferred stocks and common stocks. All bonds and stocks acquired and fully disposed of during the year are not to be demand in this Part
*The items with reference to each issue of bonds and stocks acquired at public offerings may be totaled in one line and the word "Various" inserted in Columns 2 and 3
***CUSIP numbers entered are to conform to those as provided and published by the Securities Valuation Office. See Annual Statement instructions.
††If bonds are serial issues give amounts maturing each year. Securities acquired under a reverse repurchase agreement must be identified.

35

Form 2

ANNUAL STATEMENT FOR THE YEAR 1989 OF THE ....

(Name)

SCHEDULE D—PART 4

Showing all Long-Term Bonds and Stocks SOLD, REDEEMED or otherwise DISPOSED OF During Year

Bonds, preferred stocks and common stocks to be grouped separately showing sub-totals for each group.

Description‡			2	3	4	5	6	7	8	9	10	11	12	13	14
CUSIP Identification***	Give complete and accurate description of each bond and stock, including location of all street railway, bank, trust and miscellaneous companies.††		Disposal Date**	Name of Purchaser (If matured or called under redemption option, so state and give price at which called.)	No. of Shares of Stock	Consideration (Excluding Accrued Interest and Dividends)	Par Value of Bonds	Actual Cost (Excluding Accrued Interest and Dividends)	Book Value at Disposal Date	Increase by Adjustment in Book Value During Year	Decrease by Adjustment in Book Value During Year	Profit on Disposal	Loss on Disposal	Interest on Bonds Received During Year†	Dividends on Stocks Received During Year†

TOTALS

269999

‡Enter as separate summary items the totals of Columns 6 to 14 of Part 5 for bonds, preferred stocks, and common stocks. All bonds and stocks acquired and fully disposed of during the year are not to be demand in this Part.

**Companies may at their option summarize all bonds of the same issue called, matured or redeemed during the year and amd disposal dates.

***CUSIP numbers entered are to conform to those as provided by the Securities Valuation Office. See Annual Statement instructions

****From entry in the previous year's Annual Statement, if owned at that time, from the purchase confirmation (or certificate) if purchased subsequently. Leave blank for private placements.

†Including accrued interest and dividends on bonds and stocks disposed of.

††If bonds are serial issues give amounts maturing each year. Securities sold under a reverse repurchase agreement must be identified.

ANNUAL STATEMENT FOR THE YEAR 1989 OF THE ....

.... (Name)

SCHEDULE D—PART 5

Showing all Long-Term Bonds and Stocks **ACQUIRED** During the Current Year and Fully **DISPOSED OF** During the Current Year

Bonds, preferred stocks and common stocks to be grouped separately showing sub-totals for each group.

1 Description		2	3	4	5	6	7	8	9	10	11	12	13	14	15
CUSIP Identification***	Give complete and accurate description of each bond and stock, including location of all street railway, bank, trust and miscellaneous companies.††	Date Acquired*	Name of Vendor*	Disposal Date**	Name of Purchaser (If matured or called under redemption option, so state and give price at which called.)	Par Value (Bonds) or Number of Shares (Stocks)	Cost to Company (Excluding Accrued Interest and Dividends)	Consideration (Excluding Accrued Interest and Dividends)	Book Value at Disposal Date	Increase by Adjustment in Book Value During Year	Decrease by Adjustment in Book Value During Year	Profit on Disposal	Loss on Disposal	Interest and Dividends Received During Year†	Paid for Accrued Interest and Dividends
BONDS															
099999	Sub-totals — Bonds														
STOCKS															
239999	Sub-totals — Stocks														
739999	GRAND TOTALS														

*The items with reference to each issue of bonds and stocks acquired at public offerings, may be totaled in one line and the word "Various" inserted in Columns 2 and 3

**Companies may at their option summarize all bonds of the same issue called, matured or redeemed during the year and omit disposal dates.

***CUSIP numbers entered are to conform to those as provided and published by the Securities Valuation Office. See Annual Statement Instructions.

†Including accrued interest and dividends on bonds and stocks disposed of.

††If bonds are serial issues give amounts maturing each year. Securities acquired or disposed of under a reverse repurchase agreement must be identified

37

ANNUAL STATEMENT FOR THE YEAR 1989 OF THE ....
(Name)

SCHEDULE D — PART 6 — SECTION 1

Questionnaire Relating to the Valuation of Shares of Certain Subsidiary, Controlled or Affiliated Companies

1 Name of Subsidiary, Controlled or Affiliated Company	2 Do Insurer's Admitted Assets Include Intangible Assets Connected with Holding of Such Company's Stock?	3 If Yes, Amount of Such Intangible Assets	Common Stock of Such Company Owned by Insurer on Statement Date		6 NAIC Valuation Method
			4 No. of Shares	5 % of Outstanding	
999999	TOTAL		XXXX	XXXX	XXXX

Amount of Insurer's Capital and Surplus (Page 3, Item 26 of previous year's statement filed by the insurer with its domiciliary insurance department): $ ....

SCHEDULE D — PART 6 — SECTION 2

1 Name of Lower-tier Company	2 Name of Company Listed in Section 1 which controls Lower-tier Company	3 Amount of Intangible Assets Included in Amount Shown in Column 3, Section 1	Common Stock of Lower-tier Company Owned Indirectly by Insurer on Statement Date	
			4 No. of Shares	5 % of Outstanding
999999	TOTAL		XXXX	XXXX

Form 2

SCHEDULE DA — PART 1

Showing All **SHORT-TERM INVESTMENTS**† Owned December 31 of Current Year

1 Description**	2 § Date Acquired	3 § Name of Vendor	4 § Interest		5 § Date of Maturity		6 Book Value	7 Increase or (Decrease) by Adjustment in Book Value During Year	8 Par Value	9 Rate Used To Obtain Statement Value	10 Statement Value (Excluding Accrued Interest)	11 Actual Cost (Excluding Accrued Interest)	Interest		13 Paid for Accrued Interest	14 NAIC Designation††	15 Effective Rate of Interest at Which Purchase Was Made §
			Rate Of	*How Paid	Yr.	Mo.							12.1 Amount Due and Accrued Dec. 31 of Current Year on Bonds not in default	12.2 Gross Amount Received			
CUSIP Identification***	Give complete and accurate description of all investments owned including identifying the kind of investment vehicle or other than short-term bond																
179999 Totals							†††		XXX				XXX		XXX	XXX

* Insert Initial Letters of months in which interest is payable

** Where an investment is payable in a foreign currency, the par value and the purchase price in that currency should be included as a part of the description

*** CUSIP numbers entered are to conform to those as provided and published by the Securities Valuation Office. See Annual Statement instructions.

† Include all investments whose maturities (or repurchase dates under Repurchase Agreements) at time of acquisition were one year or less. Identify "Repos" and certificates of deposit in Column 1 and for "Repos" show repurchase date

†† Insert the NAIC Designation for such security printed in the NAIC Valuation of Securities Manual

††† Includes $ .... other than accrual of discount and amortization of premium

§ Purchases of various issues of the same issuer of short-term investments may be totalled on one line and the word "various" inserted in the columns.

39

Form 2

ANNUAL STATEMENT FOR THE YEAR 1989 OF THE ....
(Name)

SCHEDULE DA—PART 2

Verification of SHORT-TERM INVESTMENTS Between Years

	1 Total*	2 Bonds	3 Collateral Loans	4 Mortgage Loans	5 Other Short-term Investment Assets**	6 Investments in Parent, Subsidiaries and Affiliates
1. Book value, previous year						
2. Cost of short-term investments acquired						
3. Increase by adjustment in book value						
4. Profit on disposal of short-term investments						
5. Subtotals (Total of items 2 to 4)						
6. Consideration received on disposal of short-term investments						
7. Decrease by adjustment in book value						
8. Loss on disposal of short-term investments						
9. Subtotals (Total of items 6 to 8)						
10. Book value, current year						
11. Income collected during year (Part 1, Line 6.2, Column 3)						
12. Income earned during year (Part 1, Line 6.2, Column 8)						

* Column 1 amounts equal the sum of Columns 2 through 6; Column 1, Line 10 equals Part 1, Column 6, Total
** Indicate the category of such assets, for example, joint ventures, transportation equipment: _____

ANNUAL STATEMENT FOR THE YEAR 1989 OF THE ....

(Name)

SCHEDULE DB — PART A — SECTION 1

Showing All Financial Options Owned December 31 of Current Year

Separate financial options into 2 groups, put options and call options, within each group. Show separately fixed income, equity and other financial options. Show subtotals for each group and category.

1 Description of all financial options owned, including description of underlying security(s) or contract(s)	2 Expiration Date	3 Exercise Price	4 Indication of Existence of Hedge*	5 Date Acquired	6 Actual Cost	7 Increase/(Decrease) by Adjustment in Book Value	8 Book Value	9 Market Value	10 Statement Value	11 Gain/(Loss) (a) Recognized	11 Gain/(Loss) (b) Deferred
459999 Grand Totals											

SCHEDULE DB — PART A — SECTION 2

Showing All Financial Options Acquired During Current Year

1 Description of all financial options acquired, including description of underlying security(s) or contract(s). Summary amounts by group may be shown for non-affiliated entities.	2 Expiration Date	3 Exercise Price	4 Indication of Existence of Hedge*	5 Name of Vendor	6 Date Acquired	7 Actual Cost
459999 Grand Total						

*Has a comprehensive description of the hedge program been made available to the domiciliary state? _____ If not, attach a description with this statement.

Form 2

ANNUAL STATEMENT FOR THE YEAR 1989 OF THE ....

(Name)

SCHEDULE DB — PART A — SECTION 3

Showing All Financial Options Terminated During Current Year

Separate financial options into 2 groups: put options and call options, within each group show separately fixed income, equity and other financial options. Show subtotals for each group and category

1 Description of financial options terminated including description of underlying security(s) or contract(s)	2 Expiration Date	3 Exercise Price	4 Indicate Exercise, Expiration or Sale	5 Date Acquired	6 Date Terminated	7 Actual Cost	8 Increase/(Decrease) by Adjustment in Book Value During Year	9 Book Value at Termination Date	10 Consideration Received on Termination	11 Premiums Allocated to Purchase Cost or Sale Proceeds on Exercise	12 Gain/(Loss) on Termination		
											(a) Deferred	(b) Recognized	(c) Used to Adjust Basis of Hedge
459999 Grand Totals													

SCHEDULE DB—PART A—SECTION 4

Verification Between Years of Book Value of Financial Options Owned

1. Book value, December 31, previous year (Sec. 4, Line 7, previous year) ....
2. Cost of options acquired (Section 2, Column 7) ....
3. Increase/(decrease) by adjustment in book value of options (Sum of Section 1, Column 7 and Section 3, Column 8) ....
4. Deduct (gain)/loss on termination of options:
   (a) deferred (Sec. 3, Col. 12a) ....
   (b) recognized (Sec. 3, Col. 12b) ....
   (c) used to adjust basis of hedge (Sec. 3, Col. 12c) ....
5. Deduct consideration received on termination of options (Section 3, Column 10) ....
6. Deduct premiums allocated to purchase cost or sale proceeds on exercise (Section 3, Column 11) ....
7. Book value of options owned, December 31, current year (Section 1, Column 8, current year) ....

Form 2

(Name)

SCHEDULE DB — PART B — SECTION 1
Showing All Financial Options Written and In-Force December 31 of Current Year

Separate financial options into 2 groups; put options and call options, within each group, show separately fixed income, equity and other financial options. Show subtotals for each group and category.

1	2	3	4	5	6	7	8	9	10 Gain/(Loss)	
Description of financial options written and in-force including description of underlying security(s) or contract(s)	XX	Expiration Date	Exercise Price	Indication of Existence of Hedge*	Date Issued	Consideration Received	Market Value	Statement Value	(a) Recognized	(b) Deferred

459999   Grand Totals

SCHEDULE DB — PART B — SECTION 2
Showing All Financial Options Written During Current Year

1	2	3	4	5	6	7
Description of all financial options issued, including description of underlying security(s) or contract(s). Summary amounts by group may be shown for non-affiliated entities.	XX	Expiration Date	Exercise Price	Indication of Existence of Hedge*	Date Issued	Consideration Received

459999   Grand Total

* Has a comprehensive description of the hedge program been made available to the domiciliary state? _____   If not, attach a description with this statement.
XX If a call option, indicate 'no' if the underlying investment was not owned at the time option was written; otherwise leave blank.

43

Form 2

ANNUAL STATEMENT FOR THE YEAR 1989 OF THE ....

(Name)

Separate financial options into 2 groups, put options and call options written each group. Show separately fixed income equity and other financial options. Show subtotals for each group and category

SCHEDULE DB — PART B — SECTION 3
Showing All Financial Options Written That Were Terminated During Current Year

1	2	3	4	5	6	7	8	9	10		
									Gain/(Loss) on Termination		
Description of all financial options terminated including description of underlying security(s) or contract(s)	Expiration Date	Exercise Price	Date Issued	Date Terminated	Indication of Exercise, Expiration or Closing Purchase Transaction	Consideration Received	Cost of Termination	Premiums Allocated to Purchase Cost or Sale Proceeds on Exercise	(a) Deferred	(b) Recognized	(c) Used to Adjust Basis of Hedge
4399999 Grand Totals											

SCHEDULE DB—PART B—SECTION 4
Verification Between Years of Consideration Received For Financial Options Written

1. Consideration received for financial options written and outstanding, previous year (Sec. 4, Line 6, previous year) ....
2. Consideration received for options written during year (Sec. 2, Col. 7) ....
3. Deduct cost of terminating options by closing purchase transaction during year (Sec. 3, Col. 8) ....
4. Deduct gain/(loss) on termination:
    (a) deferred (Sec. 3, Col. 10a)
    (b) recognized (Sec. 3, Col. 10b)
    (c) used to adjust basis of hedge (Sec. 3, Col. 10c)
5. Deduct premiums allocated to purchase cost or sale proceeds on exercise (Sec. 3, Col. 9) ....
6. Consideration received for financial options written and outstanding, current year (Sec. 1, Col. 7, current year) ....

Form 2

(Name)

SCHEDULE DB—PART C—SECTION 1
Showing All Financial Futures Contracts Open December 31 of Current Year

Separate financial futures contracts into 2 groups, long positions and short positions, within each group, show separate interest rate futures and other financial futures contracts. Show subtotals for each group and category.

1	2	3	4	5	6 Futures Contracts			7 Margin Information			
					(a) Original Price	(b) Current Price	(c) Difference	(a) Initial Deposit Requirement	Variance Margin		
									(b) Deferred Gain/(Loss)	(c) Recognized Gain/(Loss)	
Description of all financial futures contracts open	Number of Contracts	Date of Maturity	Indication of Existence of Hedge*	XX							

299999   Grand Totals

SCHEDULE DB—PART C—SECTION 2
Showing All Financial Futures Contracts Opened During the Current Year

1	2	3	4 Date of Opening Position	5 Date of Maturity	6 XX	7 Indication of Existence of Hedge*	8 Original Price of Futures Contracts	9 Initial Margin Deposit Requirement
Description of each financial futures contract executed. Summary amounts by group may be shown for non-affiliated entities.	Number of Contracts	Name of Vendor						

299999   Grand Total

* Has a comprehensive description of the hedge program been made available to the domiciliary state? _____ If not, attach a description with this statement.
XX If contract requires the company to deliver securities at the contract maturity date, indicate "no" if the underlying instruments were not owned at the time the futures contract was opened; otherwise leave blank.

45

Form 2

ANNUAL STATEMENT FOR THE YEAR 1989 OF THE ....
(Name)

SCHEDULE DB—PART C—SECTION 3

Showing All Financial Futures Contracts That Were Terminated During Current Year

Separate financial futures contracts into 2 groups, long positions and short positions, within each group, show separately interest rate futures and other financial futures contracts. Show subtotals for each group and category

1	2	3	4	5 Futures Contracts			6 Margin Information		
Description of each financial futures contract terminated	Number of Contracts	Date of Termination	Indication of Existence of Hedge*	(a) Original Price	(b) Closing Transaction Price	(c) Gain/(Loss) on Termination	(a) Gain/(Loss) Utilized to Adjust Basis of Hedge	(b) Gain/(Loss) Recognized In Current Year	(c) Gain/(Loss) Deferred Over Year End

299999 Grand Totals

*Has a comprehensive description of the hedge program been made available to the domiciliary state? .... If not, attach a description with this statement.

SCHEDULE DB—PART C—SECTION 4

Verification Between Years of Deferred Gain/(Loss) on Financial Futures Contracts

1. Deferred gain/(loss), December 31, previous year (Sec. 4, Line 6, previous year) ....

2. Change in deferred gain/(loss) on open contracts (Difference between years—Sec. 1, Col. 7b) ....

3. a. Gain/(loss) on contracts terminated during the year (Sec. 3, Col. 5c) ....
   b. Less
   (i) Gain/(loss) used to adjust basis of hedge (Sec. 3, Col. 6a) ....
   (ii) Gain/(loss) recognized in current year (Sec. 3, Col. 6b) ....
   (iii) Subtotal (Line 3b(i) plus 3b(ii)) ....
   c. Subtotal (Line 3a minus Line 3b(iii)) ....

4. Subtotal (Line 1 + Line 2 + Line 3c) ....

5. Less:
   Disposition of gain/(loss) on contracts terminated in prior years:
   (a) recognized ....
   (b) used to adjust basis of hedge ....

6. Deferred gain/(loss), December 31, current year (Line 4 minus Line 5) ....

Form 2

(Name)

SCHEDULE F — PART 1A — SECTION 1

Ceded Reinsurance as of December 31, Current Year

Federal ID Number	Name of Reinsurer*	Location**	†	Reinsurance Recoverable on Paid Losses, Days Overdue					Reinsurance Recoverable on Unpaid Losses	Unearned Premiums (Estimated)	Reinsurance Premiums Ceded
				(a) Current and 1-29	(b) 30-90	(c) 91-180	(d) Over 180	(e) Total	2	3	4
0599999	Totals										

* All companies should be listed in straight alphabetical order within the following groups with subtotals shown for each group: Affiliates; U.S. insurers and U.S. branches of alien insurers; pools, associations and similar underwriting facilities; and all other insurers.
** Show the precise location of the reinsurance company.
† Insert in this column, if applicable, the following letter designation. (I) Reinsurer subject to delinquency proceedings i.e. conservation, rehabilitation or liquidation, or in the case of an alien reinsurer, equivalent proceedings.

47

ANNUAL STATEMENT FOR THE YEAR 1989 OF THE ....
(Name)

SCHEDULE F — PART 1A — SECTION 2

Assumed Reinsurance as of December 31, Current Year (To be filed not later than April 1)

Federal ID Number	Name of Reinsured*	Location**	1 Reinsurance Payable on Paid Losses	2 Reinsurance Payable on Unpaid Losses	3 Unearned Premiums (Estimated)
059999	Grand Totals				

*All companies should be listed in straight alphabetical order within the following groups with subtotals shown for each group: Affiliates; U.S. insurers and U.S. branches of alien insurers; pools, associations and similar underwriting facilities, and all other insurers.
**Show the precise location of the reinsurance company.

ANNUAL STATEMENT FOR THE YEAR 1989 OF THE ....
(Name)

SCHEDULE F — PART 1B

Portfolio Reinsurance Effected or (Cancelled) during Current Year

Federal ID Number	Name of Company	1 Date of Contract	2 Amount of Original Premiums	3 Amount of Reinsurance Premiums
	(a) Reinsurance Ceded			
019999	Total Reinsurance Ceded by Portfolio			
	(b) Reinsurance Assumed			
029999	Total Reinsurance Assumed by Portfolio			

ANNUAL STATEMENT FOR THE YEAR 1989 OF THE

(Name)

SCHEDULE F — PART 2A

Funds Withheld on Account of Reinsurance in Unauthorized Companies as of December 31, Current Year

Federal ID Number	Name of Reinsurer	1 Unearned Premiums (Debit)	2 (a) Paid and Unpaid Losses Recoverable (Total of amounts in Cols. 1 + 2 of Schedule F, Part 1A, Section I, for unauthorized companies) (Debit)	2 (b) Incurred But Not Reported Losses Recoverable (Estimates of amounts recoverable from unauthorized companies) (Debit)	2 (c) Paid and Unpaid Allocated Loss Adjustment Expenses Recoverable (Debit)	3 Total 1 + 2a + 2b + 2c	4 Deposits by and Funds Withheld from Reinsurers (Credit)	5 Miscellaneous Balances (Credit)	6 Sum of 4 + 5 but not in excess of 3
999999	TOTALS								

NOTES: Total of Column 6 to agree with deduction taken in Item 13d, Page 3.
Securities held on deposit or held in a trust account should be valued at their fair market value.
NAIC published market values must be used when available.
Amounts included in Column 4 should be identified separately as letters of credit (L), trust agreements (T), funds deposited by and withheld from reinsurer (F), or other (O).
Letters of credit and trust agreements are not to be included in assets or liabilities on Pages 2 or 3 or supporting pages or exhibits.

ANNUAL STATEMENT FOR THE YEAR 1989 OF THE .... (Name)

SCHEDULE F — PART 2B — SECTION 1

Provision for overdue authorized reinsurance as of December 31, Current Year

Federal ID Number	Name of Reinsurer	1 Amounts 90 Days Overdue	2 Reinsurance Recoverable on Paid Losses	3 Amounts Received Prior 90 Days	4 Col 1 divided by (Col 2 + Col 3)	5 Amounts in Column 1 for Companies Reporting Less than 20%, in Column 4
	TOTALS					

NOTES: (1) Amounts in dispute should be excluded from Columns 1 and 2.
(2) If the results of the calculation in Column 4 exceeds 20%, complete Schedule F, Part 2B, Section 2.
(3) Carry Column 5 total to Schedule F, Part 2B, Section 2 for calculation of Provisions for Overdue Authorized Reinsurance

SCHEDULE F — PART 2B — SECTION 2

Provision for overdue authorized reinsurance as of December 31, Current Year

Federal ID Number	Name of Reinsurer	1 Unearned Premiums (Debit)	2 (a) Paid and Unpaid Losses Recoverable (Amounts in Cols. 1(e) + 2 of Sch F, Part 1A Section 1 for authorized companies) (Debit)	2 (b) Incurred but Not Reported Losses Recoverable (Estimates of amounts recoverable from authorized companies) (Debit)	2 (c) Paid and Unpaid Allocated Loss Adjustment Expenses Recoverable (Debit)	3 Total 1 + 2a + 2b + 2c	4 Deposits by and Funds Withheld from Reinsurers (Credit)	5 Miscellaneous Balances (Credit)	6 Sum of 4 + 5 but not in excess of 3
	TOTALS								

NOTES: Securities held on deposit or held on a trust account should be valued at their fair market value
NAIC published market values must be used when available
Amounts included in Column 4 should be identified separately as letters of credit (L), trust agreements (T), funds deposited by and withheld from reinsurer (F) or other (O).
Letters of credit and trust agreements are not to be included in assets or liabilities on Pages 2 or 3 or supporting pages or exhibits.

CALCULATION OF PROVISION FOR OVERDUE AUTHORIZED REINSURANCE
(1) Total from Column 5 of Schedule F, Part 2B, Section 1 ....
(2) Total from Column 3 of Schedule F, Part 2B, Section 2 ....
(3) Total from Column 6 of Schedule F, Part 2B, Section 2 ....
(4) (1) + (2) − (3) ....
(5) Total Provision for Overdue Authorized Reinsurance (.20 × (4))
Enter this amount on Page 3, Item 13c

ANNUAL STATEMENT FOR THE YEAR 1989 OF THE ....

(Name)

SCHEDULE H—ACCIDENT AND HEALTH EXHIBIT

(To be filed not later than April 1)

PART 1.—ANALYSIS OF UNDERWRITING OPERATIONS

	1 Total		2 Group Accident and Health		3 Credit[b] (Group and Individual)		4 Collectively Renewable		5 Non-Cancellable		6 Guaranteed Renewable		Other Individual Policies					
													7 Non-Renewable for Stated Reasons Only		8 Other Accident Only		9 All Other	
	Amount	%	Amount	%	Amount	%	Amount	%	Amount	%	Amount	%	Amount	%	Amount	%	Amount	%
1 Premiums written																		
2 Premiums earned (see note b)																		
3 Incurred claims																		
4 Increase in policy reserves																		
5 Commissions*																		
6 General insurance expenses																		
7 Taxes, licenses and fees																		
8 Total expenses incurred																		
8A Aggregate write-ins for deductions																		
9 Gain from underwriting before dividends to policyholders																		
10 Dividends to policyholders																		
11 Gain from underwriting after dividends to policyholders																		

DETAILS OF WRITE-INS AGGREGATED AT ITEM 8A FOR DEDUCTIONS

08401																		
08402																		
08403																		
08404																		
08405																		
08498 Summary of remaining write-ins for Item 8A from overflow page																		
08499 Total (Items 8401 thru 8405 plus 8498 (Schedule H Part 1 Item 8A)																		

† In each column of Part 1, show the percentages of Line 2 for Lines 3 through 11 inclusive.
* Includes $ .... reported as "Policy, membership and other fees retained by agents."
(a) Business not exceeding 120 months duration.
(b) Premiums earned and before adjustment for the increase in policy reserves which has been treated as a separate deduction.

ANNUAL STATEMENT FOR THE YEAR 1989 OF THE ....

(Name)

SCHEDULE H—ACCIDENT AND HEALTH EXHIBIT (Continued)

(To be filed not later than April 1)

	1 Total	2 Group Accident and Health	3 Credit[a] (Group and Individual)	4 Collectively Renewable	5 Non-Cancellable	6 Guaranteed Renewable	7 Non-Renewable for Stated Reasons Only	8 Other Accident Only	9 All Other
							Other Individual Policies		
PART 2—RESERVES AND LIABILITIES									
A. Premium Reserves:									
1. Unearned premiums									
2. Advance premiums									
3. Reserve for rate credits									
4. Total premium reserves, current year									
5. Total premium reserves, previous year									
6. Increase in total premium reserves									
B. Policy Reserves:									
1. Additional reserves									
2. Reserve for future contingent benefits (deferred maternity and other similar benefits)**									
3. Total policy reserves, current year									
4. Total policy reserves, previous year									
5. Increase in policy reserves									
C. Claim Reserves and Liabilities:									
1. Total current year									
2. Total previous year									
3. Increase									
PART 3—TEST OF PREVIOUS YEAR'S CLAIM RESERVES AND LIABILITIES									
1. Claims paid during the year:									
a. On claims incurred prior to current year									
b. On claims incurred during current year									
2. Claim reserves and liabilities, December 31, current year:									
a. On claims incurred prior to current year									
b. On claims incurred during current year									
3. Test:									
a. Line 1a and 2a									
b. Claim reserves and liabilities, December 31, previous year									
c. Line a minus Line b									
PART 4—REINSURANCE									
A. Reinsurance assumed:									
1. Premiums written									
2. Premiums earned (see note b)									
3. Incurred claims									
4. Commissions									
B. Reinsurance Ceded:									
1. Premiums written									
2. Premiums earned (see note b)									
3. Incurred claims									
4. Commissions									

a Business not exceeding 120 months duration.
** If not included in claim reserves.
(b) Premiums earned are before adjustment for the increase in policy reserves which has been treated as a separate deduction.

ANNUAL STATEMENT FOR THE YEAR 1989 OF THE ....
(Name)

SCHEDULE M—PART 1

Showing all direct or indirect payments of more than $100 (exclusive of expenses paid in connection with settlement of losses, claims and salvage under policy contracts) in connection with any matter, measure or proceeding before legislative bodies, officers or departments of government during the year, excluding company's share of such expenditures made by organizations listed in Part 4 below.

1 Payee		2	3
Name	Address	Amount Paid	Matter, Measure or Proceeding

SCHEDULE M—PART 2

Showing all payments (other than salary, compensation, emoluments and dividends) to or on behalf of any officer, director or employee which exceeded $1,000 or amounted in the aggregate to more than $10,000 during the year. (Excluding reimbursement of expenditures for transportation, board and lodging of Company Auditors, Inspectors, Claims Investigators and Adjusters, and Special Agents, and excluding payments listed in Part 1.)

1 Name of Payee	2 Amount Paid	3 Occasion of Expense

ANNUAL STATEMENT FOR THE YEAR 1989 OF THE ....
(Name)

SCHEDULE M—PART 3

Showing all payments for legal expenses which exceeded $500 or aggregated more than $5,000 during the year, exclusive of payments in connection with settlement of losses, claims and salvage under policy contracts. (Excluding payments listed in Part 1.)

1 Payee		2 Amount Paid	3 Occasion of Expense
Name	Address		

SCHEDULE M—PART 4

Showing all payments in excess of $1,000 to each Trade Association, Service Organization, Statistical, Actuarial or Rating Bureau during the year. (A service organization is defined as every person, partnership, association or corporation who or which formulates rules, establishes standards, or assists in the making of rates, rules, or standards for the information or benefit of insurers or rating organizations.)

1 Payee		2 Amount Paid	3 Occasion of Expense
Name	Address		

ANNUAL STATEMENT FOR THE YEAR 1989 OF THE ....
(Name)

SCHEDULE N

Showing all Banks, Trust Companies, Savings and Loan and Building and Loan Associations in which deposits were maintained by the company at any time during the year and the balances, if any (according to Company's records) on December 31, of the current year. Exclude balances represented by a negotiable instrument.

1 Depository* (Give Full Name and Location. State if depository is a parent, subsidiary or affiliate.) Show rate of interest and maturity date in the case of certificates of deposit or time deposits.	2 Amount of Interest Received During Year	3 Amount of Interest Accrued December 31 of Current Year	4 Balance
OPEN DEPOSITORIES			
019999 TOTALS—Open Depositories			
SUSPENDED DEPOSITORIES			
029999 TOTALS—Suspended Depositories			
039999 GRAND TOTALS—All Depositories			

TOTALS OF DEPOSITORY BALANCES ON THE LAST DAY OF EACH MONTH DURING THE CURRENT YEAR

January		April		July		October	
February		May		August		November	
March		June		September		December	

* In each case where the depository is not incorporated and subject to governmental supervision, the word "PRIVATE" in capitals and in parentheses, thus — (PRIVATE), should be inserted to the left of the name of the depository. Any deposit in a suspended depository which is taken credit for should have a star placed opposite the amount in the schedule.

Deposits in federally insured depositories not exceeding $40,000 may be combined and reported opposite the caption "Deposits in (insert number) depositories which do not exceed the $40,000 amount in any one depository."

Short-Term Negotiable Certificates of Deposit to be reported in Schedule DA. Long-Term Negotiable Certificates of Deposit to be reported in Schedule D.

ANNUAL STATEMENT FOR THE YEAR 1989 OF THE ....
(Name)

SCHEDULE P — ANALYSIS OF LOSSES AND LOSS EXPENSES

Notes to Schedule P

(1) The Parts of Schedule P
　Part 1 — detailed information on losses and loss expenses
　Part 2 — history of incurred losses and allocated expenses
　Part 3 — history of loss and allocated expense payments
　Part 4 — (deleted discount information now in Part 1 and Notes to Financial Statements. Reserved for future use.)
　Part 5 — schedule for claims-made policies
　Part 6 — history of bulk and incurred but not reported reserves
　Schedule P Interrogatories

(2) Lines of business A through M are groupings of the lines of business used on page 14 the state page

(3) Reinsurance A, B, C, and D (lines N to Q) are
　Reinsurance A = nonproportional property (1988 and subsequent)
　Reinsurance B = nonproportional liability (1988 and subsequent)
　Reinsurance C = financial lines (1988 and subsequent)
　Reinsurance D = old Schedule O line 30 (1987 and prior)

(4) The Instructions to Schedule P contain directions necessary for filling out Schedule P

SCHEDULE P—PART 1—SUMMARY
(000 omitted)

1	Premiums Earned			Loss and Loss Expense Payments								12
Years In Which Premiums Were Earned and Losses Were Incurred	2 Direct and Assumed	3 Ceded	4 Net (2 − 3)	Loss Payments		Allocated Loss Expense Payments		9 Salvage and Subrogation Received	10 Uncollected Loss Expense Payments	11 Total Net Paid (5 − 6 − 7 − 8 − 10)		Number of Claims Reported— Direct and Assumed
				5 Direct and Assumed	6 Ceded	7 Direct and Assumed	8 Ceded					
1. Prior	XXXX	XXXX	XXXX									XXXX
2. 1980												XXXX
3. 1981												XXXX
4. 1982												XXXX
5. 1983												XXXX
6. 1984												XXXX
7. 1985												XXXX
8. 1986												XXXX
9. 1987												XXXX
10. 1988												XXXX
11. 1989												XXXX
12. Totals	XXXX	XXXX	XXXX									XXXX

Note: For "prior," report amounts paid or received in current year only. Report cumulative amounts paid or received for specific years.
Report loss payments net of salvage and subrogation received.

1	Losses Unpaid				Allocated Loss Expenses Unpaid				21	22	23
Years In Which Premiums Were Earned and Losses Were Incurred	Case Basis		Bulk + IBNR		Case Basis		Bulk + IBNR		Unallocated Loss Expenses Unpaid	Total Net Losses and Expenses Unpaid	Number of Claims Outstanding— Direct and Assumed
	13 Direct and Assumed	14 Ceded	15 Direct and Assumed	16 Ceded	17 Direct and Assumed	18 Ceded	19 Direct and Assumed	20 Ceded			
1. Prior											XXXX
2. 1980											XXXX
3. 1981											XXXX
4. 1982											XXXX
5. 1983											XXXX
6. 1984											XXXX
7. 1985											XXXX
8. 1986											XXXX
9. 1987											XXXX
10. 1988											XXXX
11. 1989											XXXX
12. Totals											XXXX

Years In Which Premiums Were Earned and Losses Were Incurred	Total Losses and Loss Expenses Incurred			Loss and Loss Expense Percentage (Incurred/Premiums Earned)			Discount for Time Value of Money		32 Inter-Company Pooling Participation Percentage	Net Balance Sheet Reserves After Discount	
	24 Direct and Assumed	25 Ceded	26 Net*	27 Direct and Assumed	28 Ceded	29 Net	30 Loss	31 Loss Expense		33 Losses Unpaid	34 Loss Expenses Unpaid
1. Prior	XXXX	XXXX	XXXX	XXXX	XXXX	XXXX			XXXX		
2. 1980											
3. 1981											
4. 1982											
5. 1983											
6. 1984											
7. 1985											
8. 1986											
9. 1987											
10. 1988											
11. 1989											
12. Totals	XXXX	XXXX	XXXX	XXXX	XXXX	XXXX			XXXX		

*Net = (24 − 25) = (11 + 22)

ANNUAL STATEMENT FOR THE YEAR 1989 OF THE ....
(Name)

SCHEDULE P — PART 2 — SUMMARY

Years in Which Losses Were Incurred	INCURRED LOSSES AND ALLOCATED EXPENSES REPORTED AT YEAR END (000 OMITTED)										DEVELOPMENT**	
	2 1980	3 1981	4 1982	5 1983	6 1984	7 1985	8 1986	9 1987	10 1988	11 1989	12 One Year	13 Two Year
1 Prior	.											
2 1980												
3 1981	XXXX											
4 1982	XXXX	XXXX										
5 1983	XXXX	XXXX	XXXX									
6 1984	XXXX	XXXX	XXXX	XXXX								
7 1985	XXXX	XXXX	XXXX	XXXX	XXXX							
8 1986	XXXX	XXXX	XXXX	XXXX	XXXX	XXXX						
9 1987	XXXX	XXXX	XXXX	XXXX	XXXX	XXXX	XXXX					XXXX
10 1988	XXXX	XXXX	XXXX	XXXX	XXXX	XXXX	XXXX	XXXX				XXXX
11 1989	XXXX	XXXX	XXXX	XXXX	XXXX	XXXX	XXXX	XXXX	XXXX		XXXX	XXXX

*Reported reserves only Subsequent development relates only to subsequent payments and reserves
**Current year less first or second prior year, showing (redundant) or adverse

12 Totals

SCHEDULE P — PART 3 — SUMMARY

Years in Which Losses Were Incurred	CUMULATIVE PAID LOSSES AND ALLOCATED EXPENSES REPORTED AT YEAR END (000 OMITTED)										12 Number of Claims Closed With Loss Payment	13 Number of Claims Closed Without Loss Payment
	2 1980	3 1981	4 1982	5 1983	6 1984	7 1985	8 1986	9 1987	10 1988	11 1989		
1 Prior	000										XXXX	XXXX
2 1980											XXXX	XXXX
3 1981	XXXX										XXXX	XXXX
4 1982	XXXX	XXXX									XXXX	XXXX
5 1983	XXXX	XXXX	XXXX								XXXX	XXXX
6 1984	XXXX	XXXX	XXXX	XXXX							XXXX	XXXX
7 1985	XXXX	XXXX	XXXX	XXXX	XXXX						XXXX	XXXX
8 1986	XXXX	XXXX	XXXX	XXXX	XXXX	XXXX					XXXX	XXXX
9 1987	XXXX	XXXX	XXXX	XXXX	XXXX	XXXX	XXXX				XXXX	XXXX
10 1988	XXXX	XXXX	XXXX	XXXX	XXXX	XXXX	XXXX	XXXX			XXXX	XXXX
11 1989	XXXX	XXXX	XXXX	XXXX	XXXX	XXXX	XXXX	XXXX	XXXX		XXXX	XXXX

Note: Net of salvage and subrogation received

SCHEDULE P — PART 6 — SUMMARY

Years In Which Losses Were Incurred	BULK AND INCURRED BUT NOT REPORTED RESERVES ON LOSSES AND ALLOCATED EXPENSES AT YEAR END (000 OMITTED)									
	2 1980	3 1981	4 1982	5 1983	6 1984	7 1985	8 1986	9 1987	10 1988	11 1989
1 Prior										
2 1980										
3 1981	XXXX									
4 1982	XXXX	XXXX								
5 1983	XXXX	XXXX	XXXX							
6 1984	XXXX	XXXX	XXXX	XXXX						
7 1985	XXXX	XXXX	XXXX	XXXX	XXXX					
8 1986	XXXX	XXXX	XXXX	XXXX	XXXX	XXXX				
9 1987	XXXX	XXXX	XXXX	XXXX	XXXX	XXXX	XXXX			
10 1988	XXXX	XXXX	XXXX	XXXX	XXXX	XXXX	XXXX	XXXX		
11 1989	XXXX	XXXX	XXXX	XXXX	XXXX	XXXX	XXXX	XXXX	XXXX	

ANNUAL STATEMENT FOR THE YEAR 1989 OF THE ....
(Name)

SCHEDULE P—PART 1A—HOMEOWNERS/FARMOWNERS
(000 omitted)

1	Premiums Earned			Loss and Loss Expense Payments							12
Years In Which Premiums Were Earned and Losses Were Incurred	2	3	4	Loss Payments		Allocated Loss Expense Payments		9	10	11	Number of Claims Reported— Direct and Assumed
	Direct and Assumed	Ceded	Net (2 - 3)	5 Direct and Assumed	6 Ceded	7 Direct and Assumed	8 Ceded	Salvage and Subrogation Received	Unallocated Loss Expense Payments	Total Net Paid (5 - 6 - 7 - 8 - 10)	
1. Prior	XXXX	XXXX	XXXX								XXXX
2. 1980											XXXX
3. 1981											XXXX
4. 1982											XXXX
5. 1983											XXXX
6. 1984											XXXX
7. 1985											XXXX
8. 1986											XXXX
9. 1987											XXXX
10. 1988											XXXX
11. 1989											XXXX
12. Totals	XXXX	XXXX	XXXX								XXXX

Note: For "prior," report amounts paid or received in current year only. Report cumulative amounts paid or received for specific years.
Report loss payments net of salvage and subrogation received.

Years In Which Premiums Were Earned and Losses Were Incurred	Losses Unpaid				Allocated Loss Expenses Unpaid				21	22	23
	Case Basis		Bulk - IBNR		Case Basis		Bulk - IBNR		Unallocated Loss Expenses Unpaid	Total Net Losses and Expenses Unpaid	Number of Claims Outstanding— Direct and Assumed
	13 Direct and Assumed	14 Ceded	15 Direct and Assumed	16 Ceded	17 Direct and Assumed	18 Ceded	19 Direct and Assumed	20 Ceded			
1. Prior											
2. 1980											
3. 1981											
4. 1982											
5. 1983											
6. 1984											
7. 1985											
8. 1986											
9. 1987											
10. 1988											
11. 1989											
12. Totals											

Years In Which Premiums Were Earned and Losses Were Incurred	Total Losses and Loss Expenses Incurred			Loss and Loss Expense Percentage (Incurred/Premiums Earned)			Discount for Time Value of Money		32	Net Balance Sheet Reserves After Discount	
	24 Direct and Assumed	25 Ceded	26 Net*	27 Direct and Assumed	28 Ceded	29 Net	30 Loss	31 Loss Expense	Inter-Company Pooling Participation Percentage	33 Losses Unpaid	34 Loss Expenses Unpaid
1. Prior	XXXX	XXXX	XXXX	XXXX	XXXX	XXXX			XXXX		
2. 1980											
3. 1981											
4. 1982											
5. 1983											
6. 1984											
7. 1985											
8. 1986											
9. 1987											
10. 1988											
11. 1989											
12. Totals	XXXX	XXXX	XXXX	XXX	XXXX	XXXX			XXXX		

*Net = (24 - 25) = (11 + 22)

ANNUAL STATEMENT FOR THE YEAR 1989 OF THE ....
(Name)

SCHEDULE P—PART 1B—PRIVATE PASSENGER AUTO LIABILITY/MEDICAL
(000 omitted)

	Premiums Earned			Loss and Loss Expense Payments								12
Years In Which Premiums Were Earned and Losses Were Incurred	2 Direct and Assumed	3 Ceded	4 Net (2 - 3)	Loss Payments		Allocated Loss Expense Payments		9 Salvage and Subrogation Received	10 Unallocated Loss Expense Payments	11 Total Net Paid (5 - 6 - 7 - 8 - 10)		Number of Claims Reported— Direct and Assumed
				5 Direct and Assumed	6 Ceded	7 Direct and Assumed	8 Ceded					
1 Prior	XXXX	XXXX	XXXX									XXXX
2 1980												
3 1981												
4 1982												
5 1983												
6 1984												
7 1985												
8 1986												
9 1987												
10 1988												
11 1989												
12 Totals	XXXX	XXXX	XXXX									XXXX

Note: For "prior" report amounts paid or received in current year only. Report cumulative amounts paid or received for specific years.
Report loss payments net of salvage and subrogation received

	Losses Unpaid				Allocated Loss Expenses Unpaid				21	22	23
Years In Which Premiums Were Earned and Losses Were Incurred	Case Basis		Bulk - IBNR		Case Basis		Bulk - IBNR		Unallocated Loss Expenses Unpaid	Total Net Losses and Expenses Unpaid	Number of Claims Outstanding— Direct and Assumed
	13 Direct and Assumed	14 Ceded	15 Direct and Assumed	16 Ceded	17 Direct and Assumed	18 Ceded	19 Direct and Assumed	20 Ceded			
1 Prior											
2 1980											
3 1981											
4 1982											
5 1983											
6 1984											
7 1985											
8 1986											
9 1987											
10 1988											
11 1989											
12 Totals											

Years In Which Premiums Were Earned and Losses Were Incurred	Total Losses and Loss Expenses Incurred			Loss and Loss Expense Percentage (Incurred Premiums Earned)			Discount for Time Value of Money		32 Inter-Company Pooling Participation Percentage	Net Balance Sheet Reserves After Discount	
	24 Direct and Assumed	25 Ceded	26 Net*	27 Direct and Assumed	28 Ceded	29 Net	30 Loss	31 Loss Expense		33 Losses Unpaid	34 Loss Expenses Unpaid
1 Prior	XXXX	XXXX	XXXX	XXXX	XXXX	XXXX			XXXX		
2 1980											
3 1981											
4 1982											
5 1983											
6 1984											
7 1985											
8 1986											
9 1987											
10 1988											
11 1989											
12 Totals	XXXX	XXXX	XXXX	XXX	XXXX	XXXX			XXXX		

*Net = (24 - 25) = (11 - 22)

ANNUAL STATEMENT FOR THE YEAR 1989 OF THE ....
(Name)

SCHEDULE P—PART 1C—COMMERCIAL AUTO/TRUCK LIABILITY/MEDICAL
(000 omitted)

1 Years In Which Premiums Were Earned and Losses Were Incurred	Premiums Earned			Loss and Loss Expense Payments							12 Number of Claims Reported— Direct and Assumed
	2 Direct and Assumed	3 Ceded	4 Net (2 – 3)	Loss Payments		Allocated Loss Expense Payments		9 Salvage and Subrogation Received	10 Unallocated Loss Expense Payments	11 Total Net Paid (5 – 6 + 7 – 8 + 10)	
				5 Direct and Assumed	6 Ceded	7 Direct and Assumed	8 Ceded				
1. Prior	XXXX	XXXX	XXXX								XXXX
2. 1980											
3. 1981											
4. 1982											
5. 1983											
6. 1984											
7. 1985											
8. 1986											
9. 1987											
10. 1988											
11. 1989											
12. Totals	XXXX	XXXX	XXXX								XXXX

Note: For "prior," report amounts paid or received in current year only. Report cumulative amounts paid or received for specific years.
Report loss payments net of salvage and subrogation received.

Years In Which Premiums Were Earned and Losses Were Incurred	Losses Unpaid				Allocated Loss Expenses Unpaid				21 Unallocated Loss Expenses Unpaid	22 Total Net Losses and Expenses Unpaid	23 Number of Claims Outstanding— Direct and Assumed
	Case Basis		Bulk + IBNR		Case Basis		Bulk + IBNR				
	13 Direct and Assumed	14 Ceded	15 Direct and Assumed	16 Ceded	17 Direct and Assumed	18 Ceded	19 Direct and Assumed	20 Ceded			
1. Prior											
2. 1980											
3. 1981											
4. 1982											
5. 1983											
6. 1984											
7. 1985											
8. 1986											
9. 1987											
10. 1988											
11. 1989											
12. Totals											

Years In Which Premiums Were Earned and Losses Were Incurred	Total Losses and Loss Expenses Incurred			Loss and Loss Expense Percentage (Incurred/Premiums Earned)			Discount for Time Value of Money		32 Inter-Company Pooling Participation Percentage	Net Balance Sheet Reserves After Discount	
	24 Direct and Assumed	25 Ceded	26 Net*	27 Direct and Assumed	28 Ceded	29 Net	30 Loss	31 Loss Expense		33 Losses Unpaid	34 Loss Expenses Unpaid
1. Prior	XXXX	XXXX	XXXX	XXXX	XXXX	XXXX			XXXX		
2. 1980											
3. 1981											
4. 1982											
5. 1983											
6. 1984											
7. 1985											
8. 1986											
9. 1987											
10. 1988											
11. 1989											
12. Totals	XXXX	XXXX	XXXX	XXXX	XXXX	XXXX			XXXX		

*Net = (24 – 25) = (11 + 22)

ANNUAL STATEMENT FOR THE YEAR 1989 OF THE ....
(Name)

SCHEDULE P—PART 1D—WORKERS' COMPENSATION
(000 omitted)

1 Years In Which Premiums Were Earned and Losses Were Incurred	Premiums Earned			Loss and Loss Expense Payments								12 Number of Claims Reported— Direct and Assumed
	2 Direct and Assumed	3 Ceded	4 Net (2 - 3)	Loss Payments		Allocated Loss Expense Payments		9 Salvage and Subrogation Received	10 Unallocated Loss Expense Payments	11 Total Net Paid (5 - 6 + 7 - 8 + 10)		
				5 Direct and Assumed	6 Ceded	7 Direct and Assumed	8 Ceded					
1 Prior	X X X X	X X X X	X X X X									X X X X
2 1980												
3 1981												
4 1982												
5 1983												
6 1984												
7 1985												
8 1986												
9 1987												
10 1988												
11 1989												
12 Totals	X X X X	X X X X	X X X X									X X X X

Note: For "prior" report amounts paid or received in current year only. Report cumulative amounts paid or received for specific years.
Report loss payments net of salvage and subrogation received

Years In Which Premiums Were Earned and Losses Were Incurred	Losses Unpaid				Allocated Loss Expenses Unpaid				21 Unallocated Loss Expenses Unpaid	22 Total Net Losses and Expenses Unpaid	23 Number of Claims Outstanding— Direct and Assumed
	Case Basis		Bulk - IBNR		Case Basis		Bulk - IBNR				
	13 Direct and Assumed	14 Ceded	15 Direct and Assumed	16 Ceded	17 Direct and Assumed	18 Ceded	19 Direct and Assumed	20 Ceded			
1 Prior											
2 1980											
3 1981											
4 1982											
5 1983											
6 1984											
7 1985											
8 1986											
9 1987											
10 1988											
11 1989											
12 Totals											

Years In Which Premiums Were Earned and Losses Were Incurred	Total Losses and Loss Expenses Incurred			Loss and Loss Expense Percentage (Incurred Premiums Earned)			Discount for Time Value of Money		32 Inter-Company Pooling Participation Percentage	Net Balance Sheet Reserves After Discount	
	24 Direct and Assumed	25 Ceded	26 Net*	27 Direct and Assumed	28 Ceded	29 Net	30 Loss	31 Loss Expense		33 Losses Unpaid	34 Loss Expenses Unpaid
1 Prior	X X X X	X X X X	X X X X	X X X X	X X X X	X X X X			X X X X		
2 1980											
3 1981											
4 1982											
5 1983											
6 1984											
7 1985											
8 1986											
9 1987											
10 1988											
11 1989											
12 Totals	X X X X	X X X X	X X X X	X X X X	X X X X	X X X X			X X X X		

*Net   (24 - 25)   (21 - 22)

ANNUAL STATEMENT FOR THE YEAR 1989 OF THE ....
(Name)

SCHEDULE P—PART 1E—COMMERCIAL MULTIPLE PERIL
(000 omitted)

1	Premiums Earned			Loss and Loss Expense Payments							12
Years In Which Premiums Were Earned and Losses Were Incurred	2	3	4	Loss Payments		Allocated Loss Expense Payments		9	10	11	Number of Claims Reported—Direct and Assumed
	Direct and Assumed	Ceded	Net (2 − 3)	5 Direct and Assumed	6 Ceded	7 Direct and Assumed	8 Ceded	Salvage and Subrogation Received	Unallocated Loss Expense Payments	Total Net Paid (5 − 6 + 7 − 8 + 10)	
1. Prior	XXXX	XXXX	XXXX								XXXX
2. 1980											
3. 1981											
4. 1982											
5. 1983											
6. 1984											
7. 1985											
8. 1986											
9. 1987											
10. 1988											
11. 1989											
12. Totals	XXXX	XXXX	XXXX								XXXX

Note: For "prior," report amounts paid or received in current year only. Report cumulative amounts paid or received for specific years.
Report loss payments net of salvage and subrogation received.

Years In Which Premiums Were Earned and Losses Were Incurred	Losses Unpaid				Allocated Loss Expenses Unpaid				21	22	23
	Case Basis		Bulk + IBNR		Case Basis		Bulk + IBNR		Unallocated Loss Expenses Unpaid	Total Net Losses and Expenses Unpaid	Number of Claims Outstanding—Direct and Assumed
	13 Direct and Assumed	14 Ceded	15 Direct and Assumed	16 Ceded	17 Direct and Assumed	18 Ceded	19 Direct and Assumed	20 Ceded			
1. Prior											
2. 1980											
3. 1981											
4. 1982											
5. 1983											
6. 1984											
7. 1985											
8. 1986											
9. 1987											
10. 1988											
11. 1989											
12. Totals											

Years In Which Premiums Were Earned and Losses Were Incurred	Total Losses and Loss Expenses Incurred			Loss and Loss Expense Percentage (Incurred/Premiums Earned)			Discount for Time Value of Money		32	Net Balance Sheet Reserves After Discount	
	24 Direct and Assumed	25 Ceded	26 Net*	27 Direct and Assumed	28 Ceded	29 Net	30 Loss	31 Loss Expense	Inter-Company Pooling Participation Percentage	33 Losses Unpaid	34 Loss Expenses Unpaid
1. Prior	XXXX	XXXX	XXXX	XXXX	XXXX	XXXX			XXXX		
2. 1980											
3. 1981											
4. 1982											
5. 1983											
6. 1984											
7. 1985											
8. 1986											
9. 1987											
10. 1988											
11. 1989											
12. Totals	XXXX	XXXX	XXXX	XXXX	XXXX	XXXX			XXXX		

*Net = (24 − 25) = (11 + 22)

ANNUAL STATEMENT FOR THE YEAR 1989 OF THE ....
(Name)

SCHEDULE P—PART 1F—MEDICAL MALPRACTICE
(000 omitted)

1 Years In Which Premiums Were Earned and Losses Were Incurred	Premiums Earned			Loss and Loss Expense Payments								12 Number of Claims Reported— Direct and Assumed
	2 Direct and Assumed	3 Ceded	4 Net (2 – 3)	Loss Payments		Allocated Loss Expense Payments		9 Salvage and Subrogation Received	10 Unallocated Loss Expense Payments	11 Total Net Paid (5 – 6 + 7 – 8 + 10)		
				5 Direct and Assumed	6 Ceded	7 Direct and Assumed	8 Ceded					
1 Prior	X X X X	X X X X	X X X X									X X X X
2 1980												
3 1981												
4 1982												
5 1983												
6 1984												
7 1985												
8 1986												
9 1987												
10 1988												
11 1989												
12 Totals	X X X X	X X X X	X X X X									X X X X

Note: For "prior," report amounts paid or received in current year only. Report cumulative amounts paid or received for specific years.
Report loss payments net of salvage and subrogation received.

Years In Which Premiums Were Earned and Losses Were Incurred	Losses Unpaid				Allocated Loss Expenses Unpaid				21 Unallocated Loss Expenses Unpaid	22 Total Net Losses and Expenses Unpaid	23 Number of Claims Outstanding— Direct and Assumed
	Case Basis		Bulk + IBNR		Case Basis		Bulk + IBNR				
	13 Direct and Assumed	14 Ceded	15 Direct and Assumed	16 Ceded	17 Direct and Assumed	18 Ceded	19 Direct and Assumed	20 Ceded			
1 Prior											
2 1980											
3 1981											
4 1982											
5 1983											
6 1984											
7 1985											
8 1986											
9 1987											
10 1988											
11 1989											
12 Totals											

Years In Which Premiums Were Earned and Losses Were Incurred	Total Losses and Loss Expenses Incurred			Loss and Loss Expense Percentage (Incurred Premiums Earned)			Discount for Time Value of Money		32 Inter-Company Pooling Participation Percentage	Net Balance Sheet Reserves After Discount	
	24 Direct and Assumed	25 Ceded	26 Net*	27 Direct and Assumed	28 Ceded	29 Net	30 Loss	31 Loss Expense		33 Losses Unpaid	34 Loss Expenses Unpaid
1 Prior	X X X X	X X X X	X X X X	X X X X	X X X X	X X X X			X X X X		
2 1980											
3 1981											
4 1982											
5 1983											
6 1984											
7 1985											
8 1986											
9 1987											
10 1988											
11 1989											
12 Totals	X X X X	X X X X	X X X X	X X X	X X X X	X X X X			X X X X		

*Net (24 – 25) – (11 – 22)

Form 2   ANNUAL STATEMENT FOR THE YEAR 1989 OF THE ....
(Name)

SCHEDULE P—PART 1G—SPECIAL LIABILITY (OCEAN MARINE, AIRCRAFT (ALL PERILS), BOILER AND MACHINERY)
(000 omitted)

1	Premiums Earned			Loss and Loss Expense Payments							12
Years In Which Premiums Were Earned and Losses Were Incurred	2	3	4	Loss Payments		Allocated Loss Expense Payments		9	10	11	Number of Claims Reported Direct and Assumed
	Direct and Assumed	Ceded	Net (2 - 3)	5 Direct and Assumed	6 Ceded	7 Direct and Assumed	8 Ceded	Salvage and Subrogation Received	Unallocated Loss Expense Payments	Total Net Paid (5 - 6 + 7 - 8 - 10)	
1. Prior	XXXX	XXXX	XXXX								XXXX
2. 1980											XXXX
3. 1981											XXXX
4. 1982											XXXX
5. 1983											XXXX
6. 1984											XXXX
7. 1985											XXXX
8. 1986											XXXX
9. 1987											XXXX
10. 1988											XXXX
11. 1989											XXXX
12. Totals	XXXX	XXXX	XXXX								XXXX

Note: For "prior," report amounts paid or received in current year only. Report cumulative amounts paid or received for specific years.
Report loss payments net of salvage and subrogation received.

Years In Which Premiums Were Earned and Losses Were Incurred	Losses Unpaid				Allocated Loss Expenses Unpaid				21	22	23
	Case Basis		Bulk + IBNR		Case Basis		Bulk + IBNR		Unallocated Loss Expenses Unpaid	Total Net Losses and Expenses Unpaid	Number of Claims Outstanding— Direct and Assumed
	13 Direct and Assumed	14 Ceded	15 Direct and Assumed	16 Ceded	17 Direct and Assumed	18 Ceded	19 Direct and Assumed	20 Ceded			
1. Prior											
2. 1980											
3. 1981											
4. 1982											
5. 1983											
6. 1984											
7. 1985											
8. 1986											
9. 1987											
10. 1988											
11. 1989											
12. Totals											

Years In Which Premiums Were Earned and Losses Were Incurred	Total Losses and Loss Expenses Incurred			Loss and Loss Expense Percentage (Incurred-Premiums Earned)			Discount for Time Value of Money		32	Net Balance Sheet Reserves After Discount	
	24 Direct and Assumed	25 Ceded	26 Net*	27 Direct and Assumed	28 Ceded	29 Net	30 Loss	31 Loss Expense	Inter-Company Pooling Participation Percentage	33 Losses Unpaid	34 Loss Expenses Unpaid
1. Prior	XXXX	XXXX	XXXX	XXXX	XXXX	XXXX			XXXX		
2. 1980											
3. 1981											
4. 1982											
5. 1983											
6. 1984											
7. 1985											
8. 1986											
9. 1987											
10. 1988											
11. 1989											
12. Totals	XXXX	XXXX	XXXX	XXX	XXXX	XXXX			XXXX		

*Net = (24 - 25) = (11 + 22)

ANNUAL STATEMENT FOR THE YEAR 1989 OF THE .... Name ....

SCHEDULE P—PART 1H—OTHER LIABILITY
(000 omitted)

Years In Which Premiums Were Earned and Losses Were Incurred	Premiums Earned			Loss and Loss Expense Payments								Number of Claims Reported- Direct and Assumed
				Loss Payments		Allocated Loss Expense Payments		9	10	11	12	
	2 Direct and Assumed	3 Ceded	4 Net (2 - 3)	5 Direct and Assumed	6 Ceded	7 Direct and Assumed	8 Ceded	Salvage and Subrogation Received	Unallocated Loss Expense Payments	Total Net Paid (5 - 6 - 7 - 8 - 10)		
1 Prior	X X X X	X X X X	X X X X									X X X X
2 1980												
3 1981												
4 1982												
5 1983												
6 1984												
7 1985												
8 1986												
9 1987												
10 1988												
11 1989												
12 Totals	X X X X	X X X X	X X X X									X X X X

Note For "prior" report amounts paid or received in current year only. Report cumulative amounts paid or received for specific years.
Report loss payments net of salvage and subrogation received

Years In Which Premiums Were Earned and Losses Were Incurred	Losses Unpaid				Allocated Loss Expenses Unpaid				21 Unallocated Loss Expenses Unpaid	22 Total Net Losses and Expenses Unpaid	23 Number of Claims Outstanding— Direct and Assumed
	Case Basis		Bulk - IBNR		Case Basis		Bulk - IBNR				
	13 Direct and Assumed	14 Ceded	15 Direct and Assumed	16 Ceded	17 Direct and Assumed	18 Ceded	19 Direct and Assumed	20 Ceded			
1 Prior											
2 1980											
3 1981											
4 1982											
5 1983											
6 1984											
7 1985											
8 1986											
9 1987											
10 1988											
11 1989											
12 Totals											

Years In Which Premiums Were Earned and Losses Were Incurred	Total Losses and Loss Expenses Incurred			Loss and Loss Expense Percentage (Incurred Premiums Earned)			Discount for Time Value of Money		32 Inter-Company Pooling Participation Percentage	Net Balance Sheet Reserves After Discount	
	24 Direct and Assumed	25 Ceded	26 Net*	27 Direct and Assumed	28 Ceded	29 Net	30 Loss	31 Loss Expense		33 Losses Unpaid	34 Loss Expenses Unpaid
1 Prior	X X X X	X X X X	X X X X	X X X X	X X X X	X X X X			X X X X		
2 1980											
3 1981											
4 1982											
5 1983											
6 1984											
7 1985											
8 1986											
9 1987											
10 1988											
11 1989											
12 Totals	X X X X	X X X X	X X X X	X X X X	X X X X	X X X X			X X X X		

*Net = (24 - 25) = (11 - 22)

ANNUAL STATEMENT FOR THE YEAR 1989 OF THE ....
(Name)

SCHEDULE P—PART 1I—SPECIAL PROPERTY (FIRE, ALLIED LINES, INLAND MARINE, EARTHQUAKE, GLASS, BURGLARY AND THEFT)
(000 omitted)

1	Premiums Earned			Loss and Loss Expense Payments								
Years In Which Premiums Were Earned and Losses Were Incurred	2 Direct and Assumed	3 Ceded	4 Net (2 - 3)	Loss Payments		Allocated Loss Expense Payments		9 Salvage and Subrogation Received	10 Uncollected Loss Expense Payments	11 Total Net Paid (5 - 6 - 7 - 8 - 10)	12 Number of Claim Reported Direct and Assumed
				5 Direct and Assumed	6 Ceded	7 Direct and Assumed	8 Ceded				
1 Prior	XXXX	XXXX	XXXX								XXXX
2 1988											XXXX
3 1989											XXXX
4 Totals	XXXX	XXXX	XXXX								XXXX

Note: For "prior," report amounts paid or received in current year only. Report cumulative amounts paid or received for specific years.
Report loss payment net of salvage and subrogation received.

Years In Which Premiums Were Earned and Losses Were Incurred	Losses Unpaid				Allocated Loss Expenses Unpaid				21 Unallocated Loss Expenses Unpaid	22 Total Net Losses and Expenses Unpaid	23 Number of Claims Outstanding Direct and Assumed
	Case Basis		Bulk + IBNR		Case Basis		Bulk + IBNR				
	13 Direct and Assumed	14 Ceded	15 Direct and Assumed	16 Ceded	17 Direct and Assumed	18 Ceded	19 Direct and Assumed	20 Ceded			
1 Prior											
2 1988											
3 1989											
4 Totals											

Years In Which Premiums Were Earned and Losses Were Incurred	Total Losses and Loss Expenses Incurred			Loss and Loss Expense Percentage (Incurred Premiums Earned)			Discount for Time Value of Money		32 Inter-Company Pooling Participation Percentage	Net Balance Sheet Reserves After Discount	
	24 Direct and Assumed	25 Ceded	26 Net*	27 Direct and Assumed	28 Ceded	29 Net	30 Loss	31 Loss Expense		33 Losses Unpaid	34 Loss Expenses Unpaid
1 Prior	XXXX	XXXX	XXXX	XXXX	XXXX	XXXX			XXXX		
2 1988											
3 1989											
4 Totals	XXXX	XXXX	XXXX	XXX	XXXX	XXXX			XXXX		

*Net = (24 − 25) = (11 + 22)

SCHEDULE P—PART 1J—AUTO PHYSICAL DAMAGE
(000 omitted)

1	Premiums Earned			Loss and Loss Expense Payments								
Years In Which Premiums Were Earned and Losses Were Incurred	2 Direct and Assumed	3 Ceded	4 Net (2 - 3)	Loss Payments		Allocated Loss Expense Payments		9 Salvage and Subrogation Received	10 Uncollected Loss Expense Payments	11 Total Net Paid (5 - 6 - 7 - 8 - 10)	12 Number of Claims Reported— Direct and Assumed
				5 Direct and Assumed	6 Ceded	7 Direct and Assumed	8 Ceded				
1 Prior	XXXX	XXXX	XXXX								XXXX
2 1988											
3 1989											
4 Totals	XXXX	XXXX	XXXX								XXXX

Note: For "prior," report amounts paid or received in current year only. Report cumulative amounts paid or received for specific years.
Report loss payments net of salvage and subrogation received.

Years In Which Premiums Were Earned and Losses Were Incurred	Losses Unpaid				Allocated Loss Expenses Unpaid				21 Unallocated Loss Expenses Unpaid	22 Total Net Losses and Expenses Unpaid	23 Number of Claims Outstanding Direct and Assumed
	Case Basis		Bulk + IBNR		Case Basis		Bulk + IBNR				
	13 Direct and Assumed	14 Ceded	15 Direct and Assumed	16 Ceded	17 Direct and Assumed	18 Ceded	19 Direct and Assumed	20 Ceded			
1 Prior											
2 1988											
3 1989											
4 Totals											

Years In Which Premiums Were Earned and Losses Were Incurred	Total Losses and Loss Expenses Incurred			Loss and Loss Expense Percentage (Incurred/Premiums Earned)			Discount for Time Value of Money		32 Inter-Company Pooling Participation Percentage	Net Balance Sheet Reserves After Discount	
	24 Direct and Assumed	25 Ceded	26 Net*	27 Direct and Assumed	28 Ceded	29 Net	30 Loss	31 Loss Expense		33 Losses Unpaid	34 Loss Expenses Unpaid
1 Prior	XXXX	XXXX	XXXX	XXXX	XXXX	XXXX			XXXX		
2 1988											
3 1989											
4 Totals	XXXX	XXXX	XXXX	XXXX	XXXX	XXXX			XXXX		

*Net = (24 − 25) = (11 + 22)

68   ANNUAL STATEMENT FOR THE YEAR 1989 OF THE ....   Form 2

(Name)

SCHEDULE P—PART 1K—FIDELITY, SURETY, FINANCIAL GUARANTY, MORTGAGE GUARANTY
(000 omitted)

1 Years In Which Premiums Were Earned and Losses Were Incurred	Premiums Earned			Loss and Loss Expense Payments								12 Number of Claims Reported— Direct and Assumed
	2 Direct and Assumed	3 Ceded	4 Net (2 - 3)	Loss Payments		Allocated Loss Expense Payments		9 Salvage and Subrogation Received	10 Unallocated Loss Expense Payments	11 Total Net Paid (5 - 6 - 7 - 8 + 10)		
				5 Direct and Assumed	6 Ceded	7 Direct and Assumed	8 Ceded					
1 Prior	XXXX	XXXX	XXXX									XXXX
2 1988												XXXX
3 1989												XXXX
4 Totals	XXXX	XXXX	XXXX									XXXX

Note: For "prior" report amounts paid or received in current year only. Report cumulative amounts paid or received for specific years.
Report loss payments net of salvage and subrogation received.

1 Years In Which Premiums Were Earned and Losses Were Incurred	Losses Unpaid				Allocated Loss Expenses Unpaid				21 Unallocated Loss Expenses Unpaid	22 Total Net Losses and Expenses Unpaid	23 Number of Claims Outstanding— Direct and Assumed
	Case Basis		Bulk - IBNR		Case Basis		Bulk - IBNR				
	13 Direct and Assumed	14 Ceded	15 Direct and Assumed	16 Ceded	17 Direct and Assumed	18 Ceded	19 Direct and Assumed	20 Ceded			
1 Prior											
2 1988											
3 1989											
4 Totals											

1 Years In Which Premiums Were Earned and Losses Were Incurred	Total Losses and Loss Expenses Incurred			Loss and Loss Expense Percentage (Incurred/Premiums Earned)			Discount for Time Value of Money		32 Inter-Company Pooling Participation Percentage	Net Balance Sheet Reserves After Discount	
	24 Direct and Assumed	25 Ceded	26 Net*	27 Direct and Assumed	28 Ceded	29 Net	30 Loss	31 Loss Expense		33 Losses Unpaid	34 Loss Expenses Unpaid
1 Prior	XXXX	XXXX	XXXX	XXXX	XXXX	XXXX			XXXX		
2 1988											
3 1989											
4 Totals	XXXX	XXXX	XXXX	XXX	XXXX	XXXX			XXXX		

*Net = (24 - 25) ÷ (11 + 22)

SCHEDULE P—PART 1L—OTHER (INCLUDING CREDIT, ACCIDENT AND HEALTH)
(000 omitted)

1 Years In Which Premiums Were Earned and Losses Were Incurred	Premiums Earned			Loss and Loss Expense Payments								12 Number of Claims Reported— Direct and Assumed
	2 Direct and Assumed	3 Ceded	4 Net (2 - 3)	Loss Payments		Allocated Loss Expense Payments		9 Salvage and Subrogation Received	10 Unallocated Loss Expense Payments	11 Total Net Paid (5 - 6 - 7 - 8 + 10)		
				5 Direct and Assumed	6 Ceded	7 Direct and Assumed	8 Ceded					
1 Prior	XXXX	XXXX	XXXX									XXXX
2 1988												XXXX
3 1989												XXXX
4 Totals	XXXX	XXXX	XXXX									XXXX

Note: For "prior" report amounts paid or received in current year only. Report cumulative amounts paid or received for specific years.
Report loss payments net of salvage and subrogation received.

1 Years In Which Premiums Were Earned and Losses Were Incurred	Losses Unpaid				Allocated Loss Expenses Unpaid				21 Unallocated Loss Expenses Unpaid	22 Total Net Losses and Expenses Unpaid	23 Number of Claims Outstanding— Direct and Assumed
	Case Basis		Bulk - IBNR		Case Basis		Bulk - IBNR				
	13 Direct and Assumed	14 Ceded	15 Direct and Assumed	16 Ceded	17 Direct and Assumed	18 Ceded	19 Direct and Assumed	20 Ceded			
1 Prior											
2 1988											
3 1989											
4 Totals											

1 Years In Which Premiums Were Earned and Losses Were Incurred	Total Losses and Loss Expenses Incurred			Loss and Loss Expense Percentage (Incurred/Premiums Earned)			Discount for Time Value of Money		32 Inter-Company Pooling Participation Percentage	Net Balance Sheet Reserves After Discount	
	24 Direct and Assumed	25 Ceded	26 Net*	27 Direct and Assumed	28 Ceded	29 Net	30 Loss	31 Loss Expense		33 Losses Unpaid	34 Loss Expenses Unpaid
1 Prior	XXXX	XXXX	XXXX	XXXX	XXXX	XXXX			XXXX		
2 1988											
3 1989											
4 Totals	XXXX	XXXX	XXXX	XXX	XXXX	XXXX			XXXX		

*Net = (24 - 25) ÷ (11 + 22)

SCHEDULE P—PART 1M—INTERNATIONAL
(000 omitted)

1 Years In Which Premiums Were Earned and Losses Were Incurred	Premiums Earned			Loss and Loss Expense Payments								12 Number of Claims Reported— Direct and Assumed
	2 Direct and Assumed	3 Ceded	4 Net (2 − 3)	Loss Payments		Allocated Loss Expense Payments		9 Salvage and Subrogation Received	10 Unallocated Loss Expense Payments	11 Total Net Paid (5 − 6 + 7 − 8 + 10)		
				5 Direct and Assumed	6 Ceded	7 Direct and Assumed	8 Ceded					
1. Prior	XXXX	XXXX	XXXX									XXXX
2. 1980												XXXX
3. 1981												XXXX
4. 1982												XXXX
5. 1983												XXXX
6. 1984												XXXX
7. 1985												XXXX
8. 1986												XXXX
9. 1987												XXXX
10. 1988												XXXX
11. 1989												XXXX
12. Totals	XXXX	XXXX	XXXX									XXXX

Note: For "prior," report amounts paid or received in current year only. Report cumulative amounts paid or received for specific years.
Report loss payments net of salvage and subrogation received.

Years In Which Premiums Were Earned and Losses Were Incurred	Losses Unpaid				Allocated Loss Expenses Unpaid				21 Unallocated Loss Expenses Unpaid	22 Total Net Losses and Expenses Unpaid	23 Number of Claims Outstanding— Direct and Assumed
	Case Basis		Bulk + IBNR		Case Basis		Bulk + IBNR				
	13 Direct and Assumed	14 Ceded	15 Direct and Assumed	16 Ceded	17 Direct and Assumed	18 Ceded	19 Direct and Assumed	20 Ceded			
1. Prior											
2. 1980											
3. 1981											
4. 1982											
5. 1983											
6. 1984											
7. 1985											
8. 1986											
9. 1987											
10. 1988											
11. 1989											
12. Totals											

Years In Which Premiums Were Earned and Losses Were Incurred	Total Losses and Loss Expenses Incurred			Loss and Loss Expense Percentage (Incurred/Premiums Earned)			Discount for Time Value of Money		32 Inter-Company Pooling Participation Percentage	Net Balance Sheet Reserves After Discount	
	24 Direct and Assumed	25 Ceded	26 Net*	27 Direct and Assumed	28 Ceded	29 Net	30 Loss	31 Loss Expense		33 Losses Unpaid	34 Loss Expenses Unpaid
1. Prior	XXXX	XXXX	XXXX	XXXX	XXXX	XXXX			XXXX		
2. 1980											
3. 1981											
4. 1982											
5. 1983											
6. 1984											
7. 1985											
8. 1986											
9. 1987											
10. 1988											
11. 1989											
12. Totals	XXXX	XXXX	XXXX	XXX	XXXX	XXXX			XXXX		

*Net = (24 − 25) = (11 + 22)

70   ANNUAL STATEMENT FOR THE YEAR 1989 OF THE ....   Form 2

(Name)

SCHEDULE P—PART 1N—REINSURANCE A
(000 omitted)

1 Years In Which Premiums Were Earned and Losses Were Incurred	Premiums Earned			Loss and Loss Expense Payments								
	2 Direct and Assumed	3 Ceded	4 Net (2 - 3)	Loss Payments		Allocated Loss Expense Payments		9 Salvage and Subrogation Received	10 Unallocated Loss Expense Payments	11 Total Net Paid (5 - 6 + 7 - 8 + 10)	12 Number of Claims Reported— Direct and Assumed
				5 Direct and Assumed	6 Ceded	7 Direct and Assumed	8 Ceded				
1. 1988											XXXX
2. 1989											XXXX
3. Totals	XXXX	XXXX	XXXX								XXXX

Years In Which Premiums Were Earned and Losses Were Incurred	Losses Unpaid				Allocated Loss Expenses Unpaid				21 Unallocated Loss Expenses Unpaid	22 Total Net Losses and Expenses Unpaid	23 Number of Claims Outstanding— Direct and Assumed
	Case Basis		Bulk - IBNR		Case Basis		Bulk - IBNR				
	13 Direct and Assumed	14 Ceded	15 Direct and Assumed	16 Ceded	17 Direct and Assumed	18 Ceded	19 Direct and Assumed	20 Ceded			
1. 1988											XXXX
2. 1989											XXXX
3. Totals											XXXX

Years In Which Premiums Were Earned and Losses Were Incurred	Total Losses and Loss Expenses Incurred			Loss and Loss Expense Percentage (Incurred Premiums Earned)			Discount for Time Value of Money		32 Inter-Company Pooling Participation Percentage	Net Balance Sheet Reserves After Discount	
	24 Direct and Assumed	25 Ceded	26 Net*	27 Direct and Assumed	28 Ceded	29 Net	30 Loss	31 Loss Expense		33 Losses Unpaid	34 Loss Expenses Unpaid
1. 1988											
2. 1989											
3. Totals	XXXX	XXXX	XXXX	XXXX	XXXX	XXXX			XXXX		

*Net = (24 - 25) = (11 + 22)

SCHEDULE P—PART 1O—REINSURANCE B
(000 omitted)

1 Years In Which Premiums Were Earned and Losses Were Incurred	Premiums Earned			Loss and Loss Expense Payments								
	2 Direct and Assumed	3 Ceded	4 Net (2 - 3)	Loss Payments		Allocated Loss Expense Payments		9 Salvage and Subrogation Received	10 Unallocated Loss Expense Payments	11 Total Net Paid (5 - 6 + 7 - 8 + 10)	12 Number of Claims Reported— Direct and Assumed
				5 Direct and Assumed	6 Ceded	7 Direct and Assumed	8 Ceded				
1. 1988											XXXX
2. 1989											XXXX
3. Totals	XXXX	XXXX	XXXX								XXXX

Years In Which Premiums Were Earned and Losses Were Incurred	Losses Unpaid				Allocated Loss Expenses Unpaid				21 Unallocated Loss Expenses Unpaid	22 Total Net Losses and Expenses Unpaid	23 Number of Claims Outstanding— Direct and Assumed
	Case Basis		Bulk - IBNR		Case Basis		Bulk - IBNR				
	13 Direct and Assumed	14 Ceded	15 Direct and Assumed	16 Ceded	17 Direct and Assumed	18 Ceded	19 Direct and Assumed	20 Ceded			
1. 1988											XXXX
2. 1989											XXXX
3. Totals											XXXX

Years In Which Premiums Were Earned and Losses Were Incurred	Total Losses and Loss Expenses Incurred			Loss and Loss Expense Percentage (Incurred Premiums Earned)			Discount for Time Value of Money		32 Inter-Company Pooling Participation Percentage	Net Balance Sheet Reserves After Discount	
	24 Direct and Assumed	25 Ceded	26 Net*	27 Direct and Assumed	28 Ceded	29 Net	30 Loss	31 Loss Expense		33 Losses Unpaid	34 Loss Expenses Unpaid
1. 1988											
2. 1989											
3. Totals	XXXX	XXXX	XXXX	XXXX	XXXX	XXXX			XXXX		

*Net (24 25) (11 - 22)

(Name)

SCHEDULE P—PART 1P—REINSURANCE C
(000 omitted)

1 Years In Which Premiums Were Earned and Losses Incurred	Premiums Earned			Loss and Loss Expense Payments								12 Number of Claims Reported— Direct and Assumed
	2 Direct and Assumed	3 Ceded	4 Net (2 – 3)	Loss Payments		Allocated Loss Expense Payments		9 Salvage and Subrogation Received	10 Unallocated Loss Expense Payments	11 Total Net Paid (5 – 6 + 7 – 8 + 10)		
				5 Direct and Assumed	6 Ceded	7 Direct and Assumed	8 Ceded					
1. 1988												X X X X
2. 1989												X X X X
3. Totals	X X X X	X X X X	X X X X									X X X X

1 Years In Which Premiums Were Earned and Losses Were Incurred	Losses Unpaid				Allocated Loss Expenses Unpaid				21 Unallocated Loss Expenses Unpaid	22 Total Net Losses and Expenses Unpaid	23 Number of Claims Outstanding— Direct and Assumed
	Case Basis		Bulk + IBNR		Case Basis		Bulk + IBNR				
	13 Direct and Assumed	14 Ceded	15 Direct and Assumed	16 Ceded	17 Direct and Assumed	18 Ceded	19 Direct and Assumed	20 Ceded			
1. 1988											X X X X
2. 1989											X X X X
3. Totals											X X X X

1 Years In Which Premiums Were Earned and Losses Were Incurred	Total Losses and Loss Expenses Incurred			Loss and Loss Expense Percentage (Incurred/Premiums Earned)			Discount for Time Value of Money		32 Inter-Company Pooling Participation Percentage	33 Losses Unpaid	34 Loss Expenses Unpaid
	24 Direct and Assumed	25 Ceded	26 Net*	27 Direct and Assumed	28 Ceded	29 Net	30 Loss	31 Loss Expense			
1. 1988											
2. 1989											
3. Totals	X X X X	X X X X	X X X X	X X X X	X X X X	X X X X			X X X X		

*Net = (24 – 25) = (11 + 22)

SCHEDULE P—PART 1Q—REINSURANCE D
(000 omitted)

1 Years In Which Premiums Were Earned and Losses Were Incurred	Premiums Earned			Loss and Loss Expense Payments								12 Number of Claims Reported— Direct and Assumed
	2 Direct and Assumed	3 Ceded	4 Net (2 – 3)	Loss Payments		Allocated Loss Expense Payments		9 Salvage and Subrogation Received	10 Unallocated Loss Expense Payments	11 Total Net Paid (5 – 6 + 7 – 8 + 10)		
				5 Direct and Assumed	6 Ceded	7 Direct and Assumed	8 Ceded					
1. Prior	X X X X	X X X X	X X X X									X X X X
2. 1980												X X X X
3. 1981												X X X X
4. 1982												X X X X
5. 1983												X X X X
6. 1984												X X X X
7. 1985												X X X X
8. 1986												X X X X
9. 1987												X X X X
10. Totals	X X X X	X X X X	X X X X									X X X X

Note: For "prior," report amounts paid or received in current year only. Report cumulative amounts paid or received for specific years.
Report loss payments net of salvage and subrogation received.

1 Years In Which Premiums Were Earned and Losses Were Incurred	Losses Unpaid				Allocated Loss Expenses Unpaid				21 Unallocated Loss Expenses Unpaid	22 Total Net Losses and Expenses Unpaid	23 Number of Claims Outstanding— Direct and Assumed
	Case Basis		Bulk + IBNR		Case Basis		Bulk + IBNR				
	13 Direct and Assumed	14 Ceded	15 Direct and Assumed	16 Ceded	17 Direct and Assumed	18 Ceded	19 Direct and Assumed	20 Ceded			
1. Prior											X X X X
2. 1980											X X X X
3. 1981											X X X X
4. 1982											X X X X
5. 1983											X X X X
6. 1984											X X X X
7. 1985											X X X X
8. 1986											X X X X
9. 1987											X X X X
10. Totals											X X X X

1 Years In Which Premiums Were Earned and Losses Were Incurred	Total Losses and Loss Expenses Incurred			Loss and Loss Expense Percentage (Incurred/Premiums Earned)			Discount for Time Value of Money		32 Inter-Company Pooling Participation Percentage	33 Losses Unpaid	34 Loss Expenses Unpaid
	24 Direct and Assumed	25 Ceded	26 Net*	27 Direct and Assumed	28 Ceded	29 Net	30 Loss	31 Loss Expense			
1. Prior	X X X X	X X X X	X X X X	X X X X	X X X X	X X X X			X X X X		
2. 1980											
3. 1981											
4. 1982											
5. 1983											
6. 1984											
7. 1985											
8. 1986											
9. 1987											
10. Totals	X X X X	X X X X	X X X X	X X X X	X X X X	X X X X			X X X X		

*Net = (24 – 25) = (11 + 22)

(Name)

SCHEDULE P — PART 2A — HOMEOWNERS/FARMOWNERS

1 Years in Which Losses Were Incurred	INCURRED LOSSES AND ALLOCATED EXPENSES REPORTED AT YEAR END (000 OMITTED)										DEVELOPMENT**	
	2 1980	3 1981	4 1982	5 1983	6 1984	7 1985	8 1986	9 1987	10 1988	11 1989	12 One Year	13 Two Year
1. Prior	*											
2. 1980												
3. 1981	xxxx											
4. 1982	xxxx	xxxx										
5. 1983	xxxx	xxxx	xxxx									
6. 1984	xxxx	xxxx	xxxx	xxxx								
7. 1985	xxxx	xxxx	xxxx	xxxx	xxxx							
8. 1986	xxxx	xxxx	xxxx	xxxx	xxxx	xxxx						
9. 1987	xxxx	xxxx	xxxx	xxxx	xxxx	xxxx	xxxx					
10. 1988	xxxx	xxxx	xxxx	xxxx	xxxx	xxxx	xxxx	xxxx				xxxx
11. 1989	xxxx	xxxx	xxxx	xxxx	xxxx	xxxx	xxxx	xxxx	xxxx		xxxx	xxxx

12. Totals

SCHEDULE P — PART 2B — PRIVATE PASSENGER AUTO LIABILITY/MEDICAL

1 Years	2 1980	3 1981	4 1982	5 1983	6 1984	7 1985	8 1986	9 1987	10 1988	11 1989	12 One Year	13 Two Year
1. Prior	*											
2. 1980												
3. 1981	xxxx											
4. 1982	xxxx	xxxx										
5. 1983	xxxx	xxxx	xxxx									
6. 1984	xxxx	xxxx	xxxx	xxxx								
7. 1985	xxxx	xxxx	xxxx	xxxx	xxxx							
8. 1986	xxxx	xxxx	xxxx	xxxx	xxxx	xxxx						
9. 1987	xxxx	xxxx	xxxx	xxxx	xxxx	xxxx	xxxx					
10. 1988	xxxx	xxxx	xxxx	xxxx	xxxx	xxxx	xxxx	xxxx				xxxx
11. 1989	xxxx	xxxx	xxxx	xxxx	xxxx	xxxx	xxxx	xxxx	xxxx		xxxx	xxxx

12. Totals

SCHEDULE P — PART 2C — COMMERCIAL AUTO/TRUCK LIABILITY/MEDICAL

1 Years	2 1980	3 1981	4 1982	5 1983	6 1984	7 1985	8 1986	9 1987	10 1988	11 1989	12 One Year	13 Two Year
1. Prior	*											
2. 1980												
3. 1981	xxxx											
4. 1982	xxxx	xxxx										
5. 1983	xxxx	xxxx	xxxx									
6. 1984	xxxx	xxxx	xxxx	xxxx								
7. 1985	xxxx	xxxx	xxxx	xxxx	xxxx							
8. 1986	xxxx	xxxx	xxxx	xxxx	xxxx	xxxx						
9. 1987	xxxx	xxxx	xxxx	xxxx	xxxx	xxxx	xxxx					
10. 1988	xxxx	xxxx	xxxx	xxxx	xxxx	xxxx	xxxx	xxxx				xxxx
11. 1989	xxxx	xxxx	xxxx	xxxx	xxxx	xxxx	xxxx	xxxx	xxxx		xxxx	xxxx

12. Totals

SCHEDULE P — PART 2D — WORKERS' COMPENSATION

1 Years	2 1980	3 1981	4 1982	5 1983	6 1984	7 1985	8 1986	9 1987	10 1988	11 1989	12 One Year	13 Two Year
1. Prior	*											
2. 1980												
3. 1981	xxxx											
4. 1982	xxxx	xxxx										
5. 1983	xxxx	xxxx	xxxx									
6. 1984	xxxx	xxxx	xxxx	xxxx								
7. 1985	xxxx	xxxx	xxxx	xxxx	xxxx							
8. 1986	xxxx	xxxx	xxxx	xxxx	xxxx	xxxx						
9. 1987	xxxx	xxxx	xxxx	xxxx	xxxx	xxxx	xxxx					
10. 1988	xxxx	xxxx	xxxx	xxxx	xxxx	xxxx	xxxx	xxxx				xxxx
11. 1989	xxxx	xxxx	xxxx	xxxx	xxxx	xxxx	xxxx	xxxx	xxxx		xxxx	xxxx

12. Totals

SCHEDULE P — PART 2E — COMMERCIAL MULTIPLE PERIL

1 Years	2 1980	3 1981	4 1982	5 1983	6 1984	7 1985	8 1986	9 1987	10 1988	11 1989	12 One Year	13 Two Year
1. Prior	*											
2. 1980												
3. 1981	xxxx											
4. 1982	xxxx	xxxx										
5. 1983	xxxx	xxxx	xxxx									
6. 1984	xxxx	xxxx	xxxx	xxxx								
7. 1985	xxxx	xxxx	xxxx	xxxx	xxxx							
8. 1986	xxxx	xxxx	xxxx	xxxx	xxxx	xxxx						
9. 1987	xxxx	xxxx	xxxx	xxxx	xxxx	xxxx	xxxx					
10. 1988	xxxx	xxxx	xxxx	xxxx	xxxx	xxxx	xxxx	xxxx				xxxx
11. 1989	xxxx	xxxx	xxxx	xxxx	xxxx	xxxx	xxxx	xxxx	xxxx		xxxx	xxxx

*Reported reserves only. Subsequent development relates only to subsequent payments and reserves
**Current year less first or second prior year showing (redundant) or adverse

12. Totals

SCHEDULE P — PART 2F — MEDICAL MALPRACTICE

1 Years in Which Losses Were Incurred	INCURRED LOSSES AND ALLOCATED EXPENSES REPORTED AT YEAR END (000 OMITTED)										DEVELOPMENT**	
	2 1980	3 1981	4 1982	5 1983	6 1984	7 1985	8 1986	9 1987	10 1988	11 1989	12 One Year	13 Two Year
1. Prior	*											
2. 1980												
3. 1981	XXXX											
4. 1982	XXXX	XXXX										
5. 1983	XXXX	XXXX	XXXX									
6. 1984	XXXX	XXXX	XXXX	XXXX								
7. 1985	XXXX	XXXX	XXXX	XXXX	XXXX							
8. 1986	XXXX	XXXX	XXXX	XXXX	XXXX	XXXX						
9. 1987	XXXX	XXXX	XXXX	XXXX	XXXX	XXXX	XXXX					
10. 1988	XXXX	XXXX	XXXX	XXXX	XXXX	XXXX	XXXX	XXXX				XXXX
11. 1989	XXXX	XXXX	XXXX	XXXX	XXXX	XXXX	XXXX	XXXX	XXXX		XXXX	XXXX
12. Totals												

SCHEDULE P — PART 2G — SPECIAL LIABILITY (OCEAN MARINE, AIRCRAFT (ALL PERILS), BOILER AND MACHINERY)

1	2	3	4	5	6	7	8	9	10	11	12	13
1. Prior	*											
2. 1980												
3. 1981	XXXX											
4. 1982	XXXX	XXXX										
5. 1983	XXXX	XXXX	XXXX									
6. 1984	XXXX	XXXX	XXXX	XXXX								
7. 1985	XXXX	XXXX	XXXX	XXXX	XXXX							
8. 1986	XXXX	XXXX	XXXX	XXXX	XXXX	XXXX						
9. 1987	XXXX	XXXX	XXXX	XXXX	XXXX	XXXX	XXXX					
10. 1988	XXXX	XXXX	XXXX	XXXX	XXXX	XXXX	XXXX	XXXX				XXXX
11. 1989	XXXX	XXXX	XXXX	XXXX	XXXX	`XXXX	XXXX	XXXX	XXXX		XXXX	XXXX
12. Totals												

SCHEDULE P — PART 2H — OTHER LIABILITY

1	2	3	4	5	6	7	8	9	10	11	12	13
1. Prior	*											
2. 1980												
3. 1981	XXXX											
4. 1982	XXXX	XXXX										
5. 1983	XXXX	XXXX	XXXX									
6. 1984	XXXX	XXXX	XXXX	XXXX								
7. 1985	XXXX	XXXX	XXXX	XXXX	XXXX							
8. 1986	XXXX	XXXX	XXXX	XXXX	XXXX	XXXX						
9. 1987	XXXX	XXXX	XXXX	XXXX	XXXX	XXXX	XXXX					
10. 1988	XXXX	XXXX	XXXX	XXXX	XXXX	XXXX	XXXX	XXXX				XXXX
11. 1989	XXXX	XXXX	XXXX	XXXX	XXXX	XXXX	XXXX	XXXX	XXXX		XXXX	XXXX
12. Totals												

SCHEDULE P — PART 2I — SPECIAL PROPERTY (FIRE, ALLIED LINES, INLAND MARINE, EARTHQUAKE, GLASS, BURGLARY AND THEFT)

1	2	3	4	5	6	7	8	9	10	11	12	13
1. Prior	XXXX	XXXX	XXXX	XXXX	XXXX	XXXX	XXXX	*				
2. 1988	XXXX	XXXX	XXXX	XXXX	XXXX	XXXX	XXXX	XXXX				XXXX
3. 1989	XXXX	XXXX	XXXX	XXXX	XXXX	XXXX	XXXX	XXXX	XXXX		XXXX	XXXX
4. Totals												

SCHEDULE P — PART 2J — AUTO PHYSICAL DAMAGE

1	2	3	4	5	6	7	8	9	10	11	12	13
1. Prior	XXXX	XXXX	XXXX	XXXX	XXXX	XXXX	XXXX	*				
2. 1988	XXXX	XXXX	XXXX	XXXX	XXXX	XXXX	XXXX	XXXX				XXXX
3. 1989	XXXX	XXXX	XXXX	XXXX	XXXX	XXXX	XXXX	XXXX	XXXX		XXXX	XXXX
4. Totals												

SCHEDULE P — PART 2K — FIDELITY, SURETY, FINANCIAL GUARANTY, MORTGAGE GUARANTY

1	2	3	4	5	6	7	8	9	10	11	12	13
1. Prior	XXXX	XXXX	XXXX	XXXX	XXXX	XXXX	XXXX	*				
2. 1988	XXXX	XXXX	XXXX	XXXX	XXXX	XXXX	XXXX	XXXX				XXXX
3. 1989	XXXX	XXXX	XXXX	XXXX	XXXX	XXXX	XXXX	XXXX	XXXX		XXXX	XXXX
4. Totals												

*Reported reserves only. Subsequent development relates only to subsequent payments and reserves.
**Current year less first or second prior year, showing (redundant) or adverse.

(Name)

SCHEDULE P — PART 2L — OTHER (INCLUDING CREDIT, ACCIDENT AND HEALTH)

Years in Which Losses Were Incurred	INCURRED LOSSES AND ALLOCATED EXPENSES REPORTED AT YEAR END (000 OMITTED)										DEVELOPMENT**	
	2 1980	3 1981	4 1982	5 1983	6 1984	7 1985	8 1986	9 1987	10 1988	11 1989	12 One Year	13 Two Year
1 Prior	XXXX	XXXX	XXXX	XXXX	XXXX	XXXX	XXXX	*				
2 1988	XXXX	XXXX	XXXX	XXXX	XXXX	XXXX	XXXX	XXXX				XXXX
3 1989	XXXX	XXXX	XXXX	XXXX	XXXX	XXXX	XXXX	XXXX	XXXX		XXXX	XXXX
4 Totals												

SCHEDULE P — PART 2M — INTERNATIONAL

Years in Which Losses Were Incurred	1980	1981	1982	1983	1984	1985	1986	1987	1988	1989	One Year	Two Year
1 Prior	*											
2 1980												
3 1981	XXXX											
4 1982	XXXX	XXXX										
5 1983	XXXX	XXXX	XXXX									
6 1984	XXXX	XXXX	XXXX	XXXX								
7 1985	XXXX	XXXX	XXXX	XXXX	XXXX							
8 1986	XXXX	XXXX	XXXX	XXXX	XXXX	XXXX						
9 1987	XXXX	XXXX	XXXX	XXXX	XXXX	XXXX	XXXX					
10 1988	XXXX	XXXX	XXXX	XXXX	XXXX	XXXX	XXXX	XXXX				XXXX
11 1989	XXXX	XXXX	XXXX	XXXX	XXXX	XXXX	XXXX	XXXX	XXXX		XXXX	XXXX
12 Totals												

SCHEDULE P — PART 2N — REINSURANCE A

Years	1980	1981	1982	1983	1984	1985	1986	1987	1988	1989	One Year	Two Year
1 1988	XXXX	XXXX	XXXX	XXXX	XXXX	XXXX	XXXX	XXXX				XXXX
2 1989	XXXX	XXXX	XXXX	XXXX	XXXX	XXXX	XXXX	XXXX	XXXX		XXXX	XXXX
3 Totals												

SCHEDULE P — PART 2O — REINSURANCE B

Years	1980	1981	1982	1983	1984	1985	1986	1987	1988	1989	One Year	Two Year
1 1988	XXXX	XXXX	XXXX	XXXX	XXXX	XXXX	XXXX	XXXX				XXXX
2 1989	XXXX	XXXX	XXXX	XXXX	XXXX	XXXX	XXXX	XXXX	XXXX		XXXX	XXXX
3 Totals												

SCHEDULE P — PART 2P — REINSURANCE C

Years	1980	1981	1982	1983	1984	1985	1986	1987	1988	1989	One Year	Two Year
1 1988	XXXX	XXXX	XXXX	XXXX	XXXX	XXXX	XXXX	XXXX				XXXX
2 1989	XXXX	XXXX	XXXX	XXXX	XXXX	XXXX	XXXX.	XXXX	XXXX		XXXX	XXXX
3 Totals												

SCHEDULE P — PART 2Q — REINSURANCE D

Years	1980	1981	1982	1983	1984	1985	1986	1987	1988	1989	One Year	Two Year
1 Prior	*											
2 1980												
3 1981	XXXX											
4 1982	XXXX	XXXX										
5 1983	XXXX	XXXX	XXXX									
6 1984	XXXX	XXXX	XXXX	XXXX								
7 1985	XXXX	XXXX	XXXX	XXXX	XXXX							
8 1986	XXXX	XXXX	XXXX	XXXX	XXXX	XXXX						
9 1987	XXXX	XXXX	XXXX	XXXX	XXXX	XXXX	XXXX					
10 Totals												

*Reported reserves only. Subsequent development relates only to subsequent payments and reserves.
**Current year less first or second prior year, showing (redundant) or adverse.

ANNUAL STATEMENT FOR THE YEAR 1989 OF THE ....
(Name)

SCHEDULE P — PART 3A — HOMEOWNERS/FARMOWNERS

1 Years in Which Losses Were Incurred	CUMULATIVE PAID LOSSES AND ALLOCATED EXPENSES AT YEAR END (000 OMITTED)										12 Number of Claims Closed With Loss Payment	13 Number of Claims Closed Without Loss Payment
	2 1980	3 1981	4 1982	5 1983	6 1984	7 1985	8 1986	9 1987	10 1988	11 1989		
1. Prior	000										XXXX	XXXX
2. 1980											XXXX	XXXX
3. 1981	XXXX										XXXX	XXXX
4. 1982	XXXX	XXXX									XXXX	XXXX
5. 1983	XXXX	XXXX	XXXX								XXXX	XXXX
6. 1984	XXXX	XXXX	XXXX	XXXX							XXXX	XXXX
7. 1985	XXXX	XXXX	XXXX	XXXX	XXXX						XXXX	XXXX
8. 1986	XXXX	XXXX	XXXX	XXXX	XXXX	XXXX					XXXX	XXXX
9. 1987	XXXX	XXXX	XXXX	XXXX	XXXX	XXXX	XXXX				XXXX	XXXX
10. 1988	XXXX	XXXX	XXXX	XXXX	XXXX	XXXX	XXXX	XXXX			XXXX	XXXX
11. 1989	XXXX	XXXX	XXXX	XXXX	XXXX	XXXX	XXXX	XXXX	XXXX		XXXX	XXXX

SCHEDULE P — PART 3B — PRIVATE PASSENGER AUTO LIABILITY/MEDICAL

	2	3	4	5	6	7	8	9	10	11	12	13
1. Prior	000											
2. 1980												
3. 1981	XXXX											
4. 1982	XXXX	XXXX										
5. 1983	XXXX	XXXX	XXXX									
6. 1984	XXXX	XXXX	XXXX	XXXX								
7. 1985	XXXX	XXXX	XXXX	XXXX	XXXX							
8. 1986	XXXX	XXXX	XXXX	XXXX	XXXX	XXXX						
9. 1987	XXXX	XXXX	XXXX	XXXX	XXXX	XXXX	XXXX					
10. 1988	X.XXX	XXXX	XXXX	XXXX	XXXX	XXXX	XXXX	XXXX				
11. 1989	XXXX	XXXX	XXXX	XXXX	XXXX	XXXX	XXXX	XXXX	XXXX			

SCHEDULE P — PART 3C — COMMERCIAL AUTO/TRUCK LIABILITY/MEDICAL

	2	3	4	5	6	7	8	9	10	11	12	13
1. Prior	000											
2. 1980												
3. 1981	XXXX											
4. 1982	XXXX	XXXX										
5. 1983	XXXX	XXXX	XXXX									
6. 1984	XXXX	XXXX	XXXX	XXXX								
7. 1985	XXXX	XXXX	XXXX	XXXX	XXXX							
8. 1986	XXXX	XXXX	XXXX	XXXX	XXXX	XXXX						
9. 1987	XXXX	XXXX	XXXX	XXXX	XXXX	XXXX	XXXX					
10. 1988	XXXX	XXXX	XXXX	XXXX	XXXX	XXXX	XXXX	XXXX				
11. 1989	XXXX	XXXX	XXXX	XXXX	XXXX	XXXX	XXXX	XXXX	XXXX			

SCHEDULE P — PART 3D — WORKERS' COMPENSATION

	2	3	4	5	6	7	8	9	10	11	12	13
1. Prior	000											
2. 1980												
3. 1981	XXXX											
4. 1982	XXXX	XXXX										
5. 1983	XXXX	XXXX	XXXX									
6. 1984	XXXX	XXXX	XXXX	XXXX								
7. 1985	XXXX	XXXX	XXXX	XXXX	XXXX							
8. 1986	XXXX	XXXX	XXXX	XXXX	XXXX	XXXX						
9. 1987	XXXX	XXXX	XXXX	XXXX	XXXX	XXXX	XXXX					
10. 1988	XXXX	XXXX	XXXX	XXXX	XXXX	XXXX	XXXX	XXXX				
11. 1989	XXXX	XXXX	XXXX	XXXX	XXXX	XXXX	XXXX	XXXX	XXXX			

SCHEDULE P — PART 3E — COMMERCIAL MULTIPLE PERIL

	2	3	4	5	6	7	8	9	10	11	12	13
1. Prior	000											
2. 1980												
3. 1981	XXXX											
4. 1982	XXXX	XXXX										
5. 1983	XXXX	XXXX	XXXX									
6. 1984	XXXX	XXXX	XXXX	XXXX								
7. 1985	XXXX	XXXX	XXXX	XXXX	XXXX							
8. 1986	XXXX	XXXX	XXXX	XXXX	XXXX	XXXX						
9. 1987	XXXX	XXXX	XXXX	XXXX	XXXX	XXXX	XXXX					
10. 1988	XXXX	XXXX	XXXX	XXXX	XXXX	XXXX	XXXX	XXXX				
11. 1989	XXXX	XXXX	XXXX	XXXX	XXXX	XXXX	XXXX	XXXX	XXXX			

Note: Net of salvage and subrogation received.

ANNUAL STATEMENT FOR THE YEAR 1989 OF THE ....
(Name)

SCHEDULE P — PART 3F — MEDICAL MALPRACTICE

Years in Which Losses Were Incurred	CUMULATIVE PAID LOSSES AND ALLOCATED EXPENSES AT YEAR END (000 OMITTED)										12 Number of Claims Closed With Loss Payment	13 Number of Claims Closed Without Loss Payment
	2 1980	3 1981	4 1982	5 1983	6 1984	7 1985	8 1986	9 1987	10 1988	11 1989		
1 Prior	000											
2 1980												
3 1981	XXXX											
4 1982	XXXX	XXXX										
5 1983	XXXX	XXXX	XXXX									
6 1984	XXXX	XXXX	XXXX	XXXX								
7 1985	XXXX	XXXX	XXXX	XXXX	XXXX							
8 1986	XXXX	XXXX	XXXX	XXXX	XXXX	XXXX						
9 1987	XXXX	XXXX	XXXX	XXXX	XXXX	XXXX	XXXX					
10 1988	XXXX	XXXX	XXXX	XXXX	XXXX	XXXX	XXXX	XXXX				
11 1989	XXXX	XXXX	XXXX	XXXX	XXXX	XXXX	XXXX	XXXX	XXXX			

SCHEDULE P — PART 3G — SPECIAL LIABILITY (OCEAN MARINE, AIRCRAFT (ALL PERILS), BOILER AND MACHINERY)

1 Prior	000										XXXX	XXXX
2 1980											XXXX	XXXX
3 1981	XXXX										XXXX	XXXX
4 1982	XXXX	XXXX									XXXX	XXXX
5 1983	XXXX	XXXX	XXXX								XXXX	XXXX
6 1984	XXXX	XXXX	XXXX	XXXX							XXXX	XXXX
7 1985	XXXX	XXXX	XXXX	XXXX	XXXX						XXXX	XXXX
8 1986	XXXX	XXXX	XXXX	XXXX	XXXX	XXXX					XXXX	XXXX
9 1987	XXXX	XXXX	XXXX	XXXX	XXXX	XXXX	XXXX				XXXX	XXXX
10 1988	XXXX	XXXX	XXXX	XXXX	XXXX	XXXX	XXXX	XXXX			XXXX	XXXX
11 1989	XXXX	XXXX	XXXX	XXXX	XXXX	XXXX	XXXX	XXXX	XXXX		XXXX	XXXX

SCHEDULE P — PART 3H — OTHER LIABILITY

1 Prior	000											
2 1980												
3 1981	XXXX											
4 1982	XXXX	XXXX										
5 1983	XXXX	XXXX	XXXX									
6 1984	XXXX	XXXX	XXXX	XXXX								
7 1985	XXXX	XXXX	XXXX	XXXX	XXXX							
8 1986	XXXX	XXXX	XXXX	XXXX	XXXX	XXXX						
9 1987	XXXX	XXXX	XXXX	XXXX	XXXX	XXXX	XXXX					
10 1988	XXXX	XXXX	XXXX	XXXX	XXXX	XXXX	XXXX	XXXX				
11 1989	XXXX	XXXX	XXXX	XXXX	XXXX	XXXX	XXXX	XXXX	XXXX			

SCHEDULE P — PART 3I — SPECIAL PROPERTY (FIRE, ALLIED LINES, INLAND MARINE, EARTHQUAKE, GLASS, BURGLARY AND THEFT)

1 Prior	XXXX	XXXX	XXXX	XXXX	XXXX	XXXXX	XXXX	000			XXXX	XXXX
2 1988	XXXX	XXXX	XXXX	XXXX	XXXX	XXXX	XXXX	XXXX			XXXX	XXXX
3 1989	XXXX	XXXX	XXXX	XXXX	XXXX	XXXX	XXXX	XXXX	XXXX		XXXX	XXXX

SCHEDULE P — PART 3J — AUTO PHYSICAL DAMAGE

1 Prior	XXXX	XXXX	XXXX	XXXX	XXXX	XXXXX	XXXX	000				
2 1988	XXXX	XXXX	XXXX	XXXX	XXXX	XXXX	XXXX	XXXX				
3 1989	XXXX	XXXX	XXXX	XXXX	XXXX	XXXX	XXXX	XXXX	XXXX			

SCHEDULE P — PART 3K — FIDELITY, SURETY, FINANCIAL GUARANTY, MORTGAGE GUARANTY

1 Prior	XXXX	XXXX	XXXX	XXXX	XXXX	XXXXX	XXXX	000			XXXX	XXXX
2 1988	XXXX	XXXX	XXXX	XXXX	XXXX	XXXX	XXXX	XXXX			XXXX	XXXX
3 1989	XXXX	XXXX	XXXX	XXXX	XXXX	XXXX	XXXX	XXXX	XXXX		XXXX	XXXX

Note: Net of salvage and subrogation received.

ANNUAL STATEMENT FOR THE YEAR 1989 OF THE ....
(Name)

SCHEDULE P — PART 3L — OTHER (INCLUDING CREDIT, ACCIDENT AND HEALTH)

1 Years in Which Losses Were Incurred	CUMULATIVE PAID LOSSES AND ALLOCATED EXPENSES AT YEAR END (000 OMITTED)										12 Number of Claims Closed With Loss Payment	13 Number of Claims Closed Without Loss Payment
	2 1980	3 1981	4 1982	5 1983	6 1984	7 1985	8 1986	9 1987	10 1988	11 1989		
1. Prior	XXXX	XXXX	XXXX	XXXX	XXXX	XXXX	XXXX	000			XXXX	XXXX
2. 1988	XXXX	XXXX	XXXX	XXXX	XXXX	XXXX	XXXX	XXXX			XXXX	XXXX
3. 1989	XXXX	XXXX	XXXX	XXXX	XXXX	XXXX	XXXX	XXXX	XXXX		XXXX	XXXX

SCHEDULE P — PART 3M — INTERNATIONAL

1. Prior	000										XXXX	XXXX
2. 1980											XXXX	XXXX
3. 1981	XXXX										XXXX	XXXX
4. 1982	XXXX	XXXX									XXXX	XXXX
5. 1983	XXXX	XXXX	XXXX								XXXX	XXXX
6. 1984	XXXX	XXXX	XXXX	XXXX							XXXX	XXXX
7. 1985	XXXX	XXXX	XXXX	XXXX	XXXX						XXXX	XXXX
8. 1986	XXXX	XXXX	XXXX	XXXX	XXXX	XXXX					XXXX	XXXX
9. 1987	XXXX	XXXX	XXXX	XXXX	XXXX	XXXX	XXXX				XXXX	XXXX
10. 1988	XXXX	XXXX	XXXX	XXXX	XXXX	XXXX	XXXX	XXXX			XXXX	XXXX
11. 1989	XXXX	XXXX	XXXX	XXXX	XXXX	XXXX	XXXX	XXXX	XXXX		XXXX	XXXX

SCHEDULE P — PART 3N — REINSURANCE A

1. 1988	XXXX	XXXX	XXXX	XXXX	XXXX	XXXX	XXXX	XXXX			XXXX	XXXX
2. 1989	XXXX	XXXX	XXXX	XXXX	XXXX	XXXX	XXXX	XXXX	XXXX		XXXX	XXXX

SCHEDULE P — PART 3O — REINSURANCE B

1. 1988	XXXX	XXXX	XXXX	XXXX	XXXX	XXXX	XXXX	XXXX			XXXX	XXXX
2. 1989	XXXX	XXXX	XXXX	XXXX	XXXX	XXXX	XXXX	XXXX	XXXX		XXXX	XXXX

SCHEDULE P — PART 3P — REINSURANCE C

1. 1988	XXXX	XXXX	XXXX	XXXX	XXXX	XXXX	XXXX	XXXX			XXXX	XXXX
2. 1989	XXXX	XXXX	XXXX	XXXX	XXXX	XXXX	XXXX	XXXX	XXXX		XXXX	XXXX

SCHEDULE P — PART 3Q — REINSURANCE D

1. Prior	000										XXXX	XXXX
2. 1980											XXXX	XXXX
3. 1981	XXXX										XXXX	XXXX
4. 1982	XXXX	XXXX									XXXX	XXXX
5. 1983	XXXX	XXXX	XXXX								XXXX	XXXX
6. 1984	XXXX	XXXX	XXXX	XXXX							XXXX	XXXX
7. 1985	XXXX	XXXX	XXXX	XXXX	XXXX						XXXX	XXXX
8. 1986	XXXX	XXXX	XXXX	XXXX	XXXX	XXXX					XXXX	XXXX
9. 1987	XXXX	XXXX	XXXX	XXXX	XXXX	XXXX	XXXX				XXXX	XXXX

Note: Net of salvage and subrogation received.

Form 2

(Name)

SCHEDULE P—PART 5—CLAIMS - MADE
(000 omitted)

PART 5E — COMMERCIAL MULTIPLE PERIL

1 Years in Which Premiums Were Earned and Losses Were Incurred	2 Premiums Earned	3 Loss Payments	3.1 Cumulative Number of Claims Closed with Payments	3.2 Cumulative Number of Claims Closed without Payment	4 (4) Loss Expense Payments Allocated	4a Percent 4 ÷ 3	5 Unallocated	5a Percent 5 ÷ 3	6 Loss and Loss Expense Payments (3 + 4 + 5)	7 Percent 6 ÷ 2	8 Number of Claims Outstanding	9 Losses Unpaid	10 Loss Expense Unpaid	11 Total Losses and Loss Expense Incurred (6 + 9 + 10)	12 Percent 11 ÷ 2
1 1987															
2 1988															
3 1989															
4 Totals															

PART 5F — MEDICAL MALPRACTICE

1 1987															
2 1988															
3 1989															
4 Totals															

PART 5H — OTHER LIABILITY

1 1987															
2 1988															
3 1989															
4 Totals															

SCHEDULE P — PART 6A — HOMEOWNERS/FARMOWNERS

1 Years in Which Losses Were Incurred	BULK AND INCURRED BUT NOT REPORTED RESERVES ON LOSSES AND ALLOCATED EXPENSES AT YEAR END (000 OMITTED)									
	2 1980	3 1981	4 1982	5 1983	6 1984	7 1985	8 1986	9 1987	10 1988	11 1989
1. Prior										
2. 1980										
3. 1981	XXXX									
4. 1982	XXXX	XXXX								
5. 1983	XXXX	XXXX	XXXX							
6. 1984	XXXX	XXXX	XXXX	XXXX						
7. 1985	XXXX	XXXX	XXXX	XXXX	XXXX					
8. 1986	XXXX	XXXX	XXXX	XXXX	XXXX	XXXX				
9. 1987	XXXX	XXXX	XXXX	XXXX	XXXX	XXXX	XXXX			
10. 1988	XXXX	XXXX	XXXX	XXXX	XXXX	XXXX	XXXX	XXXX		
11. 1989	XXXX	XXXX	XXXX	XXXX	XXXX	XXXX	XXXX	XXXX	XXXX	

SCHEDULE P — PART 6B — PRIVATE PASSENGER AUTO LIABILITY/MEDICAL

1. Prior										
2. 1980										
3. 1981	XXXX									
4. 1982	XXXX	XXXX								
5. 1983	XXXX	XXXX	XXXX							
6. 1984	XXXX	XXXX	XXXX	XXXX						
7. 1985	XXXX	XXXX	XXXX	XXXX	XXXX					
8. 1986	XXXX	XXXX	XXXX	XXXX	XXXX	XXXX				
9. 1987	XXXX	XXXX	XXXX	XXXX	XXXX	XXXX	XXXX			
10. 1988	XXXX	XXXX	XXXX	XXXX	XXXX	XXXX	XXXX	XXXX		
11. 1989	XXXX	XXXX	XXXX	XXXX	XXXX	XXXX	XXXX	XXXX	XXXX	

SCHEDULE P — PART 6C — COMMERCIAL AUTO/TRUCK LIABILITY/MEDICAL

1. Prior										
2. 1980										
3. 1981	XXXX									
4. 1982	XXXX	XXXX								
5. 1983	XXXX	XXXX	XXXX							
6. 1984	XXXX	XXXX	XXXX	XXXX						
7. 1985	XXXX	XXXX	XXXX	XXXX	XXXX					
8. 1986	XXXX	XXXX	XXXX	XXXX	XXXX	XXXX				
9. 1987	XXXX	XXXX	XXXX	XXXX	XXXX	XXXX	XXXX			
10. 1988	XXXX	XXXX	XXXX	XXXX	XXXX	XXXX	XXXX	XXXX		
11. 1989	XXXX	XXXX	XXXX	XXXX	XXXX	XXXX	XXXX	XXXX	XXXX	

SCHEDULE P — PART 6D — WORKERS' COMPENSATION

1. Prior										
2. 1980										
3. 1981	XXXX									
4. 1982	XXXX	XXXX								
5. 1983	XXXX	XXXX	XXXX							
6. 1984	XXXX	XXXX	XXXX	XXXX						
7. 1985	XXXX	XXXX	XXXX	XXXX	XXXX					
8. 1986	XXXX	XXXX	XXXX	XXXX	XXXX	XXXX				
9. 1987	XXXX	XXXX	XXXX	XXXX	XXXX	XXXX	XXXX			
10. 1988	XXXX	XXXX	XXXX	XXXX	XXXX	XXXX	XXXX	XXXX		
11. 1989	XXXX	XXXX	XXXX	XXXX	XXXX	XXXX	XXXX	XXXX	XXXX	

SCHEDULE P — PART 6E — COMMERCIAL MULTIPLE PERIL

1. Prior										
2. 1980										
3. 1981	XXXX									
4. 1982	XXXX	XXXX								
5. 1983	XXXX	XXXX	XXXX							
6. 1984	XXXX	XXXX	XXXX	XXXX						
7. 1985	XXXX	XXXX	XXXX	XXXX	XXXX					
8. 1986	XXXX	XXXX	XXXX	XXXX	XXXX	XXXX				
9. 1987	XXXX	XXXX	XXXX	XXXX	XXXX	XXXX	XXXX			
10. 1988	XXXX	XXXX	XXXX	XXXX	XXXX	XXXX	XXXX	XXXX		
11. 1989	XXXX	XXXX	XXXX	XXXX	XXXX	XXXX	XXXX	XXXX	XXXX	

80   ANNUAL STATEMENT FOR THE YEAR 1989 OF THE ....   Form 2

(Name)

SCHEDULE P — PART 6F — MEDICAL MALPRACTICE

1 Years in Which Losses Were Incurred	BULK AND INCURRED BUT NOT REPORTED RESERVES ON LOSSES AND ALLOCATED EXPENSES AT YEAR END (000 OMITTED)									
	2 1980	3 1981	4 1982	5 1983	6 1984	7 1985	8 1986	9 1987	10 1988	11 1989
1. Prior										
2. 1980										
3. 1981	XXXX									
4. 1982	XXXX	XXXX								
5. 1983	XXXX	XXXX	XXXX							
6. 1984	XXXX	XXXX	XXXX	XXXX						
7. 1985	XXXX	XXXX	XXXX	XXXX	XXXX					
8. 1986	XXXX	XXXX	XXXX	XXXX	XXXX	XXXX				
9. 1987	XXXX	XXXX	XXXX	XXXX	XXXX	XXXX	XXXX			
10. 1988	XXXX	XXXX	XXXX	XXXX	XXXX	XXXX	XXXX	XXXX		
11. 1989	XXXX	XXXX	XXXX	XXXX	XXXX	XXXX	XXXX	XXXX	XXXX	

SCHEDULE P — PART 6G — SPECIAL LIABILITY (OCEAN MARINE, AIRCRAFT (ALL PERILS), BOILER AND MACHINERY)

1. Prior										
2. 1980										
3. 1981	XXXX									
4. 1982	XXXX	XXXX								
5. 1983	XXXX	XXXX	XXXX							
6. 1984	XXXX	XXXX	XXXX	XXXX						
7. 1985	XXXX	XXXX	XXXX	XXXX	XXXX					
8. 1986	XXXX	XXXX	XXXX	XXXX	XXXX	XXXX				
9. 1987	XXXX	XXXX	XXXX	XXXX	XXXX	XXXX	XXXX			
10. 1988	XXXX	XXXX	XXXX	XXXX	XXXX	XXXX	XXXX	XXXX		
11. 1989	XXXX	XXXX	XXXX	XXXX	XXXX	XXXX	XXXX	XXXX	XXXX	

SCHEDULE P — PART 6H — OTHER LIABILITY

1. Prior										
2. 1980										
3. 1981	XXXX									
4. 1982	XXXX	XXXX								
5. 1983	XXXX	XXXX	XXXX							
6. 1984	XXXX	XXXX	XXXX	XXXX						
7. 1985	XXXX	XXXX	XXXX	XXXX	XXXX					
8. 1986	XXXX	XXXX	XXXX	XXXX	XXXX	XXXX				
9. 1987	XXXX	XXXX	XXXX	XXXX	XXXX	XXXX	XXXX			
10. 1988	XXXX	XXXX	XXXX	XXXX	XXXX	XXXX	XXXX	XXXX		
11. 1989	XXXX	XXXX	XXXX	XXXX	XXXX	XXXX	XXXX	XXXX	XXXX	

SCHEDULE P — PART 6I — SPECIAL PROPERTY (FIRE, ALLIED LINES, INLAND MARINE, EARTHQUAKE, GLASS, BURGLARY AND THEFT)

1. Prior	XXXX	XXXX	XXXX	XXXX	XXXX	XXXX	XXXX			
2. 1988	XXXX	XXXX	XXXX	XXXX	XXXX	XXXX	XXXX	XXXX		
3. 1989	XXXX	XXXX	XXXX	XXXX	XXXX	XXXX	XXXX	XXXX	XXXX	

SCHEDULE P — PART 6J — AUTO PHYSICAL DAMAGE

1. Prior	XXXX	XXXX	XXXX	XXXX	XXXX	XXXX	XXXX			
2. 1988	XXXX	XXXX	XXXX	XXXX	XXXX	XXXX	XXXX	XXXX		
3. 1989	XXXX	XXXX	XXXX	XXXX	XXXX	XXXX	XXXX	XXXX	XXXX	

SCHEDULE P — PART 6K — FIDELITY, SURETY, FINANCIAL GUARANTY, MORTGAGE GUARANTY

1. Prior	XXXX	XXXX	XXXX	XXXX	XXXX	XXXX	XXXX			
2. 1988	XXXX	XXXX	XXXX	XXXX	XXXX	XXXX	XXXX	XXXX		
3. 1989	XXXX	XXXX	XXXX	XXXX	XXXX	XXXX	XXXX	XXXX	XXXX	

SCHEDULE P — PART 6L — OTHER (INCLUDING CREDIT, ACCIDENT AND HEALTH)

1 Years in Which Losses Were Incurred	BULK AND INCURRED BUT NOT REPORTED RESERVES ON LOSSES AND ALLOCATED EXPENSES AT YEAR END (000 OMITTED)									
	2	3	4	5	6	7	8	9	10	11
	1980	1981	1982	1983	1984	1985	1986	1987	1988	1989
1. Prior	xxxx	xxxx	xxxx	xxxx	xxxx	xxxx	xxxx			
2. 1988	xxxx	xxxx	xxxx	xxxx	xxxx	xxxx	xxxx	xxxx		
3. 1989	xxxx	xxxx	xxxx	xxxx	xxxx	xxxx	xxxx	xxxx	xxxx	

SCHEDULE P — PART 6M — INTERNATIONAL

	2	3	4	5	6	7	8	9	10	11
1. Prior										
2. 1980										
3. 1981	xxxx									
4. 1982	xxxx	xxxx								
5. 1983	xxxx	xxxx	xxxx							
6. 1984	xxxx	xxxx	xxxx	xxxx						
7. 1985	xxxx	xxxx	xxxx	xxxx	xxxx					
8. 1986	xxxx	xxxx	xxxx	xxxx	xxxx	xxxx				
9. 1987	xxxx	xxxx	xxxx	xxxx	xxxx	xxxx	xxxx			
10. 1988	xxxx	xxxx	xxxx	xxxx	xxxx	xxxx	xxxx	xxxx		
11. 1989	xxxx	xxxx	xxxx	xxxx	xxxx	xxxx	xxxx	xxxx	xxxx	

SCHEDULE P — PART 6N — REINSURANCE A

	2	3	4	5	6	7	8	9	10	11
1. 1988	xxxx	xxxx	xxxx	xxxx	xxxx	xxxx	xxxx	xxxx		
2. 1989	xxxx	xxxx	xxxx	xxxx	xxxx	xxxx	xxxx	xxxx	xxxx	

SCHEDULE P — PART 6O — REINSURANCE B

	2	3	4	5	6	7	8	9	10	11
1. 1988	xxxx	xxxx	xxxx	xxxx	xxxx	xxxx	xxxx	xxxx		
2. 1989	xxxx	xxxx	xxxx	xxxx	xxxx	xxxx	xxxx	xxxx	xxxx	

SCHEDULE P — PART 6P — REINSURANCE C

	2	3	4	5	6	7	8	9	10	11
1. 1988	xxxx	xxxx	xxxx	xxxx	xxxx	xxxx	xxxx	xxxx		
2. 1989	xxxx	xxxx	xxxx	xxxx	xxxx	xxxx	xxxx	xxxx	xxxx	

SCHEDULE P — PART 6Q — REINSURANCE D

	2	3	4	5	6	7	8	9	10	11
1. Prior										
2. 1980										
3. 1981	xxxx									
4. 1982	xxxx	xxxx								
5. 1983	xxxx	xxxx	xxxx							
6. 1984	xxxx	xxxx	xxxx	xxxx						
7. 1985	xxxx	xxxx	xxxx	xxxx	xxxx					
8. 1986	xxxx	xxxx	xxxx	xxxx	xxxx	xxxx				
9. 1987	xxxx	xxxx	xxxx	xxxx	xxxx	xxxx	xxxx			

ANNUAL STATEMENT FOR THE YEAR 1989 OF THE ....
(Name)

SCHEDULE P INTERROGATORIES

1. Computation of excess statutory reserves over statement reserves. See Instructions for explanation and formulas.

    (a) Auto Liability (private passenger and commercial)

        1989 $_____ (_____ %)   1988 $_____ (_____ %)

        1987 $_____ (_____ %)   Total $_____

    (b) Other Liability

        1989 $_____ (_____ %)   1988 $_____ (_____ %)

        1987 $_____ (_____ %)   Total $_____

    (c) Medical Malpractice

        1989 $_____ (_____ %)   1988 $_____ (_____ %)

        1987 $_____ (_____ %)   Total $_____

    (d) Workers' Compensation

        1989 $_____ (_____ %)   1988 $_____ (_____ %)

        1987 $_____ (_____ %)   Total $_____

    (e) Credit   Total $_____

    (f) All Lines Total (Report here and Page 3)   Total $_____

2. Claims-made policies: Schedule P — Part 5.
    State the amount of current year premiums earned on claims-made policies. If this amount is more than $100,000 and greater than 15% of current year premiums earned in that line,
    then you must submit a Supplemental Schedule P — Part 5; see instructions.

    (a) Commercial Multiple Peril
        (i) claims-made premiums $_____
        (ii) Part 5 required   Yes ( )   No ( )

    (b) Medical Malpractice
        (i) claims-made premiums $_____
        (ii) Part 5 required   Yes ( )   No ( )

    (c) Other Liability
        (i) claims-made premiums $_____
        (ii) Part 5 required   Yes ( )   No ( )

3. The term "Loss expense" includes all payments for legal expenses, including attorney's and witness fees and court costs, salaries and expenses of investigators, adjustors and field
    men, rents, stationery, telegraph and telephone charges, postage, salaries and expenses of office employees, home office expenses and all other payments under or on account of such
    injuries, whether the payments are allocated to specific claims or are unallocated. Are they so reported in this statement?
    Answer: Yes ( )   No ( )

4. The unallocated loss expense payments paid during the most recent calendar year should be distributed to the various years in which losses were incurred as follows: (1) 45% to the
    most recent year, (2) 5% to the next most recent year, and (3) the balance to all years, including the most recent, in proportion to the amount of loss payments paid for each year
    during the most recent calendar year. If the distribution in (1) or (2) produces an accumulated distribution to such year in excess of 10% of the premiums earned for such year,
    disregarding all distributions made under (3), such accumulated distribution should be limited to 10% of premiums earned and the balance distributed in accordance with (3). Are
    they so reported in this Statement?
    Answer: Yes ( )   No ( )

5. Do any lines in Schedule P include reserves which are reported gross of any discount to present value of future payments, but are reported net of such discounts on page 10?
                                                                                            Yes ( )   No ( )

    If Yes, proper reporting must be made in the Notes to Financial Statements, as specified in the Instructions. Also, the discounts must be reported in Schedule P — Part 1, columns 30
    and 31.

    Schedule P must be completed gross of non-tabular discounting. Work papers relating to discount calculations must be available for examination upon request.

    Discounting is allowed only if expressly permitted by the state insurance department to which this Annual Statement is being filed.

6. What were the net premiums in force at the end of the year for:

    (in thousands of dollars)   (a) Fidelity _____
                                                                                            (b) Surety _____

7. Claim count information is reported (check one)   (a) per claim _____
    If not the same in all years, explain in question 8.   (b) per claimant _____

8. The information provided in Schedule P will be used by many persons to estimate the adequacy of the current loss and expense reserves, among other things. Are there any especially significant events, coverage,
    retention or accounting changes which have occurred which must be considered when making such analyses (An extended statement may be attached)?

    _____

    _____

    _____

    _____

    _____

    _____

Form 2

(Name)

SCHEDULE X — PART 1 — UNLISTED ASSETS

*Showing all property owned by the Company or in which it had any interest, on December 31 of current year, which is not entered on any other schedule and which is not included in the financial statement for the current year

1 Description	2 From Whom Acquired	3 Date When Acquired	4 Date When Charged Off From Statement	5 Par Value	6 Actual Cost	7 Book Value When Charged Off	8 Market Value December 31 of Current Year	9 Gross Income Thereon During Year	10 Outlays Made During Year	11 Reasons for Net Carrying Property on Books
999999 TOTALS										XXXX

SCHEDULE X — PART 2

Showing all property acquired or transferred to Schedule X, Part 1, during the year except that shown in invested asset schedules and except furniture, fixtures and supplies

1 Description	2 Date of Acquisition	3 From Whom Acquired	4 Par Value	5 Actual Cost
999999 TOTALS				

SCHEDULE X — PART 3

Showing all property sold or transferred from Schedule X, Part 1, during the year except that shown in invested asset schedules

1 Description	2 Date of Acquisition	3 From Whom Acquired	4 Par Value	5 Actual Cost	6 Date of Sale	7 To Whom Sold	8 Consideration	9 Gross Income Thereon During Year	10 Outlay Thereon During Year Other Than Cost
999999 TOTALS					XXXX		XXXXXXXXXXX		

*Companies should limit entries in this schedule to items transferred from asset accounts.
NOTE: Interest, dividends and real estate income should be reported in Part 1, Line 9, Page 6; any other receipts should be reported in item 12, Page 4.

83

ANNUAL STATEMENT FOR THE YEAR 1989 OF THE ....
(Name)

SCHEDULE Y — INFORMATION CONCERNING ACTIVITIES OF INSURER MEMBERS OF A HOLDING COMPANY GROUP

NOTE: All insurer members of a Holding Company Group shall prepare a common Schedule for inclusion in each of the individual annual statements and the consolidated Fire and Casualty Annual Statement of the Group.

PART 1 — ORGANIZATIONAL CHART

Attach a chart or listing presenting the identities of interrelationships between the parent, all affiliated insurers and other affiliates, identifying all insurers as such and listing the Federal Employers Identification Number for each. The relationship of the Holding Company Group to the ultimate parent (if such parent is outside the reported holding company) should be shown. No non-insurer need be shown if it does not have any activities reported in Part 2 and its total assets are less than one-half of one percent of the total assets of the largest affiliated insurer.

Form 2

ANNUAL STATEMENT FOR THE YEAR 1989 OF THE ....

(Name)

SCHEDULE Y — (Continued)

NOTE: All insurer members of a Holding Company Group shall prepare a common Schedule for inclusion in each of the individual annual statements and the consolidated Fire and Casualty Annual Statement of the Group

PART 2 — SUMMARY OF THE INSURER'S TRANSACTIONS WITH ANY AFFILIATES

Include the aggregate of transactions, for the reporting period, within each category involving the parent company (companies), all insurance companies in the Holding Company System, and all other companies in the system with which an insurance company member had a transaction. Exclude transactions of a non-insurer with an insurance company that are of a routine nature (i.e., the purchase of insurance coverage) and cost allocation transactions that are based upon generally accepted principles of accounting.

1 Name of Insurer and Parent, Subsidiary or Affiliate	2 Shareholder Dividends	3 Capital Contributions	4 Purchases, Sales or Exchanges of Loans, Securities, Real Estate, Mortgage Loans or Other Investments	5 Receipts/ (Payments) in Connection with Guarantees or Undertakings for the Benefit of an Affiliate	6 Management Agreement, Service Contracts (including Contracts for Services Provided by the Insurer or Purchased by the Insurer from Other Affiliates) and Non-GAAP Cost Sharing Agreements	7 Receipts/ (Payments) Made Under Reinsurance Agreements	8 Any Other Material Activity not in the Ordinary Course of the Insurer's Business	9 Totals	10 Reinsurance Reserve Credits
Control Totals									

NOTE: If the nature of the transactions reported in Part 2 requires explanation with this Schedule, report such in an explanatory note immediately following Part 2

85

ANNUAL STATEMENT FOR THE YEAR 1989 OF THE ....
(Name)

SCHEDULE T — EXHIBIT OF PREMIUMS WRITTEN
Allocated by States and Territories

1 States, Etc.	1a Is Insurer Licensed? (Yes or No)	Gross Premiums, Including Policy and Membership Fees, Less Return Premiums and Premiums on Policies Not Taken		4 Dividends Paid or Credited to Policyholders on Direct Business	5 Direct Losses Paid (Deducting Salvage)	6 Direct Losses Incurred	7 Direct Losses Unpaid	8 Finance and Service Charges Not Included in Premiums	9 Direct Premiums Written for Federal Purchasing Groups (Included in Column 2)
		2 Direct Premiums Written	3 Direct Premiums Earned						
1. Alabama .... AL									
2. Alaska .... AK									
3. Arizona .... AZ									
4. Arkansas .... AR									
5. California .... CA									
6. Colorado .... CO									
7. Connecticut .... CT									
8. Delaware .... DE									
9. Dist. Columbia .... DC									
10. Florida .... FL									
11. Georgia .... GA									
12. Hawaii .... HI									
13. Idaho .... ID									
14. Illinois IL									
15. Indiana .... IN									
16. Iowa .... IA									
17. Kansas .... KS									
18. Kentucky .... KY									
19. Louisiana .... LA									
20. Maine .... ME									
21. Maryland .... MD									
22. Massachusetts .... MA									
23. Michigan .... MI									
24. Minnesota .... MN									
25. Mississippi .... MS									
26. Missouri .... MO									
27. Montana .... MT									
28. Nebraska .... NE									
29. Nevada .... NV									
30. New Hampshire .... NH									
31. New Jersey .... NJ									
32. New Mexico .... NM									
33. New York .... NY									
34. North Carolina .... NC									
35. North Dakota .... ND									
36. Ohio .... OH									
37. Oklahoma .... OK									
38. Oregon .... OR									
39. Pennsylvania .... PA									
40. Rhode Island .... RI									
41. South Carolina .... SC									
42. South Dakota .... SD									
43. Tennessee .... TN									
44. Texas .... TX									
45. Utah .... UT									
46. Vermont .... VT									
47. Virginia .... VA									
48. Washington .... WA									
49. West Virginia .... WV									
50. Wisconsin .... WI									
51. Wyoming .... WY									
52. American Samoa .... AS									
53. Guam .... GU									
54. Puerto Rico .... PR									
55. U.S. Virgin Is. VI									
56. Canada .... CN									
57. Aggregate Other Alien .. OT**									
98. *Totals	††								

DETAILS OF WRITE-INS AGGREGATED AT LINE 57 FOR OTHER ALIEN

5701									
5702									
5703									
5704									
5705									
5798 Summary of remaining write-ins for line 57 from overflow page									
5799 Totals (Items 5701 thru 5705 plus 5798) (Schedule T, Line 57)									

Explanation of basis of allocation of premiums by states, etc.

*Total for Column 2 to agree with the total of Column 1 in Part 2B, Page 8. Total for Column 5 to agree with the total of Column 1 in Part 3, Page 9.
Total for Column 6 to agree with the sum of totals for Columns 5 and 7 less the total for Column 7 in the previous annual statement.
Total for Column 7 to equal Part 3A, Page 10, totals for Columns 1a and 4a. Total for Column 8 to agree with Item 11, Page 4.
**All U.S. business must be allocated by state regardless of license status.
††Insert the number of yes responses except for Canada and Other alien.

ANNUAL STATEMENT FOR THE YEAR 1989 OF THE ....
(Name)

SUPPLEMENTAL EXHIBITS AND SCHEDULES
INTERROGATORIES

The following supplemental reports are required to be filed as part of your annual statement filing. However, in the event that your company does not transact the type of business for which the special report must be filed, your response to the specific interrogatory will be accepted in lieu of filing a "NONE" report.

1. Will Supplement A to Schedule T (Medical Malpractice Supplement) be filed with this Department by March 1?   Yes [ ]   No [ ]
   If answer is no, please explain: ....
   ....
   ....

2. Will Schedule SIS (Stockholder Information Supplement) be filed with this Department by March 1?   Yes [ ]   No [ ]
   If answer is no, please explain: ....
   ....
   ....

3. Will the Financial Guaranty Insurance Exhibit be filed with this Department by March 1?   Yes [ ]   No [ ]
   If answer is no, please explain: ....
   ....
   ....

4. Will the Insurance Expense Exhibit be filed with this Department by April 1?   Yes [ ]   No [ ]
   If answer is no, please explain: ....
   ....
   ....

5. Will Schedule H be filed with this Department by April 1?   Yes [ ]   No [ ]
   If answer is no, please explain: ....
   ....
   ....

6. Will Schedule F, Part 1A, Section 2 be filed with this Department by April 1?   Yes [ ]   No [ ]
   If answer is no, please explain: ....
   ....
   ....

7. Will the Statement of Opinion relating to loss and loss adjustment expense reserves be filed with this Department by April 1?   Yes [ ]   No [ ]
   If answer is no, please explain: ....
   ....
   ....

8. Will the Products Liability Supplement be filed with this Department by May 1?   Yes [ ]   No [ ]
   If answer is no, please explain: ....
   ....
   ....

9. Will the Credit Life and Accident & Health Experience Exhibit be filed with this Department by May 1?   Yes [ ]   No [ ]
   If answer is no, please explain: ....
   ....
   ....

10. Will the Accident and Health Policy Experience Exhibit be filed with this Department by June 30?   Yes [ ]   No [ ]
    If answer is no, please explain: ....
    ....
    ....

11. Will the Medicare Supplement Insurance Experience Exhibit be filed with this Department by June 30?   Yes [ ]   No [ ]
    If answer is no, please explain: ....
    ....
    ....

ANNUAL STATEMENT FOR THE YEAR 1989 OF THE ....
(Name)

OVERFLOW PAGE FOR WRITE-INS

Appendix B

INSURANCE EXPENSE EXHIBIT — 1989

For the Year Ended December 31, 1989

OF THE .... INSURANCE COMPANY

ADDRESS (City, State and Zip Code) ....

NAIC Group Code .... NAIC Company Code .... Employers ID Number ....

Contact Person .... Title .... Telephone ....

REPORT TO THE STATE OF

(To Be Filed Not Later Than April 1, 1990)

GENERAL INSTRUCTIONS

All modifications and/or changes made in the Annual Statement affecting this exhibit must be filed in writing with the appropriate Insurance Department if Annual Statement is subsequently changed once it has been filed with the state department.

(1) Refer to instructions for Uniform Classifications of Expenses for definitions of Expense Groups and instructions for allocation of expenses to lines of business.

(2) Compute all ratios to nearest third place and express as percentages, e.g., 48.3.

(3) There should be submitted with this exhibit a detailed statement or footnote with respect to any item or items requiring special comment or explanation.

(4) Report all amounts to the nearer thousand or through truncation of digits below a thousand. (Example: $602,503 may be reported as $603 by rounding or as $602 by truncation).

(5) **An individual company expense exhibit must be submitted. Pooled expense exhibits will not be accepted. The individual expense exhibit must reconcile to the individual company's annual statement.**

PART I—ALLOCATION TO EXPENSE GROUPS

Operating Expense Classifications	1 Loss Adjustment Expenses	Other Underwriting Expenses			5 Investment Expenses	6 Total Expenses
		2 Acquisition, Field Supervision and Collection Expenses	3 General Expenses	4 Taxes Licenses and Fees		
1. Claim adjustment services:						
a. Direct						
b. Reinsurance assumed						
c. Reinsurance ceded						
d. Net claim adjustment services (a + b − c)						
2. Commission and brokerage:						
a. Direct						
b. Reinsurance assumed						
c. Reinsurance ceded						
d. Contingent—net						
e. Policy and membership fees						
f. Net commission and brokerage (a + b − c + d + e)						
3. Allowances to managers and agents						
4. Advertising						
5. Boards, bureaus and associations						
6. Surveys and underwriting reports						
7. Audit of assureds' records						
8. Salaries						
9. Employee relations and welfare						
10. Insurance						
11. Directors' fees						
12. Travel and travel items						
13. Rent and rent items						
14. Equipment						
15. Printing and stationery						
16. Postage, telephone and telegraph, exchange and express						
17. Legal and auditing						
17a. Totals (Items 3 to 17)						
18. Taxes, licenses and fees:						
a. State and local insurance taxes						
b. Insurance department licenses and fees						
c. Payroll taxes						
d. All other (excl. Fed. and foreign income and real estate)						
e. Total taxes, licenses and fees (a + b + c + d)						
19. Real estate expenses						
20. Real estate taxes						
21. Aggregate write-ins for miscellaneous operating expenses						
22. TOTAL EXPENSES INCURRED						
Details of write-ins aggregated at item 21 for miscellaneous operating expenses						
2101						
2102						
2103						
2104						
2199 TOTALS (Line 21)						

AFFIDAVIT

STATE OF .... } ss.

COUNTY OF ....

.... and ....

(Name)   (Title)*   (Name)   (Title)

of ....(Hereinafter called the Insurer), being duly sworn, each for himself declares:

1. That he is familiar with the matters to which the within exhibits, the answers, and the information, if any, refer.

2. That he is duly authorized to make, and does make, the following declaration on behalf of the insurer.

3. That the within exhibits, the answers, and the information, if any, are full and true statements of the matters respectively described herein, according to his best knowledge, information and belief.

4. That the insurer has reported all amounts in thousands, as required.

Subscribed and sworn to before me this

.... day of 1990   ....

....

*At least one signatory must be an officer of the insurer.

INSURANCE EXPENSE EXHIBIT OF THE ....
.... (Name)

A. PREMIUMS, LOSSES, EXPENSES AND NET INCOME, AND PERCENTAGES TO EARNED PREMIUMS.	1 Fire		2 Allied Lines		3 Farmowners Multiple Peril		4 Homeowners Multiple Peril		5 Commercial Multiple Peril		8 Ocean Marine
	Amount	%	Amount	%	Amount	%	Amount	%	Amount	%	Amount
1. Net Premiums Written (Annual Statement Pg. 8, Part 2B, Col. 4)		xxx		xxx		xxx		xxx		xxx	
2. Net Premiums Earned (Annual Statement Pg. 7, Part 2, Col. 4)		100.0		100.0		100.0		100.0		100.0	
3. Net Losses Incurred (Annual Statement Pg. 9, Part 3, Col. 7)											
4. Loss Adjustment Expenses Incurred (Part I, Col. 1, Line 22)											
5. Commission and Brokerage Incurred (Part I, Col. 2, Line 2 (f))											
6. Other Acquisition, Field Supervision and Collection Expenses Incurred (Part I, Col. 2, Line 22 minus Line 2 (f))											
7. General Expenses Incurred (Part I, Col. 3, Line 22)											
8. Taxes, Licenses and Fees Incurred (Part I, Col. 4, Line 22)											
9. Total Expenses Incurred (Lines 4, 5, 6, 7 and 8)											
10. Net Investment Gain or Loss and Other Income** (Sum of Items 9A and 13, Page 4, of Annual Statement)											
11. Dividends to Policyholders (Item 14A, Page 4, of Annual Statement)											
12. Net Income before federal and foreign income taxes (Line 2 plus 10 minus 3, 9 and 11, to agree with Item 14B, Pg. 4 of Annual Statement)											

B. ADJUSTED DIRECT PREMIUMS AND EXPENSES (SEE NOTE C) AND PERCENTAGES TO ADJUSTED DIRECT PREMIUMS WRITTEN*

	1 Fire		2 Allied Lines		3 Farmowners Multiple Peril		4 Homeowners Multiple Peril		5 Commercial Multiple Peril		8 Ocean Marine
13. Direct Premiums Written (Annual Statement Pg. 8, Part 2B, Col. 1)		xxx		xxx		xxx		xxx		xxx	
14. Adjusted Direct Premiums Written (See Note C)		100.0		100.0		100.0		100.0		100.0	
15. Adjusted Direct Premiums Earned		100.0		100.0		100.0		100.0		100.0	
16. Adusted Direct Losses Incurred											
17. Adjusted Directed Loss Adjustment Expenses Incurred											
18. Direct Commission and Brokerage Incurred (Part I, Line 2 (a) plus direct contingent commission and policy and membership fees)		xxx		xxx		xxx		xxx		xxx	
19. Adjusted Direct Commission and Brokerage Incurred (See Note C)											

A.

	17 Other Liability		Auto Liability				Auto Physical Damage				22 Aircraft (all perils)		23 Fidelity		24 Surety		25 Glass	
			19.1, 19.2 Private Passenger		19.3, 19.4 Commercial		21.1 Private Passenger		21.2 Commercial									
	Amount	%	Amount	%	Amount	%	Amount	%	Amount	%	Amount	%	Amount	%	Amount	%	Amount	%
1.		xxx		xxx		xxx		xxx		xxx		xxx		xxx		xxx		xxx
2.		100.0		100.0		100.0		100.0		100.0		100.0		100.0		100.0		100.0
3.																		
4.																		
5.																		
6.																		
7.																		
8.																		
9.																		
10.																		
11.																		
12.																		

B.*

	17 Other Liability		19.1, 19.2 Private Passenger		19.3, 19.4 Commercial		21.1 Private Passenger		21.2 Commercial		22 Aircraft		23 Fidelity		24 Surety		25 Glass	
13.		xxx		xxx		xxx		xxx		xxx		xxx		xxx		xxx		xxx
14.		100.0		100.0		100.0		100.0		100.0		100.0		100.0		100.0		100.0
15.		100.0		100.0		100.0		100.0		100.0		100.0		100.0		100.0		100.0
16.																		
17.																		
18.		xxx		xxx		xxx		xxx		xxx		xxx		xxx		xxx		xxx
19.																		

*Expenses other than commission and brokerage can be developed from Section A.

NOTE C—To relate equitably expenses incurred to premiums where pooling agreements or similar arrangements exist between companies within a group and where companies operate, through pools or associations and each company participates in the expenses on a basis of a fixed percentage, each company's direct premiums, for the purpose of this exhibit shall be adjusted to produce its participation in the aggregate direct premiums of the group and further adjusted by substituting for the actual direct premiums on business written through associations, the participation of the company in the aggregate direct premiums of all members of each such association. No adjustment shall be necessary where the premiums of any syndicate or pool, included in direct premiums written (Annual Statement, Page 8, Part 2B, Column 1) for any line of business, amount to less than 2% of the total direct premiums written in that line of business.

Adjusted Direct premiums Earned (Line 15) may be obtained by assuming the same percentages to Line 14 as earned to written percentages on a net basis.

NOTE that commissions shall be adjusted to correspond with the adjusted premiums.

NOTE D—Change in reserve for deferred maternity and other similar benefits to be reflected in Net Premiums Earned or

Net Losses Incurred. State which ....

**Instructions for Allocating Net Investment Gain or Loss and Other Income to the Lines of Business for Line 10

A. Adusted mean invested assets = Annual Statement Page 2, Lines 1 + 3 + 4 − 5 +6.1 + 6.2 + 7 for current and prior years, divided by 2.
B. Adjusted investment income = Annual Statement Page 6, Part 1. Column 8. Lines 10-11-12-2.1-2.11-2.2-2.21.
C. Adjusted Acquisition Expenses = IEE Part II Lines 5 + 6 + 8 plus ½ of Line 7, for the appropriate line of business.

	9 Inland Marine		10 Financial Guaranty		11 Medical Malpractice		12 Earthquake		13 Group Accident and Health (See Note D)		14 Credit Accident and Health (Group and Individual)***		15 Other Accident and Health (See Note D)		16 Workers' Compensation	
%	Amount	%	Amount	%	Amount	%	Amount	%	Amount	%	Amount	%	Amount	%	Amount	%
	xxx		xxx		xxx		xxx		xxx		xxx		xxx		xxx	1.
100.0		100.0		100.0		100.0		100.0		100.0		100.0		100.0	2.
																3.
																4.
																5.
																6.
																7.
																8.
																9.
																10.
																11.
																12.
	xxx		xxx		xxx		xxx		xxx		xxx		xxx		xxx	13.
100.0		100.0		100.0		100.0		100.0		100.0		100.0		100.0	14.
100.0		100.0		100.0		100.0		100.0		100.0		100.0		100.0	15.
																16.
																17.
	xxx		xxx		xxx		xxx		xxx		xxx		xxx		xxx	18.
																19.

	26 Burglary and Theft		27 Boiler and Machinery		28 Credit		29 International		30 Reinsurance 30A + B + C + D		31A		31B		32 Total Underwriting Operations (Columns 1 through 31B)		33 Capital and Surplus Accounts	34 Grand Total (Columns 32 plus 33)	
Amount	%	Amount	%	Amount	%	Amount	%	Amount	%	Amount	%	Amount	%	Amount	%	Amount	Amount	
	xxx		xxx		xxx		xxx		xxx		xxx		xxx		xxx	xxx		1.
	100.0		100.0		100.0		100.0		100.0		100.0		100.0		100.0	xxx		2.
																xxx		3.
																xxx		4.
																xxx		5.
																xxx		6.
																xxx		7.
																xxx		8.
																		9.
																xxx		10.
																		11.
																		12.
	xxx		xxx		xx		xxx	xxx	xxx		xxx		xxx		xxx	xxx		13.
	100.0		100.0		100.0		100.0	xxx	xxx		100.0		100.0		100.0	xxx		14.
	100.0		100.0		100.0		100.0	xxx	xxx		100.0		100.0		100.0	xxx		15.
								xxx	xxx							xxx		16.
								xxx	xxx							xxx		17.
	xxx		xxx		xxx		xxx	xxx	xxx		xxx		xxx		xxx	xxx		18.
								xxx	xxx							xxx		19.

D. Written Premium = IEE Part II Line 1 for the appropriate line of business.

E. Agents' balances = Annual Statement Page 2, Lines 9.1 + 9.2 + 10 + 11.

F. Unearned premiums = Annual Statement Page 3, Line 9.

G. Adjusted mean unearned premiums attributable to each line of business = $(\frac{1}{2}(1 - \frac{C \cdot E}{D \cdot F})) \times$ (Annual Statement Page 7, Part 2, Colums 2 + 3 for the appropriate line of business. If negative, set equal to zero. Limit to a maximum of $\frac{1}{2}$ Page 7, Part 2, Columns 2 - 3.

H. Adjusted mean loss and loss expense reserves attributable to each line of business = ($\frac{1}{2}$ Annual Statement Page 10 Columns 5 + 6) + ($\frac{1}{2}$ Annual Statement Page 9, Column 6) + ($\frac{1}{2}$ previous Annual Statement Page 10, Column 6), for the appropriate line of business.

I. Investment income attributable to each line of business = (G + H) × B ÷ A.

J. Investment income attributable to capital and surplus accounts = Annual Statement Page 4, Line 8, less the sum of I for all lines of business.

K. Realized capital gains attributable to capital and surplus accounts = Annual Statement Page 4, Line 9.

L. Other income attributable to each line of business = Annual Statement Page 4, Lines (5 − 13) − (Annual Statement Page 4, Line 1) × (Annual Statement Page 7, Part 2, Column 4) for the appropriate line of business.

Interrogatory. Has Line 10 above been completed in accordance with these instructions. Answer _____ If not, explain

***Business not exceeding 120 months duration.

PART III—CITING ADJUSTMENT FOR EFFECT OF PREMIUM DISCOUNTS AND RETROSPECTIVE RATING
Summary of Workers' Compensation Expenses and Percentages to Earned Premium

Category	Item	Amount	Percentage of Total Premium
Regular Business (Excluding War Projects*)	1. Net Earned Premiums (Line 2, Col. 16 Part II in part)		XXX
	2. Adjustment for Premium Discounts and Retrospective Rating		XXX
	3. Net Earned Premiums—Standard Basis (1) + (2)		XXX
War Projects*	4. Net Earned Premiums (Line 2, Col. 16 Part II in part)		XXX
Total Business	5. Total—Net Earned Premiums—Standard Basis on Regular Business plus War Projects (3) + (4)		100.0%
Expenses Incurred	6. Loss adjustment expenses (Line 4, Col. 16 Part II)		
	7. Commission and brokerage (Line 5, Col. 16 Part II)		
	8. Other Acquisition, Field Supervision and Collection Expenses (Line 6, Col. 16 Part II)		
	9. General Expenses (Line 7, Col. 16 Part II)		
	10. Taxes, Licenses and Fees (Line 8, Col. 16 Part II)		
	11. Total Expenses excluding Federal and foreign income taxes (Line 9, Col. 16 Part II)		
	12. Effect of Expense Graduation		
	13. Total of Item 11 plus Item 12.		

*War Projects or National Defense Projects written under the Comprehensive Rating Plan or at an approved deviation from standard rates. The sum of Lines 1 and 4 should equal Line 2, Col. 16, Part II in the Insurance Expense Exhibit.

PART IV—EXHIBIT OF WORKERS' COMPENSATION EARNED PREMIUMS AND INCURRED LOSSES BY STATES (DIRECT BUSINESS)

1 State	Code	2 Earned Premiums (Direct Business)	3 Incurred Losses (a) (Direct Business)	4 Loss Percentage 3 ÷ 2
Alabama	01			
Alaska	54			
Arizona	02			
Arkansas	03			
California	04			
Colorado	05			
Connecticut	06			
Delaware	07			
Dist. of Columbia	08			
Florida	09			
Georgia	10			
Hawaii	52			
Idaho	11			
Illinois	12			
Indiana	13			
Iowa	14			
Kansas	15			
Kentucky	16			
Louisiana	17			
Maine	18			
Maryland	19			
Massachusetts	20			
Michigan	21			
Minnesota	22			
Mississippi	23			
Missouri	24			
Montana	25			
Nebraska	26			
New Hampshire	28			
New Jersey	29			
New Mexico	30			
New York	31			
North Carolina	32			
Oklahoma	35			
Oregon	36			
Pennsylvania	37			
Rhode Island	38			
South Carolina	39			
South Dakota	40			
Tennessee	41			
Texas	42			
Utah	43			
Vermont	44			
Virginia	45			
Wisconsin	48			
All Other	80			
(1) Total—Direct Business	81			
(2) Reinsurance Assumed	82			
(3) Reinsurance Ceded	83			
(4) Total—Net Basis, (1) + (2) − (3)	84			
(5) Other Reconciliation Items	85			
(6) Grand Total	86	(b)	(c)	

NOTES: (a) The reserves for unpaid losses used in calculating incurred losses should be the company's individual
  estimates of outstanding claims, including reserves for claims incurred but not reported.
  (b) Per Line 2, Column 16 of Insurance Expense Exhibit. (Part II)
  (c) Per Line 3, Column 16 of Insurance Expense Exhibit. (Part II)

Appendix C

Summary of NAIC Annual Statement Analytical Schedules

- Schedule A: Real Estate Owned

  The information provided includes a description of a real estate, date acquired, name of vendor, method of acquisition, encumbrances, cost, book value, market value less encumbrances, related income and expense and rental value of space occupied by the company and/or affiliates, date of sale, name of purchaser, amount received, and profit or loss on sale.

- Schedule B: Mortgages Owned

  This schedule shows all mortgages owned at year end and all mortgage loans made, increased, discharged, reduced or disposed of during the year, and other data related to mortgages.

- Schedule BA: Other Invested Assets Owned, Acquired, and Disposed of

  Transportation equipment, timber deeds, mineral rights, and other sundry items held as invested assets at the end of the year are shown in Part 1. Other invested assets acquired during the year are shown in Part 2 and those disposed of during the year are listed in Part 3.

- Schedule C: Collateral Loans

  Outstanding loans that have been secured by collateral in case of default are itemized here. These loans are shown on the balance sheet as invested assets. Loans that exceed the market value of the collateral must be reduced to such market value through the nonadmitted process of Exhibit 1.

- Schedule D: Bonds and Stocks Owned

  This schedule is divided into several parts and subsections. Two sections are in summary form, one summarizing investments by country (US, Canada, and Other) and by investment classification (Government, State, Subdivision of State, Railroads, Public Utilities, Banks and Insurance, Industrial and Miscellaneous, and Affiliated). The other section reflects investments by quality ratings assigned by the NAIC and by maturity date if any (1 year or less, 1 to 5 years, 5 to 10 years, 10 to 20 years and over 20 years). The parts itemize all bonds, common stocks, preferred stocks and options, owned, acquired, issued, redeemed, sold, or expired during the accounting period. Information is given concerning the securities' cost, book value, market value, interest rate, dividend yield, and maturity date. The final parts of the schedule ask questions concerning affiliated companies and stock options.

- Schedule F: Reinsurance Ceded and Assumed

Reinsurance recoverable on paid and unpaid losses is shown in the initial part of the schedule. This schedule consists of several parts and subsections. Part 1A—Section 1 reflects ceded reinsurance balances by assuming reinsurer and displays amounts due on paid losses on an aged basis, recoverable on unpaid losses (deducted from gross outstanding claims), the reinsurers unearned premiums and the gross reinsurance premium ceded. Part 1A—Section 2 reflects assumed reinsurance by reinsurer and displays the amount payable on paid losses, on unpaid losses, and the reinsurance. Unearned premium—for the purpose of these sections, loss adjustment expenses are included in the recoverable amounts.

Part 1B reflects Portfolio Reinsurance transactions during the year by reinsurer with separate totals for assumed and for ceded transactions. It shows the date of the reinsurance contract(s), and amount of original premium and reinsurance premium.

Part 2A summarizes by reinsurance company cessions to unauthorized companies and shows amounts due therefrom on paid and unpaid losses less funds deposited by and/or withheld from such companies.

Part 2B in Sections 1 and 2 ages amounts due from authorized reinsurers. Depending on the stratification of the aging totals, this aging can result in overdue (nonadmitted) reinsurance balances developed on a mandated formula basis. Effectively, underdue portions of reinsurance balances can be partially classed as overdue under the formula.

- Schedule H: Accident and Health Insurance Exhibit

Part 1 is an Analysis of Underwriting Operations (after dividends to policyholders if any) by type of A and H contract

(Group, Credit, Individual, and sub classifications of each). Part 2 analyzes reserves for premiums, future benefits, and claims also by type of contract. Part 3 is a one year development of the claim reserves at the end of the previous year. Part 4 details experience on reinsurance assumed and ceded separately by the same subclassifications.

- Schedule M: Expense Payments to Others

    The purpose of this schedule is to disclose payments that do not represent employee compensation, expense reimbursement, or insurance benefits. Payments in excess of $100 to legislative or other governmental bodies must be listed in Part 1. Payments to officers, directors, or employees that exceed $1,000 or amount in the aggregate to more than $10,000 during the year are shown in Part 2. Part 3 lists legal expenses greater than $500/$5,000 paid during the year for reasons other than loss and salvage settlements. All payments greater than $1,000 to industry trade associations and service bureaus are itemized in Part 4.

- Schedule N: Deposits in Banks

    It is common for property-liability insurers to maintain a number of bank accounts. Some are used to pay operating expenses while others may be used for loss disbursements or investment purposes. All deposits maintained at any time during the year and related interest thereon in banks, trust companies, and savings institutions must be shown in this schedule. Total depository balances on the last day of each month are listed. Balances remaining at the statement date in each institution also are disclosed.

- Schedule P: Loss and Loss Expense Reserve Detail and Calendar-Accident Year Data for Claims By Major Line of Business and Reinsurance

    This schedule has several parts and subparts. The first section sets forth the dollar detail and ratios of loss and loss expense to premiums earned for the past ten years for long tail lines and three years for short tail lines on an incurred year (financial statement) basis and is used to determine excess statutory reserves as well as loss ratio trends as reported. Another section shows the development of losses incurred for similar ten and three subsequent calendar years on an accident year basis. A separate set of interrogatories relating to loss and loss adjusting accounting and reserving policies and the calculation of excess reserves, if any, completes the schedule.

- Schedule X: Unlisted Assets

  Schedule X reflects, in a format similar to Schedule D and its parts, Unlisted Assets. Unlisted assets generally are items owned that have little or doubtful value. Worthless securities are the most frequent item reflected in Schedule X, but it could also include notes receivable from judgment proof entities, or royalty interests from dormant oil wells.

- Schedule Y: Transactions with Affiliates

  This schedule lists transactions occurring during the year between the filing insurer, its insurance affiliates and any other affiliated company. Asset transfers, contractual commitments, management contracts, and an organizational chart identifying all affiliated entities is to be included in this schedule.

- Schedule T: Exhibit of Premiums Written

  This schedule reflects in summary form by state, territory, possession, Canada, and other alien locations direct (No assumed or ceded reinsurance included) transactions for:

  Premiums written, Premiums earned, Dividends to policyholders, Losses paid, Losses incurred, Losses unpaid, Finance charges, and Premiums written for Federal purchasing groups.

  Totals of each column should agree with the respective totals on parts 2 and 3 of the Underwriting and Investment Exhibit. The line items for each state should agree with the Annual Statement for the respective state found on page 14.

  Respective states can utilize these data for tax and rate making verification purposes.

Appendix D

NAIC Cash Flow Ratios

Each version of the cash flow ratio uses a somewhat different definition of liquid resources available to cover any shortfall in operating cash flow. Funds provided from investments sold, matured or repaid and funds applied to acquire new investments do not enter the calculations. In all three calculations, if operating cash flow is positive, the ratio is assigned a value of 999 indicating that a cash deficiency does not exist.

Version A

The most narrow definition of liquid resources is used in this cash flow ratio; only cash on hand or deposit and maturing bonds are recognized in the ratio's numerator.

Step	Data Source	Data Description
A.	Page 5, Line 10	Funds (cash) provided from operations
B.	Page 5, Line 15.5	Total other funds applied
C.	A−B	Operating cash flow
D.	Page 2, Line 6.1	Cash on hand and on deposit
E.	Page 2, Line 6.2	Bonds maturing in one year or less
F.	D + E	Liquid resources
Ratio:	F÷C	

If C is positive, Result is 999
If C is negative, treat as positive for remainder of test

Version B

This version of the ratio includes the value of investments in preferred and common stock of nonaffiliated firms as a component of liquid resources.

Step	Data Source	Data Description
A.	Page 5, Line 10	Funds provided from operations
B.	Page 5, Line 15.5	Total other funds applied
C.	A−B	Operating cash flow
D.	Page 2, Line 6.1	Cash on hand and on deposit

E.	Schedule D, Part 1A, Line 5.5, Column 2	Bonds maturing in one year or less
F.	Page 2, Lines 2.1+2.2	Preferred plus common stocks
G.	Schedule D Summary Column 3, Line 47 + Line 65, Column 3	Market value of Affiliated Preferred and Common Stocks
H.	D + E + F − G	Liquid resources
Ratio:	H÷C	

If C is positive, Result is 999

If C is negative, treat as positive for remainder of test

Version C

This version of the ratio includes the value of investments in common stocks of nonaffiliated firms as a component of liquid resources but excludes the value of investments in all preferred stocks.

Step	Data Source	Data Description
A.	Page 5, Line 10	Funds provided from operations
B.	Page 5, Line 15.5	Total other funds applied
C.	A−B	Operating cash flow
D.	Page 2, Line 6.1	Cash on hand and on deposit
E.	Schedule D, Part 1A, Line 5.5, Column 2	Bond maturing in one year or less
F.	Schedule D Summary Lines 52+56+60+64, Column 3	Market value of Common Stocks, Nonaffiliates
G.	D + E + F	Liquid resources
Ratio:	G÷C	

If C is positive, Result is 999

If C is negative, treat as positive for remainder of test